U H University
Coll

Microsoft® Visual Basic® 2005 Step by Step

Michael Halvorson

PUBLISHED BY
Microsoft Press
A Division of Microsoft Corporation
One Microsoft Way
Redmond, Washington 98052-6399

Library of Congress Control Number 2005933122

Printed and bound in the United States of America.

2 3 4 5 6 7 8 9 QWT 8 7 6 5

Distributed in Canada by H.B. Fenn and Company Ltd.A CIP catalogue record for this book is available from the British Library.

Microsoft Press books are available through booksellers and distributors worldwide. For further information about international editions, contact your local Microsoft Corporation office or contact Microsoft Press International directly at fax (425) 936-7329. Visit our Web site at www.microsoft.com/mspress. Send comments to mspinput@microsoft.com.

Acquisitions Editor: Ben Ryan
Project Editor: Melissa von Tschudi-Sutton
Production: Online Training Solutions, Inc.

Body Part No. X11-44966

5000720036

University of Hertfordshire

College Lane, Hatfield, Herts. AL10 9AB

Learning and Information Services

Michael Halvorson

PUBLISHED BY
Microsoft Press
A Division of Microsoft Corporation
One Microsoft Way
Redmond, Washington 98052-6399

Library of Congress Control Number 2005933122

Printed and bound in the United States of America.

2 3 4 5 6 7 8 9 QWT 8 7 6 5

Distributed in Canada by H.B. Fenn and Company Ltd. A CIP catalogue record for this book is available from the British Library.

Microsoft Press books are available through booksellers and distributors worldwide. For further information about international editions, contact your local Microsoft Corporation office or contact Microsoft Press International directly at fax (425) 936-7329. Visit our Web site at www.microsoft.com/mspress. Send comments to mspinput@microsoft.com.

Microsoft, Microsoft, ActiveX, DataTips, Excel, FrontPage, IntelliSense, Microsoft Press, MSDN, MS-DOS, Outlook, PowerPoint, Visual Basic, Visual C#, Visual C++, Visual InterDev, Visual J#, Visual J++, Visual Studio, Visual Web Developer, Windows, Windows NT, and Windows Server are either registered trademarks or trademarks of Microsoft Corporation in the United States and/or other countries. Other product and company names mentioned herein may be the trademarks of their respective owners.

The example companies, organizations, products, domain names, e-mail addresses, logos, people, places, and events depicted herein are fictitious. No association with any real company, organization, product, domain name, e-mail address, logo, person, place, or event is intended or should be inferred.

This book expresses the author's views and opinions. The information contained in this book is provided without any express, statutory, or implied warranties. Neither the authors, Microsoft Corporation, nor its resellers, or distributors will be held liable for any damages caused or alleged to be caused either directly or indirectly by this book.

Acquisitions Editor: Ben Ryan
Project Editor: Melissa von Tschudi-Sutton
Production: Online Training Solutions, Inc.

Body Part No. X11-44966

For Kim

with love and friendship

Table of Contents

Part II   Programming Fundamentals

5   Visual Basic Variables and Formulas, and the .NET Framework 115

6   Using Decision Structures. 149

13   Exploring Text Files and String Processing. 301

Part III   Designing the User Interface

14   Managing Windows Forms and Controls at Run Time 329

Acknowledgments

Over the years working on Visual Basic, I have had a lot of help from a number of people, whom I now want to thank. I first learned about Microsoft Visual Basic 1.0 (or *Thunder*, as it was code-named) in 1990 from Adam Rauch and Nevet Basker while working as an acquisitions editor at Microsoft Corporation. Among the early advocates of this product, I want to thank Brian Overland, Mitch Waite, Michael Young, Ross Nelson, and John Clark Craig, who converted their enthusiasm for Visual Basic into important early books about Visual Basic programming. David Rygmyr, a friend and colleague who co-authored three books with me about QuickBasic programming in the late 1980s, also deserves special mention here for helping me to understand how closely Basic would be tied to Microsoft's future, and for his great creativity in writing about software.

Between the March 1991 debut of Visual Basic 1.0 and the November 2005 release of Microsoft Visual Studio 2005, I have written eight books about Visual Basic programming, with localized versions appearing in over a dozen languages. During these years, I have incurred numerous debts to talented product managers, program managers, developers, testers, writers, professors, publishing colleagues, and product support personnel. Although each person cannot be listed, I would especially like to thank Min Yee, Patty Stonesifer, Bill Gates, Chris Banks, Jim Brown, Russell Steele, Dean Holmes, Gerry Zyfers, Lucinda Rowley, Mary DeJong, Robert Lyon, Dail Magee, Jr., Jim Fuchs, Marc Young, Jean Ross, Julie Xiao, Emma Gibson, Chris Kinata, Barry Preppernau, Dick Brown, Denise Bankaitis, Laura Sackerman, Lisa Theobald, Danielle Voeller, Casey Doyle, Eric Stroo, Megan Sheppard, Deb Vogel, Tom Button, Eric Peterson, Rob Howard, Chris Dias, Omar Khan, Jon Roskill, Jay Roxe, and Larry Edison. Your ideas, hard work, and support have been very valuable to me. In addition, I would like to thank Jan Shanahan for organizing an excellent technical conference in March 2005 that helped me to further understand and exploit the powerful new features in Microsoft Visual Basic 2005—the best version of Visual Basic yet.

For the publication of this book, I also have many debts. I would especially like to thank product manager Ben Ryan, who had a strong vision for this book from the beginning, developed marketing and release plans for this and other Visual Studio titles, and (most important for a technical writer) responded quickly and with good humor to all my beta software and scheduling questions. Also at Microsoft Learning, project editor Melissa von Tschudi-Sutton skillfully managed this book's production schedule, organized the team's project servers, and answered many questions about house style and the publishing process. Special thanks also to Robert Lyon for organizing technical support and contributing in important technical ways to this book, and to Bill Teel for performing his usual magic with screen shots and electronic images.

At Online Training Solutions, Inc. (OTSI), I was extremely well handled by a number of talented publishing professionals—many of whom I have worked with since the mid-1980s. The book's copy editing team improved the manuscript in many important ways, including sorting out and enforcing style rules for how elements in the Visual Studio IDE should be printed and discussed. Joyce Cox, undoubtedly one of the most experienced and thoughtful editors in the computer book industry, also provided valuable editorial support and advice throughout the project, for which I am very grateful. Steve Lambert, the book's primary technical reviewer, offered valuable peer support and tested the programs and exercises in each chapter with extreme vigilance. I first worked with Steve in 1986, and it has been a great pleasure to discuss coding techniques with him again. Joan Preppernau, Steve's daughter and also vice president and chief operating officer of OTSI, brought her typical good humor and organizational skills to the project, and I benefited from her patient leadership greatly. Susie Bayers, project editor at OTSI, was also a great source of support. Susie coordinated the book's tight production schedule, tracked down missing documents, and transferred files to and from our project server.

Finally, I would like to thank my wife, Kim, and my sons, Henry and Felix, for their support and patience as this book made its way from manuscript to printed form in the spring, summer, and fall of 2005. In particular, Kim has borne the burden of being married to a compulsive writer and late-night programmer with grace and understanding for many years now. I am very grateful for your wisdom and encouragement, Kim.

Introduction

Welcome to *Microsoft Visual Basic 2005 Step by Step*, a comprehensive introduction to Visual Basic programming using the Microsoft Visual Basic 2005 software. I've designed this practical, hands-on tutorial with a variety of skill levels in mind. The result is that new programmers can learn software development fundamentals in the context of useful, real-world applications, and experienced Visual Basic programmers can quickly master the essential tools and programming techniques offered in the Visual Basic 2005 upgrade.

Complementing this comprehensive approach is the book's structure—4 topically organized parts, 20 chapters, and 54 step-by-step exercises and sample programs. By using this book, you'll quickly learn how to create professional-quality Visual Basic 2005 applications for the Microsoft Windows operating system and a variety of Web browsers. You'll also have fun!

What is Visual Basic 2005?

Visual Basic 2005 is a development tool that you can use to build applications that perform useful work and look great within a variety of settings. Using Visual Basic 2005, you can create applications for the Windows operating system, the Web, hand-held devices, and a host of other environments and settings. The most important advantage of Visual Basic is that it has been designed to increase productivity in your daily development work—especially if you need to use information in databases or create solutions for the Internet—but an important additional benefit is that once you become comfortable with the development environment in Microsoft Visual Studio 2005, you can use the same tools to write programs for Microsoft Visual C++ 2005, Microsoft Visual C# 2005, Microsoft Visual J# 2005, and other third-party tools and compilers.

Visual Basic .NET Versions

The first version of Visual Basic .NET (Microsoft Visual Basic .NET 2002) was released in February 2002. The second release (Microsoft Visual Basic .NET 2003) was widely available in March 2003. After a long period of development and integration work, Microsoft released Visual Basic 2005 in late 2005. Visual Basic 2005 is now so tightly integrated with Visual Studio that it is only available as a component in the Visual Studio 2005 programming suite, which includes the Visual C#, Visual C++, and Visual J# compilers and other Microsoft .NET development tools. However, Visual Studio 2005 is sold in several different product configurations, including Standard Edition, Professional Edition, Team Suite, and Express Edition. I've written this book to be compatible with all editions of Visual Basic 2005 and Visual Studio 2005, but especially with the tools and techniques available in Visual Studio Standard Edition and Visual Studio Professional Edition. Although Visual Basic 2005 is similar in many ways to Visual Basic .NET 2003, there are many important differences and improvements, so I recommend that you complete the exercises in this book using the Visual Basic 2005 software.

> **Note** The Visual Basic 2005 software is not included with this book! The CD-ROM distributed with most versions of this book contains practice files, sample databases, and other useful information that requires the Visual Basic 2005 software (sold separately) for use.

Finding Your Best Starting Point in This Book

This book is designed to help you build skills in a number of essential areas. You can use this book if you're new to programming, switching from another programming language, or upgrading from Visual Basic 6 or Visual Basic .NET 2003. Use the following table to find your best starting point in this book.

If you are	Follow these steps
New	
To programming	1. Install the practice files as described in the section "Installing the Practice Files on Your Computer" later in this introduction.
	2. Learn basic skills for using Visual Basic 2005 by working sequentially from Chapter 1 through Chapter 17.
	3. Complete Part IV, "Database and Web Programming," as your level of interest or experience dictates.
Upgrading	
From Visual Basic .NET 2002 or 2003	1. Install the practice files as described in the section "Installing the Practice Files on Your Computer."
	2. Complete Chapters 1 through 4, skim Chapters 5 through 17, and complete Chapters 18 through 20.
	3. For a discussion of specific features that have changed in this upgrade, read Chapters 1, 4, 5, 7, 8, and 13.
From Visual Basic 6	1. Install the practice files as described in the section "Installing the Practice Files on Your Computer."
	2. Read Chapters 1 through 4 carefully to learn the new features of the Visual Studio 2005 development environment.
	3. Pay special attention to the "Upgrade Notes: Migrating Visual Basic 6 Code to Visual Basic 2005" sidebars near the beginning of each chapter, which highlight the significant differences between Visual Basic 6 and Visual Basic 2005.
	4. Skim Chapters 5 through 13 to review the fundamentals of event-driven programming, using variables, and writing decision structures. Give special attention to Chapters 5, 6, 9, and 12.
	5. Work sequentially from Chapters 14 through 20 to learn the new Visual Basic 2005 features related to user interface design, database programming, and Web programming.

If you are Referencing	Follow these steps
This book after working through the chapters	1. Use the index to locate information about specific topics, and use the table of contents to locate information about general topics.
	2. Use the Upgrading Index to see a list of the new features in Visual Basic 2005 and how Visual Basic 6 program code should be upgraded.
	3. Read the Quick Reference at the end of each chapter for a brief review of the major tasks in the chapter. The Quick Reference topics are listed in the same order as they're presented in the chapter.

System Requirements

You'll need the following hardware and software to complete the exercises in this book:

- Microsoft Windows XP Professional Edition with Service Pack 2 or Microsoft Windows XP Home Edition with Service Pack 2, Microsoft Windows Server 2003 with Service Pack 1, or Microsoft Windows 2000 with Service Pack 4 (Microsoft Windows 2000 Datacenter Server is not supported)

- Microsoft Visual Studio 2005 Standard Edition or Microsoft Visual Studio 2005 Professional Edition

- 600 MHz Pentium or compatible processor (1 GHz Pentium recommended)

- 192 MB RAM (256 MB or more recommended)

- Video (800 x 600 or higher resolution) monitor with at least 256 colors (1024 x 768 High Color 16-bit recommended)

- CD-ROM or DVD-ROM drive

- Microsoft Mouse or compatible pointing device

> **Note** This book and the practice files were tested using Visual Studio 2005 Standard and Visual Studio 2005 Professional. You might notice a few differences if you're using other editions of Visual Studio 2005. In particular, if you're using Visual Studio 2005 Express Edition, a few features will be unavailable to you.

Prerelease Software

This book was reviewed and tested against the August 2005 Community Technical Preview (CTP) of Visual Studio 2005. The August CTP was the last preview before the final release of Visual Studio 2005. This book is expected to be fully compatible with the final release of Visual Studio 2005 and Visual Basic 2005. If there are any changes or corrections for this book, they will be collected and added to an easy-to-access Microsoft Knowledge Base article on the Web. See the "Support for This Book" section for more information.

Installing and Using the Practice Files

The CD-ROM inside this book contains the practice files that you'll use as you perform the exercises in the book. For example, when you're learning how to display database tables on a form by using the *GridDataView* control, you'll open one of the practice files—an academic database named Students.mdb—and then use Visual Studio database programming tools to access the database. By using the practice files, you won't waste time creating files that aren't relevant to the exercise. Instead, you can concentrate on learning how to master Visual Basic 2005 programming techniques. With the files and the step-by-step instructions in the chapters, you'll also learn by doing, which is an easy and effective way to acquire and remember new skills.

Important   Before you break the seal on the CD-ROM, be sure that this book matches your version of the software. This book is designed for use with Visual Studio 2005 and the Visual Basic 2005 programming language. To find out what software you're running, you can check the product package, or you can start the software, open a project, and then click About Microsoft Visual Studio on the Help menu at the top of the screen.

Installing the Practice Files

Installing the practice files on your hard disk requires approximately 7.2 MB of disk space. Follow these steps to install the practice files on your computer's hard disk so that you can use them with the exercises in this book.

1. Remove the CD from the package inside this book, and insert it into your CD-ROM drive.

Note   An end user license agreement should open automatically. If this agreement does not appear, open My Computer on the desktop or Start menu, double-click the icon for your CD-ROM drive, and then double-click StartCD.exe.

2. Review the end user license agreement. If you accept the terms, select the accept option, and then click Next.

   A menu appears with options related to the book.

3. Click Install Practice Files.

4. Follow the onscreen instructions.

> **Note** For best results when using the practice files with this book, accept the prese-lected installation location, which by default is c:\vb05sbs. If you change the installation location, you'll need to manually adjust the paths in several practice files to locate essential components, such as artwork and database files, when you use them.

5. When the files have been installed, remove the CD-ROM from your drive and replace it in the package inside the back cover of your book.

   If you accepted the default settings, a folder named c:\vb05sbs has been created on your hard disk, and the practice files have been placed in that folder. You'll find one folder in c:\vb05sbs for each chapter in the book. (Some of the files represent completed projects, and others will require that you enter some program code.) If you have trouble running any of the practice files, refer to the text in the book that describes those files.

Using the Practice Files

Each chapter in this book explains when and how to use the practice files for that chapter. When it's time to use a practice file, the book lists instructions for how to open the file. The chapters are built around scenarios that simulate real programming projects so that you can easily apply the skills you learn to your own work.

> **Note** Visual Basic 2005 features a new file format for its projects and solutions. Accordingly, you won't be able to open the practice files for this book if you're using an older version of the Visual Basic or Visual Studio software. To see what version of Visual Basic or Visual Studio you're using, click the About command on the Help menu.

Visual Studio is extremely customizable and can be configured to open and save projects and solutions in different ways. The instructions in this book generally rely on the default setting for Visual Studio. For more information about how settings within the development environment affect how you write programs and use the practice files, see the section "Customizing IDE Settings to Match Step by Step Exercises" in Chapter 1, "Exploring the Visual Studio Integrated Development Environment."

For those of you who like to know all the details, here's a list of the Visual Basic projects included on the CD-ROM. Each project is located in its own folder and has several support files. Look at all the things you will be doing!

Project	Description
Chapter 1	
MusicTrivia	A simple trivia program that welcomes you to the programming course and displays a digital photo.
Chapter 2	
Lucky7	Your first program—a game that simulates a Las Vegas Lucky Seven slot machine.
Chapter 3	
Birthday	A program that uses the *DateTimePicker* control to pick a date.
CheckBox	A program that demonstrates the *CheckBox* control and its properties.
Hello	A "Hello, world!" program that demonstrates the *Label* and *TextBox* controls.
Input Controls	The user interface for a graphical ordering environment, assembled using several powerful input controls.
WebLink	A demonstration of the *LinkLabel* control that opens a Web browser in your Visual Basic application.
Chapter 4	
Menu	Demonstrates how to use Visual Studio dialog box controls, toolbars, and menus.
Chapter 5	
Advanced Math	Advanced use of operators for integer division, remainder division, exponentiation, and string concatenation.
Basic Math	Basic use of operators for addition, subtraction, multiplication, and division.
Constant Tester	Uses a constant to hold a fixed mathematical entity.
Data Types	A demonstration of Visual Basic fundamental data types and their use with variables.
Framework Math	Demonstrates the .NET Framework classes with mathematical methods.
Input Box	Receives input with the *InputBox* function.
Variable Test	Declares and uses variables to store information.
Chapter 6	
Select Case	Uses a Select Case decision structure and a *ListBox* control to display a welcome message in several languages.
User Validation	Uses the If...Then...Else decision structure and a *MaskedTextBox* control to manage a logon process.

Project	Description
Chapter 7	
Celsius Conversion	Converts temperatures from Fahrenheit to Celsius by using a Do loop.
Digital Clock	A simple digital clock program that demonstrates the *Timer* control.
For Loop	Demonstrates using a For...Next loop to display text in a *TextBox* control, and using the *Chr* function to create a Wrap character.
For Loop Icons	Uses a global counter variable in an event procedure as an alternative to loops. This program also displays images by using a *PictureBox* control.
Timed Password	Demonstrates how to use a *Timer* control to create a logon program with a password time-out feature.
Windows Version Snippet	Shows how to use the new Insert Snippet command to display the current version of Windows running on a user's computer.
Chapter 8	
Debug Test	A simulated debugging problem, designed to be solved using the Visual Studio debugging tools.
Chapter 9	
Disc Drive Error	A program that crashes when a CD drive is used incorrectly. This project is used as the basis of a Visual Basic error handler.
Disc Drive Handler	A project with a completed error handler for loading files that demonstrates the Try...Catch syntax.
Chapter 10	
Text Box Sub	A general-purpose Sub procedure that adds items to a list box.
TrackWins	A clean version of the Lucky7 slot machine project from Chapter 2, which you enhance by using public variables and a function that computes the game's win rate.
Chapter 11	
Array Class Sorts	A program that shows you how to create and manipulate large integer arrays. Demonstrates the *Array.Sort* and *Array.Reverse* methods and how to use a *ProgressBar* control to give the user visual feedback during long sorts.
Dynamic Array	Computes the average temperature for any number of days by using a dynamic array.
Fixed Array	Computes the average weekly temperature by using a fixed-length array.
Chapter 12	
Controls Collection	Uses a For Each loop and the Visual Studio *Controls* collection to move objects on a form.
URL Collection	Demonstrates a user-defined collection containing a list of Web addresses (URLs) recently visited by the user.

Project	Description
Chapter 13	
Quick Note	A simple note-taking utility that demonstrates the *FileOpen* function and the *TextBox*, *MenuStrip*, and *SaveFileDialog* controls.
Sort Text	A text file editor with a menu bar that demonstrates how to manage Open, Close, Save As, Insert Date, Sort Text, and Exit commands in a program. Contains a *ShellSort* module for sorting arrays that can be added to other programming projects.
Text Browser	Displays the contents of a text file in a Visual Basic program. Demonstrates menu commands, a Try...Catch error handler, and the *FileOpen* and *LineInput* functions, and serves as a foundation for the other programs in this chapter.
Chapter 14	
Add Controls	Demonstrates how controls are added to a Windows Form at run time by using program code (not the Designer).
Anchor and Dock	Uses the *Anchor* and *Dock* properties of a form to align objects at run time.
Desktop Bounds	Uses the *StartPosition* and *DesktopBounds* properties to position a Windows form at run time. Also demonstrates the *FormBorderStyle* property, *Rectangle* structure, and *ShowDialog* method.
Lucky Seven Help	The enhanced Lucky7 program (TrackWins) from Chapter 10, which is enhanced again through the addition of a second form to display Help information.
Chapter 15	
Draw Shapes	Demonstrates a few of the useful graphics methods in the *System .Drawing* namespace, including *DrawEllipse*, *FillRectangle*, and *DrawCurve*.
Moving Icon	Animates an icon on the form, moving it from the top of the form to the bottom each time that you click the Move Down button.
Transparent Form	Demonstrates how to change the transparency of a form by using the *Me* object and the *Opacity* property.
Zoom In	Simulates zooming in, or magnifying, an object on a form (in this case, the planet Earth).
Chapter 16	
Form Inheritance	Uses the Visual Studio Inheritance Picker to create a form that inherits its characteristics and functionality from another form.
Person Class	Demonstrates how to create new classes, properties, and methods in a Visual Basic project. The new *Person* class is an employee record with first name, last name, and date of birth fields, and it contains a method that computes the current age of an employee.
Chapter 17	
Print Dialogs	Demonstrates how to create Print Preview and Page Setup dialog boxes.

Project	Description
Print File	A project that handles more sophisticated printing tasks, including printing a multipage text file with wrapping lines. Includes lots of code to use in your own projects.
Print Graphics	Prints graphics from within a Visual Basic program by using an error handler, the *Print* method, and the *DrawImage* method.
Print Text	Demonstrates how simple text is printed in a Visual Basic program.
Chapter 18	
ADO Form	Demonstrates how ADO.NET is used to establish a connection to a Microsoft Access database and display information from it.
Chapter 19	
DataGridView Sample	Shows how the *DataGridView* control is used to display multiple tables of data on a form. Also demonstrates how navigation bars, datasets, and table adapters are interconnected and bound to objects on a form.
Chapter 20	
Chap20	Demonstrates using Visual Web Developer and ASP.NET to create a car loan calculator that runs in a Web browser, offers Help information, and displays database records.

Uninstalling the Practice Files

Use the following steps to remove the practice files added to your hard drive by the Visual Basic 2005 Step by Step installation program.

1. In Control Panel, open Add Or Remove Programs.
2. From the list of Currently Installed Programs, select Microsoft Visual Basic 2005 Step by Step.
3. Click Remove.
4. Follow the onscreen instructions to remove the practice files

Conventions and Features in This Book

Before you start the exercises in this book, you can save time by understanding how I provide instructions and the elements I use to communicate information about Visual Basic programming. The following lists identify stylistic conventions, discuss helpful features of the book, and point out a few elements that are especially useful for readers who plan to upgrade Visual Basic 6 applications to Visual Basic 2005.

Conventions

- The names of all program elements—controls, objects, methods, functions, properties, and so on—appear in italic.

- Hands-on exercises for you to follow are given in numbered lists of steps (1, 2, and so on). A round bullet (●) indicates an exercise that has only one step.

- Text that you need to type appears in bold.

- As you work through steps, you'll occasionally see tables with lists of properties that you'll set in Visual Studio. Text properties appear within quotes, but you don't need to type the quotes.

- A plus sign (+) between two key names means that you must press those keys at the same time. For example, "Press Alt+Tab" means that you hold down the Alt key while you press Tab.

- Elements labeled Note, Tip, More Info, or Important provide additional information or alternative methods for a step. You should read these before continuing with the exercise.

Other Features

- You can learn special programming techniques, background information, or features related to the information being discussed by reading the sidebars that appear throughout the chapters. These sidebars often highlight difficult terminology or suggest future areas for exploration.

- You can learn about options or techniques that build on what you learned in a chapter by trying the One Step Further exercise at the end of that chapter.

- You can get a quick reminder of how to perform the tasks you learned by reading the Quick Reference at the end of a chapter.

Upgrading Visual Basic 6 Programs

- The Upgrading Index, located before the comprehensive index, lists in one place the major differences between Visual Basic 6 and Visual Basic 2005 and provides page citations to information in the book about these differences.

- "Upgrade Notes" sidebars, near the beginning of each chapter, provide a basic overview, or executive summary, of the features in Visual Basic 2005 for Visual Basic 6 users. Use these sidebars if you're interested in how Visual Basic has changed in the context of an individual topic, such as variable declaration, Toolbox controls, or database programming. (Readers upgrading from Visual Basic .NET 2002 or 2003 to Visual Basic 2005 are welcome to review these notes as well, but moving to Visual Basic 2005 will be easier for you.)

Helpful Support Links

You are invited to check out the following links that provide support for the Visual Studio 2005 software and this book's contents:

Visual Studio 2005 Software Support

For questions about the Visual Studio 2005 software, I recommend two Microsoft Web sites:

- *http://msdn.microsoft.com/vbasic* (the Microsoft MSDN home page for Visual Basic)
- *http://www.microsoft.com/communities* (technical communities related to Microsoft software products and technologies)

Both Web sites give you access to professional Visual Basic developers, Microsoft employees, Visual Basic blogs, newsgroups, webcasts, technical chats, and interesting user groups. For additional information about these and other electronic and printed resources, see Appendix A, "Where To Go For More Information."

Online Companion Content

The online companion content page has content and links related to this book, including a link to the Microsoft Press Technology Updates Web page. (As technologies related to this book are updated, links to additional information will be added to the Microsoft Press Technology Updates Web page. Visit the page periodically for updates on Visual Studio 2005 and other technologies.) The online companion content page for this book can be found at:

http://www.microsoft.com/mspress/companion/0-7356-2131-4/

Microsoft Press Web Site

The Microsoft Press Web site has descriptions for the complete line of Microsoft Press books, information about ordering titles, notice of special features and events, additional content for Microsoft Press books, and much more.

http://www.microsoft.com/learning/books/

Support for this Book

Every effort has been made to ensure the accuracy of this book and the contents of the CD. As corrections or changes are collected, they will be added to a Microsoft Knowledge Base article on the Web. To view the list of known corrections for this book, visit the following Web site:

http://support.microsoft.com/kb/905036/

In addition, Microsoft Press provides general support information for its books and companion CDs at the following Web site:

http://www.microsoft.com/learning/support/books/

Questions and Comments

If you have comments or questions that are not answered by visiting the sites above, please send them to Microsoft Press via e-mail to

mspinput@microsoft.com

Or via postal mail to

Microsoft Press
Attn: Step by Step Series Editor
One Microsoft Way
Redmond, WA 98052-6399

Please note that Microsoft software product support is not offered through the above addresses.

Part I
Getting Started
with Microsoft Visual Basic 2005

Chapter 1
Exploring the Visual Studio Integrated Development Environment

After completing this chapter, you will be able to:

- Start Microsoft Visual Studio 2005.

- Use the Visual Studio Integrated Development Environment.

- Open and run a Microsoft Visual Basic program.

- Change property settings.

- Move, resize, dock, and auto hide tool windows.

- Open a Web browser within Visual Studio.

- Use new Help commands and customize Help.

- Customize Integrated Development Environment settings to match this book's step-by-step instructions.

- Save your changes, and exit Visual Studio.

Microsoft Visual Basic 2005 is an important upgrade and enhancement of the popular Visual Basic development system and an iterative upgrade of the Microsoft Visual Basic .NET 2003 software. This chapter gives you the skills you need to quickly and efficiently get up and running with the Visual Studio 2005 Integrated Development Environment (IDE)—the place where you will write Visual Basic programs. You should read this chapter whether you are new to Visual Basic programming or you have used previous versions of Visual Basic or Visual Studio.

In this chapter, you'll learn how to start Visual Studio 2005 and how to use the IDE to open and run a simple program. You'll learn the essential Visual Studio menu commands and programming procedures; you'll open and run a simple Visual Basic program named Music Trivia; you'll change a programming setting called a *property*; and you'll practice moving, sizing, docking, and auto hiding tool windows. You'll also learn how to open a Web browser within Visual Studio, how to get more information by using online Help, and how to exit the development environment and save your changes.

Upgrade Notes: Migrating Visual Basic 6 Code to Visual Basic 2005

Microsoft Visual Basic 6.0 has been an extremely successful product. Even though Visual Basic 6 was released in 1998, many software developers, including a large number of professional programmers who work outside of North America, continue to use this tool to develop and modify applications for Microsoft Windows. If you are thinking about upgrading to Visual Basic 2005 but are most comfortable with the commands and features in Visual Basic 6, there are some important product features and migration tips that you should be aware of. To help programmers who are moving from Visual Basic 6, I plan to start each chapter of this book with a sidebar that highlights the feature changes that you should be aware of. (If you are not upgrading from Visual Basic 6, simply skip the sidebar.)

Remember that you don't need *any* programming experience to learn Visual Basic 2005 using this book. But if you have some Visual Basic 6 knowledge already, you will benefit from an executive summary spelling out the differences. So to begin with, here is my list of upgrade notes for Chapter 1:

■ Visual Basic is now a full member of Visual Studio—it shares the Visual Studio development environment with Microsoft Visual C++ 2005, Microsoft Visual C# 2005, Microsoft Visual J# 2005, and several other programming tools. Although Visual Basic, Visual C++, Visual C#, and Visual J# are still different programming languages, they share the same IDE.

■ As part of its new development environment, Visual Studio offers a new Start Page pane, which shows recently used projects and lets you open new or existing source files. Additional links in the Start Page pane provide access to Visual Studio Web sites, news and articles about Visual Studio programming, and contacts within the Visual Studio development community.

■ The Visual Studio development environment contains several new and modified programming tools. The Project window is now called Solution Explorer, and help information is delivered through a new tool called Microsoft Document Explorer. You'll find that the Toolbox has changed quite a bit—it's now subdivided into several functional categories, such as Common Controls, Components, and Data.

■ Most of the programming tool windows (including the Toolbox) have an auto hide feature that hides the tool as a tab when it isn't needed. Auto hiding tools saves you design and coding space within the development environment.

■ Projects are now saved in a different way. You give your project a name *before* you create it, and the files that you create remain in memory for testing and debugging until you choose to save (or discard) them. The project itself is spread over several

files and folders—even more than in Visual Basic 6. In Visual Basic 6, programs
that are made up of multiple projects are called *project groups*; now they're called
solutions.

- To upgrade Visual Basic 6 applications to Visual Basic 2005, you can use a tool
  called the Visual Basic Upgrade Wizard, which starts automatically when you
  open a Visual Basic 6 program in Visual Studio. The Upgrade Wizard isn't a complete solution for migrating Visual Basic 6 applications. However, the wizard efficiently handles most repetitive code changes and can even swap Visual Basic 6
  controls for Visual Studio 2005 controls on forms. In addition to this upgrade
  tool, which prepares a complete migration report, you can also use the Upgrade
  Visual Basic 6 command on the Visual Studio Tools menu to quickly translate a
  line of Visual Basic 6 code and insert it into a Visual Basic 2005 project.

- If you open Visual Basic .NET 2002 or 2003 projects in Visual Studio 2005, they
  are converted automatically via the Visual Studio Conversion Wizard.

The Visual Studio Development Environment

Although the programming language you'll be learning in this book is Visual Basic, the development environment you'll be using to write programs is called the Microsoft Visual Studio
Integrated Development Environment, or IDE for short. Visual Studio is a powerful and customizable programming workshop that contains all the tools you need to build robust programs for Windows and the Web quickly and efficiently. Most of the features in the Visual
Studio IDE apply equally to Visual Basic, Visual C++, Visual C#, and Visual J#. Use the following procedures to start Visual Studio now.

Important   If you haven't yet installed this book's practice files, work through "Finding Your
Best Starting Point" and "About the CD-ROM and Practice Files" in this book's Introduction. (I
recommend that you place the project files and related subfolders in the c:\vb05sbs folder.)
Then return to this chapter.

Start Visual Studio 2005

1. On the Windows taskbar, click Start, point to All Programs, and then point to the
    Microsoft Visual Studio 2005 folder.

    The folders and icons in the Microsoft Visual Studio 2005 folder appear in a list.

> **Note**   To perform the steps in this book, you must have a version of the Microsoft Visual Studio 2005 software installed. Most of the procedures that I describe are designed to work with either Visual Studio 2005 Standard Edition or Visual Studio 2005 Professional Edition. If you are especially lucky, you might have access to Visual Studio 2005 Team Suite or Visual Studio 2005 Team Foundation tools as well. If this is the case, you'll be able to follow the procedures in this book without difficulty, but you will also have access to some cool advanced features and capabilities. However, even though it is tempting, don't try to use this book if you have an earlier version of the Visual Basic software. If that's your situation, you'll be better served by locating an earlier (and perhaps lower priced!) edition of my book, such as *Microsoft Visual Basic .NET Step by Step Version 2003* (which describes the Visual Basic .NET 2003 software) or *Microsoft Visual Basic Professional 6.0 Step by Step* (which describes the Visual Basic 6 software).

2. Click the Microsoft Visual Studio 2005 icon.

    Visual Studio starts, and you see the development environment on the screen with its many menus, tools, and component windows. (These windows are sometimes called *tool windows*.) You also should see a Start Page containing a set of links, MSDN articles, and project options. In Visual Studio 2005, the Start Page is much improved and has become a comprehensive source of information about your project, as well as resources within the Visual Basic development community. The new Community menu on the Visual Studio menu bar provides access to many of the same resources.

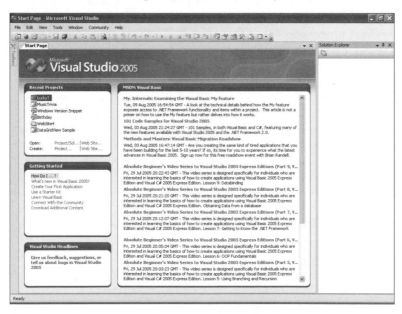

    The first thing most developers do when they start Visual Studio is open an existing project—either a completed solution they want to work with again or an ongoing development project. Try opening an existing project that I created for you—the Music Trivia program.

Open a Visual Basic project

1. Click the Open Projects/Solutions link in the Start Page.

    The Open Project dialog box appears on the screen with several options. (You can also display this dialog box by clicking the Open Project command on the File menu or by pressing Ctrl+O.) Even if you haven't used Visual Studio before, the Open Project dialog box will seem straightforward because it resembles the familiar Open dialog box in Microsoft Word or Microsoft Excel.

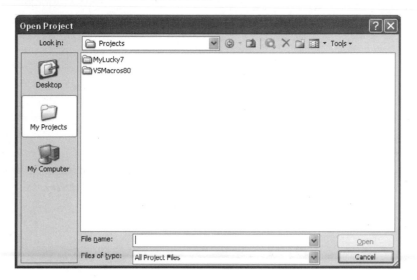

> **Tip**   In the Open Project dialog box, you see a number of shortcut icons along the left side of the window. The My Projects icon is particularly useful; it opens the Projects folder inside the My Documents\Visual Studio 2005 folder on your system. By default, Visual Studio saves your projects in this Projects folder, giving each project its own sub-folder. The folder VSMacros80 contains the macro files for Visual Studio 2005 (which is also called Visual Studio version 8.0 in some parts of the software).

2. Browse to the c:\vb05sbs folder on your hard disk.

    The c:\vb05sbs folder is the default location for this book's extensive sample file collection, and you'll find the files there if you followed the setup instructions in "About the CD-ROM and Practice Files" at the beginning of this book. If you didn't install the sample files, close this dialog box and install them now by using the CD-ROM included with this book. Then return to this procedure and continue.

3. Open the chap01\musictrivia folder, and then double-click the MusicTrivia solution file. (If your system shows file name extensions, this file will end with .sln.)

Visual Studio loads the MusicTrivia form, properties, and program code for the Music-Trivia solution. The Start Page probably is still visible, but in the upper-right corner of the screen, Solution Explorer lists some of the files in the solution.

> **Troubleshooting**   If you see an error message indicating that the project you want to open is in a newer file format, you might be trying to load Visual Basic 2005 files into the older Visual Basic .NET 2002 or 2003 software. (Earlier versions of Visual Basic cannot open the Visual Basic 2005 projects included on the companion CD-ROM.) To check which version of Visual Basic you're using, click the About command on the Help menu.

Visual Studio provides a special check box named Always Show Solution to control several options related to solutions within the IDE. The check box is located on the Projects and Solutions/General tab of the Options dialog box, which you open by clicking the Options command on the Tools menu. If the check box is selected, a subfolder is created for each new solution, placing the project and its files in a separate folder beneath the solution. Also, if you select the Always Show Solution check box, a few options related to solutions appear in the IDE, such as commands on the File menu and a solution entry in Solution Explorer. If you like the idea of creating separate folders for solutions and seeing solution-related commands and settings, select this check box.

Projects and Solutions

In Visual Studio, programs under development are typically called *projects* or *solutions* because they contain many individual components, not just one file. Visual Basic 2005 programs include a project file (.vbproj) and a solution file (.sln), and if you examine these files within a file browsing utility such as Windows Explorer, you'll notice that the solution file icons have a tiny 8 in them, an indication of their version number. (Visual Basic 2005 is referred to as VB 8 internally.)

A project file contains information specific to a single programming task. A solution file contains information about one or more projects. Solution files are useful to manage multiple related projects and are similar to project group files (.vbg) in Visual Basic 6. The samples included with this book typically have a single project for each solution, so opening the project file (.vbproj) has the same effect as opening the solution file (.sln). But for a multi-project solution, you will want to open the solution file. Visual Basic 2005 offers a new file format for its projects and solutions, but the basic terminology that you might have learned while using Visual Basic .NET 2002 or 2003 still applies.

The Visual Studio Tools

At this point, you should take a few moments to study the Visual Studio IDE and identify some of the programming tools and windows that you'll be using as you complete this course. If you've written Visual Basic programs before, you'll recognize many (but probably not all) of the programming tools. Collectively, these features are the components that you use to construct, organize, and test your Visual Basic programs. A few of the programming tools also help you learn more about the resources on your system, including the larger world of databases and Web site connections available to you. There are also several powerful Help tools.

The *menu bar* provides access to most of the commands that control the development environment. Menus and commands work as they do in all Windows-based programs, and you can access them by using the keyboard or the mouse. Located below the menu bar is the *Standard toolbar*, a collection of buttons that serve as shortcuts for executing commands and controlling the Visual Studio IDE. If you've used Excel or Word, the toolbar should be a familiar concept. To activate a button on the toolbar, use your mouse to click the button. You can see the full list of available toolbars by right-clicking the toolbar in the IDE.

Along the bottom of the screen is the Windows *taskbar*. You can use the taskbar to switch between various Visual Studio components and to activate other Windows-based programs. You might also see taskbar icons for Microsoft Internet Explorer, antivirus utilities, and other programs installed on your system.

The following illustration shows some of the tools and windows in the Visual Studio IDE. Don't worry that this illustration looks different from your current development environment view. You'll learn more about these elements (and how you adjust your views) as you work through the chapter.

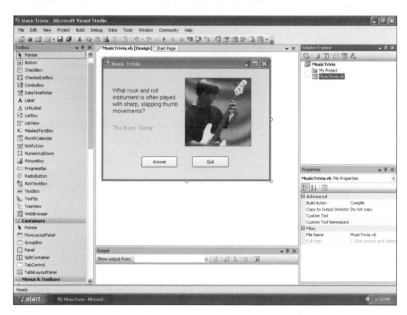

The main tools visible in this Visual Studio IDE are the Designer, Solution Explorer, the Properties window, the Toolbox, and the Output window. You might also see more specialized tools such as Server Explorer and Object Browser, or they may appear as tabs within the IDE. Because no two developers' preferences are exactly alike, it is difficult to predict what you'll see if your Visual Studio software has already been used. (What I show is essentially the "out of the box" view.)

If a tool isn't visible and you want to see it, click the View menu and select the tool. Because the View menu has expanded steadily over the years, Microsoft has moved some of the less frequently used View tools to a submenu called Other Windows. Check there if you don't see what you need.

The exact size and shape of the tools and windows depend on how your development environment has been configured. With Visual Studio, you can align and attach, or *dock*, windows to make visible only the elements that you want see. You can also partially conceal tools as *tabbed documents* along the edge of the development environment and then switch back and forth between documents quickly. Trying to sort out which tools are important to you now and which you can learn about later is a difficult early challenge when you're learning the busy Visual Studio interface. Your development environment will probably look best if you set your monitor and Windows desktop settings so that they maximize your screen space, but even then things can get a little crowded. (For example, I'm using a screen resolution of 1024 × 768 for some of the full-size screen shots in this book. You can change the screen resolution by right-clicking the Windows desktop and clicking Properties.)

The purpose of all this tool complexity is to add many new and useful features to the IDE while providing clever mechanisms for managing the clutter. These mechanisms include features such as docking, auto hiding, floating, and a few other window states that I'll describe later. If you're just starting out with Visual Basic, the best way to deal with this feature tension is to hide the tools that you don't plan to use often to make room for the important ones. The crucial tools for beginning Visual Basic programming—the ones you'll start using right away in this book—are Solution Explorer, the Properties window, the Designer, and the Toolbox. You won't use the Server Explorer, Class View, Resource View, Object Browser, or Debug windows until later in the book.

In the following exercises, you'll start experimenting with the crucial tools in the Visual Studio IDE. You'll also learn how to display a Web browser within Visual Studio and how to hide the tools that you won't use for a while.

The Designer

If you completed the last exercise, the MusicTrivia project is loaded in the Visual Studio development environment. However, the user interface, or *form*, for the project might not yet be visible in Visual Studio. (More sophisticated projects might contain several forms, but this simple trivia program needs only one.) To make the form of the MusicTrivia project visible in the IDE, you display it by using Solution Explorer.

Display the Designer

1. Locate the Solution Explorer window near the upper-right corner of the Visual Studio development environment. If you don't see Solution Explorer (if it is hidden as a tab in a location that you cannot see or isn't currently visible), click Solution Explorer on the View menu to display it.

   When the MusicTrivia project is loaded, Solution Explorer looks like this:

2. Click the MusicTrivia.vb form in the Solution Explorer window.

   All form files, including this one, have a tiny form icon next to them so that you can easily identify them. When you click the form file, Visual Studio highlights it in Solution Explorer, and some information about the file appears in the Properties window (if it is visible).

3. Click the View Designer button in Solution Explorer to display the program's user interface.

   The MusicTrivia form is displayed in the Designer, as shown here:

Notice that a tab for the Start Page is still visible near the top of the Designer. You can click this tab to display the Start Page, where you can view articles and Web links, or open additional project files. To return to Designer view, click the MusicTrivia.vb [Design] tab near the top of the MusicTrivia form.

Now try running a Visual Basic program with Visual Studio.

> **Tip**   If you don't see the Start Page and MusicTrivia.vb [Design] tabs, your development environment might be in Multiple Documents view instead of Tabbed Documents view. To change this option, click Options on the Tools menu. On the left side of the Options dialog box, click the Environment folder, and then click General. On the right, under Window Layout, click the Tabbed Documents option, and then click OK. The next time you start Visual Studio, the various windows that you open have tabs, and you can switch between them with a simple button click.

Running a Visual Basic Program

Music Trivia is a simple Visual Basic program designed to familiarize you with the programming tools in Visual Studio. The form you see now has been customized with five objects (two labels, a picture, and two buttons), and I've added three lines of program code to make the trivia program ask a simple question and display the appropriate answer. (The program "gives away" the answer now because it is currently in design mode, but the answer is hidden when you run the program.) You'll learn more about creating objects and adding program code in the next chapter. For now, try running the program in the Visual Studio IDE.

Run the Music Trivia program

1. Click the Start Debugging button (the green right-pointing arrow) on the Standard toolbar to run the Music Trivia program in Visual Studio.

> **Tip**   You can also press F5 or click the Start Debugging command on the Debug menu to run a program in the Visual Studio development environment. Note that the placement of the Start command is different than it is in the Visual Basic 6 IDE, and that it has a different name.

Visual Studio loads and compiles the project into an *assembly* (a structured collection of modules, data, and manifest information for a program), prepares the program for testing or *debugging*, and then (if the compilation is successful) runs the program in the development environment. While the program is running, an icon for the program appears on the Windows taskbar. After a moment, you see the MusicTrivia form again, this time with the photograph and answer label hidden from view, as shown here:

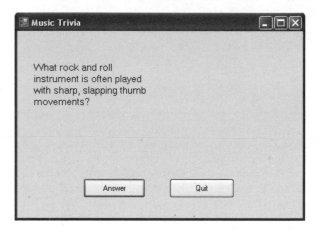

Music Trivia now asks its important question: What rock and roll instrument is often played with sharp, slapping thumb movements?

2. Click the Answer button to reveal the solution to the question.

The program displays the answer (The Bass Guitar) below the question and then displays a photograph of an obscure Seattle bass player demonstrating the technique. The test program works.

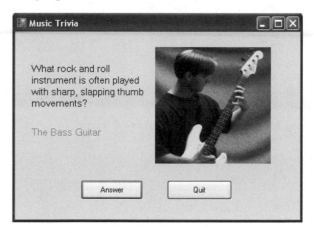

3. Click Quit to close the program.

The form closes, and the Visual Studio IDE becomes active again.

The Properties Window

You use the Properties window to change the characteristics, or *property settings*, of the user interface elements on a form. A property setting is a *quality* of one of the objects in your program. You can change property settings by using the Properties window while you're creating your user interface, or you can add program code via the Code Editor to change one or more property settings while your program is running. For example, the trivia question that the Music Trivia program displays can be modified to appear in a different font or font size or with a different alignment. (With Visual Studio, you can display text in any font installed on your system, just as you can in Excel or Word.)

The Properties window contains an Object list that itemizes all the user interface elements (objects) on the form. The window also lists the property settings that can be changed for each object. You can click one of two convenient buttons to view properties alphabetically or by category. You'll practice changing the Font property of the first label in the Music Trivia program now.

Change a property

1. Click the *Label1* object on the form. (*Label1* contains the text "What rock and roll instrument is often played with short, slapping thumb movements?")

    To work with an object on a form, you must first select the object. When you select an object, resize handles surround it, and the property settings for the object are displayed in the Properties window.

2. Click the Properties Window button on the Standard toolbar.

    The Properties window might or might not be visible in Visual Studio, depending on how it's been configured and used on your system. It usually appears below Solution Explorer on the right side of the development environment. (If it is visible, you don't need to click the button, but you should click the window to activate it.)

    You'll see a window similar to the following:

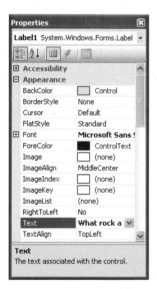

The Properties window lists all the property settings for the first label object (*Label1*) on the form. (In Visual Basic 2005, over 50 properties are associated with labels.) Property names are listed in the left column of the window, and the current setting for each property is listed in the right column. Because there are so many properties (including some that are rarely modified), Visual Studio organizes them into categories and displays them in outline view. If a category has a plus sign (+) next to it, you can click the collection title to display all the properties in that category. If a category has a minus sign (-) next to it, the properties are all visible, but you can hide the list under the category name by clicking the minus sign.

> **Tip** The Properties window has two handy buttons that you can use to further organize properties. Clicking the Alphabetical button lists all the properties in alphabetical order and puts them in just a few categories. Clicking the Categorized button organizes the property list into many logical categories. I recommend this view if you are new to Visual Studio.

3. Scroll in the Properties window list box until the *Font* property is visible.

   The Properties window scrolls like a regular list box. If you are in categorized view, Font is in the Appearance category.

4. Click the *Font* property name (in the left column).

   The current font (Microsoft Sans Serif) is partially displayed in the right column, and a button with three dots on it appears by the font name. This button is called an *ellipsis button* and indicates that a dialog box is available to customize the property setting.

5. Click the Font ellipsis button in the Properties window.

   Visual Studio displays the Font dialog box, which you can use to specify new formatting characteristics for the text in the selected label on your form. The Font dialog box contains more than one formatting option; for each option you select, a different property setting will be modified.

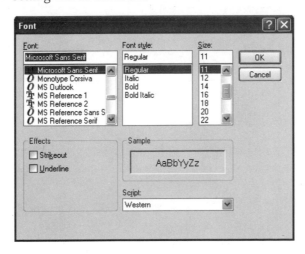

6. Change the size of the font from 11 point to 12 point, and then change the font style from Regular to Italic. Click OK to confirm your changes.

   Visual Studio records your changes and adjusts the property settings accordingly. You can examine the changes by viewing your form in the Designer or by expanding the Font category in the Properties window.

   Now change a property setting for the *Label2* object (the label that contains the text "The Bass Guitar").

7. In the Designer, click the second label object (*Label2*).

   When you select the object, resize handles surround it.

8. Click the *Font* property in the Properties window.

   The *Label2* object has its own unique set of property settings. Although the property names are the same as those of the *Label1* object, the values in the property settings are distinct and allow the *Label2* object to act independently on the form.

9. Click the Font ellipsis button, set the font style to Bold, and then click OK.

10. Scroll to the *ForeColor* property in the Properties window, and then click it in the left column.

11. Click the ForeColor arrow in the right column, click the Custom tab, and then click a dark purple color.

    The text in the *Label2* object is now bold and purple on the form.

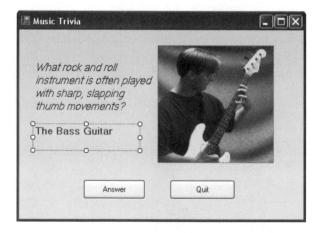

Congratulations! You've just learned how to set properties in a Visual Basic program by using the Visual Studio Properties window—one of the important skills in becoming a Visual Basic programmer.

> ## Thinking About Properties
>
> In Visual Basic, each user interface element in a program (including the form itself) has a set of definable properties. You can set properties at design time by using the Properties window. Properties can also be referenced in code to do meaningful work while the program runs. (User interface elements that receive input often use properties to convey information to the program.) At first, you might find properties a difficult concept to grasp. Viewing them in terms of something from everyday life can help.
>
> Consider this bicycle analogy: a bicycle is an object you use to ride from one place to another. Because a bicycle is a physical object, it has several inherent characteristics. It has a brand name, a color, gears, brakes, and wheels, and it's built in a particular style. (It might be a touring bike, a mountain bike, or a bicycle built for two.) In Visual Basic terminology, these characteristics are *properties* of the bicycle object. Most of the bicycle's properties were defined when the bicycle was built. But others (tires, travel speed, and options such as reflectors and mirrors) are properties that change while the bicycle is used. The bike might even have intangible (that is, invisible) properties, such as age, current owner, or rental status. As you work with Visual Basic, you'll use object properties of both types—visible and invisible.

Moving and Resizing the Programming Tools

With numerous programming tools to contend with on the screen, the Visual Studio IDE can become a pretty busy place. To give you complete control over the shape and size of the elements in the development environment, Visual Studio lets you move, resize, dock, and auto hide most of the interface elements that you use to build programs.

To move one of the tool windows in Visual Studio, simply click the title bar and drag the object to a new location. If you align one window along the edge of another window, it attaches to that window, or *docks* itself. Dockable windows are advantageous because they always remain visible. (They don't become hidden behind other windows.) If you want to see more of a docked window, simply drag one of its borders to view more content.

If you want to completely close a window, click the Close button in the upper-right corner of the window. You can always open the window again later by clicking the appropriate command on the View menu.

If you want an option somewhere between docking and closing a window, you might try auto hiding a tool window at the side of the Visual Studio IDE by clicking the tiny Auto Hide push-pin button on the right side of the tool's title bar. This action removes the window from the docked position and places the title of the tool at the edge of the development environment in an unobtrusive tab. When you auto hide a window, you'll notice that the tool window remains visible as long as you keep the mouse pointer in the area of the window. When you move the mouse to another part of the IDE, the window slides out of view.

To restore a window that you have auto hidden, click the tool tab at the edge of the development environment or hold your mouse over the tab. (You can recognize a window that is auto hidden because the pushpin in its title bar is pointing sideways.) By holding the mouse pointer over the title, you can use the tools in what I call "peek-a-boo" mode—in other words, to quickly display an auto hidden window, click its tab, check or set the information you need, and then move the mouse to make the window disappear. If you ever need the tool displayed permanently, click the Auto Hide pushpin button again so that the point of the pushpin faces down, and the window then remains visible.

An exciting capability of Visual Studio 2005 is the ability to display windows as tabbed documents (windows with tab handles that partially hide behind other windows) and to dock windows by using docking guides, as shown in the following illustration.

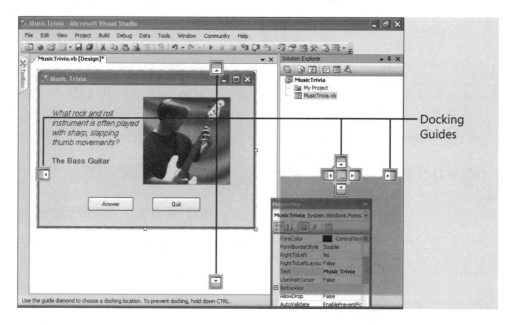

Docking guides are changeable icons that appear on the surface of the IDE when you move a window or tool from a docked position to a new location. Because the docking guides are associated with shaded, rectangular areas of the IDE, you can preview the results of your docking maneuver before you actually make it. In my opinion, this fixes a major problem with previous versions of the Visual Studio IDE, which had impressive collections of development tools that were cumbersome to customize.

Docking and auto hiding techniques definitely take some practice to master. Use the following exercises to hone your windows management skills and experiment with the features of the Visual Studio development environment. After you complete the exercises here, feel free to configure the Visual Studio tools in a way that seems comfortable for you.

Moving and Resizing Tool Windows

To move and resize one of the programming tool windows in Visual Studio, follow these steps. This exercise demonstrates how to manipulate the Properties window, but you can work with a different tool window if you want to.

Move and resize the Properties window

1. If the Properties window isn't visible in the development environment, click the Properties Window button on the Standard toolbar.

    The Properties window is activated in the IDE, and its title bar is highlighted.

2. Double-click the Properties window title bar to display the window as a floating (non-docked) window.

3. Using the Properties window title bar, drag the window to a new location in the development environment, but don't dock it (yet).

    Moving windows around the Visual Studio IDE gives you some flexibility with the tools and the look of your development environment.

    Now you'll resize the Properties window to see more object property settings at once.

4. Move the mouse to the lower-right corner of the Properties window until it becomes a resizing pointer.

5. Drag the lower-right border of the window down and to the right to enlarge the window.

    Your Properties window is now bigger:

You can work more quickly and with more clarity of purpose in a bigger window. Feel free to move or resize a window when you need to see more of it.

Docking Tool Windows

If a tool window is floating over the development environment, you can return it to its original docked position by double-clicking the window's title bar. (Notice that you used this same technique in the previous exercise to expand a docked window. Double-clicking a title bar works like a *toggle*, a state that switches back and forth between two standard positions.) You can also attach or dock a floating tool in a different place. You might want to do this if you need to make more room in Visual Studio for a particular programming task, such as creating a user interface with the Designer. Try docking the Properties window in a different location now.

Dock the Properties window

1. Verify that the Properties window (or another tool that you want to dock) is floating over the Visual Studio IDE in an undocked position.

    If you completed the previous exercise, the Properties window is undocked now.

2. Drag the title bar of the Properties window to the top, bottom, right, or left edge of the development environment (your choice!), taking care to drag the mouse pointer over one of the docking guides (small arrows) on the edge of the Visual Studio IDE, or the collection of four docking guides in the center.

    As you move the mouse over a docking guide, the Properties window snaps into place, and a blue shaded rectangle indicates how your window will appear when you release the mouse button. Note that there are several valid docking locations for tool windows in Visual Studio, so you might want to try two or three different spots until you find one that looks right to you. (A window should be located in a place that's handy and not in the way of other needed tools.)

3. Release the mouse button to dock the Properties window.

   The window snaps into place in its new home.

> **Tip** To switch between dockable, tabbed document, and floating window styles, right-click the window's title bar (or tab, if it is a tabbed document), and select the option that you want to use. Although the Properties window works very well as a dockable window, you'll probably find that larger windows (the Visual Studio Start Page, for example) work best as tabbed document windows.

4. Try docking the Properties window several more times in different places to get the hang of how docking works.

   I guarantee that although a few of these window procedures seem confusing at first, after a while they'll become routine for you. In general, you want to create window spaces that have enough room for the information you need to see and use while you work on more important tasks in the Designer and in the Code Editor.

Hiding Tool Windows

To hide a tool window, click the Auto Hide pushpin button on the right side of the title bar to conceal the window beneath a tool tab on the edge of the IDE, and click it again to restore the window to its docked position. You can also use the Auto Hide command on the Window menu (or right-click a title bar and select Auto Hide) to auto hide a tool window. Give it a try now.

Use the auto hide feature

1. Locate the Auto Hide pushpin button on the title bar of the Properties window.

   The pushpin is currently in the "down," or "pushed in," position, meaning that the Properties window is "pinned" open and auto hide is disabled.

2. Click the pushpin button in the Properties window title bar.

   The Properties window slides off the screen and is replaced by a small tab named Properties. The benefit of enabling auto hide, of course, is that the process frees up additional work area in Visual Studio. But the hidden window is also quickly accessible.

3. Hold the mouse pointer over the Properties tab. (You can also click the Properties tab if you want.)

   The Properties window immediately slides back into view.

4. Click elsewhere within the IDE, and the window disappears again.

5. Finally, display the Properties window again, and then click the pushpin button on the Properties window title bar.

   The Properties window returns to its familiar docked position, and you can use it without worrying about it sliding away.

Spend some time moving, resizing, docking, and auto hiding tool windows in Visual Studio now, to create your version of the perfect work environment. As you work through this book, you'll want to adjust your window settings periodically to adapt your work area to the new tools you're using. When the need arises, come back to this section and practice your skills again.

> **Tip**   Visual Studio 2005 now lets you save your window and programming environment settings and copy them to a second computer or share them with members of your programming team. To experiment with this new feature, click the Import/Export Settings command on the Tools menu and follow the wizard instructions to export (save) or import (load) settings from a file.

Opening a Web Browser Within Visual Studio

A handy new feature in Visual Studio 2005 is the ability to open a simple Web browser within the development environment. The browser appears as a tabbed document window in the IDE, so it takes up little space but can be opened immediately when needed. You could open a stand-alone Web browser (such as Internet Explorer) and keep it nearby on the Windows taskbar, but running a Web browser *within* Visual Studio makes examining Web sites and copying data into Visual Studio even easier. Try using the Visual Studio Web browser now.

Open the Visual Studio Web browser

1. Click the Other Windows submenu on the View menu, and then click the Web Browser command.

   The Web Browser window appears, as shown here:

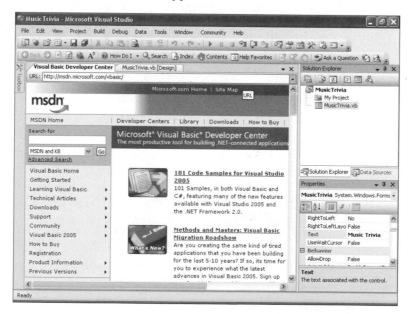

The browser is a tabbed document window by default, but you can change it into a floating window or a docked window by right-clicking the window title bar and then clicking the Floating or Dockable commands.

2. Experiment with the browser and how it functions within the IDE.

Although the browser is more basic than Internet Explorer or another full-featured browser, you will soon find it a useful addition to the Visual Studio tool collection.

3. When you're finished, click the Close button on the right side of the Web browser title bar to close the window. (If your browser window appears as a tabbed window, you might need to change it to a floating window first.)

4. If the Help toolbar is still visible in the IDE, right-click the Help toolbar, and then click Help in the pop-up menu to remove it.

Getting Help

Visual Studio includes an electronic reference center called Microsoft Visual Studio 2005 Documentation that you can use to learn more about the Visual Studio IDE, the Visual Basic programming language, resources in the .NET Framework, online communities that specialize in Visual Basic and Visual Studio, and the remaining tools in the Visual Studio suite. Take a moment to explore these Help resources now before moving on to the next chapter, where you'll build your first program.

Two Sources for Help: Local Help Files and Online Content

Major improvements have been made in the content of the Visual Studio help information and the tools that provide access to this help. Essentially, there are two basic resources for electronic help within Visual Studio:

- You can access the local help files that were installed during the Visual Studio 2005 setup process. (These files are stored on discs labeled MSDN Library in your Visual Studio software package.)

- You can access online (Internet-based) help via MSDN Online, MSDN newsgroups, and a collection of developer Web sites sponsored by Microsoft called the .NET Code Wise Community. The .NET Code Wise Community is especially valuable, because the group includes professional developers who are using Visual Studio and Visual Basic 2005 to write real-world applications; the content and advice they offer is continually updated and therefore reflects current trends, concerns, and triumphs within the VB programming community.

Configure your Help system now to offer both local and online help resources as you learn about Visual Basic.

Set Help system options

1. Click How Do I? on the Help menu to open the Help system.

    Visual Studio offers its help through an HTML-based tool called Microsoft Document Explorer. You can use several commands on the Community and Help menus to open Document Explorer. Each command opens and configures Document Explorer to display a different type of help information. How Do I? is one of the best starting places; it presents a hierarchical list of common programming tasks that you can use to quickly find the information you need. Your screen looks something like this:

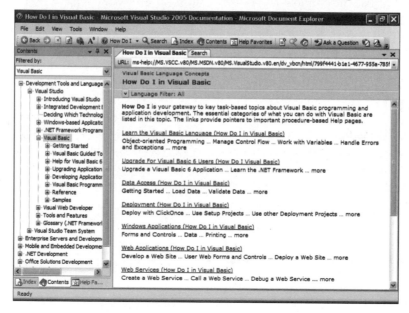

2. Click one or more topics within the How Do I? list to explore the type of material provided.

    For Visual Basic 2005, the Help system contains hundreds of technical descriptions and tutorials (many with sample code). Now you'll configure Help to display just the content that you want when it opens.

3. On the Microsoft Document Explorer menu bar, click Tools, and then click the Options command.

    You are presented with customization options that you can use to configure how the Help system works and (most importantly) what resources Help checks when it searches for information.

4. Click the Online topic under the Help category, if it is not already selected.

    Your screen looks similar to the following:

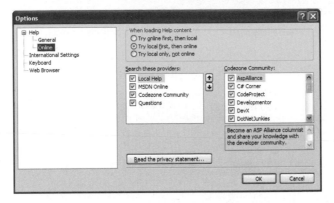

My recommendation is that you set your online options as shown in this screen—essentially, the default settings. First select the middle option button to load Help content first from local sources on your hard disk and then from online sources. Next be sure that MSDN Online and Codezone (the .NET Code Wise community) are selected so that Visual Studio loads recent articles from VB developers each time that you use the Search command. If you find after a while that you prefer one or two Codezone communities over the others, you can adjust the search order or remove items from the list.

5. Select the configuration options that make sense to you, and then click OK to save them.

You can return to the Options menu within Document Explorer any time that the Help system is open. Now try using another new feature in Visual Studio 2005, the Help favorites list, which operates much like the Favorites list within Internet Explorer.

Maintain a Favorites list within Help

1. On the Document Explorer toolbar, click the Add to Help Favorites button (the one next to the Help Favorites button, with the icon of a page with a plus sign (+) on it).

    When you click this button, Document Explorer adds the article that is currently visible to your preferred list of Help documents. Now you can always have your favorite Help resources organized and right at your fingertips!

2. Click the Search tab at the top of the Document Explorer window.

    The Search window opens, providing a tool that you can use to make specific text-based searches within your local and online help resources.

3. Click the Language arrow (a content filter), and remove the check marks from all languages except Visual Basic.

    You can configure the Help system to limit your search to just the languages, technologies, and topics that you want by using the filter arrows. Because you are just starting with Visual Studio, you might want to limit your search to just Visual Basic for now.

4. In the Search text box, type **data controls**, and press Enter.

Visual Studio searches for the text string "data controls" in your local help files and online in MSDN, newsgroup, and Codezone communities. Pay particular attention to the Sort By list box in the Search window, which you can use to select how articles found by Search are displayed. Rumor has it that the Visual Studio 2005 team worked pretty hard to make these Search results easier to understand and use than they have been in the past. Along these lines, note especially the new Visual Studio 2005 feature that creates an abstract for each search result found. This abstract gives you a better opportunity to evaluate a search's potential relevance.

5. Click the Save Search button on the Document Explorer toolbar.

> **Tip**   In addition to help articles, you can save important search results in your Favorites list.

Your screen looks similar to the following illustration. Notice that the Help Favorites window now holds the two new favorites that you have saved.

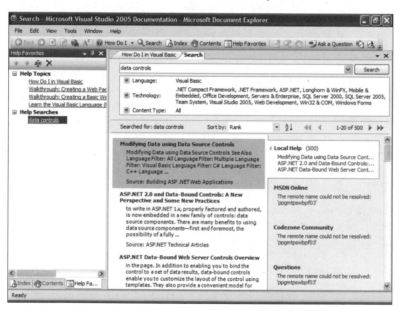

6. Click the Rename button in the Help Favorites window. (You can also right-click the search that you saved, and then click Rename.)

Document Explorer highlights the name that you used for your search and allows you to rename it so that your favorite more closely matches the actual search. This step is optional, but I find it useful.

7. Type **binding data to controls**, and press Enter.

Document Explorer changes the name of the search within your Favorites list. I chose this title because it seemed clearer to me than my original search string. (However, you might want to specify a different title that more closely matches the search results that you have achieved.)

8. Click How Do I? in the Help Favorites window.

   The first article that you saved appears in Document Explorer. Now you'll practice deleting a favorite, a skill that becomes important when your list of favorite Help articles grows long and you need to thin it out.

9. Click the Delete button in the Help Favorites window.

10. If you are prompted to confirm your intention to delete this favorite, click Yes.

   The How Do I? article is deleted from your favorites list (but not from the Help system).

11. Click the Close button on the Document Explorer title bar.

   There are additional Help features to learn and experiment with, but now is a good time for me to summarize the important Help commands and for you to turn to the writing of your first program in Chapter 2.

Summary of Help Commands

Here is a short compilation of useful Help commands and their uses within the Visual Studio IDE:

To get Help information	Do this
Organized by programming task	On the Visual Studio Help menu, click How Do I?
About the feature or command you're currently using	On the Visual Studio Help menu, click Dynamic Help.
By topic or activity	On the Visual Studio Help menu, click Contents.
While working in the Code Editor	Click the keyword or program statement you're interested in, and then press F1.
While working in a dialog box	Click the Help button (question mark) in select dialog boxes (for example, the dialog box displayed when you choose the Options command on the Tools menu).
By searching for a specific keyword	On the Help menu, click Search, and type the term you're looking for. Filter and organize the search results using the Sort By list box.
From MSDN and independent Visual Studio Web sites	On the Community menu, click Developer Center or Codezone Community.
About contacting Microsoft for product support	On the Help menu, click Technical Support.

Customizing IDE Settings to Match Step-by-Step Exercises

Like the tool windows and the Help system, the compiler settings within the Visual Studio development environment are highly customizable. It is important to review a few of these settings now so that your version of Visual Studio is configured in a way that is compatible with the step-by-step programming exercises that follow. You will also learn how to customize Visual Studio generally so that as you gain programming experience, you can set up Visual Studio in the way that is most productive for you.

Setting the IDE for Visual Basic Development

The first setting that you need to check was established when Visual Studio was first installed on your machine. During setup, you were asked how you wanted Visual Studio to configure your general development environment. Since Visual Studio is a multi-purpose programming tool, you had many options—Visual Basic development, Visual C++ development, Visual C# development, Visual J++ development, Web development, and even a general-purpose programming environment that closely matches Visual Studio .NET 2003. The selection you made configured not only the Code Editor and the development tools available to you, but also the menu and toolbar commands, and the contents of several tool windows. For this reason, if you plan to use this book to learn Visual Basic programming but originally configured your software for a different language, a few of the menu commands and procedures described in this book will not exactly match your current software configuration. (The location of the Open Browser command, discussed above, is one example.)

Fortunately, you can fix this inconsistency and practice changing your environment settings by using the Import and Export Settings command on the Tools menu. The following steps show you how to change your environment setting to Visual Basic development, the recommended setting for this book.

Set the IDE for Visual Basic development

1. On the Tools menu, click Import and Export Settings.

   You can use the wizard that appears to save your environment settings for use on another computer, load settings from another computer, or reset your settings—the option that you want to select now.

2. Click Reset All Options, and then click Next.

   Visual Studio asks you if you want to save your current settings in a file before you configure the IDE for a different type of programming. It is always a good idea to save your current settings as a backup, so that you can return to them if the new ones don't work out.

3. Verify that the Yes, Save My Settings button is selected, and note the file name and folder location in which Visual Studio plans to save the settings.

   If you want to go back to these settings, you'll use this same wizard and the Import Selected Environmental Settings button to restore them.

...

4. Click Next to view the default list of settings that you can use for Visual Studio.

   You see the following list of options:

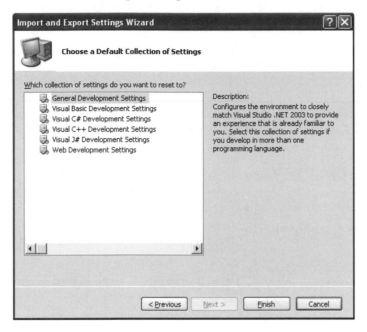

5. Click Visual Basic Development Settings, and click Finish.

   The wizard switches your IDE settings, including menu commands, toolbars, and settings within a few dialog boxes, tool windows, and the Code Editor. If a Help window is still open from an earlier exercise, you see a warning reminding you that the Help system cannot be updated fully until you close and restart Help.

   Feel free to repeat this customization process any time that you need to reset your settings (for example, if you make a customization mistake that you regret), or if you want to customize Visual Studio for another programming tool.

6. Click Close to close the wizard.

Checking Project and Compiler Settings

If you just reset your environment settings for Visual Basic development, you are now ready to begin the programming exercises. But if you didn't reset your settings—for example, if you were already configured for Visual Basic development and have been using Visual Studio 2005 for a while, or if your computer is a shared resource used by other programmers who might have modified the default settings (perhaps in a college computer lab)—complete the following steps to verify that your settings related to projects, solutions, and the Visual Basic compiler match those that I use in the book.

Check project and compiler settings

1. Click the Options command on the Tools menu to display the Options dialog box.

   The Options dialog box is your window to many of the customizable settings within Visual Studio. To see all the settings that you can adjust, click to select the Show All Settings check box in the lower-left corner of the dialog box.

2. Click the Projects And Solutions category and the General item in the Options dialog box.

   This group of check boxes and options configures the Visual Studio project and solution settings. So that your software matches the settings used in this book, adjust your settings to match those shown in the following dialog box:

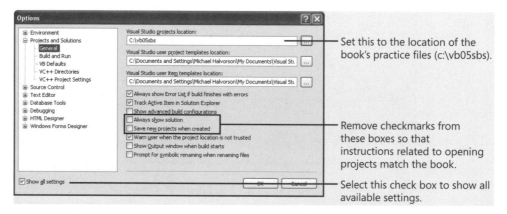

— Set this to the location of the book's practice files (c:\vb05sbs).

— Remove checkmarks from these boxes so that instructions related to opening projects match the book.

— Select this check box to show all available settings.

In particular, I recommend that you clear the check marks from the Always Show Solution and Save New Projects When Created check boxes. The first option creates a second folder for your program's solution file, which is not necessary for solutions that contain only one project (the situation for most programs in this book). The second option (in contrast with Visual Studio .NET 2003 and Visual Basic 6) causes Visual Studio to postpone saving your project until you click the Save All command on the File menu and provide a location for saving the file. This "delayed save" feature allows you to create a test program, compile and debug the program, and even run it without actually saving the project on disk—a useful feature when you want to create a quick test program that you might want to discard instead of saving. (An equivalent situation in word-processing terms is when you open a new Word document, enter an address for a mailing label, print the address, and then exit Word without saving the file.) With this default setting, the exercises in this book prompt you to save your projects after you create them, although you can also save your projects in advance by selecting the Save New Projects When Created check box.

You'll also notice that I have highlighted the c:\vb05sbs folder as the location for Visual Studio projects, the default location for this book's sample files. Most of the projects that you create will be stored in this folder, and they will have a "My" prefix to distinguish them from the completed project I provide for you to examine.

After you have adjusted these settings, you're ready to check three Visual Basic compiler settings.

3. Click the VB Defaults item in the Options dialog box.

    Visual Studio displays a list of three compiler settings: Option Explicit, Option Strict, and Option Compare. Your screen looks like this:

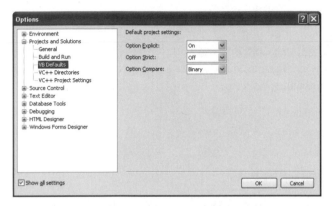

Although a detailed description of these settings is beyond the scope of Chapter 1, you'll want to verify that Option Explicit is set to On and Option Strict is set to Off—the default settings for Visual Basic programming within Visual Studio. Option Explicit On is a setting that requires you to declare a variable before using it in a program—a very good programming practice that I want to encourage. Option Strict Off allows variables and objects of different types to be combined under certain circumstances without generating a compiler error. (For example, a number can be assigned to a text box object without error.) Although this is a potentially worrisome programming practice, Option Strict Off is a useful setting for certain types of demonstration programs. If you don't keep this setting, a few projects will display error messages when you run them.

4. Feel free to examine additional settings in the Options dialog box related to your programming environment and Visual Studio. When you're finished, click OK to close the Options dialog box.

You're ready to exit Visual Studio and start programming.

One Step Further: Exiting Visual Studio

Each chapter in this book concludes with a section entitled "One Step Further" that enables you to practice an additional skill related to the topic at hand. After the "One Step Further" tutorial, I've compiled a Quick Reference table that reprises the important concepts discussed in each chapter.

When you're finished using Visual Studio for the day, save any projects that are open, and close the development environment. Give it a try.

Exit Visual Studio

1. Save any changes you've made to your program by clicking the Save All button on the Standard toolbar.

   As you learned in the preceding section, the default behavior in Visual Studio 2005 is that you give your program a name when you begin a project or solution, but you don't specify a file location and save the project until you click the Save All button or the Save All command on the File menu. You've made a few changes to your project, so you should save your changes now.

2. On the File menu, click the Exit command.

   The Visual Studio program closes. Time to move on to your first program in Chapter 2!

Chapter 1 Quick Reference

To	Do this
Start Visual Studio	Click Start on the taskbar, point to All Programs, point to the Microsoft Visual Studio 2005 folder, and then click the Microsoft Visual Studio 2005 program icon.
Open an existing project	Start Visual Studio. Click Open Project on the File menu. *or* On the Start Page, click Project/Solution at the bottom of the Recent Projects pane.
Compile and run a program	Click the Start Debugging button on the Standard toolbar. *or* Press F5.
Set properties	Click the object on the form whose properties you want to set, and then if the Properties window is not open, click the Properties Window button on the Standard toolbar. In the Properties window, click the property name in the left column, and then change the property setting in the corresponding right column.
Resize a tool window	Display the tool as a floating window (if it is currently docked), and resize it by dragging its edges.
Move a tool window	Display the tool as a floating window (if it is in a docked state), and then drag its title bar.
Dock a tool window	With the mouse pointer, drag the window's title bar over a docking guide to preview how it will appear, and then release the mouse button to snap the tool into place.
Auto hide a docked tool window	Click the Auto Hide pushpin button on the right side of the title bar of the tool window. The window hides behind a small tab at the edge of the development environment until you hold the mouse over it.
Disable auto hide for a docked tool window	Click the tool tab, and then click the Auto Hide pushpin button.

To	Do this
Get help	Start the Help system (hosted by the Microsoft Document Explorer) by clicking a command on the Community or Help menu.
Customize Help	In Document Explorer, click the Options command on the Tools menu.
Configure the Visual Studio environment for Visual Basic development	Click the Import and Export Settings command on the Tools menu, click Reset All Settings and the Next button. Click Yes, Save My Current Settings, and the Next button. Finally click Visual Basic Development Settings and the Finish button, and then click Close.
Customize IDE settings	Click the Options command on the Tools menu, and then customize Visual Studio settings by category. To view and customize project settings, click the General item in the Projects And Solutions category. To view and customize compiler settings, click the VB Defaults item in the Projects And Solutions category.
Exit Visual Studio	On the File menu, click Exit.

Chapter 2
Writing Your First Program

After completing this chapter, you will be able to:

- Create the user interface for a new program.
- Set the properties for each object in your user interface.
- Write program code.
- Save and run the program.
- Build an executable file.

As you learned in Chapter 1, the Microsoft Visual Studio 2005 Integrated Development Environment (IDE) contains several powerful tools to help you run and manage your programs. Visual Studio also contains everything you need to build your own applications for Microsoft Windows and the Web from the ground up.

Upgrade Notes: Migrating Visual Basic 6 Code to Visual Basic 2005

If you're experienced with Microsoft Visual Basic 6, you'll notice some new features in Microsoft Visual Basic 2005, including the following:

- The Visual Studio 2005 IDE provides a few different menus and toolbars with which you can build your programs. For example, Visual Basic 6 includes the Format, Run, and Add-Ins menus, which aren't included in Visual Studio. Most of the commands have been relocated—for example, you'll find many of the Run menu commands on the Debug menu.

- The *CommandButton* control is named the *Button* control in Visual Studio 2005, and many of its properties and methods have changed. For example, the *Caption* property is now named the *Text* property.

- Some of the properties and methods for the *Label* control are new or have changed. For example, the *Caption* property is now named the *Text* property, and the *TextAlign* property has more alignment options than the previous *Alignment* property.

- The *Image* control has been removed from Visual Studio. To display pictures, use the *PictureBox* control.

In this chapter, you'll learn how to create a simple but attractive user interface with the controls in the Visual Studio Toolbox. Next you'll learn how to customize the operation of these controls with property settings. Then you'll see how to identify just what your program should do by writing program code. Finally, you'll learn how to save and run your new program (a Las Vegas–style slot machine) and how to compile it as an executable file.

Lucky Seven: Your First Visual Basic Program

The Windows-based application you're going to construct is Lucky Seven, a game program that simulates a lucky number slot machine. Lucky Seven has a simple user interface and can be created and compiled in just a few minutes using Visual Basic. (If you'd like to run a completed version of Lucky Seven before you start, you can find it in the c:\vb05sbs\chap02\lucky7 folder on your hard disk.) Here's what your program will look like when it's finished:

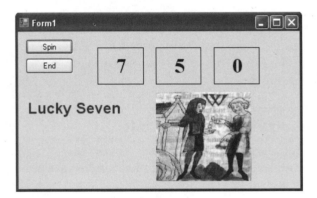

Programming Steps

The Lucky Seven user interface contains two buttons, three lucky number boxes, a digital photo depicting your winnings, and the label "Lucky Seven." I produced these elements by creating seven objects on the Lucky Seven form and then changing several properties for each object. After I designed the interface, I added program code for the Spin and End buttons to process the user's button clicks and produce the random numbers. To re-create Lucky Seven, you'll follow three essential programming steps in Visual Basic:

1. Create the user interface.
2. Set the properties.
3. Write the program code.

The following table summarizes the process for Lucky Seven.

Programming step	Number of items
1. Create the user interface.	7 objects
2. Set the properties.	13 properties
3. Write the program code.	2 objects

Creating the User Interface

In this exercise, you'll start building Lucky Seven by first creating a new project and then using controls in the Toolbox to construct the user interface.

Create a new project

1. Start Visual Studio 2005.

2. On the Visual Studio File menu, click New Project.

> **Tip**   You can also start a new programming project by clicking the blue Project link to the right of Create at the bottom of the Recent Projects pane on the Start Page.

The New Project dialog box appears.

3. In the Project Types area of the dialog box, click a few + signs to more fully display the programming options available to you. Your screen looks something like this:

The New Project dialog box provides access to the major project types available for writing Windows applications. If you indicated during setup that you are a Visual Basic programmer, Visual Basic is your primary development option (as shown here), but the other languages in Visual Studio (Visual C#, Visual J++, and C++) are always available through this dialog box. Although you will select a basic Windows application project in this exercise, this dialog box is also the gateway to other types of development projects, such as a console application, smart device (.NET compact Framework) application, starter kit, or Visual Studio deployment project. Web development options are not available through this dialog box. To create a Web application (something you'll try later in the book), you would click the New Web Site command on the File menu.

4. Click the Windows Application icon in the Templates area of the dialog box, if it is not already selected.

    Visual Studio prepares the development environment for Visual Basic Windows application programming.

5. In the Name text box, type **MyLucky7**.

    Visual Studio assigns the name MyLucky7 to your project. (You'll specify a folder location for the project later.)

> **Tip**   If your New Project dialog box contains Location and Solution Name text boxes, you need to specify a folder location and solution name for your new programming project now. The presence of these text boxes is controlled by a check box in the Tools/ Options dialog box, but this is no longer the default setting for Visual Basic 2005. Throughout this book, you will be instructed to save your projects (or discard them) *after* you have completed the programming exercise. For more information about this "delayed saving" feature and about restoring Visual Studio to its default settings, see "Customizing IDE Settings to Match Step-by-Step Exercises" in Chapter 1.

6. Click OK to create the new project in Visual Studio.

    Visual Studio cleans the slate for a new programming project and displays the blank Windows form that you will use to build your user interface.

Now you'll enlarge the form and create the two buttons in the interface.

Create the user interface

1. Position the mouse pointer over the lower-right corner of the form until its shape changes to a resizing pointer, and then drag to increase the size of the form to make room for the objects in your program.

    As you resize the form, scroll bars might appear in the Designer to give you access to the entire form you're creating. Depending on your screen resolution and the Visual Studio tools you have open, you might not be able to see the entire form at once. Don't worry about this—your form can be small or it can fill the entire screen because the scroll bars give you access to the entire form.

    Size your form so that it is about the size of the form shown here. If you want to match my example exactly, you can use the width and height dimensions (485 pixels x 278 pixels) shown in the lower-right corner of the screen.

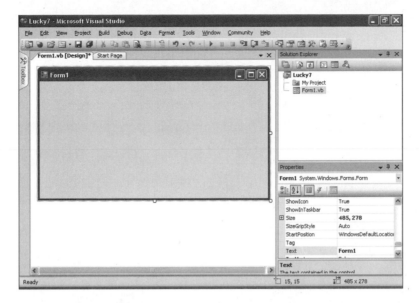

To see the entire form without obstruction, you can resize or close the other programming tools, as you learned in Chapter 1. (Return to Chapter 1 if you have questions about resizing windows or tools.)

Now you'll practice adding a button object on the form.

2. Click the Toolbox tab to display the Toolbox window in the IDE.

    The Toolbox contains all of the controls that you'll use to build Visual Basic programs in this book. The controls suitable for creating a Windows application are visible now because you selected the Windows Application project type earlier. Controls are organized by type, and by default the Common Controls category is visible. (If the Toolbox is not visible now, click Toolbox on the View menu to display it.)

3. Double-click the *Button* control in the Toolbox, and then move the mouse pointer away from the Toolbox.

    Visual Studio creates a default-sized button object on the form and hides the Toolbox, as shown here:

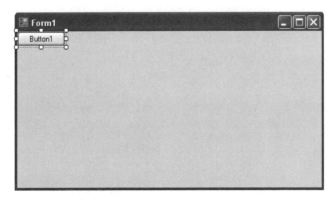

The button is named *Button1* because it is the first button in the program. (You should make a mental note of this button name—you'll see it again when you write your program code.) The new button object is selected and enclosed by resize handles. When Visual Basic is in *design mode* (that is, whenever the Visual Studio IDE is active), you can move objects on the form by dragging them with the mouse, and you can resize them by using the resize handles. While a program is running, however, the user can't move interface elements unless you've changed a property in the program to allow this. You'll practice moving and resizing the button now.

Move and resize a button

1. Position the mouse pointer over the button so that it changes to a four-headed arrow, and then drag the button down and to the right.

   The button moves across the surface of the form. If you move the object near the edge of the form or another object (if other objects are present), it automatically aligns itself to a hidden grid when it is an inch or so away. A little blue "snapline" also appears to help you gauge the distance of this object from the edge of the form or the other object. Unlike previous versions of Visual Studio, a grid is not displayed on the form by default, but you can use the snapline to judge distances with almost the same effect.

> **Tip**   If you want to display the design mode grid as in Microsoft Visual Studio .NET 2003 and Visual Basic 6, click the Options command on the Tools menu, click Windows Form Designer, and then click General. Set ShowGrid to True, and set LayOutMode to SnapToGrid. You will need to close and reopen the project for the change to take effect.

2. Position the mouse pointer on the lower-right corner of the button.

   When the mouse pointer rests on a resize handle of a selected object, it becomes a resizing pointer. You can use the resizing pointer to change the size of an object.

3. Enlarge the button by dragging the pointer down and to the right.

   When you release the mouse button, the button changes size and snaps to the grid.

4. Use the resizing pointer to return the button to its original size, and then move the button back to its original location on the form.

Now you'll add a second button to the form, below the first button.

Add a second button

1. Click the Toolbox tab to display the Toolbox.

2. Click the *Button* control in the Toolbox (single-click this time), and then move the mouse pointer over the form.

   The mouse pointer changes to crosshairs and a button icon. The crosshairs are designed to help you draw the rectangular shape of the button on the form, and you can use this method as an alternative to double-clicking to create a control of the default size.

3. Drag the pointer down and to the right. Release the mouse button to complete the button, and watch it snap to the form.

4. Resize the button object so that it is the same size as the first button, and then move it below the first button on the form. (Use the snapline feature to help you.)

> **Tip**   At any time, you can delete an object and start over again by selecting the object on the form and then pressing Delete. Feel free to create and delete objects to practice creating your user interface.

Now you'll add the labels used to display the numbers in the program. A *label* is a special user interface element designed to display text, numbers, or symbols when a program runs. When the user clicks the Lucky Seven program's Spin button, three random numbers appear in the label boxes. If one of the numbers is a 7, the user wins.

Add the number labels

1. Double-click the *Label* control in the Toolbox.

   Visual Studio creates a label object on the form. If you're familiar with earlier versions of Visual Studio or Visual Basic, you'll notice that the label object is smaller than in previous versions by default. It is just large enough to hold the text contained in the object, but it can also be resized.

2. Drag the *Label1* object to the right of the two button objects.

   Your form looks something like this:

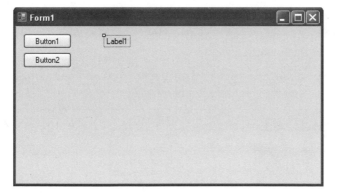

3. Double-click the *Label* control in the Toolbox to create a second label object.

   This label object will be named *Label2* in the program.

4. Double-click the *Label* control again to create a third label object.

5. Move the second and third label objects to the right of the first one on the form.

   Allow plenty of space between the three labels because you will use them to display large numbers when the program runs.

Now you'll use the *Label* control to add a descriptive label to your form. This will be the fourth and final label in the program.

6. Double-click the *Label* control in the Toolbox.

7. Drag the *Label4* object below the two command buttons.

    When you've finished, your four labels should look like those in the following illustration. (You can move your label objects if they don't look quite right.)

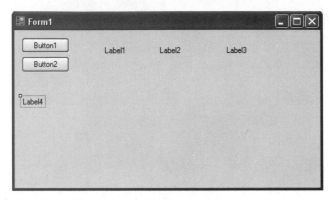

Now you'll add a picture box to the form to graphically display the payout you'll receive when you draw a 7 and hit the jackpot. A *picture box* is designed to display bitmaps, icons, digital photos, and other artwork in a program. One of the best uses for a picture box is to display a JPEG image file.

Add a picture

1. Click the *PictureBox* control in the Toolbox.

2. Using the control's drawing pointer, create a large rectangular box below the second and third labels on the form.

    Leave a little space below the labels for their size to grow as I mentioned earlier. When you've finished, your picture box object looks similar to this:

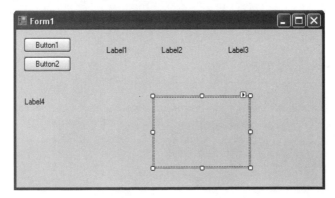

This object will be named *PictureBox1* in your program; you'll use this name later in the program code.

Now you're ready to customize your interface by setting a few properties.

Setting the Properties

As you discovered in Chapter 1, you can change properties by selecting objects on the form and changing their settings in the Properties window. You'll start by changing the property settings for the two buttons.

Set the button properties

1. Click the first button (*Button1*) on the form.

    The button is selected and is surrounded by resize handles.

2. Click the Properties window title bar.

> **Tip**   If the Properties window isn't visible, click the Properties Window command on the View menu, or press F4.

3. Resize the Properties window (if necessary) so that there is plenty of room to see the property names and their current settings.

    Once you get used to setting properties, you will probably use the Properties window without enlarging it, but making it bigger helps when you first try to use it. The Properties window in the following illustration is a good size for setting properties:

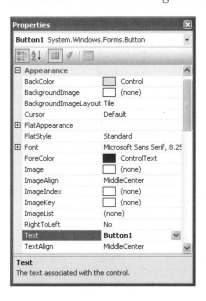

    The Properties window lists the settings for the first button. These include settings for the background color, text, font height, and width of the button. Because there are so many properties, Visual Studio organizes them into categories and displays them in outline view. If you want to see the properties in a category, click the plus sign (+) next to the category title.

4. Scroll in the Properties window until you see the *Text* property located in the Appearance category.

5. Double-click the *Text* property in the left column of the Properties window.

   The current *Text* setting ("Button1") is highlighted in the Properties window.

6. Type **Spin**, and press Enter.

   The *Text* property changes to "Spin" in the Properties window and on the button on the form. Now you'll change the *Text* property of the second button to "End". (You'll select the second button in a new way this time.)

7. Open the Object list at the top of the Properties window.

   A list of the interface objects in your program appears as follows:

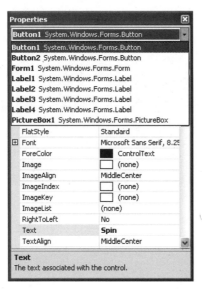

8. Click Button2 System.Windows.Forms.Button (the second button) in the list box.

   The property settings for the second button appear in the Properties window, and Visual Studio highlights Button2 on the form.

9. Double-click the current *Text* property ("Button2"), type **End**, and then press Enter.

   The text of the second button changes to "End".

> **Tip**   Using the Object list is a handy way to switch between objects in your program. You can also switch between objects on the form by clicking each object.

Now you'll set the properties for the labels in the program. The first three labels will hold the random numbers generated by the program and will have identical property settings. (You'll set most of them as a group.) The descriptive label settings will be slightly different.

Set the number label properties

1. Click the first number label (*Label1*), hold down the Shift key, click the second and third number labels, and then release the Shift key. (If the Properties window is in the way, move it to a new place.)

    A selection rectangle and resize handles appear around each label you click. You'll change the *TextAlign*, *BorderStyle*, and *Font* properties now so that the numbers that will appear in the labels will be centered, boxed, and identical in font and point size. (All of these properties are located in the Appearance category of the Properties window.) You'll also set the *AutoSize* property to False so that you can change the size of the labels according to your precise specifications. (The *AutoSize* property is located in the Layout category.)

> **Tip** When more than one object is selected, only those properties that can be changed for the group are displayed in the Properties window.

2. Click the *AutoSize* property in the Properties window, and then click the arrow that appears to the right.

3. Set the *AutoSize* property to False so that you can size the labels manually.

4. Click the *TextAlign* property, and then click the arrow that appears to the right.

    A graphical assortment of alignment options appears in the list box; you can use these settings to align text anywhere within the borders of the label object.

5. Click the center option (MiddleCenter).

    The *TextAlign* property for each of the selected labels changes to MiddleCenter.

6. Click the *BorderStyle* property, and then click the arrow that appears to the right.

    The valid property settings (None, FixedSingle, and Fixed3D) appear in the list box.

7. Click FixedSingle in the list box to add a thin border around each label.

8. Click the *Font* property, and then click the ellipsis button (the button with three dots that's located next to the current font setting).

    The Font dialog box appears.

9. Change the font to Times New Roman, the font style to Bold, and the point size to 24, and then click OK.

    The label text appears in the font, style, and size you specified.

    Now you'll set the text for the three labels to the number 0—a good "placeholder" for the numbers that will eventually fill these boxes in your game. (Because the program produces the actual numbers, you could also delete the text, but putting a placeholder here gives you something to base the size of the labels on.)

10. Click a blank area on the form to remove the selection from the three labels, and then click the first label.

11. Double-click the *Text* property, type **0**, and then press Enter.

The text of the *Label1* object is set to 0. You'll use program code to set this property to a random "slot machine" number later in this chapter.

12. Change the text in the second and third labels on the form to **0** also.

13. Move and resize the labels now so that they are appropriately spaced.

Your form looks something like this:

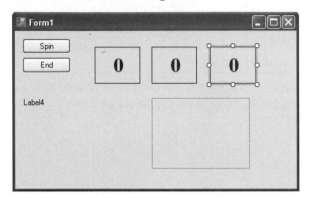

Now you'll change the *Text*, *Font*, and *ForeColor* properties of the fourth label.

Set the descriptive label properties

1. Click the fourth label object (*Label4*) on the form.

2. Change the *Text* property in the Properties window to **Lucky Seven**.

3. Click the *Font* property, and then click the ellipsis button.

4. Use the Font dialog box to change the font to Arial, the font style to Bold, and the point size to 18. Then click OK.

The font in the *Label4* object is updated, and the label is resized automatically to hold the larger font size because the object's *AutoSize* property is set to True.

5. Click the *ForeColor* property in the Properties window, and then click the arrow in the second column.

Visual Studio displays a list box with Custom, Web, and System tabs for setting the foreground colors (the color of text) of the label object. The Custom tab offers many of the colors available in your system. The Web tab sets colors for Web pages and lets you pick colors using their common names. The System tab displays the current colors used for user interface elements in your system.

6. Click the purple color on the Custom tab.

The text in the label box changes to purple.

Now you're ready to set the properties for the last object.

The Picture Box Properties

When the person playing your game hits the jackpot (that is, when at least one 7 appears in the number labels on the form), the picture box object will contain a picture of a person dispensing money. This picture is a digitized image from an unpublished fourteenth-century German manuscript stored in JPEG format. (As a history professor, I run across these things.) You need to set the *SizeMode* property to accurately size the picture and set the *Image* property to specify the name of the JPEG file that you will load into the picture box. You also need to set the *Visible* property, which specifies the picture state at the beginning of the program.

Set the picture box properties

1. Click the picture box object on the form.

2. Click the *SizeMode* property in the Properties window (listed in the Behavior category), click the arrow to the right, and then click StretchImage.

    Setting *SizeMode* to StretchImage before you open a graphic causes Visual Studio to resize the graphic to the exact dimensions of the picture box. (Typically, you set this property before you set the *Image* property.)

3. Click the *Image* property in the Properties window, and then click the ellipsis button in the second column.

    The Select Resource dialog box appears.

4. Click the Local Resource option, and then click the Import button.

5. In the Open dialog box, navigate to the c:\vb05sbs\chap02 folder.

    This folder contains the digital photo PayCoins.jpg.

6. Select PayCoins.jpg, and then click Open.

    A medieval illustration of one person paying another appears in the Select Resource dialog box. (The letter *W* represents winning.)

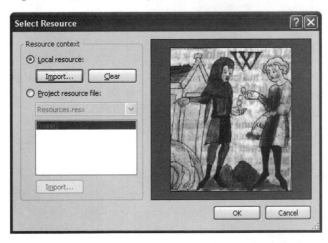

7. Click OK.

The PayCoins photo is loaded into the picture box. Because the photo is relatively small (24 KB), it opens quickly on the form.

8. Resize the picture box object now to fix any distortion problems that you see in the image.

I sized my picture box object to be 148 pixels wide by 138 pixels high. You can match this size by using the width and height dimensions located on the lower-right side of the Visual Studio IDE. (The dimensions of the selected object are given on the lower-right side, and the location on the form of the object's upper-left corner is given to the left of the its dimensions.)

This particular image displays best when the picture box object retains a square shape.

> **Note**   As you look at the picture box object, you might notice a tiny shortcut arrow near the upper-right corner. This arrow is a button that you can click to quickly change a few common picture box settings and open the Select Resource dialog box. (The shortcut arrow is a new feature in Visual Studio 2005, and you'll see it again in Chapter 4, "Working with Menus, Toolbars, and Dialog Boxes," when you use the *ToolStrip* control.)

Now you'll change the *Visible* property to False so that the image will be invisible when the program starts.

9. Click the *Visible* property in the Behavior category of the Properties window, and then click the arrow to the right.

The valid settings for the *Visible* property appear in a list box.

10. Click False to make the picture invisible when the program starts.

Setting the *Visible* property to False affects the picture box when the program runs, but not now while you're designing it. Your completed form looks similar to this:

> **Tip**   You can also double-click property names that have True and False settings (so-called *Boolean* properties), to toggle back and forth between True and False. Default Boolean properties are shown in regular type, and changed settings appear in bold.

11. You're done setting properties for now, so if your Properties window is floating, double-click its title bar to return it to the docked position.

Writing the Code

Now you're ready to write the code for the Lucky Seven program. Because most of the objects you've created already "know" how to work when the program runs, they're ready to receive input from the user and process it. The inherent functionality of objects is one of the great strengths of Visual Studio and Visual Basic—after objects are placed on a form and their properties are set, they're ready to run without any additional programming. However, the "meat" of the Lucky Seven game—the code that actually calculates random numbers, displays them in boxes, and detects a jackpot—is still missing from the program. This computing logic can be built into the application only by using program statements—code that clearly spells out what the program should do at each step of the way. Because the Spin and End buttons drive the program, you'll associate the code for the game with those buttons. You enter and edit Visual Basic program statements in the Code Editor.

In the following steps, you'll enter the program code for Lucky Seven in the Code Editor.

Reading Properties in Tables

In this chapter, you've set the properties for the Lucky Seven program step by step. In future chapters, the instructions to set properties will be presented in table format unless a setting is especially tricky. Here are the properties you've set so far in the Lucky Seven program in table format, as they'd look later in the book. Settings you need to type in are shown in quotation marks. You shouldn't type the quotation marks.

Object	Property	Setting
Button1	Text	"Spin"
Button2	Text	"End"
Label1, Label2, Label3	AutoSize	False
	BorderStyle	Fixed Single
	Font	Times New Roman, Bold, 24-point
	Text	"0"
	TextAlign	MiddleCenter
Label4	Text	"Lucky Seven"
	Font	Arial, Bold, 18-point
	ForeColor	Purple
PictureBox1	Image	"c:\vb05sbs\chap02\paycoins.jpg"
	SizeMode	StretchImage
	Visible	False

Use the Code Editor

1. Double-click the End button on the form.

   The Code Editor appears as a tabbed document window in the center of the Visual
   Studio IDE, as shown here:

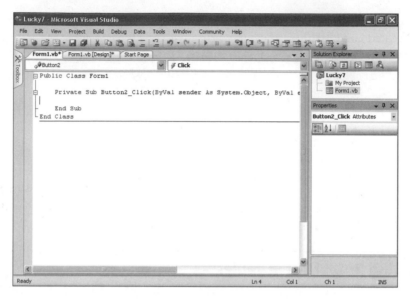

Inside the Code Editor are program statements associated with the current form. Program statements that are used together to perform some action are typically grouped in
a programming construct called a *procedure*. A common type of procedure is a Sub procedure, sometimes called a *subroutine*. Sub procedures include a *Sub* keyword in the first
line and end with *End Sub*. Procedures are typically executed when certain events occur,
such as when a button is clicked. When a procedure is associated with a particular
object and an event, it is called an *event handler* or an *event procedure*.

When you double-clicked the End button (*Button2*), Visual Studio automatically added
the first and last lines of the *Button2_Click* event procedure, as the following code shows.
(The first line was wrapped to stay within the book margins.) You'll notice other lines of
code in the Code Editor, which Visual Studio has added to define important characteristics of the form. However, readers familiar with Visual Basic 2002 and 2003 will see
less boilerplate code than in previous versions of Visual Basic. The code block beginning
with the words `Windows Form Designer generated code` has been removed.

```
Private Sub Button2_Click(ByVal sender As System.Object, _
  ByVal e As System.EventArgs) Handles Button2.Click

End Sub
```

The body of a procedure fits between these lines and is executed whenever a user acti-
vates the interface element associated with the procedure. In this case, the event is a
mouse click, but as you'll see later in the book, it could also be a different type of event.

2. Type **End**, and then press the Down Arrow key.

After you type the statement, the letters turn blue and are indented, indicating that Visual Basic recognizes *End* as one of several hundred unique reserved words, or *keywords*, within the Visual Basic language. You use the *End* keyword to stop your program and remove it from the screen. In this case, *End* is also a complete *program statement*, a self-contained instruction executed by the *Visual Basic compiler*, the part of Visual Studio that processes or *parses* each line of Visual Basic *source code*, combining the result with other resources to create an executable file. Program statements are a little like complete sentences in a human language—statements can be of varying lengths but must follow the grammatical "rules" of the compiler. In Visual Studio 2005, program statements can be composed of keywords, properties, object names, variables, numbers, special symbols, and other values. You'll learn more about how program statements are constructed in Chapter 5, "Visual Basic Variables and Formulas, and the .NET Framework."

As you enter program statements and make other edits, the Code Editor handles many of the formatting details for you, including adjusting indentation and spacing and adding any necessary parentheses. The exact spelling, order, and spacing of items within program statements is referred to as *statement syntax*.

When you pressed the Down Arrow key, the *End* statement was indented to set it apart from the *Private Sub* and *End Sub* statements. This indenting scheme is one of the programming conventions you'll see throughout this book to keep your programs clear and readable. The group of conventions regarding how code is organized in a program is often referred to as *program style*.

Now that you've written the code associated with the End button, you'll write code for the Spin button. These program statements will be a little more extensive and will give you a chance to learn more about statement syntax and program style. You'll study many of the program statements later in this book, so you don't need to know everything about them now. Just focus on the general structure of the code and on typing the program statements exactly as they are printed.

Write code for the Spin button

1. Click the View Designer button in the Solution Explorer window to display your form again.

> **Note**   When the Code Editor is visible, you won't be able to see the form you're working on. The View Designer button is one mechanism you can use to display it again. (If more than one form is loaded in Solution Explorer, click the form you want to display first.) You can also click the Form1.vb [Design] tab at the top edge of the Code Editor. If you don't see tabs at the top of the Code Editor, enable Tabbed Documents view in the Options dialog box, as discussed in a Tip in Chapter 1.

2. Double-click the Spin button.

    After a few moments, the Code Editor appears, and an event procedure associated with the *Button1* button appears near the *Button2* event procedure.

    Although you changed the text of this button to "Spin", its name in the program is still *Button1*. (The name and the text of an interface element can be different to suit the needs of the programmer.) Each object can have several procedures associated with it, one for each event it recognizes. The click event is the one you're interested in now because users will click the Spin and End buttons when they run the program.

3. Type the following program lines between the *Private Sub* and *End Sub* statements. Press Enter after each line, press Tab to indent, and take care to type the program statements exactly as they appear here. (The Code Editor will scroll to the left as you enter the longer lines.) If you make a mistake (usually identified by a jagged underline), delete the incorrect statements and try again.

> **Tip** As you enter the program code, Visual Basic formats the text and displays different parts of the program in color to help you identify the various elements. When you begin to type a property, Visual Basic also displays the available properties for the object you're using in a list box, so you can double-click the property or keep typing to enter it yourself. If Visual Basic displays an error message, you might have misspelled a program statement. Check the line against the text in this book, make the necessary correction, and continue typing. (You can also delete a line and type it from scratch.) In addition, Visual Basic might add necessary code automatically. For example, when you type the following code, Visual Basic automatically adds the *End If* line. Readers of previous editions of this book have found this first typing exercise to be the toughest part of this chapter—"But Mr. Halvorson, I know I typed it just as you wrote it!"—so please give this program code your closest attention. I promise you, it works!

```
PictureBox1.Visible = False     ' hide picture
Label1.Text = CStr(Int(Rnd() * 10))     ' pick numbers
Label2.Text = CStr(Int(Rnd() * 10))
Label3.Text = CStr(Int(Rnd() * 10))
' if any number is 7 display picture and beep
If (Label1.Text = "7") Or (Label2.Text = "7") _
Or (Label3.Text = "7") Then
    PictureBox1.Visible = True
    Beep()
End If
```

When you've finished, the Code Editor looks as shown in the following graphic:

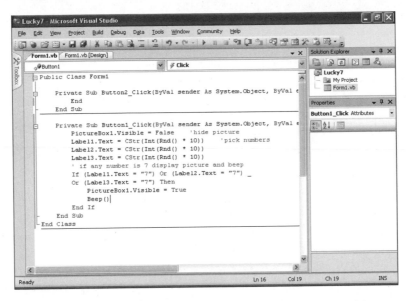

4. Click the Save All command on the File menu to save your additions to the program.

    The Save All command saves everything in your project—the project file, the form file, any code modules, and other related components in your application. Since this is the first time that you have saved your project, the Save Project dialog box appears prompting you for the name and location of the project. (If your copy of Visual Studio is configured to prompt you for a location when you first create your project, you won't see the Save Project dialog box now—Visual Studio just saves your changes.)

5. Click the Browse button to the right of the Location text box, and select a location for your files.

    I recommend that you use the c:\vb05sbs\chap02 folder (the location of the book's sample files), but the location is up to you. Since you used the "My" prefix when you originally opened your project, this version won't overwrite the Lucky7 practice file that I built for you on disk.

> **Note**   If you want to save just the item you are currently working on (the form, the code module, or something else), you can use the Save command on the File menu. If you want to save the current item with a different name, you can use the Save As command.

A Look at the *Button1_Click* Procedure

The *Button1_Click* procedure is executed when the user clicks the Spin button on the form. The procedure uses some pretty complicated statements, and because I haven't formally introduced them yet, it might look a little confusing. However, if you take a closer look, you'll probably see a few things that look familiar. Taking a peek at the contents of these procedures will give you a feel for the type of program code you'll be creating later in this book. (If you'd rather not stop for this preview, feel free to skip to the next section, "Running Visual Basic Applications.")

The *Button1_Click* procedure performs three tasks:

- It hides the digital photo.
- It creates three random numbers for the number labels.
- It displays the photo when the number 7 appears.

Let's look at each of these steps individually.

Hiding the photo is accomplished with the following line:

```
PictureBox1.Visible = False    ' hide picture
```

This line is made up of two parts: a program statement and a comment.

The `PictureBox1.Visible = False` program statement sets the *Visible* property of the picture box object (*PictureBox1*) to False (one of two possible settings). You might remember that you set this property to False once before by using the Properties window. You're doing it again now in the program code because the first task is a spin and you need to clear away a photo that might have been displayed in a previous game. Because the property will be changed at run time and not at design time, you must set the property by using program code. This is a handy feature of Visual Basic, and I'll talk about it more in Chapter 3, "Working with Toolbox Controls."

The second part of the first line (the part displayed in green type on your screen) is called a *comment*. Comments are explanatory notes included in program code following a single quotation mark ('). Programmers use comments to describe how important statements work in a program. These notes aren't processed by Visual Basic when the program runs; they exist only to document what the program does. You'll want to use comments often when you write Visual Basic programs to leave an easy-to-understand record of what you're doing.

The next three lines handle the random number computations. Does this concept sound strange? You can actually make Visual Basic generate unpredictable numbers within specific guidelines—in other words, you can create random numbers for lottery contests, dice games, or other statistical patterns. The *Rnd* function in each line creates a random number between 0 and 1 (a number with a decimal point and several decimal places), and the *Int* function returns the integer portion of the result of multiplying the random number by 10. This computation creates random numbers between 0 and 9 in the program—just what you need for this particular slot machine application.

```
Label1.Text = CStr(Int(Rnd() * 10))    ' pick numbers
```

You then need to jump through a little hoop in your code. You need to copy these random numbers into the three label boxes on the form, but first the numbers need to be converted to text with the *CStr* (convert to string) function. Notice how *CStr*, *Int*, and *Rnd* are all connected together in the program statement—they work collectively to produce a result like a mathematical formula. After the computation and conversion, the values are assigned to the *Text* properties of the first three labels on the form, and the assignment causes the numbers to be displayed in bold, 24-point, Times New Roman format in the three number labels.

The following illustration shows how Visual Basic evaluates one line of code step by step to generate the random number 7 and copy it to a label object. Visual Basic evaluates the expression just like a mathematician solving a mathematical formula.

Example:
```
Label1.Text = CStr(Int(Rnd() * 10))
```

Code	Result
Rnd()	0.7055475
Rnd() * 10	7.055475
Int(Rnd() * 10)	7
CStr(Int(Rnd() * 10))	"7"
Label1.Text = CStr(Int(Rnd() * 10))	7

The last group of statements in the program checks whether any of the random numbers is 7. If one or more of them is, the program displays the medieval manuscript depiction of a payout, and a beep announces the winnings.

```
' if any number is 7 display picture and beep
If (Label1.Text = "7") Or (Label2.Text = "7") _
Or (Label3.Text = "7") Then
    PictureBox1.Visible = True
    Beep()
End If
```

Each time the user clicks the Spin button, the *Button1_Click* procedure is executed, or *called*, and the program statements in the procedure are run again.

Running Visual Basic Applications

Congratulations! You're ready to run your first real program. To run a Visual Basic program from the development environment, you can do any of the following:

■ Click Start Debugging on the Debug menu.

- Click the Start Debugging button on the Standard toolbar.

- Press F5.

Try running your Lucky Seven program now. If Visual Basic displays an error message, you might have a typing mistake or two in your program code. Try to fix it by comparing the printed version in this book with the one you typed, or load Lucky7 from your hard disk and run it.

Run the Lucky Seven program

1. Click the Start Debugging button on the Standard toolbar.

   The Lucky Seven program compiles and runs in the IDE. After a few seconds, the user interface appears, just as you designed it.

2. Click the Spin button.

   The program picks three random numbers and displays them in the labels on the form, as follows:

   Because a 7 appears in the first label box, the digital photo depicting the payoff appears, and the computer beeps. You win! (The sound you hear depends on your Sounds And Multimedia setting (or the Sounds And Devices setting) in Windows Control Panel. To make this game sound really cool, change the Default Beep sound to something more dynamic.)

3. Click the Spin button 15 or 16 more times, watching the results of the spins in the number boxes.

   About half the time you spin, you hit the jackpot—pretty easy odds. (The actual odds are about 2.8 times out of 10; you're just lucky at first.) Later on you might want to make the game tougher by displaying the photo only when two or three 7s appear, or by creating a running total of winnings.

4. When you've finished experimenting with your new creation, click the End button.

   The program stops, and the development environment reappears on your screen.

> **Tip**   If you run this program again, you might notice that Lucky Seven displays exactly the same sequence of random numbers. There is nothing wrong here—the Visual Basic *Rnd* function was designed to display a repeating sequence of numbers at first so that you can properly test your code using output that can be reproduced again and again. To create truly "random" numbers, use the *Randomize* function in your code, as shown in the exercise at the end of this chapter. The .NET Framework, which you'll learn to use later, also supplies random number functions.

Sample Projects on Disk

If you didn't build the MyLucky7 project from scratch (or if you did build the project and want to compare what you created to what I built for you as I wrote the chapter), take a moment to open and run the completed Lucky7 project, which is located in the c:\vb05sbs\chap02\lucky7 folder on your hard disk (the default location for the Chapter 2 practice files). If you need a refresher course on opening projects, see the detailed instructions in Chapter 1. If you are asked if you want to save changes to the MyLucky7 project, be sure to click Save.

This book is a step by step tutorial, so you will benefit most from building the projects on your own and experimenting with them. But after you have completed the projects, it is often a good idea to compare what you have with the practice file "solution" that I provide, especially if you run into trouble. To make this easy, I will give you the name of the solution files on disk before you run the completed program in most of the step-by-step exercises.

After you have compared the MyLucky7 project to the Lucky7 solution files on disk, re-open MyLucky7, and prepare to compile it as an executable file. If you didn't create MyLucky7, use my solution file to complete the exercise.

Building an Executable File

Your last task in this chapter is to complete the development process and create an application for Windows, or an *executable file*. Windows applications created with Visual Studio have the file name extension .exe and can be run on any system that contains Microsoft Windows and the necessary support files. (Visual Basic installs these support files—including the .NET Framework files—automatically.) If you plan to distribute your applications, see "Deploying Your Application" later in the chapter.

At this point, you need to know that Visual Studio can create two types of executable files for your project: a debug build and a release build.

Debug builds are created automatically by Visual Studio when you create and test your program. They are stored in a folder called bin\debug within your project folder. The debug executable file typically contains debugging information that makes the program run slightly slower.

Release builds are optimized executable files stored in the bin\release folder within your project. To customize the settings for your release build, you click the [*ProjectName*] Properties command on the Project menu, and then click the Compile tab, where you see a list of compilation options that looks like this:

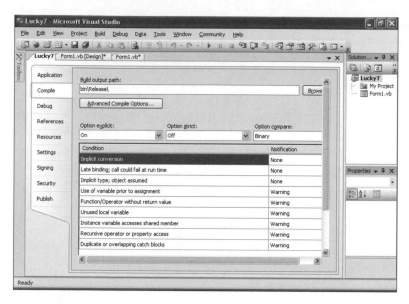

Try creating a release build named MyLucky7.exe now.

Create an executable file

1. On the Build menu, click the Build MyLucky7 command.

    The Build command creates a bin\release folder in which to store your project (if the folder doesn't already exist) and compiles the source code in your project. The result is an executable file named MyLucky7.exe. To save you time, Visual Studio often creates temporary executable files while you develop your application; however, it's always a good idea to recompile your application manually with the Build or Rebuild commands when you reach an important milestone.

    Try running this program outside the Visual Studio IDE now by using the Run command on the Start menu.

2. On the Windows taskbar, click Start, and then click Run.

    The Run dialog box appears.

3. Click Browse, and then navigate to the c:\vb05sbs\chap02\mylucky7\bin\release folder.

4. Click the MyLucky7.exe application icon, click Open, and then click OK.

5. The Lucky Seven program loads and runs in Windows.

6. Click Spin a few times to verify the operation of the game, and then click End.

> **Tip**   You can also run Windows applications, including compiled Visual Basic programs, by opening Windows Explorer and double-clicking the executable file. To create a short-cut icon for MyLucky7.exe on the Windows desktop, right-click the Windows desktop, point to New, and then click Shortcut. When you're prompted for the location of your application file, click Browse, and select the MyLucky7.exe executable file. Click the OK, Next, and Finish buttons. Windows places an icon on the desktop that you can double-click to run your program.

7. On the File menu, click Exit to close Visual Studio and the MyLucky7 project.

The Visual Studio development environment closes.

Deploying Your Application

Visual Studio helps you distribute your Visual Basic applications by providing several options for *deployment*—that is, for installing the application on one or more computer systems. Whereas Visual Basic 6 requires a sophisticated setup program that copies dynamic-link libraries (DLLs) and support files and registers the application with the operating system, Visual Studio 2005 applications are compiled as *assemblies*—deployment units consisting of one or more files necessary for the program to run. Assemblies contain four elements: Microsoft intermediate language (MSIL) code, metadata, a manifest, and supporting files and resources.

Assemblies are so comprehensive and self-describing that Visual Studio applications don't need to be formally registered with the operating system to run. This means that theoretically a Visual Basic 2005 application can be installed by simply copying the assembly for the program to a second computer that has the .NET Framework installed—a process called *XCOPY installation*, after the MS-DOS XCOPY command that copies a complete directory (folder) structure from one location to another. In practice, however, it isn't practical to deploy Visual Basic applications by using a copy procedure such as XCOPY (via the command prompt) or Windows Explorer. For commercial applications, an installation program with a graphical user interface is usually preferred, and it's often desirable to register the program with the operating system so that it can be uninstalled later by using Add/Remove Programs in Control Panel.

To manage the installation process, Visual Studio 2005 allows developers to add a setup or *Windows Installer* project to their solutions, which automatically creates a setup program for the application. This setup project can be customized to allow for different methods of installation, such as CD-ROMs or Web servers. Best of all, in Visual Studio 2005 you can utilize a technology called *ClickOnce* to create a Web-based installation service for desktop applications that users can access on their own with minimal interaction. Although the advanced options related to deployment and security go beyond the scope of this book, you can get started with these features at any time by using the Publish command on the Build menu, or by using the New Project command on the File menu to create a custom Windows Installer project. (Select the Setup And Deployment option under Other Project Types to see a list of setup templates and wizards.) The Properties command on the Project menu has a Publish tab that you can use to customize your application's setup settings.

One Step Further: Adding to a Program

You can restart Visual Studio at any time and work on a programming project you've stored on disk. You'll restart Visual Studio now and add a *Randomize* statement to the Lucky Seven program.

Reload Lucky Seven

1. On the Windows taskbar, click Start, point to All Programs, point to Microsoft Visual Studio 2005, and then click the Microsoft Visual Studio 2005 program icon.

   A list of the projects that you've most recently worked on appears on the Visual Studio Start Page. Because you just finished working with Lucky Seven, the MyLucky7 project should be first on the list.

2. Click the MyLucky7 link to open the Lucky Seven project.

   The Lucky Seven program opens, and the MyLucky7 form appears. (If you don't see the form, click Form1.vb in Solution Explorer, and then click the View Designer button.)

   Now you'll add the *Randomize* statement to the *Form_Load* procedure, a special procedure that is associated with the form and that is executed each time the program is started.

3. Double-click the form (not one of the objects) to display the *Form_Load* procedure.

   The *Form_Load* procedure appears in the Code Editor, as shown here:

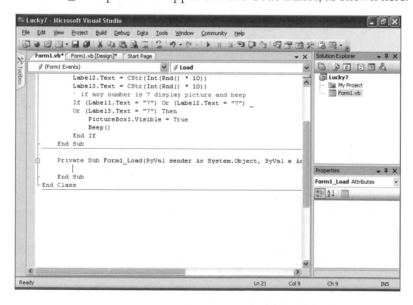

4. Type **Randomize**, and then press the Down Arrow key.

    The *Randomize* statement is added to the program and will be executed each time the program starts. *Randomize* uses the system clock to create a truly random starting point, or *seed*, for the *Rnd* statement used in the *Button1_Click* procedure. As I mentioned earlier, without the *Randomize* statement, the Lucky Seven program produces the same string of random spins every time you restart the program. With *Randomize* in place, the program spins randomly every time it runs, and the numbers don't follow a recognizable pattern.

5. Run the new version of Lucky Seven, and then save the project. If you plan to use the new version a lot, you might want to create a new .exe file, too.

6. When you're finished, click Close Project on the File menu.

    The files associated with the Lucky Seven program are closed.

Chapter 2 Quick Reference

To	Do this
Create a user interface	Use Toolbox controls to place objects on your form, and then set the necessary properties. Resize the form and the objects as appropriate.
Move an object	Position the mouse pointer over the object until the four-headed arrow appears, and then drag the object.
Resize an object	Click the object to select it, and then drag the resize handle attached to the part of the object you want to resize.
Delete an object	Click the object, and then press the Delete key.
Open the Code Editor	Double-click an object on the form (or the form itself). *or* Select a form or a module in Solution Explorer, and then click the View Code button.
Write program code	Type Visual Basic program statements associated with objects in the Code Editor.
Save a program	On the File menu, click the Save All command. *or* Click the Save All button on the Standard toolbar.
Save a form file	Make sure the form is open, and then on the File menu, click the Save command. *or* Click the Save button on the Standard toolbar.
Create an .exe file	On the Build menu, click the Build or Rebuild command.
Deploy an application by using ClickOnce technology	Click the Publish command on the Build menu, and then use the Publish wizard to specify the location and settings for the application.

To	Do this
Reload a project	On the File menu, click the Open Project command.
	or
	On the File menu, point to Recent Projects, and then click the desired project.
	or
	Click the project in the recent projects list on the Visual Studio Start Page.

Chapter 3
Working with Toolbox Controls

After completing this chapter, you will be able to:

- Use *TextBox* and *Button* controls to create a Hello World program.

- Use the *DateTimePicker* control to display your birth date.

- Use *CheckBox*, *RadioButton*, *ListBox*, and *ComboBox* controls to process user input.

- Use the *LinkLabel* control and the *Process.Start* method to display a Web page by using your system's default browser.

As you learned in earlier chapters, Microsoft Visual Studio 2005 controls are the graphical tools you use to build the user interface of a Microsoft Visual Basic program. Controls are located in the development environment's Toolbox, and you use them to create objects on a form with a simple series of mouse clicks and dragging motions.

Upgrade Notes: Migrating Visual Basic 6 Code to Visual Basic 2005

If you're experienced with Microsoft Visual Basic 6, you'll notice some new features in Microsoft Visual Basic 2005, including the following:

- A new control named *DateTimePicker* helps you prompt the user for date and time information. The new *LinkLabel* control is designed to display and manage Web links on a form.

- The *OptionButton* control has been replaced with a new *RadioButton* control.

- The *Frame* control has been replaced with a new *GroupBox* control.

- The *ListIndex* property of the *ListBox* control has been replaced with a property called *SelectedIndex*. The same change was made to the *ComboBox* control.

- There is no longer an *Image* control. You use the *PictureBox* control instead.

- Images are added to picture box objects by using the *System.Drawing.Image.From-File* method (not the *LoadPicture* function).

- Microsoft Windows applications are now started within a program by using the *System.Diagnostics.Process.Start* method.

Windows forms controls are specifically designed for building Windows applications, and you'll find them organized on the All Windows Forms tab of the Toolbox, although many of the controls are also accessible in tabs such as Common Controls, Containers, and Printing. (You used a few of these controls in the previous chapter.) You'll learn about other controls, including the tools you use to build database applications and Web pages, later in the book.

In this chapter, you'll learn how to display information in a text box, work with date and time information on your system, process user input, and display a Web page within a Visual Basic program. The exercises in this chapter will help you design your own Visual Basic applications and will teach you more about objects, properties, and program code.

The Basic Use of Controls: The Hello World Program

A great tradition in introductory programming books is the Hello World program, which demonstrates how the simplest utility can be built and run in a given programming language. In the days of character-based programming, Hello World was usually a two-line or three-line program typed in a program editor and assembled with a stand-alone compiler. With the advent of complex operating systems and programming tools, however, the typical Hello World has grown into a more sophisticated program containing dozens of lines and requiring several programming tools for its construction. Fortunately, creating a Hello World program is still quite simple with Visual Studio and Visual Basic 2005. You can construct a complete user interface by creating two objects, setting two properties, and entering one line of code. Give it a try.

Create a Hello World program

1. Start Visual Studio 2005 if it isn't already open.

2. On the File menu, click New Project.

    Visual Studio displays the New Project dialog box, which prompts you for the name of your project and for the template that you want to use.

> **Note**   Use the following instructions each time you want to create a new project on your hard disk.

3. Ensure that the Visual Basic project type and the Windows category are selected, and then click the Windows Application template.

    These selections indicate that you'll be building a stand-alone Visual Basic application that will run under Windows.

4. Remove the default project name (WindowsApplication1) from the Name text box, and then type **MyHello**.

> **Note** Throughout this book, I ask you to create sample projects with the *My* prefix, to distinguish your own work from the practice files I include on the companion CD-ROM.

The New Project dialog box now looks like this:

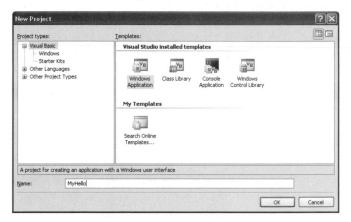

5. Click OK to create your new project.

    The new project is created, and a blank form appears in the Designer, as shown in the following illustration. The two controls you'll use in this exercise, *Button* and *TextBox*, are visible in the Toolbox, which appears in the illustration as a docked window. If your programming tools are configured differently, take a few moments to organize them as shown in the illustration. (Chapter 1, "Exploring the Visual Studio Integrated Development Environment," describes how to configure the IDE if you need a refresher course.)

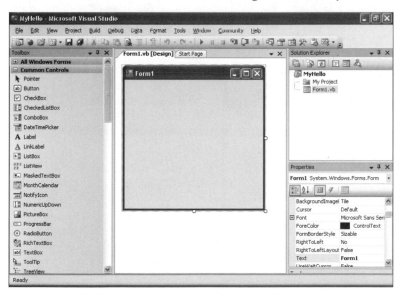

6. Click the *TextBox* control on the Common Controls tab of the Toolbox.

7. Draw a text box similar to this:

Text boxes are used to display text on a form or to get user input while a program is running. How a text box works depends on how you set its properties and how you reference the text box in the program code. In this program, a text box object will be used to display the message "Hello, world!" when you click a button object on the form.

> **Note**   Readers who have used earlier versions of Visual Basic will notice that the *Text-Box* control no longer contains a default *Text* property value of "TextBox1" as it did previously. The default text box is now empty.

You'll add a button to the form now.

8. Click the *Button* control in the Toolbox.

9. Draw a button below the text box on the form.

Your form looks something like this:

As you learned in Chapter 2, "Writing Your First Program," buttons are used to get the most basic input from a user. When a user clicks a button, he or she is requesting that the program perform a specific action immediately. In Visual Basic terms, the user is using the button to create an *event* that needs to be processed in the program. Typical buttons in a program are the OK button, which a user clicks to accept a list of options and to indicate that he or she is ready to proceed; the Cancel button, which a user clicks to discard a list of options; and the Quit button, which a user clicks to exit the program. In each case, you should use these buttons in the standard way so that they work as expected when the user clicks them. A button's characteristics (like those of all objects) can be modified with property settings and references to the object in program code.

10. Set the following property for the button object by using the Properties window:

Object	Property	Setting
Button1	*Text*	"OK"

For more information about setting properties and reading them in tables, see the section entitled "The Properties Window" in Chapter 1.

11. Double-click the OK button, and type the following program statement between the *Private Sub Button1_Click* and *End Sub* statements in the Code Editor:

```
TextBox1.Text = "Hello, world!"
```

> **Note** After you type the *TextBox1* object name and a period, Visual Studio displays a list box containing all the valid properties for text box objects, to jog your memory if you've forgotten the complete list. You can select a property from the list by double-clicking it, or you can continue typing to enter it yourself. (I usually just keep typing, unless I'm exploring new features.)

The statement you've entered changes the *Text* property of the text box to "Hello, world!" when the user clicks the button at run time. (The equal sign (=) assigns everything between the quotation marks to the *Text* property of the *TextBox1* object.) This example changes a property at run time—one of the most common uses of program code in a Visual Basic program.

Now you're ready to run the Hello World program.

Run the Hello World program

> **Tip** The complete Hello World program is located in the c:\vb05sbs\chap03\hello folder.

1. Click the Start Debugging button on the Standard toolbar.

The Hello World program compiles and, after a few seconds, runs in the Visual Studio IDE.

2. Click OK.

The program displays the greeting "Hello, world!" in the text box, as shown here:

When you clicked the OK button, the program code changed the *Text* property of the empty *TextBox1* text box to "Hello, world!" and displayed this text in the box. If you didn't get this result, repeat the steps in the previous section, and build the program again. You might have set a property incorrectly or made a typing mistake in the program code. (Syntax errors appear with a jagged underline in the Code Editor.)

3. Click the Close button in the upper-right corner of the Hello World program window to stop the program.

> **Note**   To stop a program running in Visual Studio, you can also click the Stop Debugging button on the Standard toolbar to close the program.

4. Click the Save All button on the Standard toolbar to save your new project to disk.

Visual Studio now prompts you for a name and a location for the project.

5. Click the Browse button.

The Project Location dialog box opens. You use this dialog box to specify the location of your project and to create new folders for your projects if necessary. Although you can save your projects in any location (the My Documents\Visual Studio 2005\Projects folder is a common location), in this book I instruct you to save your projects in the c:\vb05sbs folder, the default location for your *Step by Step* practice files. If you ever want to remove all the files associated with this programming course, you'll know just where the files are, and you'll be able to remove them easily by deleting the entire folder.

6. Click the Desktop icon in the Project Location dialog box, double-click the My Computer icon, and then browse to the c:\vb05sbs\chap03 folder.

7. Click the Open button to open the folder you specified.

8. Clear the check mark from the Create Directory For Solution check box if it is selected.

   Because this solution contains only one project (which is the case for most of the solutions in this book), you don't need to create a separate root folder to hold the solution files for the project. (However, you can create an extra folder if you want.)

9. Click Save to save the project and its files.

Congratulations—you've joined the ranks of programmers who've written a Hello World program. Now let's try another control.

Using the *DateTimePicker* Control

Some Visual Basic controls display information, and others gather information from the user or process data behind the scenes. In this exercise, you'll work with the *DateTimePicker* control, which prompts the user for a date or time by using a graphical calendar with scroll arrows. Although your use of the control will be rudimentary at this point, experimenting with *DateTimePicker* will give you an idea of how much Visual Basic controls can do for you automatically and how you process the information that comes from them.

The Birthday Program

The Birthday program uses a *DateTimePicker* control and a *Button* control to prompt the user for the date of his or her birthday. It then displays that information by using a message box. Give it a try now.

Build the Birthday program

1. On the File menu, click Close Project to close the MyHello project.

   The files associated with the Hello World program close.

2. On the File menu, click New Project.

   The New Project dialog box appears.

3. Create a new Visual Basic Windows Application project named **MyBirthday**.

   The new project is created, and a blank form appears in the Designer.

4. Click the *DateTimePicker* control in the Toolbox.

5. Draw a date time picker object in the middle of the form, as shown on the next page.

The date time picker object by default displays the current date, but you can adjust the displayed date by changing the object's *Value* property. Displaying the date is a handy design guide—it lets you size the date time picker object appropriately when you're creating it.

6. Click the *Button* control in the Toolbox, and then add a button object below the date time picker.

    You'll use this button to display your birth date and to verify that the date time picker works correctly.

7. In the Properties window, change the *Text* property of the button object to **Show My Birthday**.

    Now you'll add a few lines of program code to a procedure associated with the button object. This is an event procedure because it runs when an event, such as a mouse click, occurs, or *fires,* in the object.

8. Double-click the button object on the form to display its default event procedure, and then type the following program statements between the *Private Sub* and *End Sub* statements in the *Button1_Click* event procedure:

```
MsgBox("Your birth date was " & DateTimePicker1.Text)
MsgBox("Day of the year: " & _
  DateTimePicker1.Value.DayOfYear.ToString())
```

These program statements display two message boxes (small dialog boxes) with information from the date time picker object. The first line uses the *Text* property of the date time picker to display the birth date information you select when using the object at run time. The *MsgBox* function displays the string value "Your birth date was" in addition to the textual value held in the date time picker's *Text* property. These two pieces of information are joined together by the string concatenation operator (&). You'll learn more about the *MsgBox* function and the string concatenation operator in Chapter 5, "Visual Basic Variables and Formulas, and the .NET Framework."

The second and third lines collectively form one program statement and have been broken by the line continuation character (_) because the statement was a bit too long to print in this book.

> **Note** Program lines can be more than 65,000 characters long in the Visual Studio Code Editor, but it's usually easiest to work with lines of 80 or fewer characters. You can divide long program statements among multiple lines by using a space and a line continuation character (_) at the end of each line in the statement, except the last line. (You cannot use a line continuation character to break a string that's in quotation marks, however.) I use the line continuation character in this exercise to break the second line of code into two parts.

The statement `DateTimePicker1.Value.DayOfYear.ToString()` uses the date time picker object to calculate the day of the year in which you were born, counting from January 1. This is accomplished by the *DayOfYear* property and the *ToString* method, which converts the numeric result of the date calculation to a textual value that's more easily displayed by the *MsgBox* function.

Methods are special statements that perform an action or a service for a particular object, such as converting a number to a string or adding items to a list box. Methods differ from properties, which contain a value, and event procedures, which execute when a user manipulates an object. Methods can also be shared among objects, so when you learn how to use a particular method, you'll often be able to apply it to several circumstances. We'll discuss several important methods as you work through this book.

After you enter the code for the *Button1_Click* event procedure, the Code Editor looks similar to this:

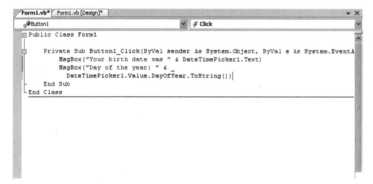

9. Click the Save All button to save your changes to disk, and specify c:\vb05sbs\chap03 as the folder location.

Now you're ready to run the Birthday program.

Run the Birthday program

> **Tip**   The complete Birthday program is located in the c:\vb05sbs\chap03\birthday folder.

1. Click the Start Debugging button on the Standard toolbar.

    The Birthday program starts to run in the IDE. The current date is displayed in the date time picker.

2. Click the arrow in the date time picker to display the object in calendar view.

    Your form looks like the following illustration, with a different date.

3. Click the Left scroll arrow to look at previous months on the calendar.

    Notice that the text box portion of the object also changes as you scroll the date. The "today" value at the bottom of the calendar doesn't change, however.

    Although you can scroll all the way back to your exact birthday, you might not have the patience to scroll month by month. To move to your birth year faster, select the year value in the date time picker text box and enter a new year.

4. Select the four-digit year in the date time picker text box.

    When you select the date, the date time picker closes.

5. Type your birth year in place of the year that's currently selected, and then click the arrow again.

    The calendar reappears in the year of your birth.

6. Click the scroll arrow again to locate the month in which you were born, and then click the exact day on which you were born.

    If you didn't know the day of the week you were born on, now you can find out!

When you select the final date, the date time picker closes, and your birth date is displayed in the text box. You can click the button object to see how this information is made available to other objects on your form.

7. Click the Show My Birthday button.

    Visual Basic executes your program code and displays a message box containing the day and date of your birth. Notice how the two dates match:

8. Click OK in the message box.

    A second message box appears indicating the day of the year on which you were born—everything seems to work! You'll find this control to be quite capable—not only does it remember the new date or time information that you enter, but it also keeps track of the current date and time, and it can display this date and time information in a variety of useful formats.

> **Note**   To configure the date time picker object to display times instead of dates, set the object's *Format* property to Time.

9. Click OK to close the message box, and then click the Close button on the form.

    You're finished using the *DateTimePicker* control for now.

A Word About Terminology

So far in this book I've used several different terms to describe items in a Visual Basic program. Do you know what all these items are yet? It's worth listing several of them now to clear up any confusion.

■ **Program statement**   A program statement is a line of code in a Visual Basic program, a self-contained instruction executed by the Visual Basic compiler that performs useful work within the application. Program statements can vary in length (some contain only one Visual Basic keyword!), but all program statements must follow syntax rules defined and enforced by the Visual Basic compiler. In Visual Studio 2005, program statements can be composed of keywords, properties, object names, variables, numbers, special symbols, and other values. (See Chapter 2 and Chapter 5.)

- **Keyword**   A keyword is a reserved word within the Visual Basic language that is recognized by the Visual Basic compiler and performs useful work. (For example, the *End* keyword stops program execution.) Keywords are one of the basic building blocks of program statements; they work together with objects, properties, variables, and other values to form complete lines of code and (therefore) instructions for the compiler and operating system. Most keywords are shown in blue type in the Code Editor. (See Chapter 2.)

- **Variable**   A variable is a special container used to hold data temporarily in a program. The programmer creates variables by using the *Dim* statement and then uses these variables to store the results of a calculation, file names, input, and so on. Numbers, names, and property values can be stored in variables. (See Chapter 5.)

- **Control**   A control is a tool you use to create objects on a Visual Basic form. You select controls from the Toolbox and use them to draw objects with the mouse on a form. You use most controls to create user interface elements, such as buttons, picture boxes, and list boxes. (See especially Chapters 2 through 4.)

- **Object**   An object is a user interface element that you create on a Visual Basic form with a control in the Toolbox. In Visual Basic, the form itself is also an object. You can move, resize, and customize objects by using property settings. Objects have what is known as *inherent functionality*–they know how to operate and can respond to certain situations on their own. (A list box "knows" how to scroll, for example.) You can program Visual Basic objects by using customized event procedures for different situations in a program. (See Chapters 1 through 4.)

- **Class**   A class is a blueprint or template for one or more objects that defines what the object does. Accordingly, a class defines what an object can do but is not the object itself. In Visual Basic .NET 2003 and Visual Basic 2005, you can use existing Visual Studio classes (like *System.Math* and *System.Windows.Forms.Form*), and you can build your own classes and *inherit* properties, methods, and events from them. (Inheritance allows one class to acquire the pre-existing interface and behavior characteristics of another class.) Although classes might sound esoteric at this point, they are a key feature of Visual Studio 2005, and in this book, you will use them to build user interfaces rapidly and to extend the work that you do to other programming projects. (See Chapters 5 and 16.)

- **Namespace**   A namespace is a hierarchical library of classes organized under a unique name, such as *System.Windows* or *System.Diagnostics*. To access the classes and underlying objects within a namespace, you place an *Imports* statement at the top of your program code. Every project in Visual Studio also has a root namespace, which is set using the project's Properties page. Namespaces are referred to as object libraries or class libraries in Visual Studio books and documentation. (See Chapter 5.)

■ **Property**   A property is a value, or characteristic, held by an object. For example, a button object has a *Text* property to specify the text that appears on the button and an *Image* property to specify the path to an image file that should appear on the button face. In Visual Basic, properties can be set at design time by using the Properties window or at run time by using statements in the program code. In code, the format for setting a property is

```
Object.Property = Value
```

where *Object* is the name of the object you're customizing, *Property* is the characteristic you want to change, and *Value* is the new property setting. For example,

```
Button1.Text = "Hello"
```

could be used in the program code to set the *Text* property of the *Button1* object to "Hello". (See Chapters 1 through 3.)

■ **Event procedure**   An event procedure is a block of code that's executed when an object is manipulated in a program. For example, when the *Button1* object is clicked, the *Button1_Click* event procedure is executed. Event procedures typically evaluate and set properties and use other program statements to perform the work of the program. (See Chapters 1 through 3.)

■ **Method**   A method is a special statement that performs an action or a service for a particular object in a program. In program code, the notation for using a method is

```
Object.Method(Value)
```

where *Object* is the name of the object you want to work with, *Method* is the action you want to perform, and *Value* is an optional argument to be used by the method. For example, the statement

```
ListBox1.Items.Add("Check")
```

uses the *Add* method to put the word *Check* in the *ListBox1* list box. Methods and properties are often identified by their position in a collection or object library, so don't be surprised if you see long references such as *System.Drawing.Image.FromFile*, which would be read as "the *FromFile* method, which is a member of the *Image* class, which is a member of the *System.Drawing* object library." (See Chapters 1 through 5.)

Controls for Gathering Input

Visual Basic provides several mechanisms for gathering input in a program. *Text boxes* accept typed input, *menus* present commands that can be clicked or chosen with the keyboard, and *dialog boxes* offer a variety of elements that can be chosen individually or selected in a group. In this exercise, you'll learn how to use four important controls that help you gather input in several different situations. You'll learn about the *RadioButton*, *CheckBox*, *ListBox*, and *Combo-Box* controls. You'll explore each of these objects as you use a Visual Basic program called Input Controls, which is the user interface for a simple, graphics-based ordering system. As you run the program, you'll get some hands-on experience with the input objects. In the next chapter, I'll discuss how these objects can be used along with menus in a full-fledged program.

As a simple experiment, try using the *CheckBox* control now to see how user input is processed on a form and in program code.

Experiment with the *CheckBox* control

1.   On the File menu, click Close Project to close the Birthday project.

2.   On the File menu, click New Project.

     The New Project dialog box appears.

3.   Create a new Visual Basic Windows Application project named **MyCheckBox**.

     The new project is created, and a blank form appears in the Designer.

4.   Click the *CheckBox* control in the Toolbox.

5.   Draw two check box objects on the form, one above the other.

     Check boxes appear as objects on your form just as other objects do. You'll have to click the Checkbox in the Toolbox a second time for the second check box.

6.   Using the *PictureBox* control, draw two square picture box objects beneath the two check boxes.

7.   Set the following properties for the check box and picture box objects:

Object	Property	Setting
CheckBox1	Checked	True
	Text	"Calculator"
CheckBox2	Text	"Copy machine"
PictureBox1	Image	c:\vb05sbs\chap03\calcultr.bmp
	SizeMode	StretchImage
PictureBox2	SizeMode	StretchImage

In this walkthrough, you'll use the check boxes to display and hide images of a calculator and a copy machine. The *Text* property of the check box object determines the contents of the check box label in the user interface. With the *Checked* property, you can set a default value for the check box. Setting *Checked* to True places a check mark in the box, and setting *Checked* to False (the default setting) removes the check mark. I use the *Size-Mode* properties in the picture boxes to size the images so that they stretch to fit in the picture box.

Your form looks something like this:

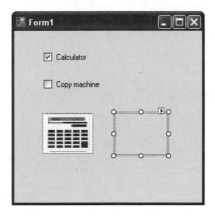

8. Double-click the first check box object to open the *CheckBox1_CheckedChanged* event procedure in the Code Editor, and then enter the following program code:

```
If CheckBox1.CheckState = 1 Then
    PictureBox1.Image = System.Drawing.Image.FromFile _
      ("c:\vb05sbs\chap03\calcultr.bmp")
    PictureBox1.Visible = True
Else
    PictureBox1.Visible = False
End If
```

The *CheckBox1_CheckedChanged* event procedure runs only if the user clicks in the first check box object. The event procedure uses an If...Then decision structure (described in Chapter 6, "Using Decision Structures") to confirm the current status, or *state*, of the first check box, and it displays a calculator picture from the c:\vb05sbs\chap03 folder if a check mark is in the box. The *CheckState* property holds a value of 1 if there's a check mark present and 0 if there's no check mark present. I use the *Visible* property to display the picture if a check mark is present or to hide the picture if a check mark isn't present. Notice that I wrapped the long line that loads the image into the picture box object by using the line continuation (_) character.

9. Click the View Designer button in Solution Explorer to display the form again, double-click the second check box, and then add the following code to the *CheckBox2_Checked-Changed* event procedure:

```
If CheckBox2.CheckState = 1 Then
    PictureBox2.Image = System.Drawing.Image.FromFile _
      ("c:\vb05sbs\chap03\copymach.bmp")
    PictureBox2.Visible = True
Else
    PictureBox2.Visible = False
End If
```

This event procedure is almost identical to the one that you just entered; only the names of the image (copymach.bmp), the check box object (*CheckBox2*), and the picture box object (*PictureBox2*) are different.

10. Click the Save All button on the Standard toolbar to save your changes, specifying the c:\vb05sbs\chap03 folder as the location.

Run the CheckBox program

> **Tip**   The complete CheckBox program is located in the c:\vb05sbs\chap03\checkbox folder.

1. Click the Start Debugging button on the Standard toolbar.

    Visual Basic runs the program in the IDE. The calculator image appears in a picture box on the form, and the first check box contains a check mark.

2. Select the Copy Machine check box.

    Visual Basic displays the copy machine image, as shown here:

3. Experiment with different combinations of check boxes, selecting or clearing the boxes several times to test the program. The program logic you added with a few short lines of

Visual Basic code manages the boxes perfectly. (You'll learn much more about program code in upcoming chapters.)

4. Click the Close button on the form to end the program.

The Input Controls Demo

Now that you've had a little experience with check boxes, run and examine the Input Controls demonstration program that I created to simulate a graphical ordering environment that makes more extensive use of check boxes, radio buttons, a list box, and a combo box. If you work in a business that does a lot of order entry, you might want to expand this program into a full-featured graphical order entry program. After you experiment with Input Controls, spend some time learning how the four input controls work in the program. They were created in a few short steps by using Visual Basic and the techniques you just learned.

Run the Input Controls program

1. On the File menu, click Open Project.

   The Open Project dialog box appears.

2. Open the c:\vb05sbs\chap03\input controls folder, and then double-click the Input Controls project file (Input Controls.vbproj).

   As I mentioned earlier, you may open either the project file (Input Controls.vbproj) or the solutions file (Input Controls.sln) to open solutions with only one project. In either case, the Input Controls project opens in the IDE.

3. If the project's form isn't visible, click the Form1.vb form in Solution Explorer, and then click the View Designer button.

4. Move or close the windows that block your view of the form so that you can see how the objects are laid out.

   You see a form similar to this:

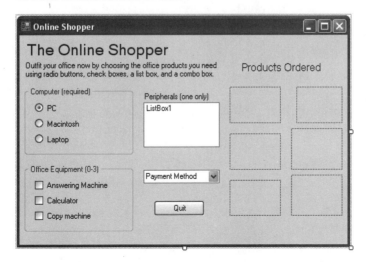

The Input Controls form contains radio button, check box, list box, combo box, picture box, button, and label objects. These objects work together to create a simple order entry program that demonstrates how the Visual Basic input objects work. When the Input Controls program is run, it loads images from the c:\vb05sbs\chap03\input controls folder and displays them in the six picture boxes on the form.

> **Note**   If you installed the practice files in a location other than the default c:\vb05sbs folder, the statements in the program that load the artwork from the disk contain an incorrect path. (Each statement begins with c:\vb05sbs\chap03\input controls, as you'll see soon.) If this is the case, you can make the program work by renaming your practice files folder \vb05sbs or by changing the paths in the Code Editor by using the editing keys or the Quick Replace command on the Edit menu.

5. Click the Start Debugging button on the Standard toolbar.

    The program runs in the IDE.

6. Click the Laptop radio button in the Computer box.

    The image of a laptop computer appears in the Products Ordered area on the right side of the form. The user can click various options, and the current choice is depicted in the order area on the right. In the Computer box, a group of radio buttons is used to gather input from the user.

    Radio buttons force the user to choose one (and only one) item from a list of possibilities. (Radio buttons are called option buttons in Visual Basic 6.) When radio buttons are placed inside a group box object on a form, the radio buttons are considered to be part of a group, and only one option can be chosen. To create a group box, click the *Group-Box* control on the Containers tab of the Toolbox, and then draw the control on your form. (The *GroupBox* control replaces the *Frame* control in Visual Basic 6.) You can give the group of radio buttons a title (as I have) by setting the *Text* property of the group box object. When you move a group box object on the form, the controls within it also move.

7. Click to select the Answering Machine, Calculator, and Copy Machine check boxes in the Office Equipment box.

    Check boxes are used in a program so that the user can select more than one option at a time from a list. Click to clear the Calculator check box again, and notice that the picture of the calculator disappears from the order area. Because each user interface element responds to click events as they occur, order choices are reflected immediately. The code that completes these tasks is nearly identical to the code you entered earlier in the CheckBox program.

8. Click Satellite Dish in the Peripherals list box.

    A picture of a satellite dish is added to the order area.

List boxes are used to get a single response from a list of choices. They are created with the *ListBox* control, and might contain many items to choose from. (Scroll bars appear if the list of items is longer than the list box.) Unlike radio buttons, a list box doesn't require that the user be presented with a default selection. And from a programmatic standpoint, items in a list box can be added to, removed from, or sorted while the program is running. If you would like to see check marks next to the items in your list box, use the *CheckedListBox* control in the Toolbox instead of the *ListBox* control.

9. Now choose U.S. Dollars (sorry, no credit) from the payment list in the Payment Method combo box.

    Combo boxes, or drop-down list boxes, are similar to regular list boxes, but they take up less space. (The "combo" in a combo box basically comes from a "combination" of an editable text box and a drop-down list.) Visual Basic automatically handles the opening, closing, and scrolling of the list box. All you do as a programmer is create the combo box by using the *ComboBox* control in the Toolbox, set the *Text* property to provide directions or a default value, and then write code to add items to the combo box and to process the user's combo box selection. You'll see examples of each task in the program code for the Input Controls demonstration in the next section.

    After you make your order selections, your screen looks something like this:

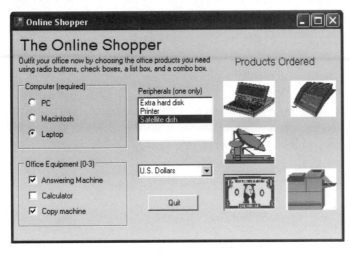

10. Practice making a few more changes to the order list in the program (try different computers, peripherals, and payment methods), and then click the Quit button in the program to exit.

    When you click Quit, the program closes, and the IDE appears.

Looking at the Input Controls Program Code

Although you haven't had much formal experience with program code yet, it's worth taking a quick look at a few event procedures in Input Controls to see how the program processes input from the user interface elements. In these procedures, you'll see the *If...Then* and *Select*

Case statements at work. You'll learn about these and other decision structures in Chapter 6. For now, concentrate on the *CheckState* property, which changes when a check box is selected, and the *SelectedIndex* property, which changes when a list box is selected.

Examine check box and list box code

1. Be sure the program has stopped running, and then double-click the Answering Machine check box in the Office Equipment group box to display the *CheckBox1_CheckedChanged* event procedure in the Code Editor.

   You see the following program code:

   ```
   'If the CheckState property for a check box is 1, it has a mark in it
   If CheckBox1.CheckState = 1 Then
       PictureBox2.Image = System.Drawing.Image.FromFile _
         ("c:\vb05sbs\chap03\input controls\answmach.bmp")
       PictureBox2.Visible = True
   Else
       'If there is no mark, hide the image
       PictureBox2.Visible = False
   End If
   ```

   As you learned in Chapter 2, the first line of this event procedure is a comment. Comments are displayed in green type and are simply notes written by the programmer to describe what's important or interesting about this particular piece of program code. (Comments are also occasionally generated by automated programming tools that compile programs or insert code snippets.) I wrote this comment to remind myself that the *CheckState* property contains a crucial value in this routine—a value of 1 if the first check box was checked.

   The rest of the event procedure is nearly identical to the one you just wrote in the Check-Box program. If you scroll down in the Code Editor, you see a similar event procedure for the *CheckBox2* and *CheckBox3* objects.

2. At the top edge of the Code Editor, click the Form1.vb [Design] tab to display the form again, and then double-click the Peripherals list box on the form.

   The *ListBox1_SelectedIndexChanged* event procedure appears in the Code Editor. You see the following program statements:

   ```
   'The item you picked (0-2) is held in the SelectedIndex property
   Select Case ListBox1.SelectedIndex
       Case 0
           PictureBox3.Image = System.Drawing.Image.FromFile _
             ("c:\vb05sbs\chap03\input controls\harddisk.bmp")
       Case 1
           PictureBox3.Image = System.Drawing.Image.FromFile _
             ("c:\vb05sbs\chap03\input controls\printer.bmp")
       Case 2
           PictureBox3.Image = System.Drawing.Image.FromFile _
             ("c:\vb05sbs\chap03\input controls\satedish.bmp")
   End Select
   ```

Here you see code that executes when the user clicks an item in the Peripherals list box in the program. In this case, the important keyword is *ListBox1.SelectedIndex*, which is read "the *SelectedIndex* property of the first list box object." After the user clicks an item in the list box, the *SelectedIndex* property returns a number that corresponds to the location of the item in the list box. (The first item is numbered 0, the second item is numbered 1, and so on.)

In the previous code, *SelectedIndex* is evaluated by the Select Case decision structure, and a different image is loaded depending on the value of the *SelectedIndex* property. If the value is 0, a picture of a hard disk is loaded; if the value is 1, a picture of a printer is loaded; and if the value is 2, a picture of a satellite dish is loaded. You'll learn more about how the Select Case decision structure works in Chapter 6.

3. At the top edge of the Code Editor, click the Form1.vb [Design] tab to display the form again, and then double-click the form (not any of the objects) to display the code associated with the form itself.

The *Form1_Load* event procedure appears in the Code Editor. This is the procedure that's executed each time the Input Controls program is loaded into memory. Programmers put program statements in this special procedure when they want them executed every time a form loads. (Your program can display more than one form, or none at all, but the default behavior is that Visual Basic loads and runs the *Form1_Load* event procedure each time the user runs the program.) Often, as in the Input Controls program, these statements define an aspect of the user interface that couldn't be created by using the controls in the Toolbox or the Properties window.

Here's what the *Form1_Load* event procedure looks like for this program:

```
'These program statements run when the form loads
PictureBox1.Image = System.Drawing.Image.FromFile _
  ("c:\vb05sbs\chap03\input controls\pcomputr.bmp")
'Add items to a list box like this:
ListBox1.Items.Add("Extra hard disk")
ListBox1.Items.Add("Printer")
ListBox1.Items.Add("Satellite dish")
'Combo boxes are also filled with the Add method:
ComboBox1.Items.Add("U.S. Dollars")
ComboBox1.Items.Add("Check")
ComboBox1.Items.Add("English Pounds")
```

Three lines in this event procedure are comments displayed in green type. The second line in the event procedure loads the personal computer image into the first picture box. (This line is broken in two using a space and the line continuation character, but the compiler still thinks of it as one line.) Loading an image establishes the default setting reflected in the Computer radio button group box. Note also that text between double quotes is displayed in red type.

The next three lines add items to the Peripherals list box (*ListBox1*) in the program. The words in quotes will appear in the list box when it appears on the form. Below the list box program statements, the items in the Payment Method combo box (*ComboBox1*) are specified. The important keyword in both these groups is *Add*, which is a special function, or method, that adds items to list box and combo box objects.

You're finished using the Input Controls program. Take a few minutes to examine any other parts of the program you're interested in, and then move on to the next exercise.

One Step Further: Using the *LinkLabel* Control

Providing access to the Web is now a standard feature of many Windows applications, and with Visual Studio 2005, adding this functionality is easier than ever. You can create a Visual Basic program that runs from a Web server by creating a Web Forms project and using controls in the Toolbox optimized for the Web. Alternatively, you can use Visual Basic to create a Windows application that opens a Web browser within the application, providing access to the Web while remaining a Windows program running on a client computer. We'll postpone writing Web Forms projects for a little while longer in this book, but in the following exercise you'll learn how to use the *LinkLabel* Toolbox control to create a Web link in a Windows program that provides access to the Internet through Microsoft Internet Explorer or the default Web browser on your system.

> **Note**   To learn more about writing Web-aware Visual Basic 2005 applications, read Chapter 20, "Creating Web Sites and Web Pages Using Microsoft Visual Web Developer and ASP.NET."

Create the WebLink program

1. On the File menu, click Close Project to close the Input Controls project.

2. On the File menu, click New Project.

    The New Project dialog box appears.

3. Create a new Visual Basic Windows Application project named **MyWebLink**.

    The new project is created, and a blank form appears in the Designer.

4. Click the *LinkLabel* control in the Toolbox, and draw a rectangular link label object on your form.

    Link label objects look like label objects, except that all label text is displayed in blue underlined type on the form.

5. Set the *Text* property of the link label object to the URL for the Microsoft Press home page:

    http://www.microsoft.com/learning/books/

    Your form looks like this:

6. Click the form in the IDE to select it. (Click the form itself, not the link label object.)

   This is the technique you use to view the properties of the default form, Form1, in the Properties window. Like other objects in your project, the form also has properties that you can set.

7. Set the *Text* property of the form object to **Web Link Test**.

   The *Text* property for a form controls what appears on the form's title bar at design time and when the program runs. Although this customization isn't related exclusively to the Web, I thought you'd enjoy picking up that skill now, before we move on to other projects. (We'll customize the title bar in most of the programs we build.)

8. Double-click the link label object, and then type the following program code in the *LinkLabel1_LinkClicked* event procedure:

```
' Change the color of the link by setting LinkVisited to True.
LinkLabel1.LinkVisited = True
' Use the Process.Start method to open the default browser
' using the Microsoft Press URL:
System.Diagnostics.Process.Start _
  ("http://www.microsoft.com/learning/books/")
```

I've included comments in the program code to give you some practice entering them. As soon as you enter the single quote character ('), Visual Studio changes the color of the line to green, identifying the line as a comment. Comments are for documentation purposes only—they aren't evaluated or executed by the compiler.

The two program statements that aren't comments control how the link works. Setting the *LinkVisited* property to True gives the link that dimmer color of purple, which indicates in many browsers that the HTML document associated with the link has already been viewed. Although setting this property isn't necessary to display a Web page, it's a good programming practice to provide the user with information in a way that's consistent with other applications.

The second program statement (which I have broken into two lines) runs the default Web browser (such as Internet Explorer) if the browser isn't already running. (If the browser is running, the URL just loads immediately.) The *Start* method in the *Process* class performs the important work, by starting a process or executable program session in memory for the browser. The *Process* class, which manages many other aspects of program execution, is a member of the *System.Diagnostics* namespace. By including an Internet address or a URL along with the *Start* method, I'm letting Visual Basic know that I want to view a Web site, and Visual Basic is clever enough to know that the default system browser is the tool that would best display that URL, even though I didn't identify the browser by name.

An exciting feature of the *Process.Start* method is that it can be used to run other Windows applications, too. If I did want to identify a particular browser by name to open the URL, I could have specified one using the following syntax. (Here I'll request the Internet Explorer browser.)

```
System.Diagnostics.Process.Start("IExplore.exe", _
  "http://www.microsoft.com/learning/books/")
```

Here two arguments are used with the *Start* method, separated by a comma. The exact location for the program named IExplore.exe on my system isn't specified, but Visual Basic will search the current system path for it when the program runs.

If I wanted to run a different application with the *Start* method—for example, if I wanted to run the Microsoft Word application and open the document c:\myletter.doc—I could use the following syntax:

```
System.Diagnostics.Process.Start("Winword.exe", _
  "c:\myletter.doc")
```

As you can see, the *Start* method in the *Process* class is very useful.

Now that you've entered your code, you should save your project. (If you experimented with the *Start* syntax as I showed you, restore the original code shown at the beginning of step 8 first.)

9. Click the Save All button on the Standard toolbar to save your changes, and specify c:\vb05sbs\chap03 as the location.

You can now run the program.

Run the WebLink program

> **Tip** The complete WebLink program is located in the c:\vb05sbs\chap03\weblink folder.

1. Click the Start button on the Standard toolbar to run the WebLink program.

The form opens and runs, showing its Web site link and handsome title bar text.

2.   Click the link to open the Web site at *http://www.microsoft.com/learning/books/.*

Recall that it's only a happy coincidence that the link label *Text* property contains the same URL as the site you named in the program code. (It is not necessary that these two items match.) You can enter any text you like in the link label. You can also use the *Image* property for a link label to specify a picture to display in the background of the link label. The following figure shows what the Microsoft Press Web page looks like (in English) when the WebLink program displays it using Internet Explorer.

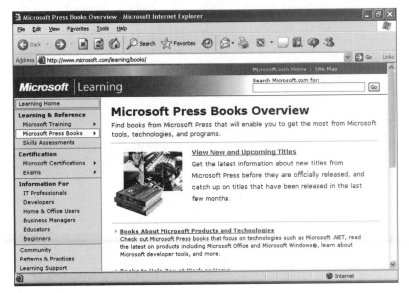

3.   Display the form again. (Click the Web Link Test form icon on the Windows taskbar if the form isn't visible.)

Notice that the link now appears in a dimmed style. Like a standard Web link, your link label communicates that it's been used (but is still active) by the color and intensity that it appears in.

4.   Click the Close button on the form to quit the test utility.

You're finished writing code in this chapter, and you're gaining valuable experience with some of the Toolbox controls available for creating Windows Forms applications. Let's keep going!

Chapter 3 Quick Reference

To	Do this
Create a text box	Click the *TextBox* control, and draw the box.
Create a button	Click the *Button* control, and draw the button.
Change a property at run time	Change the value of the property by using program code. For example: `Label1.Text = "Hello!"`
Create a radio button	Use the *RadioButton* control. To create multiple radio buttons, place more than one button object inside a box that you create by using the *GroupBox* control.
Create a check box	Click the *CheckBox* control, and draw a check box.
Create a list box	Click the *ListBox* control, and draw a list box.
Create a drop-down list box	Click the *ComboBox* control, and draw a drop-down list box.
Add items to a list box	Include statements with the *Add* method in the *Form1_Load* event procedure of your program. For example: `ListBox1.Items.Add "Printer"`
Use a comment in code	Type a single quotation mark (') in the Code Editor, and then type a descriptive comment that will be ignored by the compiler. For example: `' Use the Process.Start method to start IE`
Display a Web page	Create a link to the Web page by using the *LinkLabel* control, and then open the link in a browser by using the *Process.Start* method in program code.

Working with Menus, Toolbars, and Dialog Boxes

After completing this chapter, you will be able to:

- Add menus to your programs by using the *MenuStrip* control.
- Process menu and toolbar selections by using event procedures and the Code Editor.
- Add toolbars and buttons by using the *ToolStrip* control.
- Use the *OpenFileDialog* and *ColorDialog* controls to create standard dialog boxes.
- Add access keys and shortcut keys to menus.

In Chapter 3, "Working with Toolbox Controls," you used several Microsoft Visual Studio 2005 controls to gather input from the user while he or she used a program. In this chapter, you'll learn how to present choices to the user by creating professional-looking menus, toolbars, and dialog boxes.

A menu is located on the menu bar and contains a list of related commands; a toolbar contains buttons and other tools that perform useful work in a program. Most menu and toolbar commands are executed immediately after they're clicked; for example, when the user clicks the Copy command on the Edit menu, information is copied to the Clipboard immediately. If a menu command is followed by an ellipsis (...), however, clicking the command displays a dialog box requesting more information before the command is carried out, and many toolbar buttons also display dialog boxes.

In this chapter, you'll learn how to use the *MenuStrip* and *Toolstrip* controls to add a professional look to your application's user interface. You'll also learn how to process menu, toolbar, and dialog box commands.

Upgrade Notes: Migrating Visual Basic 6 Code to Visual Basic 2005

If you're experienced with Microsoft Visual Basic 6, you'll notice some new features in Microsoft Visual Basic 2005, including the following:

- Menus are no longer created by using the Visual Basic 6 Menu Editor tool. Instead, you create a menu strip object on your form by using the *MenuStrip* control and then customize the object by using property settings and the Menu Designer. However, menu choices are still processed with program code.

- The Visual Basic 6 *Toolbar* and *Coolbar* controls have been replaced by the *ToolStrip* control.

- Standard dialog boxes are no longer created by using the *CommonDialog* control. Instead, you use one of eight Windows Forms controls that add standard dialog boxes to your project. These controls are *OpenFileDialog*, *SaveFileDialog*, *FolderBrowserDialog*, *FontDialog*, *ColorDialog*, *PrintDialog*, *PrintPreviewDialog*, and *PageSetupDialog*.

- Forms now feature the *ShowDialog* method and the *DialogResult* property, making it easier to create custom forms that look and act like standard dialog boxes.

Adding Menus by Using the *MenuStrip* Control

The *MenuStrip* control is a tool that adds menus to your programs, which you can customize with property settings in the Properties window. (*MenuStrip* is an enhanced version of the *MainMenu* control that was distributed with Microsoft Visual Basic .NET 2002 and 2003.) With *MenuStrip*, you can add new menus, modify and reorder existing menus, and delete old menus. You can also create a standard menu configuration automatically, and you can enhance your menus with special effects, such as access keys, check marks, and keyboard shortcuts. The menus look perfect—just like a professional Microsoft Windows application— but *MenuStrip* only creates the *visible* part of your menus and commands. You still need to write event procedures that process the menu selections and make the commands perform useful work. In the following exercise, you'll take your first steps with this process by using the *MenuStrip* control to create a Clock menu containing commands that display the current date and time.

Create a menu

1. Start Visual Studio.

2. On the File menu, click New Project.

   The New Project dialog box appears.

3. Create a new Windows Application project named **MyMenu**.

4. Click the *MenuStrip* control on the Menus & Toolbars tab of the Toolbox, and then draw a menu control on your form.

Don't worry about the location—Visual Studio will move the control and resize it automatically. Your form looks like the one shown here:

The menu strip object doesn't appear on your form, but below it. That's different from Visual Basic 6, which in one way or another displays all objects on the form itself—even those that don't have a visual representation when the program ran, such as the *Timer* control. But in Visual Studio, non-visible objects, such as menus and timers, are displayed in the IDE in a separate pane named the *component tray*, and you can select them, set their properties, or delete them right from this pane.

In addition to the menu strip object in the component tray, Visual Studio displays a visual representation of the menu you created at the top of the form. The Type Here tag encourages you to click the tag and enter the title of your menu. After you enter the first menu title, you can enter submenu titles and other menu names by pressing the arrow keys and typing additional names. Best of all, you can come back to this in-line Menu Designer later and edit what you've done or add additional menu items—the menu strip object is fully customizable and with it you can create an exciting menu-driven user interface like the ones you've seen in the best Windows applications.

5. Click the Type Here tag, type **Clock**, and then press Enter.

The word "Clock" is entered as the name of your first menu, and two additional Type Here tags appear with which you can create submenu items below the new Clock menu or additional menu titles. The submenu item is currently selected.

6. Type **Date** to create a Date command for the Clock menu, and then press Enter.

Visual Studio adds the Date command to the menu and selects the next submenu item.

7. Type **Time** to create a Time command for the menu, and then press Enter.

You now have a Clock menu with two menu commands, Date and Time. You could continue to create additional menus or commands, but what you've done is sufficient for this example program. Your form looks like the one shown here:

8.   Click the form to close the Menu Designer.

The Menu Designer closes, and your form appears in the IDE with a new Clock menu. You're ready to start customizing the menu now.

Adding Access Keys to Menu Commands

With most applications, you can access and execute menu commands by using the keyboard. For example, in Visual Studio you can open the File menu by pressing the Alt key and then pressing the F key. Once the File menu is open, you can open a project by pressing the P key. The key that you press in addition to the Alt key and the key that you press to execute a command in an open menu are called *access keys*. You can identify the access key of a menu item because it's underlined.

Visual Studio makes it easy to provide access key support. To add an access key to a menu item, activate the Menu Designer, and then type an ampersand (&) before the appropriate letter in the menu name. When you open the menu at run time (when the program is running), your program automatically supports the access key.

> **Note**   By default, Microsoft Windows 2000, Microsoft Windows XP, and Microsoft Windows Server 2003 don't display the underline for access keys in a program until you press the Alt key for the first time. In Windows 2000, you can turn off this option on the Effects tab of the Display control panel. In Windows XP and Windows Server 2003, you can turn off this option by using the Effects button on the Appearance tab of the Display Properties control panel.

Try adding access keys to the Clock menu now.

Menu Conventions

By convention, each menu title and menu command in a Windows application has an initial capital letter. File and Edit are often the first two menu names on the menu bar, and Help is usually the last. Other common menu names are View, Format, and Window. No matter what menus and commands you use in your applications, take care to be clear and consistent with them. Menus and commands should be easy to use and should have as much in common as possible with those in other Windows–based applications. As you create menu items, use the following guidelines:

- Use short, specific captions consisting of one or two words at most.

- Assign each menu item an access key. Use the first letter of the item if possible, or the access key that is commonly assigned (such as x for Exit).

- Menu items at the same level must have a unique access key.

- If a command is used as an on/off toggle, place a check mark to the left of the item when it's active. You can add a check mark by setting the *Checked* property of the menu command to True in the Properties window.

- Place an ellipsis (...) after a menu command that requires the user to enter more information before the command can be executed. The ellipsis indicates that you'll open a dialog box if the user selects this item.

Add access keys

1. Click the Clock menu name on the form, pause a moment, and then click it again.

   The menu name is highlighted, and a blinking I-beam (text-editing cursor) appears at the end of the selection. With the I-beam, you can edit your menu name or add the ampersand character (&) for an access key. (If you double-clicked the menu name, the Code Editor might have opened. If that happened, close the Code Editor and repeat step 1.)

2. Press the Left Arrow key five times to move the I-beam to just before the Clock menu name.

   The I-beam blinks before the letter C in Clock.

3. Type & to define the letter C as the access key for the Clock menu.

   An ampersand appears in the text box in front of the word Clock.

4. Click the Date command in the menu list, and then click Date a second time to display the I-beam.

5. Type & before the letter D.

   The letter D is now defined as the access key for the Date command.

6. Click the Time command in the menu list, and then click the command a second time to display the I-beam.

7. Type **&** before the letter T.

   The letter T is now defined as the access key for the Time command.

8. Press Enter.

   Pressing Enter locks in your text-editing changes. Your form looks this:

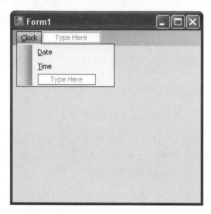

Now you'll practice using the Menu Designer to switch the order of the Date and Time commands on the Clock menu. Changing the order of menu items is an important skill because at times you'll think of a better way to define your menus.

Change the order of menu items

1. Click the Clock menu on the form to display its menu items.

   To change the order of a menu item, simply drag the item to a new location on the menu. Try it now.

2. Drag the Time menu on top of the Date menu, and then release the mouse button.

   Dragging one menu item on top of another menu item means that you want to place the first menu item ahead of the second menu item on the menu. As quickly as that, Visual Studio moved the Time menu item ahead of the Date item.

You've finished creating the user interface for the Clock menu. Now you'll use the menu event procedures to process the user's menu selections in the program.

> **Note** To delete a menu item from a menu, click the unwanted item in the menu list, and then press the Delete key. (If you try this now, remember that Visual Studio also has an Undo command, located on both the Edit menu and the Standard toolbar, so you can reverse the effects of the deletion.)

Processing Menu Choices

After menus and commands are configured by using the menu strip object, they also become new objects in your program. To make the menu objects do meaningful work, you need to write event procedures for them. Menu event procedures typically contain program statements that display or process information on the user interface form and modify one or more menu properties. If more information is needed from the user to process the selected command, you can write your event procedure so that it displays a dialog box or one of the input controls you used in Chapter 3.

In the following exercise, you'll add a label object to your form to display the output of the Time and Date commands on the Clock menu.

Add a label object to the form

1. Click the *Label* control in the Toolbox.

2. Create a label in the middle of the form.

   The label object appears on the form and bears the name *Label1* in the program code. If you find later that this label is too small later to fit the text, you can resize it as you would any object on a form. See the following graphic for the size I've used.

3. Set the following properties for the label:

Object	Property	Setting
Label1	AutoSize	False
	BorderStyle	FixedSingle
	Font	Microsoft Sans Serif, Bold, 14-point
	Text	(empty)
	TextAlign	MiddleCenter

Your form looks similar to this:

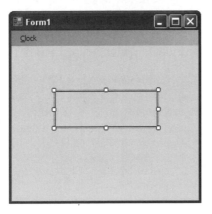

Now you'll add program statements to the Time and Date event procedures to process the menu commands.

> **Note**   In the following exercises, you'll enter program code to process menu choices. It's OK if you're still a bit hazy on what program code does and how you use it—you'll learn much more about program statements in Chapters 5 through 7.

Edit the menu event procedures

1. Click the Clock menu on the form to display its commands.

2. Double-click the Time command in the menu to open an event procedure for the command in the Code Editor.

    The *TimeToolStripMenuItem_Click* event procedure appears in the Code Editor. The name *TimeToolStripMenuItem_Click* includes the name *Time* that you gave this menu command. The words *ToolStripMenuItem* indicate that in its underlying technology, the *MenuStrip* control is related to the *ToolStrip* control. (We'll see further examples of that later in this chapter.) The *_Click* syntax means that this is the event procedure that runs when a user clicks the menu item.

    We'll keep this menu name for now, but if you wanted to create your own internal names for menu objects, you could select the object, open the Properties window, and change the *Name* property. Although I won't bother with that extra step in this chapter, later in the book you'll practice renaming objects in your program to conform more readily to professional programming practices.

3. Type the following program statement:

    ```
    Label1.Text = TimeString
    ```

    This program statement displays the current time (from the system clock) in the *Text* property of the *Label1* object, replacing the previous *Label1* text (if any). *TimeString* is a property that contains the current time formatted for display or printing. You can use *TimeString* at any time in your programs to display the time accurately down to the second. (*TimeString* is essentially a replacement for the older Visual Basic *TIME$* statement.)

> **Note**   The Visual Basic *TimeString* property returns the current system time. You can set the system time by using the Date/Time icon in Windows Control Panel; you can change the system time format by using the Regional Options (or Regional and Language Options) icon in Control Panel.

4. Press the Down Arrow key.

Visual Basic interprets the line and adjusts capitalization and spacing, if necessary. (Visual Basic checks each line for syntax errors as you enter it.)

> **Tip**   You can enter a line by pressing Enter, Up Arrow, or Down Arrow.

5. Click the View Designer button in Solution Explorer, and then double-click the Date command on the Clock menu.

The *DateToolStripMenuItem_Click* event procedure appears in the Code Editor. This event procedure is executed when the user clicks the Date command on the Clock menu.

6. Type the following program statement:

```
Label1.Text = DateString
```

This program statement displays the current date (from the system clock) in the *Text* property of the *Label1* object, replacing the previous *Label1* text. The *DateString* property is also available for general use in your programs. Assign *DateString* to the *Text* property of an object whenever you want to display the current date on a form.

> **Note**   The Visual Basic *DateString* property returns the current system date. You can set the system date by using the Date And Time icon in Control Panel; you can change the system date format by using the Regional Options (or Regional And Language Options) icon in Control Panel.

7. Press the Down Arrow key to enter the line.

Your screen looks similar to this:

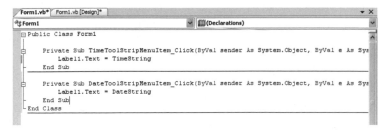

You've finished entering the menu demonstration program. Now you'll save your changes to the project and prepare to run it.

8. Click the Save All button on the Standard toolbar, and then specify the c:\vb05sbs\chap04 folder as the location.

Run the Menu program

> **Tip** The complete Menu program is located in the c:\vb05sbs\chap04\menu folder.

1. Click the Start Debugging button on the Standard toolbar.

   The Menu program runs in the IDE.

2. Click the Clock menu on the menu bar.

   The Clock menu appears.

3. Click the Time command.

   The current system time appears in the label box, as shown here:

   Now you'll try displaying the current date by using the access keys on the menu.

4. Press and release the Alt key.

   The Clock menu opens and the first item on it is highlighted.

5. Press D to display the current date.

   The current date appears in the label box.

6. Click the Close button on the program's title bar to stop the program.

Congratulations! You've created a working program that makes use of menus and access keys. In the next exercise, you'll learn how to use toolbars.

System Clock Properties and Functions

You can use various properties and functions to retrieve chronological values from the system clock. You can use these values to create custom calendars, clocks, and alarms in your programs. The following table lists the most useful system clock functions. For more information, check the Visual Studio online Help.

Property or Function	Description
TimeString	This property sets or returns the current time from the system clock.
DateString	This property sets or returns the current date from the system clock.
Now	This property returns an encoded value representing the current date and time. This property is most useful as an argument for other system clock functions.
Hour (*date*)	This function extracts the hour portion of the specified date/time value (0 through 23).
Minute (*date*)	This function extracts the minute portion of the specified date/time value (0 through 59).
Second (*date*)	This function extracts the second portion of the specified date/time value (0 through 59).
Month (*date*)	This function extracts a whole number representing the month (1 through 12).
Year (*date*)	This function extracts the year portion of the specified date/time value.
Weekday (*date*)	This function extracts a whole number representing the day of the week (1 is Sunday, 2 is Monday, and so on).

Adding Toolbars with the *ToolStrip* Control

Parallel to the *MenuStrip* control, you can use the Visual Studio *ToolStrip* control to quickly add toolbars to your program's user interface. The *ToolStrip* control is placed on a Visual Basic form but resides in the component tray in the IDE, just like the *MenuStrip* control. In Visual Studio 2005, you can add a variety of new features to your toolbars, including labels, combo boxes, text boxes, and split buttons. Toolbars look especially exciting when you add them, but remember that as with menu commands, you must write an event procedure for each button that you want to use in your program. Still, compared with earlier versions of Visual Basic, it is amazing how much toolbar programming and configuring the IDE does for you. Practice creating a toolbar now.

Create a toolbar

1. Click the *ToolStrip* control on the Menus & Toolbars tab of the Toolbox, and then draw a toolbar control on your form.

   Don't worry about the location—Visual Studio will create a toolbar on your form automatically and extend it across the window. The tool strip object itself appears below the form in the component tray. On the form, the default toolbar contains one button. Now you'll use a special shortcut feature to populate the toolbar automatically.

2. Click the tiny shortcut arrow in the upper-right corner of the new toolbar.

    The shortcut arrow points to the right and looks similar to the shortcut arrow we saw in the *PictureBox* control in Chapter 2, "Writing Your First Program." When you click the arrow, a window opens that includes a few of the most common toolbar tasks and properties. You can configure the toolbar quickly with these commands.

3. Click Insert Standard Items.

    Visual Studio adds a collection of standard toolbar buttons to the toolbar, including New, Open, Save, Print, Cut, Copy, Paste, and Help. Your form looks similar to this:

It is not necessary for you to start with a full toolbar of buttons as I have done here—I'm merely demonstrating one of the useful "automatic" features of Visual Studio 2005. You could also create the buttons on your toolbar one by one using the ToolStrip editing commands, as I shall demonstrate shortly. But for many applications, clicking Insert Standard Items is a time-saving feature. Remember, however, that although these toolbar buttons look professional, they are not functional yet. They need event procedures to make them work.

4. Click the Add ToolStripButton button on the right side of the toolbar, then click the Button item.

    Add ToolStripButton adds additional items to your toolbar, such as buttons, labels, split buttons, text boxes, combo boxes, and other useful interface elements. You've now created a custom toolbar button; by default it contains a picture of a mountain and a sun.

5. Right-click the new button, point to DisplayStyle, and click ImageAndText.

    Your new button displays both text and a graphical image on the toolbar. Visual Studio names your new button *ToolStripButton1* in the program, and this name appears by default on the toolbar.

6. Change the ToolStripButton1 object's *Text* property to Color, which is the name of your button on the form, and then press Enter.

    The Color button appears on the toolbar. You'll use this button later in the program to change the color of text on the form. Now insert a custom bitmap for your button.

7. Right-click the Color button, and then click the Set Image command.

8. Click Local Resource (if it is not already selected), and then the Import button.

9. Browse to the c:\vb05sbs\chap04 folder, click the ColorButton bitmap file that I created for you, click Open, then click OK.

    Visual Studio loads the pink, blue, and yellow paint icon into the Color button, as shown in the following illustration:

Your new button is complete, and you have learned how to add your own buttons to the toolbar, in addition to the default items supplied by Visual Studio. Now you'll learn how to delete and rearrange toolbar buttons.

Move and delete toolbar buttons

1. Drag the new Color button to the left side of the toolbar.

    Visual Studio lets you rearrange your toolbar buttons by using simple click-and-drag movements.

2. Right-click the second button in the toolbar (New), then click the Delete command.

    The New button is removed from the toolbar. With the Delete command, you can delete unwanted buttons, which makes it easy to customize the standard toolbar buttons provided by the *ToolStrip* control.

3. Delete the Save and Print buttons, but be sure to keep the Color and Open buttons.

Now you'll learn to use dialog box controls and connect them to toolbar buttons.

Using Dialog Box Controls

Visual Studio contains eight standard dialog box controls on the Dialogs and Printing tabs of the Toolbox. These dialog boxes are ready-made, so you don't need to create your own custom dialog boxes for the most common tasks in Windows applications, such as opening, saving, and printing files. In many cases, you'll still need to write the event procedure code that connects these dialog boxes to your program, but the user interfaces are built for you and conform to the standards for common use among Windows applications.

The eight standard dialog box controls available to you are listed in the following table. With a few important exceptions, they're similar to the objects provided by the *CommonDialog* control in Visual Basic 6. The *PrintPreviewControl* control isn't listed here, but you'll find it useful if you use the *PrintPreviewDialog* control.

Control Name	Purpose
OpenFileDialog	Gets the drive, folder name, and file name for an existing file
SaveFileDialog	Gets the drive, folder name, and file name for a new file
FontDialog	Lets the user choose a new font type and style
ColorDialog	Lets the user select a color from a palette
FolderBrowserDialog	Lets the user navigate through a computer's folder structure
PrintDialog	Lets the user set printing options
PrintPreviewDialog	Displays a print preview dialog box like the Microsoft Word program does
PageSetupDialog	Lets the user control page setup options, such as margins, paper size, and layout

In the following exercises, you'll practice using the *OpenFileDialog* and *ColorDialog* controls. The *OpenFileDialog* control lets your program open bitmap files, and the *ColorDialog* control enables your program to change the color of the clock output. You'll connect these dialog boxes to the toolbar that you just created, although you could just as easily connect them to menu commands.

Add *OpenFileDialog* and *ColorDialog* controls

1. Click the *OpenFileDialog* control on the Dialogs tab of the Toolbox, and then click the form.

    An open file dialog object appears in the component tray.

2. Click the *ColorDialog* control on the Dialogs tab of the Toolbox, and then click the form again.

    The component tray now looks like this:

Just like the menu strip and tool strip objects, the open file dialog and color dialog objects appear in the component tray, and they can be customized with property settings.

Now you'll create a picture box object by using the *PictureBox* control. As you've seen, the picture box object displays artwork on a form. This time, you'll display artwork in the picture box by using the open file dialog object.

Add a picture box object

1. Click the *PictureBox* control in the Toolbox.

2. Draw a picture box object on the form, below the label.

3. Use the shortcut arrow in the picture box object to set the *SizeMode* property of the picture box to StretchImage.

Now you'll create event procedures for the Color and Open buttons on the toolbar.

Event Procedures That Manage Common Dialog Boxes

After you create a dialog box object, you can display the dialog box in a program by doing the following:

- Type the dialog box name with the *ShowDialog* method in an event procedure associated with a toolbar button or menu command.

- If necessary, set one or more dialog box properties by using program code before opening the dialog box.

- Use program code to respond to the user's dialog box selections after the dialog box has been manipulated and closed.

In the following exercise, you'll enter the program code for the *openToolStripButton_Click* event procedure, the routine that executes when the Open command is clicked. You'll set the *Filter* property in the *OpenFileDialog1* object to define the file type in the Open common dialog box. (You'll specify Windows bitmaps.) Then you'll use the *ShowDialog* method to display the Open dialog box. After the user has selected a file and closed this dialog box, you'll display the file he or she selected in a picture box by setting the *Image* property of the picture box object to the file name the user selected.

Edit the Open button event procedure

1. Double-click the Open button on your form's toolbar.

The *openToolStripButton_Click* event procedure appears in the Code Editor.

2.   Type the following program statements in the event procedure. Be sure to type each line exactly as it's printed here, and press the Down Arrow key after the last line.

```
OpenFileDialog1.Filter = "Bitmaps (*.bmp)|*.bmp"
If OpenFileDialog1.ShowDialog() = DialogResult.OK Then
    PictureBox1.Image = System.Drawing.Image.FromFile _
      (OpenFileDialog1.FileName)
End If
```

The first three statements in the event procedure refer to three different properties of the open file dialog object. The first statement uses the *Filter* property to define a list of valid files. (In this case, the list has only one item: *.bmp.) This is important for the Open dialog box because a picture box object can display a number of file types, including:

- Bitmaps (.bmp files)

- Windows metafiles (.emf and .wmf files)

- Icons (.ico files)

- Joint Photographic Experts Group format (.jpg and .jpeg files)

- Portable Network Graphics format (.png files)

- Graphics Interchange Format (.gif files)

To add additional items to the *Filter* list, you can type a pipe symbol (|) between items. For example, this program statement

```
OpenFileDialog1.Filter = "Bitmaps (*.bmp)|*.bmp|Metafiles (*.wmf)|*.wmf"
```

allows both bitmaps and Windows metafiles to be chosen in the Open dialog box.

The second statement in the event procedure displays the Open dialog box in the program. *ShowDialog* is similar to the *Show* method in Visual Basic 6, but it can be used with any Windows form. The *ShowDialog* method returns a result named *DialogResult*, which indicates the button on the dialog box that the user clicked. To determine whether the user clicked the Open button, an If...Then decision structure is used to check whether the returned result equals *DialogResult.OK*. If it does, a valid .bmp file path should be stored in the *FileName* property of the open file dialog object. (You'll learn more about the syntax of If...Then decision structures in Chapter 6, "Using Decision Structures.")

The third statement uses the file name selected in the dialog box by the user. When the user selects a drive, folder, and file name and then clicks Open, the complete path is passed to the program through the *OpenFileDialog1.FileName* property. The *System.Drawing.Image.FromFile* method, which loads electronic artwork, is then used to copy the specified Windows bitmap into the picture box object. (I broke this statement with the line continuation character (_) because it was rather long.)

Now you'll write an event procedure for the Color button that you added to the toolbar.

Write the Color button event procedure

1. Display the form again, and then double-click the Color button on the toolbar that you added to the form.

    An event procedure named *ToolStripButton1_Click* appears in the Code Editor. The object name includes *Button1* because it was the first non-standard button that you added to the toolbar. (You can change the name of this object to something more intuitive, such as *colorToolStripButton*, by clicking the button on the form and changing the *Name* property in the Properties window.)

2. Type the following program statements in the event procedure:

    ```
    ColorDialog1.ShowDialog()
    Label1.ForeColor = ColorDialog1.Color
    ```

    The first program statement uses the *ShowDialog* method to open the color dialog box. As you learned earlier in this chapter, *ShowDialog* is the method you use to open any form as a dialog box, including a form created by one of the standard dialog box controls that Visual Studio provides. The second statement in the event procedure assigns the color that the user selected in the dialog box to the *ForeColor* property of the *Label1* object. You might remember *Label1* from earlier in this chapter—it's the label box you used to display the current time and date on the form. You'll use the color returned from the color dialog box to set the color of the text in the label.

    Note that the Color dialog box can be used to set the color of any user interface element that supports color. Other possibilities include the background color of the form, the colors of shapes on the form, and the foreground and background colors of objects.

3. Click the Save All button on the Standard toolbar to save your changes.

Controlling Color Choices by Setting Color Dialog Box Properties

If you want to further customize the color dialog box, you can control what color choices the dialog box presents to the user when the dialog box opens. You can adjust these color settings by using the Properties window, or by setting properties by using program code before you display the dialog box with the *ShowDialog* method. The following table describes the most useful properties of the *ColorDialog* control. Each property should be set with a value of True to enable the option or False to disable the option.

Property	Meaning
AllowFullOpen	Set to True to enable the Define Custom Colors button in the dialog box.
AnyColor	Set to True if the user can select any color shown in the dialog box.
FullOpen	Set to True if you want to display the Custom Colors area when the dialog box first opens.
ShowHelp	Set to True if you want to enable the Help button in the dialog box.
SolidColorOnly	Set to True if you want the user to select only solid colors (dithered colors—those that are made up of pixels of different colors—are disabled).

Now you'll run the Menu program and experiment with the menus and dialog boxes you've created.

Run the Menu program

> **Tip** The complete Menu program is located in the c:\vb05sbs\chap04\menu folder.

1. Click the Start Debugging button on the Standard toolbar.

   The program runs, and the Clock menu and the toolbar appear at the top of the screen.

2. On the form's toolbar, click Open.

   The Open dialog box appears. It looks great, doesn't it? Notice the Bitmaps (*.bmp) entry in the Files Of Type box. You defined this entry with the statement

   ```
   OpenFileDialog1.Filter = "Bitmaps (*.bmp)|*.bmp"
   ```

   in the *openToolStripButton_Click* event procedure. The first part of the text in quotes—Bitmaps (*.bmp)—specifies which items are listed in the Files Of Type box. The second part—*.bmp—specifies the file name extension of the files that are to be listed in the dialog box.

3. Open the c:\windows folder (or another folder that contains bitmap images) on your hard disk, and scroll past the list of folders to see the bitmap files.

   A standard collection of bitmaps appears. Most of these files were included with the Windows operating system, and you might have added to the collection yourself.

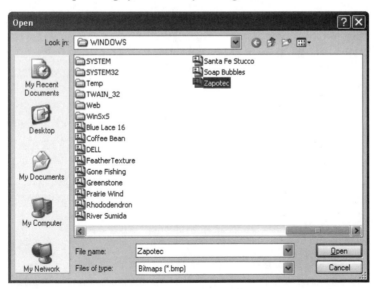

4. Select one of the bitmap files, and then click the Open button.

A picture of the bitmap appears in the picture box. (I've selected the Zapotec.bmp file.) Your form looks similar to this:

Now you'll practice using the Clock menu.

5. On the Clock menu, click the Time command.

    The current time appears in the label box.

6. Click the Color button on the toolbar.

    The Color dialog box appears, as shown here:

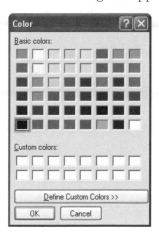

The Color dialog box contains elements that you can use to change the color of the clock text in your program. The current color setting, black, is selected.

7. Click the blue box, and then click the OK button.

    The Color dialog box closes, and the color of the text in the clock label changes to blue, as shown on the next page.

8. On the Clock menu, click the Date command.

   The current date is displayed in blue type. Now that the text color has been set in the label, it remains blue until the color is changed again or the program closes.

9. Close the program.

   The application terminates, and the Visual Studio IDE appears.

That's it! You've learned several important commands and techniques for creating menus, toolbars, and dialog boxes in your programs. After you learn more about program code, you'll be able to put these skills to work in your own programs.

Adding Nonstandard Dialog Boxes to Programs

What if you need to add a dialog box to your program that isn't provided by one of the eight dialog box controls in Visual Studio? No problem—but you'll need to do a little extra design work. As you'll learn in future chapters, a Visual Basic program can use more than one form to receive and display information. To create nonstandard dialog boxes, you need to add new forms to your program, add input and output objects, and process the dialog box clicks in your program code. (These techniques will be discussed in Chapter 14, "Managing Windows Forms and Controls at Run time.") In the next chapter, you'll learn how to use two handy dialog boxes that are specifically designed for receiving text input (*InputBox*) and displaying text output (*MsgBox*). These dialog boxes help bridge the gap between the dialog box controls and the dialog boxes that you need to create on your own.

One Step Further: Assigning Shortcut Keys to Menus

The *MenuStrip* control lets you assign shortcut keys to your menus. *Shortcut keys* are key combinations that a user can press to activate a command without using the menu bar. For example, on a typical Edit menu in a Windows application, such as Microsoft Word, you can copy selected text to the Clipboard by pressing Ctrl+C. With the *MenuStrip* control's *ShortcutKeys* property, you can customize this setting. Try assigning two shortcut keys to the Clock menu in the Menu program now.

Assign shortcut keys to the Clock menu

1. Make sure that your program has stopped running and is in design mode.

   You can modify a program only when it isn't running.

2. Click the Clock menu, and then click the Time command to highlight it.

   Before you set the shortcut key for a menu command, you must select it. You assign a shortcut key by setting the *ShortcutKeys* property for the command by using the Properties window. (In Visual Basic .NET 2002 and 2003, this property was named *Shortcut*.) The menu strip object provides an easy way for you to do this.

3. Open the Properties window, click the *ShortcutKeys* property, and then click the arrow in the second column

   A pop-up menu appears that helps you assign the shortcut key.

4. Click the Ctrl check box, click the Key list box, and select the letter T in the list.

   The Properties window looks like this:

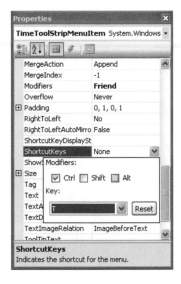

> **Tip** Visual Basic normally displays the shortcut key combination in the menu when you run the program, to give users a hint about which keys to press. To hide shortcut key combinations from the user (if you're running out of space), set the *ShowShortcutKeys* property to False. The shortcut key still works, but users won't see a visual reminder for it. You can also set what will be displayed within the program as a shortcut key by setting the *ShortcutKeyDisplayString* property.

5. Click the Date command, and then change its *ShortcutKeys* property setting to Ctrl+D.

   Now you'll run the program and try the shortcut keys.

6. Click the Start Debugging button on the Standard toolbar.

7. Press Ctrl+D to run the Date command.

   The current date appears in the program.

8. Press Ctrl+T to run the Time command.

   The current time appears in the program.

9. Click the Clock menu.

   The shortcut keys are listed beside the Time and Date commands, as shown in the following illustration. Visual Basic adds these key combinations when you define the shortcuts by using the *ShortcutKeys* property.

10. Close the program.

    The Menu program ends, and the development environment appears.

You're ready to move deeper into writing programs now, in the part of the book I call "Programming Fundamentals."

Chapter 4 Quick Reference

To	Do this
Create a menu item	Click the *MenuStrip* control, and draw a menu on your form. Click the Type Here tag on your form, and type the name of the menus and commands that you want to create.
Add an access key to a menu item	Click the menu item twice to display the I-beam, and then type an ampersand (&) followed by the letter you want to use as an access key.
Assign a shortcut key to a menu item	Set the *ShortcutKeys* property of the menu item by using the Properties window. A list of common shortcut keys is provided.
Change the order of menu items	Drag the menu item you want to move to a new location.
Add a toolbar to your program	Click the *ToolStrip* control, and draw a toolbar on your form. Right-click buttons to customize them. Double-click buttons and write event procedures to configure them.
Use a standard dialog box in your program	Add one of the eight standard dialog box controls to your form, and then customize it with property settings and program code. Dialog box controls are located on the Dialogs and Printing Toolbar tabs.
Display an Open dialog box	Add the *OpenFileDialog* control to your form. Display the dialog box with the *ShowDialog* method. The *FileName* property contains the name of the file selected.
Display a Color dialog box	Add the *ColorDialog* control to your form. Display the dialog box with the *ShowDialog* method. The *Color* property contains the color the user selected.

Part II
Programming Fundamentals

Chapter 5

Visual Basic Variables and Formulas, and the .NET Framework

After completing this chapter, you will be able to:

- Use variables to store data in your programs.
- Get input by using the *InputBox* function.
- Display messages by using the *MsgBox* function.
- Work with different data types.
- Use variables and operators to manipulate data.
- Use methods in the .NET Framework.
- Use mathematical operators and functions in formulas.

In Part I, you learned how to create the user interface of a Microsoft Visual Basic 2005 program and how to build and run a program in the Microsoft Visual Studio 2005 development environment. In the nine chapters in Part II, you'll learn more about Visual Basic program code—the statements and keywords that form the core of a Visual Basic program. You'll learn how to manage information within programs and control how your code is executed, and you'll learn how to use decision structures, loops, timers, arrays, collections, and text files. You'll also learn how to debug your programs and handle run-time errors if they occur. After you complete Part II, you'll be ready for more advanced topics, such as customizing the user interface, database programming, and Web programming.

In this chapter, you'll learn how to use variables and constants to store data temporarily in your program, and how to use the *InputBox* and *MsgBox* functions to gather and present information by using dialog boxes. You'll also learn how to use functions and formulas to perform calculations, and how to use mathematical operators to perform tasks such as multiplication and string concatenation. Finally, you'll learn how to tap into the powerful classes and methods of the Microsoft .NET 2.0 Framework to perform mathematical calculations and other useful work.

Upgrade Notes: Migrating Visual Basic 6 Code to Visual Basic 2005

If you're experienced with Microsoft Visual Basic 6, you'll notice some new features in Visual Basic 2005, including the following:

- To encourage better programming practices and cleaner program code, all Visual Basic 2005 variables must be declared before they're used. The implicit declaration of variables (using variables without declaring them) is allowed only if you use the *Option Explicit Off* statement—a practice that's discouraged.

- Visual Basic no longer supports the *Variant* data type. You should declare all variables by using *Dim* and the keyword *As* to identify the type of data that they'll hold.

- There are several new fundamental data types, and some of the older data types now support different ranges. For example, there's a 16-bit *Short* data type, a 32-bit *Integer* data type, and a 64-bit *Long* data type. The Visual Basic 6 *Currency* data type has been replaced with the *Decimal* data type.

- Beginning with Microsoft Visual Studio .NET 2002, Visual Basic offered a program statement and compiler setting named *Option Strict*, which (when enabled) required that variables be of the same data type when they are added, compared, or combined. In Visual Basic 2005, this compiler setting is turned off by default, meaning that variables of different data types can be combined under certain circumstances without generating a compiler error. (To check your compiler setting, click Options on the Tools menu, click Projects And Solutions, and then click VB Defaults.) The designers of Visual Studio offer this setting as a "professional grade" protection against unwanted type-mismatch errors, and it can be a useful safety measure in larger programming projects. (If you enable *Option Strict*, you'll need to become familiar with data type conversion functions such as *CInt*, *CLng*, and *CType* to make different types of data compatible.) However, in this book I assume that you have *Option Strict* set to False, and in a few cases the sample programs will not run correctly if you have *Option Strict* set to True.

- Visual Basic 2005 offers shortcut symbols for certain basic mathematical operations, such as addition (+), subtraction (-), and multiplication (*). With these shortcuts, you can write a formula such as X = X + 2 by using the syntax X += 2.

- Visual Basic 2005 no longer provides built-in keywords, such as *Abs* or *Cos*, for mathematical operations. Instead, you must use the methods in the *System.Math* class library of the .NET Framework for mathematical functions. The functionality of these methods is similar to the familiar Visual Basic 6 functions, although a few names have changed (for example, *Sqr* is now *Sqrt*).

- Visual Studio includes a *MessageBox* object, which is an alternative to the *MsgBox* function for displaying message boxes. To display a message box, you use the *MessageBox.Show* method.

The Anatomy of a Visual Basic Program Statement

As you learned in Chapter 2, "Writing Your First Program," a line of code in a Visual Basic program is called a *program statement*. A program statement is any combination of Visual Basic keywords, properties, object names, variables, numbers, special symbols, and other values that collectively create a valid instruction recognized by the Visual Basic compiler. A complete program statement can be a simple keyword, such as

```
End
```

which halts the execution of a Visual Basic program, or it can be a combination of elements, such as the following statement, which uses the *TimeString* property to assign the current system time to the *Text* property of the *Label1* object:

```
Label1.Text = TimeString
```

The rules of construction that must be used when you build a programming statement are called statement syntax. Visual Basic shares many of its syntax rules with earlier versions of the BASIC programming language and with other language compilers. The trick to writing good program statements is learning the syntax of the most useful language elements and then using those elements correctly to process the data in your program. Fortunately, Visual Basic does a lot of the toughest work for you, so the time you spend writing program code is relatively short, and the results can be reused in future programs.

In the following chapters, you'll learn the most important Visual Basic keywords and program statements, as well as many of the objects, properties, and methods provided by Visual Studio controls and the .NET Framework. You'll find that these keywords and objects complement nicely the programming skills you've already learned and will help you write powerful programs in the future. The first topics, variables and data types, are critical features of nearly every program.

Using Variables to Store Information

A *variable* is a temporary storage location for data in your program. You can use one or many variables in your code, and they can contain words, numbers, dates, properties, or other values. By using variables, you can assign a short and easy-to-remember name to each piece of data you plan to work with. Variables can hold information entered by the user at run time, the result of a specific calculation, or a piece of data you want to display on your form. In short, variables are handy containers that you can use to store and track almost any type of information.

Using variables in a Visual Basic program requires some planning. Before you can use a variable, you must set aside memory in the computer for the variable's use. This process is a little like reserving a seat at a theater or a baseball game. I'll cover the process of making reservations for, or *declaring*, a variable in the next section.

Setting Aside Space for Variables: The *Dim* Statement

In Microsoft Visual Basic .NET 2003 and Visual Basic 2005, you must explicitly declare your variables before using them. This is a change from Visual Basic 6 and earlier versions of Visual Basic, where (under certain circumstances) you can declare variables implicitly—in other words, simply by using them and without a *Dim* statement. This practice is flexible but rather risky—it creates the potential for variable confusion and misspelled variable names, which introduces potential bugs into the code that might or might not be discovered later.

To declare a variable in Visual Basic 2005, type the variable name after the *Dim* statement. (Dim stands for *dimension*.) This declaration reserves room in memory for the variable when the program runs and lets Visual Basic know what type of data it should expect to see later. Although this declaration can be done at any place in the program code (as long as the declaration happens before the variable is used), most programmers declare variables in one place at the top of their event procedures or code modules.

For example, the following statement creates space for a variable named *LastName* that will hold a textual, or *string*, value:

```
Dim LastName As String
```

Note that in addition to identifying the variable by name, I've used the *As* keyword to give the variable a particular type, and I've identified the type by using the keyword *String*. (You'll learn about other data types later in this chapter.) A string variable contains textual information: words, letters, symbols—even numbers. I find myself using string variables a lot; they hold names, places, lines from a poem, the contents of a file, and many other "wordy" data.

Why do you need to declare variables? Visual Basic wants you to identify the name and the type of your variables in advance so that the compiler can set aside the memory the program will need to store and process the information held in the variables. Memory management might not seem like a big deal to you (after all, modern personal computers have lots of RAM and gigabytes of free hard disk space), but in some programs, memory can be consumed quickly, and it's a good practice to take memory allocation seriously even as you take your first steps as a programmer. As you'll soon see, different types of variables have different space requirements and size limitations.

> **Note**   In some earlier versions of Visual Basic, specific variable types (such as *String* or *Integer*) aren't required—information is simply held by using a generic (and memory hungry) data type called *Variant*, which can hold data of any size or format. Variants are not supported in Visual Basic 2005. Although they are handy for beginning programmers, their design makes them slow and inefficient, and they allow variables to be converted from one type to another too easily—often causing unexpected results.

After you declare a variable, you're free to assign information to it in your code by using the assignment operator (=). For example, the following program statement assigns the last name "Jefferson" to the *LastName* variable:

```
LastName = "Jefferson"
```

Note that I was careful to assign a textual value to the *LastName* variable because its data type is *String*. I can also assign values with spaces, symbols, or numbers to the variable, such as

```
LastName = "1313 Mockingbird Lane"
```

but the variable is still considered a string value. The number portion could only be used in a mathematical formula if it were first converted to an integer or a floating-point value by using one of a handful of conversion functions I'll discuss later in this book.

After the *LastName* variable is assigned a value, it can be used in place of the name "Jefferson" in your code. For example, the assignment statement

```
Label1.Text = LastName
```

displays "Jefferson" in the first label (*Label1*) on your form.

> **Note**   If you really want to declare variables "the old way" in Visual Basic 2005—that is, without explicitly declaring them by using the *Dim* statement—you can place the Option Explicit Off statement at the very top of your form's or module's program code (before any event procedures), and it will defeat the Visual Basic default requirement that variables be declared before they're used. I don't recommend this statement as a permanent addition to your code, but you might find it useful temporarily as you convert older Visual Basic programs to Visual Studio 2005.

Using Variables in a Program

Variables can maintain the same value throughout a program, or they can change values several times, depending on your needs. The following exercise demonstrates how a variable named *LastName* can contain different text values and how the variable can be assigned to object properties.

Change the value of a variable

1. Start Visual Studio.

2. On the File menu, click Open Project.

   The Open Project dialog box appears.

3. Open the Variable Test project in the c:\vb05sbs\chap05\variable test folder.

4. If the project's form isn't visible, click Form1.vb in Solution Explorer, and then click the View Designer button.

The Variable Test form appears in the Designer. Variable Test is a *skeleton program*—it contains a form with labels and buttons for displaying output, but little program code. (I create these skeleton programs now and then to save you time, although you can also create the project from scratch.) You'll add code in this exercise.

The Variable Test form looks like this:

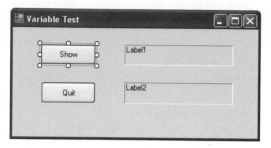

The form contains two labels and two buttons. You'll use variables to display information in each of the labels.

> **Note**   The label objects look like boxes because I set their *BorderStyle* properties to Fixed3D.

5. Double-click the Show button.

The *Button1_Click* event procedure appears in the Code Editor.

6. Type the following program statements to declare and use the *LastName* variable:

```
Dim LastName As String

LastName = "Luther"
Label1.Text = LastName

LastName = "Bodenstein von Karlstadt"
Label2.Text = LastName
```

The program statements are arranged in three groups. The first statement declares the *LastName* variable by using the *Dim* statement and the *String* type. After you type this line, Visual Studio places a jagged line under the *LastName* variable, because it has been declared but not used in the program. There is nothing wrong here—Visual Studio is just reminding you that a new variable has been created and is waiting to be used.

> **Tip**   If you finish writing your program and the variable name is still underlined, it could be a sign that you misspelled a variable name somewhere within your code.

The second and third lines assign the name "Luther" to the *LastName* variable and then display this name in the first label on the form. This example demonstrates one of the most common uses of variables in a program—transferring information to a property. As you have seen before, all string values assigned to variables are displayed in red type.

The fourth line assigns the name "Bodenstein von Karlstadt" to the *LastName* variable (in other words, it changes the contents of the variable). Notice that the second string is longer than the first and contains a few blank spaces. When you assign text strings to variables, or use them in other places, you need to enclose the text within quotation marks. (You don't need to do this with numbers.)

Finally, keep in mind another important characteristic of the variables being declared in this event procedure—they maintain their *scope*, or hold their value, only within the event procedure you're using them in. Later in this chapter, you'll learn how to declare variables so that they can be used in any of your form's event procedures.

7. Click the Form1.vb [Design] tab to display the form again.

8. Double-click the Quit button.

    The *Button2_Click* event procedure appears in the Code Editor.

9. Type the following program statement to stop the program:

    ```
    End
    ```

    Your screen looks like this:

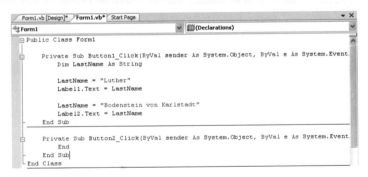

10. Click the Save All button on the Standard toolbar to save your changes.

11. Click the Start Debugging button on the Standard toolbar to run the program.

    The program runs in the IDE.

12. Click the Show button.

    The program declares the variable, assigns two values to it, and copies each value to the appropriate label on the form. The program produces the output shown on the next page.

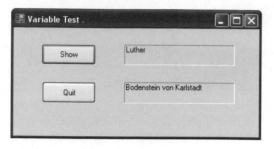

13.   Click the Quit button to stop the program.

The program stops, and the development environment returns.

Variable Naming Conventions

Naming variables can be a little tricky because you need to use names that are short but intuitive and easy to remember. To avoid confusion, use the following conventions when naming variables:

■   Begin each variable name with a letter or underscore. This is a Visual Basic require-ment. Variable names can contain only letters, underscores, and numbers.

■   Although variable names can be virtually any length, try to keep them under 33 characters to make them easier to read. (Variable names are limited to 255 charac-ters in Visual Basic 6, but that's no longer a constraint.)

■   Make your variable names descriptive by combining one or more words when it makes sense to do so. For example, the variable name *SalesTaxRate* is much clearer than *Tax* or *Rate*.

■   Use a combination of uppercase and lowercase characters and numbers. An accepted convention is to capitalize the first letter of each word in a variable; for example, *DateOfBirth*. However, some programmers prefer to use so-called camel casing (making the first letter of a variable name lowercase) to distinguish variable names from functions and module names, which usually begin with uppercase let-ters. Examples of camel casing include *dateOfBirth*, *employeeName*, and *counter*.

■   Don't use Visual Basic keywords, objects, or properties as variable names. If you do, you'll get an error when you try to run your program.

■   Optionally, you can begin each variable name with a two-character or three-character abbreviation corresponding to the type of data that's stored in the vari-able. For example, use *strName* to show that the *Name* variable contains string data. Although you don't need to worry too much about this detail now, you should make a note of this convention for later—you'll see it in the Visual Studio online Help and in many of the advanced books about Visual Basic programming. (This convention and abbreviation scheme was originally created by Microsoft Distinguished Engineer Charles Simonyi and is sometimes called the Hungarian Naming Convention.)

Using a Variable to Store Input

One practical use for a variable is to hold information from the user. Although you can often use an object such as a list box or a text box to gather this information, at times you might want to deal directly with the user and save the input in a variable rather than in a property. One way to gather input is to use the *InputBox* function to display a dialog box on the screen and then use a variable to store the text the user types. You'll try this approach in the following example.

Get input by using the *InputBox* function

1. On the File menu, point to Open, and then click Project.

   The Open Project dialog box appears.

2. Open the Input Box project in the c:\vb05sbs\chap05\input box folder.

   The Input Box project opens in the IDE. Input Box is a skeleton program.

3. If the project's form isn't visible, click Form1.vb in Solution Explorer, and then click the View Designer button.

   The form contains one label and two buttons. You'll use the *InputBox* function to get input from the user, and then you'll display the input in the label on the form.

4. Double-click the Input Box button.

   The *Button1_Click* event procedure appears in the Code Editor.

5. Type the following program statements to declare two variables and call the *InputBox* function:

```
Dim Prompt, FullName As String
Prompt = "Please enter your name."

FullName = InputBox(Prompt)
Label1.Text = FullName
```

This time, you're declaring two variables by using the *Dim* statement: *Prompt* and *FullName*. Both variables are declared using the *String* type. (You can declare as many variables as you want on the same line, as long as they are of the same type.) Note that in Visual Basic 6, this same syntax would have produced different results. *Dim* would create the *Prompt* variable using the *Variant* type (because no type was specified) and the *FullName* variable using the *String* type. But this logical inconsistency has been fixed in Visual Basic versions 2002, 2003, and 2005.

The second line in the event procedure assigns a text string to the *Prompt* variable. This message is used as a text argument for the *InputBox* function. (An *argument* is a value or an expression passed to a procedure or a function.) The next line calls the *InputBox* function and assigns the result of the call (the text string the user enters) to the *Full-Name* variable. *InputBox* is a special Visual Basic function that displays a dialog box on the screen and prompts the user for input. In addition to a prompt string, the *InputBox* function supports other arguments you might want to use occasionally. Consult the Visual Basic online Help for details.

After *InputBox* has returned a text string to the program, the fourth statement in the procedure places the user's name in the *Text* property of the *Label1* object, which displays it on the form.

> **Note** In older versions of BASIC, the *InputBox* function included a $ character at the end to help programmers remember that the function returned information in the string ($) data type. String variables were also identified with the $ symbol on occasion. These days we don't use character abbreviations for data types. *String* ($), *Integer* (%), and the other type abbreviations are now relics.

6. Save your changes.

   Do you remember which toolbar button to click to save your project? See step 10 of the previous exercise if you've forgotten.

7. Click the Start Debugging button on the Standard toolbar to run the program.

   The program runs in the IDE.

8. Click the Input Box button.

   Visual Basic executes the *Button1_Click* event procedure, and the Input Box dialog box appears on your screen, as shown here:

9. Type your full name, and then click OK.

   The *InputBox* function returns your name to the program and places it in the *FullName* variable. The program then uses the variable to display your name on the form, as shown here:

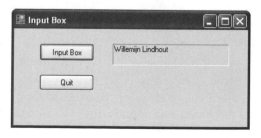

Use the *InputBox* function in your programs anytime you want to prompt the user for information. You can use this function in combination with the other input controls to regulate the flow of data into and out of a program. In the next exercise, you'll learn how to use a similar function to display text in a dialog box.

10. Click the Quit button on the form to stop the program.

   The program stops, and the development environment returns.

What Is a Function?

InputBox is a special Visual Basic keyword known as a *function*. A function is a statement that performs meaningful work (such as prompting the user for information or calculating an equation) and then returns a result to the program. The value returned by a function can be assigned to a variable, as it was in the Input Box program, or it can be assigned to a property or another statement or function. Visual Basic functions often use one or more arguments to define their activities. For example, the *InputBox* function you just executed used the *Prompt* variable to display dialog box instructions for the user. When a function uses more than one argument, commas separate the arguments, and the whole group of arguments is enclosed in parentheses. The following statement shows a function call that has two arguments:

```
FullName = InputBox(Prompt, Title)
```

Notice that I'm using italic in this syntax description to indicate that certain items are placeholders for information you specify. This is a style you'll find throughout the book and in the Visual Studio documentation.

Using a Variable for Output

You can display the contents of a variable by assigning the variable to a property (such as the *Text* property of a label object) or by passing the variable as an argument to a dialog box function. One useful dialog box function for displaying output is the *MsgBox* function. When you call the *MsgBox* function, it displays a dialog box, sometimes called a *message box*, with various options that you can specify. Like *InputBox*, it takes one or more arguments as input, and the results of the function call can be assigned to a variable. The syntax for the *MsgBox* function is

```
ButtonClicked = MsgBox(Prompt, Buttons, Title)
```

where *Prompt* is the text to be displayed in the message box; *Buttons* is a number that specifies the buttons, icons, and other options to display for the message box; and *Title* is the text displayed in the message box title bar. The variable *ButtonClicked* is assigned the result returned by the function, which indicates which button the user clicked in the dialog box.

If you're just displaying a message using the *MsgBox* function, the *ButtonClicked* variable, the assignment operator (=), the *Buttons* argument, and the *Title* argument are optional. You'll be using the *Title* argument, but you won't be using the others in the following exercise; for more information about them (including the different buttons you can include in *MsgBox* and a few more options), search for *MsgBox Function* in Visual Studio online Help.

> **Note**   Visual Basic provides both the *MsgBox* function and the *MessageBox* class for display-ing text in a message box. The *MessageBox* class is part of the *System.Windows.Forms* name-space, it takes arguments much like *MsgBox,* and it is displayed by using the *Show* method. I'll use both *MsgBox* and *MessageBox* in this book.

Now you'll add a *MsgBox* function to the Input Box program to display the name the user enters in the Input Box dialog box.

Display a message by using the *MsgBox* function

1. If the Code Editor isn't visible, double-click the Input Box button on the Input Box form.

    The *Button1_Click* event procedure appears in the Code Editor. (This is the code you entered in the last exercise.)

2. Select the following statement in the event procedure (the last line):

    ```
    Label1.Text = FullName
    ```

    This is the statement that displays the contents of the *FullName* variable in the label.

3. Press the Delete key to delete the line.

    The statement is removed from the Code Editor.

4. Type the following line into the event procedure as a replacement:

    ```
    MsgBox(FullName, , "Input Results")
    ```

    This new statement will call the *MsgBox* function, display the contents of the *Full-Name* variable in the dialog box, and place the words *Input Results* in the title bar. (The optional *Buttons* argument and the *ButtonClicked* variable are irrelevant here and have been omitted.) Your event procedure looks like this:

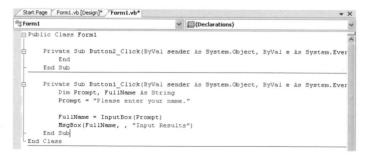

5. Click the Start Debugging button on the Standard toolbar.

6. Click the Input Box button, type your name in the input box, and then click OK.

   Visual Basic stores the input in the program in the *FullName* variable and then displays it in a message box. Your screen looks similar to this:

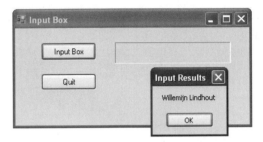

7. Click OK to close the message box. Then click Quit to close the program.

   The program closes, and the development environment returns.

Working with Specific Data Types

The *String* data type is useful for managing text in your programs, but what about numbers, dates, and other types of information? To allow for the efficient memory management of all types of data, Visual Basic provides several additional data types that you can use for your variables. Many of these are familiar data types from earlier versions of BASIC or Visual Basic, and some of the data types are new or have been changed in Visual Studio 2005 to allow for the efficient processing of data in newer 64-bit computers.

The following table lists the fundamental (or elementary) data types in Visual Basic. Experienced programmers will notice four new data types in Visual Basic 2005: *SByte*, *UShort*, *UInteger*, and *ULong*. *SByte* allows for "signed" byte values—that is, for both positive and negative numbers. *UShort*, *UInteger*, and *ULong* are "unsigned" data types—meaning that they cannot hold negative numbers. (However, as unsigned data types they offer twice the positive-number range of their signed counterparts, as shown in the table below.) You'll gain a performance advantage in your programs if you choose the right data type for your variables—a size that's neither too big nor too small. In the next exercise, you'll see how several of these data types work.

Note Variable storage size is measured in bits. The amount of space required to store one standard (ASCII) keyboard character in memory is 8 bits, which equals 1 byte.

Data type	Size	Range	Sample usage
Short	16-bit	-32,768 through 32,767	`Dim Birds As Short` `Birds = 12500`
UShort	16-bit	0 through 65,535	`Dim Days As UShort` `Days = 55000`
Integer	32-bit	-2,147,483,648 through 2,147,483,647	`Dim Insects As Integer` `Insects = 37500000`
UInteger	32-bit	0 through 4,294,967,295	`Dim Joys As UInteger` `Joys = 3000000000`
Long	64-bit	-9,223,372,036,854,775,808 to 9,223,372,036,854,775,807	`Dim WorldPop As Long` `WorldPop = 4800000004`

ULong	64-bit	0 through 18,446,744,073,709,551,615	`Dim Stars As ULong`
			`Stars = _`
			`1800000000000000000`

Single	32-bit floating point	-3.4028235E38 through 3.4028235E38	`Dim Price As Single` `Price = 899.99`
Double	64-bit floating point	-1.79769313486231E308 through 1.79769313486231E308	`Dim Pi As Double` `Pi = 3.1415926535`
Decimal	128-bit	values up to +/-79,228 × 1024	`Dim Debt As Decimal` `Debt = 7600300.50`
Byte	8-bit	0 through 255 (no negative numbers)	`Dim RetKey As Byte` `RetKey = 13`
SByte	8-bit	-128 through 127	`Dim NegVal As SByte` `NegVal = -20`
Char	16-bit	Any Unicode symbol in the range 0–65,535	`Dim UnicodeChar As Char` `UnicodeChar = "Ä"`
String	Usually 16-bits per character	0 to approximately 2 billion 16-bit Unicode characters	`Dim Dog As String` `Dog = "pointer"`
Boolean	16-bit	True or False (during conversions, 0 is converted to False, other values to True)	`Dim Flag as Boolean` `Flag = True`
Date	64-bit	January 1, 0001, through December 31, 9999	`Dim Birthday as Date` `Birthday = #3/1/1963#`

Object	32-bit	Any type can be stored in a variable of type Object	`Dim MyApp As Object`
			`MyApp = CreateObject _`
			`("Word.Application")`

Use fundamental data types in code

1. On the File menu, click Open Project.

   The Open Project dialog box appears.

2. Open the Data Types project in the c:\vb05sbs\chap05\data types folder.

3. If the project's form isn't visible, click Form1.vb in Solution Explorer, and then click the View Designer button.

   Data Types is a complete Visual Basic program that I created to demonstrate how the fundamental data types work. You'll run the program to see what the data types look like, and then you'll look at how the variables are declared and used in the program code. You'll also learn where to place variable declarations so that they're available to all the event procedures in your program.

4. Click the Start Debugging button on the Standard toolbar.

   The following application window appears:

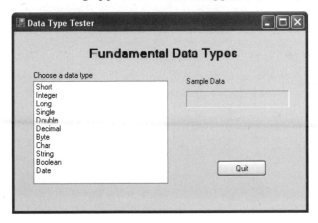

   The Data Types program lets you experiment with 11 data types, including integer, single-precision floating point, and date. The program displays an example of each type when you click its name in the list box.

5. Click the Integer type in the list box.

   The number 37,500,000 appears in the Sample Data box, as shown in the illustration on the next page. Note that with the *Short, Integer,* and *Long* data types, you can't insert or display commas. To display commas, you'll need to use the *Format* function.

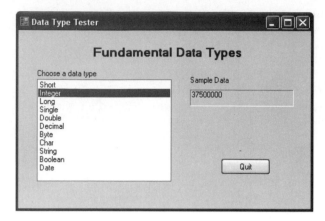

6. Click the Date type in the list box.

    The date 3/1/1963 appears in the Sample Data box.

7. Click each data type in the list box to see how Visual Basic displays it in the Sample Data box.

8. Click the Quit button to stop the program.

    Now you'll examine how the fundamental data types are declared at the top of the form and how they're used in the *ListBox1_SelectedIndexChanged* event procedure.

9. Double-click the form itself (not any objects on the form), and enlarge the Code Editor to see more of the program code.

    The Code Editor looks like this:

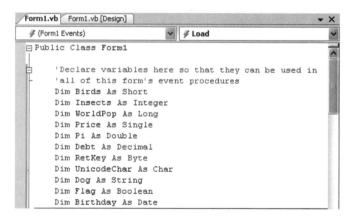

Scroll to the top of the Code Editor to see the dozen or so program statements I added to declare 11 variables in your program—one for each of the fundamental data types in Visual Basic. (I didn't create an example for the *SByte*, *UShort*, *UInteger*, and *ULong* types, because they closely resemble their signed or unsigned counterparts.) By placing each *Dim* statement here, at the top of the form's code initialization area, I'm ensuring that the variables will be valid, or will have *scope*, for all of the form's event procedures. That way, I can set the value of a variable in one event procedure and read it in another. Normally, variables are valid only in the event procedure in which they're declared. To make them valid across the form, you need to declare variables at the top of your form's code.

> **Note**   I've given each variable the same name as I did in the data types table earlier in the chapter so that you can see the examples I showed you in actual program code.

10. Scroll down in the Code Editor, and examine the *Form1_Load* event procedure.

    You'll see the following statements, which add items to the list box object in the program. (You might remember this syntax from Chapter 3, "Working with Toolbox Controls"—I used some similar statements there.)

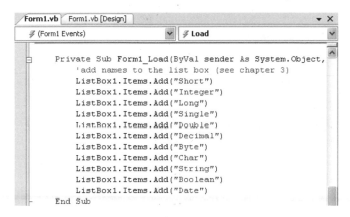

```
Private Sub Form1_Load(ByVal sender As System.Object,
    'add names to the list box (see chapter 3)
    ListBox1.Items.Add("Short")
    ListBox1.Items.Add("Integer")
    ListBox1.Items.Add("Long")
    ListBox1.Items.Add("Single")
    ListBox1.Items.Add("Double")
    ListBox1.Items.Add("Decimal")
    ListBox1.Items.Add("Byte")
    ListBox1.Items.Add("Char")
    ListBox1.Items.Add("String")
    ListBox1.Items.Add("Boolean")
    ListBox1.Items.Add("Date")
End Sub
```

11. Scroll down and examine the *ListBox1_SelectedIndexChanged* event procedure.

    The *ListBox1_SelectedIndexChanged* event procedure processes the selections you make in the list box and looks like this:

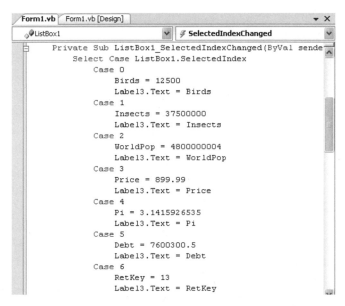

```
Private Sub ListBox1_SelectedIndexChanged(ByVal sende
    Select Case ListBox1.SelectedIndex
        Case 0
            Birds = 12500
            Label3.Text = Birds
        Case 1
            Insects = 37500000
            Label3.Text = Insects
        Case 2
            WorldPop = 4800000004
            Label3.Text = WorldPop
        Case 3
            Price = 899.99
            Label3.Text = Price
        Case 4
            Pi = 3.1415926535
            Label3.Text = Pi
        Case 5
            Debt = 7600300.5
            Label3.Text = Debt
        Case 6
            RetKey = 13
            Label3.Text = RetKey
```

The heart of the event procedure is a Select Case decision structure. In the next chapter, we'll discuss how this group of program statements selects one choice from many. For now, notice how each section of the Select Case block assigns a sample value to one of the fundamental data type variables and then assigns the variable to the *Text* property of the *Label4* object on the form. I used code like this in Chapter 3 to process list box choices, and you can use these techniques to work with list boxes and data types in your own programs.

> **Note**   If you have more than one form in your project, you need to declare variables in a slightly different way (and place) to give them scope throughout your program (that is, in each form that your project contains). The type of variable that you'll declare is a public, or global, variable, and it's declared in a *module*, a special file that contains declarations and procedures not associated with a particular form. For information about creating public variables in modules, see Chapter 10, "Creating Modules and Procedures."

12. Scroll through the *ListBox1_SelectedIndexChanged* event procedure, and examine each of the variable assignments closely.

Try changing the data in a few of the variable assignment statements and running the program again to see what the data looks like. In particular, you might try assigning values to variables that are outside their accepted range, as shown in the data types table presented earlier. If you make such an error, Visual Basic adds a jagged underline below the incorrect value in the Code Editor, and the program won't run until you change it. To learn more about your mistake, you can hold the mouse pointer over the jagged underlined value and read a short ScreenTip error message about the problem.

13. If you made any changes you want to save to disk, click the Save All button on the Standard toolbar.

User-Defined Data Types

Visual Basic also lets you create your own data types. This feature is most useful when you're dealing with a group of data items that naturally fit together but fall into different data categories. You create a *user-defined type* (UDT) by using the *Structure* statement, and you declare variables associated with the new type by using the *Dim* statement. Be aware that the *Structure* statement cannot be located in an event procedure—it must be located at the top of the form along with other variable declarations, or in a code module.

For example, the following declaration creates a user-defined data type named *Employee* that can store the name, date of birth, and hire date associated with a worker:

```
Structure Employee
    Dim Name As String
    Dim DateOfBirth As Date
    Dim HireDate As Date
End Structure
```

> After you create a data type, you can use it in the program code for the form's or module's event procedures. The following statements use the new *Employee* type. The first statement creates a variable named *ProductManager*, of the *Employee* type, and the second statement assigns the name "Greg Baker" to the *Name* component of the variable:
>
> ```
> Dim ProductManager As Employee
> ProductManager.Name = "Greg Baker"
> ```
>
> This looks a little similar to setting a property, doesn't it? Visual Basic uses the same notation for the relationship between objects and properties as it uses for the relationship between user-defined data types and component variables.

Constants: Variables That Don't Change

If a variable in your program contains a value that never changes (such as π, a fixed mathematical entity), you might consider storing the value as a constant instead of as a variable. A *constant* is a meaningful name that takes the place of a number or a text string that doesn't change. Constants are useful because they increase the readability of program code, they can reduce programming mistakes, and they make global changes easier to accomplish later. Constants operate a lot like variables, but you can't modify their values at run time. They are declared with the *Const* keyword, as shown in the following example:

```
Const Pi As Double = 3.14159265
```

This statement creates a constant named *Pi* that can be used in place of the value of π in the program code. To make a constant available to all the objects and event procedures in your form, place the statement at the top of your form along with other variable and structure declarations that will have scope in all of the form's event procedures. To make the constant available to all the forms and modules in a program (not just *Form1*), create the constant in a code module, with the *Public* keyword in front of it. For example:

```
Public Const Pi As Double = 3.14159265
```

The following exercise demonstrates how you can use a constant in an event procedure.

Use a constant in an event procedure

1. On the File menu, click Open Project.

   The Open Project dialog box appears.

2. Open the Constant Tester project in the c:\vb05sbs\chap05\constant tester folder.

3. If the project's form isn't visible, click Form1.vb in Solution Explorer, and then click the View Designer button.

   The Constant Tester form appears in the Designer. Constant Tester is a skeleton program. The user interface is finished, but you need to type in the program code.

4. Double-click the Show Constant button on the form.

The *Button1_Click* event procedure appears in the Code Editor.

5. Type the following statements in the *Button1_Click* event procedure:

```
Const Pi As Double = 3.14159265
Label1.Text = Pi
```

> **Tip**   The location you choose for your declarations should be based on how you plan to use the constants or the variables. Programmers typically keep the scope for declarations as small as possible, while still making them available for code that needs to use them. For example, if a constant is needed only in a single event procedure, you should put the constant declaration within that event procedure. However, you could also place the declaration at the top of the form's code, which would give all the event procedures in your form access to it.

6. Click the Start Debugging button on the Standard toolbar to run the program.

7. Click the Show Constant button.

The *Pi* constant appears in the label box, as shown here:

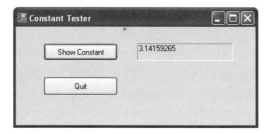

8. Click the Quit button to stop the program.

Constants are useful in program code, especially in involved mathematical formulas, such as Area = πr^2. The next section describes how you can use operators and variables to write similar formulas.

Working with Visual Basic Operators

A *formula* is a statement that combines numbers, variables, operators, and keywords to create a new value. Visual Basic contains several language elements designed for use in formulas. In this section, you'll practice working with mathematical *operators*, the symbols used to tie together the parts of a formula. With a few exceptions, the mathematical symbols you'll use are the ones you use in everyday life, and their operations are fairly intuitive. You'll see each operator demonstrated in the following exercises.

Visual Basic includes the following operators:

Operator	Description
+	Addition
–	Subtraction
*	Multiplication
/	Division
\	Integer (whole number) division
Mod	Remainder division
^	Exponentiation (raising to a power)
&	String concatenation (combination)

Basic Math: The +, –, *, and / Operators

The operators for addition, subtraction, multiplication, and division are pretty straightforward and can be used in any formula where numbers or numeric variables are used. The following exercise demonstrates how you can use them in a program.

Work with basic operators

1. On the File menu, click Open Project.

2. Open the Basic Math project in the c:\vb05sbs\chap05\basic math folder.

3. If the project's form isn't visible, click Form1.vb in Solution Explorer, and then click the View Designer button.

   The Basic Math form appears in the Designer. The Basic Math program demonstrates how the addition, subtraction, multiplication, and division operators work with numbers you type. It also demonstrates how you can use text box, radio button, and button objects to process user input in a program.

4. Click the Start Debugging button on the Standard toolbar.

   The Basic Math program runs in the IDE. The program displays two text boxes in which you enter numeric values, a group of operator radio buttons, a box that displays results, and two button objects (Calculate and Quit).

5. Type **100** in the Variable 1 text box, and then press Tab.

   The insertion point, or *focus*, moves to the second text box.

6. Type **17** in the Variable 2 text box.

   You can now apply any of the mathematical operators to the values in the text boxes.

7. Click the Addition radio button, and then click the Calculate button.

   The operator is applied to the two values, and the number 117 appears in the Result box, as shown on the next page.

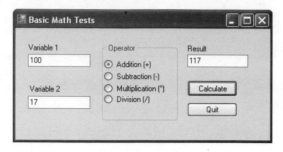

8. Practice using the subtraction, multiplication, and division operators with the two numbers in the variable boxes. (Click Calculate to calculate each formula.)

The results appear in the Result box. Feel free to experiment with different numbers in the variable text boxes. (Try a few numbers with decimal points if you like.) I used the *Double* data type to declare the variables, so you can use very large numbers.

Now try the following test to see what happens:

9. Type **100** in the Variable 1 text box, type **0** in the Variable 2 text box, click the Division radio button, and then click Calculate.

Dividing by zero is not allowed in mathematical calculations, because it produces an infinite result. But Visual Basic is able to handle this calculation and displays a value of Infinity in the Result text box. Being able to handle some divide-by-zero conditions is a feature that Visual Basic 2005 automatically provides.

10. When you've finished contemplating this and other tests, click the Quit button.

The program stops, and the development environment returns.

Now take a look at the program code to see how the results were calculated. Basic Math uses a few of the standard input controls you experimented with in Chapter 3 and an event procedure that uses variables and operators to process the simple mathematical formulas. The program declares its variables at the top of the form so that they can be used in all of the Form1 event procedures.

Examine the Basic Math program code

1. Double-click the Calculate button on the form.

The Code Editor displays the *Button1_Click* event procedure. At the top of the form's code, you'll see the following statement, which declares two variables of type *Double*:

```
'Declare FirstNum and SecondNum variables
Dim FirstNum, SecondNum As Double
```

I used the *Double* type because I wanted a large, general purpose variable type that could handle many different numbers—integers, numbers with decimal points, very big numbers, small numbers, and so on. The variables are declared on the same line by using the shortcut notation. Both *FirstNum* and *SecondNum* are of type *Double*, and are used to hold the values input in the first and second text boxes, respectively.

2. Scroll down in the Code Editor to see the contents of the *Button1_Click* event procedure. Your screen looks similar to this:

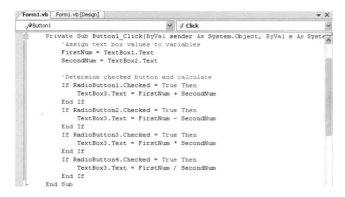

The first two statements in the event procedure transfer data entered in the text box objects into the *FirstNum* and *SecondNum* variables.

```
'Assign text box values to variables
FirstNum = TextBox1.Text
SecondNum = TextBox2.Text
```

The *TextBox* control handles the transfer with the *Text* property—a property that accepts text entered by the user and makes it available for use in the program. I'll make frequent use of the *TextBox* control in this book. When it's set to multiline and resized, it can display many lines of text—even a whole file!

After the text box values are assigned to the variables, the event procedure determines which radio button has been checked, calculates the mathematical formula, and displays the result in a third text box. The first radio button test looks like this:

```
'Determine checked button and calculate
If RadioButton1.Checked = True Then
    TextBox3.Text = FirstNum + SecondNum
End If
```

Remember from Chapter 3 that only one radio button object in a group box object can be selected at once. You can tell whether a radio button has been selected by evaluating the *Checked* property. If it's True, the button has been selected. If the *Checked* property is False, the button has not been selected. After this simple test, you're ready to compute the result and display it in the third text box object. That's all there is to using basic mathematical operators. (You'll learn more about the syntax of If...Then tests in Chapter 6, "Using Decision Structures.")

You're done using the Basic Math program.

New Shortcut Operators

An interesting feature of Visual Basic 2002, 2003, and 2005 is that you can use shortcut operators for mathematical and string operations that involve changing the value of an existing variable. For example, if you combine the + symbol with the = symbol, you can add to a variable without repeating the variable name twice in the formula. Thus, you can write the formula X = X + 6 by using the syntax X += 6. The following table shows examples of these shortcut operators.

Operation	Long-form syntax	Shortcut syntax
Addition (+)	X = X + 6	X += 6
Subtraction (-)	X = X − 6	X -= 6
Multiplication (*)	X = X * 6	X *= 6
Division (/)	X = X / 6	X /= 6
Integer division (\)	X = X \ 6	X \= 6
Exponentiation (^)	X = X ^ 6	X ^= 6
String concatenation (&)	X = X & "ABC"	X &= "ABC"

Using Advanced Operators: \, *Mod*, ^, and &

In addition to the four basic mathematical operators, Visual Basic includes four advanced operators, which perform integer division (\), remainder division (*Mod*), exponentiation (^), and string concatenation (&). These operators are useful in special-purpose mathematical formulas and text processing applications. The following utility (a slight modification of the Basic Math program) shows how you can use each of these operators in a program.

Work with advanced operators

1. On the File menu, click Open Project.

    The Open Project dialog box appears.

2. Open the Advanced Math project in the c:\vb05sbs\chap05\advanced math folder.

3. If the project's form isn't visible, click Form1.vb in Solution Explorer, and then click the View Designer button.

    The Advanced Math form appears in the Designer. The Advanced Math program is identical to the Basic Math program, with the exception of the operators shown in the radio buttons and in the program.

4. Click the Start Debugging button on the Standard toolbar.

    The program displays two text boxes in which you enter numeric values, a group of operator radio buttons, a text box that displays results, and two buttons.

5. Type **9** in the Variable 1 text box, and then press Tab.

6. Type **2** in the Variable 2 text box.

   You can now apply any of the advanced operators to the values in the text boxes.

7. Click the Integer Division radio button, and then click the Calculate button.

   The operator is applied to the two values, and the number 4 appears in the Result box, as shown here:

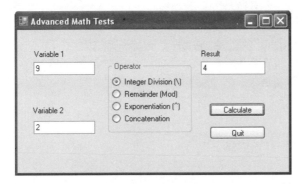

   Integer division produces only the whole number result of the division operation. Although 9 divided by 2 equals 4.5, the integer division operation returns only the first part, an integer (the whole number 4). You might find this result useful if you're working with quantities that can't easily be divided into fractional components, such as the number of adults who can fit in a car.

8. Click the Remainder radio button, and then click the Calculate button.

   The number 1 appears in the Result box. Remainder division (modulus arithmetic) returns the remainder (the part left over) after two numbers are divided. Because 9 divided by 2 equals 4 with a remainder of 1 ($2 \times 4 + 1 = 9$), the result produced by the *Mod* operator is 1. In addition to adding an early-seventies vibe to your code, the *Mod* operator can help you track "leftovers" in your calculations, such as the amount of money left over after a financial transaction.

9. Click the Exponentiation radio button, and then click the Calculate button.

   The number 81 appears in the Result box. The exponentiation operator (^) raises a number to a specified power. For example, 9 ^ 2 equals 9^2, or 81. In a Visual Basic formula, 9^2 is written 9 ^ 2.

10. Click the Concatenation radio button, and then click the Calculate button.

    The number 92 appears in the Result box. The string concatenation operator (&) combines two strings in a formula, but not through addition. The result is a combination of the "9" character and the "2" character. String concatenation can be performed on numeric variables—for example, if you're displaying the inning-by-inning score of a baseball game as they do in old-time score boxes—but concatenation is more commonly performed on string values or variables.

Because I declared the *FirstNum* and *SecondNum* variables as type *Double*, you can't combine words or letters by using the program code as written. As an example, try the following test, which causes an error and ends the program.

11. Type **birth** in the Variable 1 text box, type **day** in the Variable 2 text box, verify that Concatenation is selected, and then click Calculate.

Visual Basic is unable to process the text values you entered, so the program stops running, and an error message appears on the screen, as shown here:

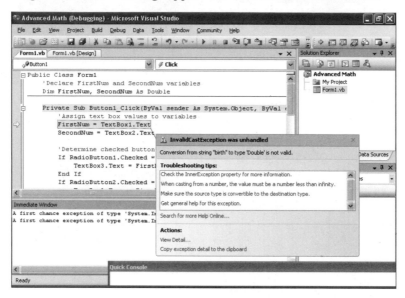

This type of error is called a *run-time error*—an error that surfaces not during the design and compilation of the program, but later, when the program is running and encounters a condition that it doesn't know how to process. If this seems odd, you might imagine that Visual Basic is simply offering you a modern rendition of the robot plea "Does not compute!" from the best science fiction films of the 1950s. The computer-speak message "Conversion from string "birth" to type 'Double' is not valid" means that the words you entered in the text boxes ("birth" and "day") could not be converted, or *cast*, by Visual Basic to variables of the type *Double*. *Double* types can only contain numbers. Period.

As we shall explore in more detail later, Visual Studio no longer leaves you hanging with this problem, but provides a dialog box with different types of information to help you resolve the run-time error. (Debugging has been a major area of improvement in Visual Studio 2005.) You have learned another important lesson about data types and when not to mix them.

12. Click the Stop Debugging button on the Standard toolbar to end the program.

Your program ends and returns you to the development environment.

> **Note** In Chapter 8, "Debugging Visual Basic Programs," you'll learn about debugging mode, which allows you to track down the defects, or *bugs*, in your program code.

Now take a look at the program code to see how variables were declared and how the advanced operators were used.

13. Scroll to the code at the top of the Code Editor.

    You see the following comment and program statement:

    ```
    'Declare FirstNum and SecondNum variables
    Dim FirstNum, SecondNum As Double
    ```

    As you might recall from the previous exercise, *FirstNum* and *SecondNum* are the variables that hold numbers coming in from the *TextBox1* and *TextBox2* objects.

14. Change the data type from *Double* to *String* so that you can properly test how the string concatenation (*&*) operator works.

15. Scroll down in the Code Editor to see how the advanced operators are used in the program code.

    You see the following code:

    ```
    'Assign text box values to variables
    FirstNum = TextBox1.Text
    SecondNum = TextBox2.Text

    'Determine checked button and calculate
    If RadioButton1.Checked = True Then
        TextBox3.Text = FirstNum \ SecondNum
    End If
    If RadioButton2.Checked = True Then
        TextBox3.Text = FirstNum Mod SecondNum
    End If
    If RadioButton3.Checked = True Then
        TextBox3.Text = FirstNum ^ SecondNum
    End If
    If RadioButton4.Checked = True Then
        TextBox3.Text = FirstNum & SecondNum
    End If
    ```

    Like the Basic Math program, this program loads data from the text boxes and places it in the *FirstNum* and *SecondNum* variables. The program then checks to see which radio button the user checked and computes the requested formula. In this event procedure, the integer division (\), remainder (*Mod*), exponentiation (^), and string concatenation (*&*) operators are used. Now that you've changed the data type of the variables to *String*, run the program again to see how the *&* operator works on text.

16. Click the Start Debugging button.

17. Type **birth** in the Variable 1 text box, type **day** in the Variable 2 text box, click Concatenation, and then click Calculate.

The program now concatenates the string values and doesn't produce a run-time error, as shown here:

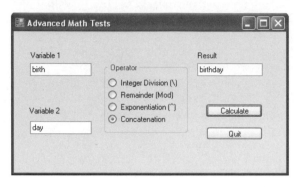

18.   Click the Quit button to close the program.

You're finished working with the Advanced Math program.

> **Tip**   Run-time errors are difficult to avoid completely—even the most sophisticated application programs, such as Microsoft Word or Microsoft Excel, sometimes run into error conditions that they can't handle, producing run-time errors, or *crashes*. Designing your programs to handle many different data types and operating conditions helps you produce solid, or *robust*, applications. In Chapter 9, "Trapping Errors Using Structured Error Handling," you'll learn about another helpful tool for preventing run-time error crashes—the structured error handler.

Working with Methods in the Microsoft .NET Framework

Now and then you'll want to do a little extra number crunching in your programs. You might need to round a number, calculate a complex mathematical expression, or introduce randomness into your programs. The math methods shown in the following table can help you work with numbers in your formulas. These methods are provided by the Microsoft .NET Framework, a class library that lets you tap into the power of the Microsoft Windows operating system and accomplish many of the common programming tasks that you need to create your projects. The .NET Framework is a major feature of Visual Studio that is shared by Visual Basic, Microsoft Visual C++, Microsoft Visual C#, Microsoft Visual J#, and other tools in Visual Studio. It's an underlying interface that becomes part of the Windows operating system itself, and it is installed on each computer that runs Visual Studio programs.

The .NET Framework is organized into classes that you can include by name in your programming projects by using the *Imports* statement. The process is quite simple, and you'll experiment with how it works now by using a math method in the *System.Math* class of the .NET Framework.

What's New in Microsoft .NET Framework 2.0?

Visual Studio 2005 includes a new version of the .NET Framework—Microsoft .NET Framework 2.0. Version 2.0 adds support for 64-bit extensions to 32-bit processors (AMD64 chips and Intel processors with EM64T technology). The 2.0 Framework also adds new classes that provide additional functionality (greater access to file systems, printers, and the Windows registry), and new classes that make it easier for you to write programs by providing a higher level of "encapsulation" for existing objects and resources. Many of the improvements in the .NET Framework will come to you automatically as you use Visual Basic 2005, and some will become useful as you explore advanced programming techniques.

The following table offers a partial list of the math methods in the *System.Math* class. The argument *n* in the table represents the number, variable, or expression you want the method to evaluate. If you use any of these methods, be sure that you put the statement

```
Imports System.Math
```

at the very top of your form's code in the Code Editor.

Method	Purpose
Abs(n)	Returns the absolute value of *n*.
Atan(n)	Returns the arctangent, in radians, of *n*.
Cos(n)	Returns the cosine of the angle *n*. The angle *n* is expressed in radians.
Exp(n)	Returns the constant *e* raised to the power *n*.
Sign(n)	Returns -1 if *n* is less than 0, 0 if *n* is 0, and +1 if *n* is greater than 0.
Sin(n)	Returns the sine of the angle *n*. The angle *n* is expressed in radians.
Sqrt(n)	Returns the square root of *n*.
Tan(n)	Returns the tangent of the angle *n*. The angle *n* is expressed in radians.

Use the *System.Math* class to compute square roots

1. On the File menu, click New Project.

   The New Project dialog box appears.

2. Create a new Visual Basic Windows Application project named **My Framework Math**.

   The new project is created, and a blank form appears in the Designer.

3. Click the *Button* control on the Windows Forms tab of the Toolbox, and create a button object at the top of your form.

4. Click the *TextBox* control in the Toolbox, and draw a text box below the button object.

5. Set the *Text* property of the button object to Square Root.

6. Double-click the button object to display the Code Editor.

7. At the very top of the Code Editor, above the `Public Class Form1` statement, type the following program statement:

```
Imports System.Math
```

The *Imports* statement adds a library of objects, properties, and methods to your project. This statement must be the first statement in your program—it must come even before the variables that you declare for the form and the `Public Class Form1` statement that Visual Basic automatically provides. The particular library you've chosen is the *System.Math* class, a collection of objects, properties, and methods provided by the .NET Framework for mathematical operations.

8. Move down in the Code Editor, and add the following code to the *Button1_Click* event procedure between the *Private Sub* and *End Sub* statements:

```
Dim Result As Double
Result = Sqrt(625)
TextBox1.Text = Result
```

These three statements declare a variable of the double type named *Result*, use the *Sqrt* method to compute the square root of 625, and assign the *Result* variable to the *Text* property of the text box object so that the answer is displayed.

9. Click the Save All button on the Standard toolbar to save your changes. Specify the c:\vb05sbs\chap05 folder as the location.

10. Click the Start Debugging button on the Standard toolbar.

The Framework Math program runs in the IDE.

11. Click the Square Root button.

Visual Basic calculates the square root of 625 and displays the result (25) in the text box. As you can see here, the *Sqrt* method works!

12. Click the Close button on the form to end the program.

To use a particular .NET Framework class in your program, include the *Imports* statement, and specify the appropriate class library. You can use this technique to use any class in the .NET Framework, and you'll see many more examples of this technique as you work through *Microsoft Visual Basic 2005 Step by Step.*

One Step Further: Establishing Order of Precedence

In the previous few exercises, you experimented with several mathematical operators and one string operator. Visual Basic lets you mix as many mathematical operators as you like in a formula, as long as each numeric variable and expression is separated from another by one operator. For example, this is an acceptable Visual Basic formula:

```
Total = 10 + 15 * 2 / 4 ^ 2
```

The formula processes several values and assigns the result to a variable named *Total*. But how is such an expression evaluated by Visual Basic? In other words, what sequence does Visual Basic follow when solving the formula? You might not have noticed, but the order of evaluation matters a great deal in this example.

Visual Basic solves this dilemma by establishing a specific *order of precedence* for mathematical operations. This list of rules tells Visual Basic which operator to use first, second, and so on when evaluating an expression that contains more than one operator.

The following table lists the operators from first to last in the order in which they are evaluated. (Operators on the same level in this table are evaluated from left to right as they appear in an expression.)

Operators	Order of Precedence
( )	Values within parentheses are always evaluated first.
^	Exponentiation (raising a number to a power) is second.
–	Negation (creating a negative number) is third.
* /	Multiplication and division are fourth.
\	Integer division is fifth.
Mod	Remainder division is sixth.
+ -	Addition and subtraction are last.

Given the order of precedence in this table, the expression

```
Total = 10 + 15 * 2 / 4 ^ 2
```

is evaluated by Visual Basic in the following steps. (Bold type is used to show each step in the order of evaluation and its result.)

```
Total = 10 + 15 * 2 / 4 ^ 2
Total = 10 + 15 * 2 / 16
Total = 10 + 30 / 16
Total = 10 + 1.875
Total = 11.875
```

Using Parentheses in a Formula

You can use one or more pairs of parentheses in a formula to clarify the order of precedence. For example, Visual Basic calculates the formula

```
Number = (8 - 5 * 3) ^ 2
```

by determining the value within the parentheses (-7) before doing the exponentiation—even though exponentiation is higher in order of precedence than subtraction and multiplication, according to the preceding table. You can further refine the calculation by placing nested parentheses in the formula. For example,

```
Number = ((8 - 5) * 3) ^ 2
```

directs Visual Basic to calculate the difference in the inner set of parentheses first, perform the operation in the outer parentheses next, and then determine the exponentiation. The result produced by the two formulas is different: the first formula evaluates to 49 and the second to 81. Parentheses can change the result of a mathematical operation, as well as make it easier to read.

Chapter 5 Quick Reference

To	Do this
Declare a variable	Type *Dim* followed by the variable name, the *As* keyword, and the variable data type in the program code. To make the variable valid in all of a form's event procedures, place this statement at the top of the code for the form, before any event procedures. For example: `Dim Country As String`
Change the value of a variable	Assign a new value with the assignment operator of (=). For example: `Country = "Japan"`

To	Do this
Get input with a dialog box	Use the *InputBox* function, and assign the result to a variable. For example: ```UserName = InputBox("what is your name?")```

Display output in a dialog box	Use the *MsgBox* function. (The string to be displayed in the dialog box can be stored in a variable.) For example:
	
	```Forecast = "Rain, mainly on the plain."```
	```MsgBox(Forecast, , "Spain Weather Report")```

Create a constant	Type the *Const* keyword followed by the constant name, the assignment operator (=), the constant data type, and the fixed value. For example: ```Const JackBennysAge As Short = 39```
Create a formula	Link together numeric variables or values with one of the seven mathematical operators, and then assign the result to a variable or a property. For example: ```Result = 1 ^ 2 * 3 \ 4 'this equals 0```
Combine text strings	Use the string concatenation operator (&). For example: ```Msg = "Hello" & "," & " world!"```
Include a class library from the .NET Framework	Place an *Imports* statement at the very top of the form's code that identifies the class library. For example: ```Imports System.Math```
Make a call to a method from an included class library	Use the method name, and include any necessary arguments so that it can be used in a formula or a program statement. For example, to make a call to the *Sqrt* method in the *System.Math* class library: ```Hypotenuse = Sqrt(x ^ 2 + y ^ 2)```

Control the evaluation order in a formula	Use parentheses in the formula. For example:
	
	```Result = 1 + 2 ^ 3 \ 4 'this equals 3```
	```Result = (1 + 2) ^ (3 \ 4) 'this equals 1```

Chapter 6
Using Decision Structures

After completing this chapter, you will be able to:

- Write conditional expressions.

- Use an *If...Then* statement to branch to a set of program statements based on a varying condition.

- Use the *MaskedTextBox* control to receive user input in a specific format.

- Short-circuit an *If...Then* statement.

- Use a *Select Case* statement to select one choice from many options in program code.

- Use the *Name* property to rename objects within a program.

- Manage mouse events and write a *MouseHover* event handler.

In the past few chapters, you used several features of Microsoft Visual Basic 2005 to process user input. You used menus, toolbars, dialog boxes, and other Toolbox controls to display choices for the user, and you processed input by using property settings, variables, operators, formulas, and the Microsoft .NET Framework.

In this chapter, you'll learn how to branch conditionally to a specific area in your program based on input you receive from the user. You'll also learn how to evaluate one or more properties or variables by using conditional expressions, and then execute one or more program statements based on the results. In short, you'll increase your programming vocabulary by creating code blocks called *decision structures* that control how your program executes, or *flows*, internally.

Upgrade Notes: Migrating Visual Basic 6 Code to Visual Basic 2005

If you're experienced with Microsoft Visual Basic 6, you'll notice some new features in Visual Basic 2005, including the following:

- Visual Basic 2005 includes two logical operators named *AndAlso* and *OrElse*. In a conditional statement that contains multiple conditions, such as an If...Then decision structure, it might not be necessary to always evaluate all the conditions. Passing over conditions is sometimes called *short-circuiting* and can be controlled by using the *AndAlso* and *OrElse* operators.

Event-Driven Programming

The programs you've written so far in this book have displayed Toolbox controls, menus, tool-bars, and dialog boxes on the screen, and with these programs, users could manipulate the screen elements in whatever order they saw fit. The programs put the user in charge, waited patiently for a response, and then processed the input predictably. In programming circles, this methodology is known as *event-driven programming*. You build a program by creating a group of "intelligent" objects that know how to respond when the user interacts with them, and then the program processes the input by using event procedures associated with the objects. The following diagram shows how an event-driven program works in Visual Basic:

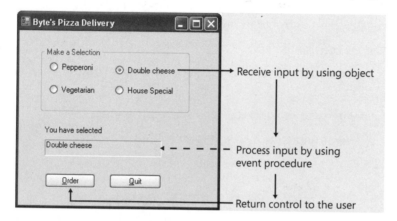

Program input can also come from the computer system itself. For example, your program might be notified when a piece of electronic mail arrives or when a specified period of time has elapsed on the system clock. The computer, not the user, triggers these events. Regardless of how an event is triggered, Visual Basic reacts by calling the event procedure associated with the object that recognized the event. So far, you've dealt primarily with the *Click*, *Checked-Changed*, and *SelectedIndexChanged* events. However, Visual Basic objects also can respond to several other types of events.

The event-driven nature of Visual Basic means that most of the computing done in your programs is accomplished by event procedures. These event-specific blocks of code process input, calculate new values, display output, and handle other tasks.

In this chapter, you'll learn how to use decision structures to compare variables, properties, and values, and how to execute one or more statements based on the results. In Chapter 7, "Using Loops and Timers," you'll use loops to execute a group of statements over and over until a condition is met or while a specific condition is true. Together, these powerful flow-control structures will help you build your event procedures so that they can respond to almost any situation.

Events Supported by Visual Basic Objects

Each object in Visual Basic has a predefined set of events to which it can respond. These events are listed when you select an object name in the Class Name list box at the top of the Code Editor and then click the Method Name arrow. (Events are visually identified in Visual Studio by a lightning bolt icon.) You can write an event procedure for any of these events, and if that event occurs in the program, Visual Basic will execute the event procedure that's associated with it. For example, a list box object supports more than 60 events, including *Click*, *DoubleClick*, *DragDrop*, *DragOver*, *GotFocus*, *KeyDown*, *KeyPress*, *KeyUp*, *LostFocus*, *MouseDown*, *MouseMove*, *MouseUp*, *MouseHover*, *TextChanged*, and *Validated*. You probably won't need to write code for more than three or four of these events in your applications, but it's nice to know that you have so many choices when you create elements in your interface. The following illustration shows a partial listing of the events for a list box object in the Code Editor:

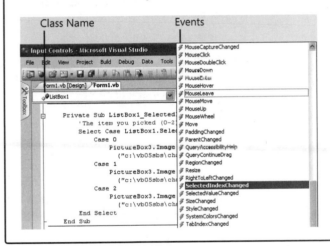

Using Conditional Expressions

One of the most useful tools for processing information in an event procedure is a conditional expression. A *conditional expression* is a part of a complete program statement that asks a True-or-False question about a property, a variable, or another piece of data in the program code. For example, the conditional expression

```
Price < 100
```

evaluates to True if the *Price* variable contains a value that is less than 100, and it evaluates to False if *Price* contains a value that is greater than or equal to 100.

You can use the following comparison operators in a conditional expression:

Comparison operator	Meaning
=	Equal to
< >	Not equal to
>	Greater than
<	Less than
>=	Greater than or equal to
<=	Less than or equal to

The following table shows some conditional expressions and their results. You'll work with conditional expressions in an exercise later in this chapter.

Conditional expression	Result
10 <> 20	True (10 is not equal to 20)
Score < 20	True if *Score* is less than 20; otherwise, False
Score = Label1.Text	True if the *Text* property of the *Label1* object contains the same value as the *Score* variable; otherwise, False
TextBox1.Text = "Bill"	True if the word "Bill" is in the first text box; otherwise, False

If...Then Decision Structures

When a conditional expression is used in a special block of statements called a *decision structure*, it controls whether other statements in your program are executed and in what order they're executed. You can use an If...Then decision structure to evaluate a condition in the program and take a course of action based on the result. In its simplest form, an If...Then decision structure is written on a single line:

```
If condition Then statement
```

where *condition* is a conditional expression, and *statement* is a valid Visual Basic program statement. For example,

```
If Score >= 20 Then Label1.Text = "You win!"
```

is an If...Then decision structure that uses the conditional expression

```
Score >= 20
```

to determine whether the program should set the *Text* property of the *Label1* object to "You win!" If the *Score* variable contains a value that's greater than or equal to 20, Visual Basic sets the *Text* property; otherwise, it skips the assignment statement and executes the next line in the event procedure. This sort of comparison always results in a True or False value. A conditional expression never results in maybe.

Testing Several Conditions in an If...Then Decision Structure

Visual Basic also supports an If...Then decision structure that you can use to include several conditional expressions. This block of statements can be several lines long and contains the important keywords *ElseIf*, *Else*, and *End If*.

```
If condition1 Then
    statements executed if condition1 is True
ElseIf condition2 Then
    statements executed if condition2 is True
[Additional ElseIf conditions and statements can be placed here]
Else
    statements executed if none of the conditions is True
End If
```

In this structure, *condition1* is evaluated first. If this conditional expression is True, the block of statements below it is executed, one statement at a time. (You can include one or more program statements.) If the first condition isn't True, the second conditional expression (*condition2*) is evaluated. If the second condition is True, the second block of statements is executed. (You can add additional *ElseIf* conditions and statements if you have more conditions to evaluate.) If none of the conditional expressions is True, the statements below the *Else* keyword are executed. Finally, the whole structure is closed by the *End If* keywords.

The following code shows how a multiple-line If...Then structure could be used to determine the amount of tax due in a hypothetical progressive tax return. (The income and percentage numbers are from the projected United States Internal Revenue Service 2005 Tax Rate Schedule for single filing status.)

```
Dim AdjustedIncome, TaxDue As Double
AdjustedIncome = 50000

If AdjustedIncome <= 7300 Then              '10% tax bracket
    TaxDue = AdjustedIncome * 0.1
ElseIf AdjustedIncome <= 29700 Then         '15% tax bracket
    TaxDue = 730 + ((AdjustedIncome - 7300) * 0.15)
ElseIf AdjustedIncome <= 71950 Then         '25% tax bracket
    TaxDue = 4090 + ((AdjustedIncome - 29700) * 0.25)
ElseIf AdjustedIncome <= 150150 Then        '28% tax bracket
    TaxDue = 14652.5 + ((AdjustedIncome - 71950) * 0.28)
ElseIf AdjustedIncome <= 326450 Then        '33% tax bracket
    TaxDue = 36548.5 + ((AdjustedIncome - 150150) * 0.33)
Else                                        '35% tax bracket
    TaxDue = 94727.5 + ((AdjustedIncome - 326450) * 0.35)
End If
```

Important   The order of the conditional expressions in your *If…Then* and *ElseIf* statements is critical. What happens if you reverse the order of the conditional expressions in the tax computation example and list the rates in the structure from highest to lowest? Taxpayers in the 10 percent, 15 percent, 25 percent, 28 percent, and 33 percent tax brackets are all placed in the 35 percent tax bracket because they all have an income that's less than or equal to 326,450. (Visual Basic stops at the first conditional expression that is True, even if others are also True.) Because all the conditional expressions in this example test the same variable, they need to be listed in ascending order to get the taxpayers to fall out in the right places. Moral: when you use more than one conditional expression, consider the order carefully.

This useful decision structure tests the double-precision variable *AdjustedIncome* at the first income level and subsequent income levels until one of the conditional expressions evaluates to True, and then determines the taxpayer's income tax accordingly. With some simple modifications, it could be used to compute the tax owed by any taxpayer in a progressive tax system, such as the one in the United States. Provided that the tax rates are complete and up to date and that the value in the *AdjustedIncome* variable is correct, the program as written will give the correct tax owed for single U.S. taxpayers for 2005. If the tax rates change, it's a simple matter to update the conditional expressions. With an additional decision structure to determine taxpayers' filing status, the program readily extends itself to include all U.S. taxpayers.

Tip   Expressions that can be evaluated as True or False are also known as *Boolean expressions*, and the True or False result can be assigned to a Boolean variable or property. You can assign Boolean values to certain object properties or Boolean variables that have been created by using the *Dim* statement and the *As Boolean* keywords.

In the next exercise, you'll use an If…Then decision structure that recognizes users as they enter a program—a simple way to get started with writing your own decision structures. You'll also learn how to use the *MaskedTextBox* control to receive input from the user in a specific format.

Validating users by using If…Then

1. Start Visual Studio, and create a new project named **My User Validation**.

   The new project is created, and a blank form appears in the Designer.

2. Click the form, and set the form's *Text* property to "User Validation".

3. Use the *Label* control to create a label on your form, and use the Properties window to set the *Text* property to "Enter your Social Security Number".

4. Use the *Button* control to create a button on your form, and set the button's *Text* property to "Sign In".

5. Click the *MaskedTextBox* control on the Common Controls tab in the Toolbox, and then create a masked text box object on your form below the label.

    The *MaskedTextBox* control is similar to the *TextBox* control that you have been using, but by using *MaskedTextBox*, you can control the format of the information entered by the user into your program. You control the format by setting the *Mask* property; you can use a predefined format supplied by the control or choose your own format. You'll use the *MaskedTextBox* control in this program to require that users enter a Social Security Number in the standard nine-digit format used by the United States Internal Revenue Service.

6. With the *MaskedTextBox1* object selected, click the *Mask* property in the Properties window, and then click the ellipses button next to it.

    The Input Mask dialog box appears, showing a list of your predefined formatting patterns, or *masks*.

7. Click Social Security Number in the list.

    The Input Mask dialog box looks like this:

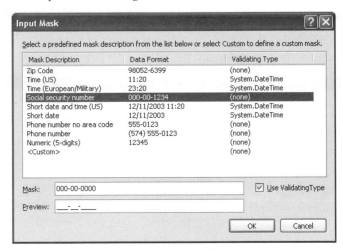

    Although you won't use it now, take a moment to note the Custom option, which you can use later to create your own input masks using numbers and placeholder characters such as a hyphen (-).

8. Click OK to accept Social Security Number as your input mask.

Visual Studio displays your input mask in the *MaskedTextBox1* object, as shown in the following illustration:

9. Double-click the Sign In button.

The *Button1_Click* event procedure appears in the Code Editor.

10. Type the following program statements in the event procedure:

```
If MaskedTextBox1.Text = "555-55-1212" Then
    MsgBox("Welcome to the system!")
Else
    MsgBox("I don't recognize this number")
End If
```

This simple If...Then decision structure checks the value of the *MaskedTextBox1* object's *Text* property, and if it equals "555-55-1212", the structure displays the message "Welcome to the system". If the number entered by the user is some other value, the structure displays the message "I don't recognize you". The beauty in this program, however, is how the *MaskedTextBox1* object automatically filters input to ensure that it is in the correct format.

11. Click the Save All button on the Standard toolbar to save your changes. Specify the c:\vb05sbs\chap06 folder as the location for your project.

12. Click the Start Debugging button on the Standard toolbar.

The program runs in the IDE. The form prompts the user to enter a Social Security number (SSN) in the appropriate format, and displays underlines and hypens to offer the user a hint of the format required.

13. Type **abcd** to test the input mask.

Visual Basic prevents the letters from being displayed, because letters do not fit the requested format. A nine-digit SSN is required.

14.   Type **1234567890** to test the input mask.

Visual Basic displays the number 123-45-6789 in the masked text box, ignoring the tenth digit that you typed. Again, Visual Basic has forced the user's input into the proper format. Your form looks like this:

15.   Click the Sign In button.

Visual Basic displays the message "I don't recognize the number", because the SSN does not match the number the If...Then decision structure is looking for.

16.   Click OK, delete the SSN from the masked text box, enter **555-55-1212** as the number, and then click Sign In again.

This time the decision structure recognizes the number and displays a welcome message. You see the following message box:

Your code has prevented an unauthorized user from using the program, and you've learned a useful skill related to controlling input from the user.

17.   Exit the program.

Using Logical Operators in Conditional Expressions

You can test more than one conditional expression in *If...Then* and *ElseIf* clauses if you want to include more than one selection criterion in your decision structure. The extra conditions are linked together by using one or more of the logical operators listed in the following table.

Logical operator	Meaning
And	If both conditional expressions are True, then the result is True.
Or	If either conditional expression is True, then the result is True.
Not	If the conditional expression is False, then the result is True. If the conditional expression is True, then the result is False.
Xor	If one and only one of the conditional expressions is True, then the result is True. If both are True or both are False, then the result is False. (*Xor* stands for exclusive *Or*.)

> **Tip** When your program evaluates a complex expression that mixes different operator types, it evaluates mathematical operators first, comparison operators second, and logical operators third.

The following table lists some examples of the logical operators at work. In the expressions, it is assumed that the *Vehicle* string variable contains the value "Bike", and the integer variable *Price* contains the value 200.

Logical expression	Result
`Vehicle = "Bike" And Price < 300`	True (both conditions are True)
`Vehicle = "Car" Or Price < 500`	True (one condition is True)
`Not Price < 100`	True (condition is False)
`Vehicle = "Bike" Xor Price < 300`	False (both conditions are True)

In the following exercise, you'll modify the My User Validation program to prompt the user for a personal identification number (PIN) during the validation process. To do this, you will add a second text box to get the PIN from the user, and then modify the *If...Then* clause in the decision structure so that it uses the *And* operator to verify the PIN.

Add password protection by using the *And* operator

1. Display the User Validation form, and use the *Label* control to add a second descriptive label to the form below the first masked text box.

2. Set the new label's *Text* property to "PIN".

3. Add a second *MaskedTextBox* control to the form below the first masked text box and the new label.

4. Click the shortcut arrow in the *MaskedTextBox2* object, and then click the Set Mask command to display the Input Mask dialog box.

5. Click the Numeric (5 digits) input mask, and then click OK.

   Like many PINs found online, this PIN will be five digits long. Again, if the user types a password of a different length or format, it will be rejected.

6. Double-click the Sign In button to display the *Button1_Click* event procedure in the Code Editor.

7. Modify the event procedure so that it contains the following code:

```
If MaskedTextBox1.Text = "555-55-1212" _
And MaskedTextBox2.Text = "54321" Then
    MsgBox("Welcome to the system!")
Else
    MsgBox("I don't recognize this number")
End If
```

   The statement now includes the *And* logical operator, which requires that the user's PIN correspond with his or her SSN before the user is admitted to the system. (In this case, the valid PIN is 54321; in a real-world program, this value would be extracted along with the SSN from a secure database.) I modified the earlier program by adding a line continuation character (_) to the end of the first line, and by adding the second line beginning with *And*.

8. Click the Start Debugging button on the Standard toolbar.

   The program runs in the IDE.

9. Type **555-55-1212** in the Social Security Number masked text box.

10. Type **54321** in the PIN masked text box.

11. Click the Sign In button.

    The user is welcomed to the program, as shown in the screen on the next page.

12.   Click OK to close the message box.

13.   Experiment with other values for the SSN and PIN.

      Test the program carefully to be sure that the welcome message is not displayed when other PINs or SSNs are entered.

14.   Click the Close button on the form when you're finished.

      The program ends, and the development environment returns.

> **Tip**   You can further customize this program by using the *PasswordChar* property in the masked text box objects, which displays a placeholder character such as an asterisk (*) when the user types. (You specify the character by using the Properties window.) Using a password character gives users additional secrecy as they enter their protected password—a standard feature of such operations.

Short-Circuiting by Using *AndAlso* and *OrElse*

Visual Basic offers two logical operators that you can use in your conditional statements, *AndAlso* and *OrElse*. These operators work the same as *And* and *Or* respectively, but offer an important subtlety in the way they're evaluated that will be new to programmers experienced with Visual Basic 6.

Consider an *If* statement that has two conditions that are connected by an *AndAlso* operator. For the statements of the If structure to be executed, both conditions must evaluate to True. If the first condition evaluates to False, Visual Basic skips to the next line or the *Else* statement immediately, without testing the second condition. This partial, or *short-circuiting*, evaluation of an *If* statement makes logical sense—why should Visual Basic continue to evaluate the *If* statement if both conditions cannot be True?

The *OrElse* operator works in a similar fashion. Consider an *If* statement that has two conditions that are connected by an *OrElse* operator. For the statements of the If structure to be executed, at least one condition must evaluate to True. If the first condition evaluates to True, Visual Basic begins to execute the statements in the If structure immediately, without testing the second condition.

Here's an example of the short-circuit situation in Visual Basic, a simple routine that uses an *If* statement and an *AndAlso* operator to test two conditions and display the message "Inside If" if both conditions are True:

```
Dim Number As Integer = 0
If Number = 1 AndAlso MsgBox("Second condition test") Then
    MsgBox("Inside If")
Else
    MsgBox("Inside Else")
End If
```

The *MsgBox* function itself is used as the second conditional test, which is somewhat unusual, but the strange syntax is completely valid and gives us a perfect opportunity to see how short-circuiting works up close. The text "Second condition test" appears in a message box only if the *Number* variable is set to 1; otherwise, the *AndAlso* operator short-circuits the *If* statement, and the second condition isn't evaluated. If you actually try this code, remember that it's for demonstration purposes only—you wouldn't want to use *MsgBox* with this syntax as a test because it doesn't really test anything. But by changing the *Number* variable from 0 to 1 and back, you can get a good idea of how the *AndAlso* statement and short-circuiting work.

Here's a second example of how short-circuiting functions in Visual Basic when two conditions are evaluated using the *AndAlso* operator. This time, a more complex conditional test (7 / HumanAge <= 1) is used after the *AndAlso* operator to determine what some people call the "dog age" of a person:

```
Dim HumanAge As Integer
HumanAge = 7
'One year for a dog is seven years for a human
If HumanAge <> 0 AndAlso 7 / HumanAge <= 1 Then
    MsgBox("You are at least one dog year old")
Else
    MsgBox("You are less than one dog year old")
End If
```

As part of a larger program that determines the so-called dog age of a person by dividing his or her current age by 7, this bare-bones routine tries to determine whether the value in the *HumanAge* integer variable is at least 7. (If you haven't heard the concept of "dog age" before, bear with me—following this logic, a 28-year-old person would be four dog years old. This has been suggested as an interesting way of relating to dogs, since dogs have a lifespan of roughly one-seventh that of humans.) The code uses two *If* statement conditions and can be used in a variety of different contexts—I used it in the *Click* event procedure for a button object. The first condition checks to see whether a non-zero number has been placed in the *HumanAge* variable—I've assumed momentarily that the user has enough sense to place a positive age into *HumanAge* because a negative number would produce incorrect results. The second condition tests whether the person is at least seven years old. If both conditions evaluate to True, the message "You are at least one dog year old" is displayed in a message box. If the person is less than seven, the message "You are less than one dog year old" is displayed.

Now imagine that I've changed the value of the *HumanAge* variable from 7 to 0. What happens? The first *If* statement condition is evaluated as False by the Visual Basic compiler, and that evaluation prevents the second condition from being evaluated, thus halting, or short-circuiting, the *If* statement and saving us from a nasty "divide by zero" error that could result if we divided 7 by 0 (the new value of the *HumanAge* variable). We wouldn't have had the same luck in Visual Basic 6. Setting the *HumanAge* variable to 0 in Visual Basic 6 would have produced a run-time error and a crash, because the entire *If* statement would have been evaluated, and division by zero isn't permitted in Visual Basic 6. In Visual Studio, we get a benefit from the short-circuiting behavior.

In summary, the *AndAlso* and *OrElse* operators in Visual Basic open up a few new possibilities for Visual Basic programmers, including the potential to prevent run-time errors and other unexpected results. It's also possible to improve performance by placing conditions that are time consuming to calculate at the end of the condition statement, because Visual Basic doesn't perform these expensive condition calculations unless it's necessary. However, you need to think carefully about all the possible conditions that your *If* statements might encounter as variable states change during program execution.

Select Case Decision Structures

With Visual Basic, you can also control the execution of statements in your programs by using Select Case decision structures. You used Select Case structures in Chapters 3 and 5 of this book when you wrote event procedures to process list box and combo box choices. A Select Case structure is similar to an If...Then...ElseIf structure, but it's more efficient when the branching depends on one key variable, or *test case*. You can also use Select Case structures to make your program code more readable.

The syntax for a Select Case structure looks like this:

```
Select Case variable
    Case value1
        statements executed if value1 matches variable
    Case value2
        statements executed if value2 matches variable
    Case value3
        statements executed if value3 matches variable
    ...
    Case Else
        statements executed if no match is found
End Select
```

A Select Case structure begins with the *Select Case* keywords and ends with the *End Select* keywords. You replace *variable* with the variable, property, or other expression that is to be the key value, or test case, for the structure. You replace *value1*, *value2*, and *value3* with numbers, strings, or other values related to the test case being considered. If one of the values matches the variable, the statements below the *Case* clause are executed, and then Visual Basic jumps to the line after the *End Select* statement and picks up execution there. You can include any number of *Case* clauses in a Select Case structure, and you can include more than one value in a *Case* clause. If you list multiple values after a case, separate them with commas.

The following example shows how a Select Case structure could be used to print an appropriate message about a person's age and cultural milestones in a program. Since the *Age* variable contains a value of 18, the string "You can vote now!" is assigned to the *Text* property of the label object. (You'll notice that the "milestones" have an American slant to them; please customize freely to match your cultural setting.)

```
Dim Age As Integer
Age = 18

Select Case Age
    Case 16
        Label1.Text = "You can drive now!"
    Case 18
        Label1.Text = "You can vote now!"
    Case 21
        Label1.Text = "You can drink wine with your meals."
    Case 65
        Label1.Text = "Time to retire and have fun!"
End Select
```

A Select Case structure also supports a *Case Else* clause that you can use to display a message if none of the preceding cases matches the *Age* variable. Here's how *Case Else* would work in the following example—note that I've changed the value of *Age* to 25 to trigger the *Case Else* clause:

```
Dim Age As Integer
Age = 25

Select Case Age
    Case 16
        Label1.Text = "You can drive now!"
    Case 18
        Label1.Text = "You can vote now!"
    Case 21
        Label1.Text = "You can drink wine with your meals."
    Case 65
        Label1.Text = "Time to retire and have fun!"
    Case Else
        Label1.Text = "You're a great age! Enjoy it!"
End Select
```

Using Comparison Operators with a Select Case Structure

You can use comparison operators to include a range of test values in a Select Case structure. The Visual Basic comparison operators that can be used are =, <>, >, <, >=, and <=. To use the comparison operators, you need to include the *Is* keyword or the *To* keyword in the expression to identify the comparison you're making. The *Is* keyword instructs the compiler to compare the test variable to the expression listed after the *Is* keyword. The *To* keyword identifies a range of values. The following structure uses *Is*, *To*, and several comparison operators to test the *Age* variable and to display one of five messages:

```
Select Case Age
    Case Is < 13
        Label1.Text = "Enjoy your youth!"
    Case 13 To 19
        Label1.Text = "Enjoy your teens!"
    Case 21
        Label1.Text = "You can drink wine with your meals."
    Case Is > 100
        Label1.Text = "Looking good!"
    Case Else
        Label1.Text = "That's a nice age to be."
End Select
```

If the value of the *Age* variable is less than 13, the message "Enjoy your youth!" is displayed. For the ages 13 through 19, the message "Enjoy your teens!" is displayed, and so on.

A Select Case decision structure is usually much clearer than an If...Then structure and is more efficient when you're making three or more branching decisions based on one variable or property. However, when you're making two or fewer comparisons, or when you're working with several different values, you'll probably want to use an If...Then decision structure.

In the following exercise, you'll see how you can use a Select Case structure to process input from a list box. You'll use the *ListBox1.Text* and *ListBox1.SelectedIndexChanged* properties to collect the input, and then you'll use a Select Case structure to display a greeting in one of four languages.

Use a Select Case structure to process input from a list box

1. On the File menu, click New Project.

    The New Project dialog box appears.

2. Create a new project named **My Select Case**.

    A blank form appears in the Designer.

3. Click the *Label* control in the Toolbox, and then draw a label near the top of the form to display a title for the program.

4. Use the *Label* control to create a second label object below the first.

    You'll use this label as a title for the list box.

5. Click the *ListBox* control in the Toolbox, and then create a list box below the second label.

6. Use the *Label* control to draw two more labels below the list box to display program output.

7. Use the *Button* control to create a small button on the bottom of the form.

8. Open the Properties window, and then set the properties shown in the following table for the objects that you have just created.

Since there are so many objects, you'll also assign *Name* properties to help you easily identify the control on the form and within your program code. (You'll find *Name* listed in parentheses near the top of the Properties window, which allows it to be listed first in the alphabetical list.) I recommend that you use the *Name* property whenever you have more than four or five objects in a program. In this example, I've given the objects names that feature a three-character prefix to identify the object type, such as btn (for button), lbl (for label), and lst (for list box).

Object	Property	Setting
Form1	*Text*	"Case Greeting"
Label1	*Font*	Times New Roman, Bold, 12-point
	Name	lblTitle
	Text	"International Welcome Program"
Label2	*Name*	lblTextBoxLabel
	Text	"Choose a country"
Label3	*Font*	10-point
	Name	lblCountry
	Text	(empty)
Label4	*AutoSize*	False
	BorderStyle	Fixed3D
	ForeColor	Red
	Name	lblGreeting
	Text	(empty)
ListBox1	*Name*	lstCountryBox
Button1	*Name*	btnQuit
	Text	"Quit"

When you've finished setting properties, your form looks similar to this:

Now you'll enter the program code to initialize the list box.

9. Double-click the form.

   The *Form1_Load* event procedure appears in the Code Editor.

10. Type the following program code to initialize the list box:

```
lstCountryBox.Items.Add("England")
lstCountryBox.Items.Add("Germany")
lstCountryBox.Items.Add("Mexico")
lstCountryBox.Items.Add("Italy")
```

   These lines use the *Add* method of the list box object to add entries to the list box on your form.

11. Click the Form1.vb [Design] tab at the top of the Code Editor to switch back to the Designer, and then double-click the list box object on your form to edit its event procedure.

   The *lstCountryBox_SelectedIndexChanged* event procedure appears in the Code Editor.

12. Type the following lines to process the list box selection made by the user:

```
lblCountry.Text = lstCountryBox.Text
Select Case lstCountryBox.SelectedIndex
    Case 0
        lblGreeting.Text = "Hello, programmer"
    Case 1
        lblGreeting.Text = "Hallo, programmierer"
    Case 2
        lblGreeting.Text = "Hola, programador"
    Case 3
        lblGreeting.Text = "Ciao, programmatore"
End Select
```

The first line copies the name of the selected list box item to the *Text* property of the third label on the form (which you renamed *lblCountry*). The most important property used in the statement is *lstCountryBox.Text*, which contains the exact text of the item selected in the list box. The remaining statements are part of the Select Case decision structure. The structure uses the *lstCountryBox.SelectedIndex* property as a test case variable and compares it to several values. The *SelectedIndex* property always contains the number of the item selected in the list box; the item at the top is 0 (zero), the second item is 1, the next item is 2, and so on. By using *SelectedIndex*, the Select Case structure can quickly identify the user's choice and display the correct greeting on the form.

13.   Display the form again, and double-click the Quit button (*btnQuit*).

      The *btnQuit_Click* event procedure appears in the Code Editor.

14.   Type **End** in the event procedure.

15.   Click the Save All button on the Standard toolbar to save your changes. Specify the c:\vb05sbs\chap06 folder as the location.

      Now run the program, and see how the *Select Case* statement works.

> **Tip**   The complete Select Case project is located in the c:\vb05sbs\chap06\select case folder.

16.   Click the Start Debugging button on the Standard toolbar to run the program.

17.   Click each of the country names in the Choose A Country list box.

      The program displays a greeting for each of the countries listed. The following illustration shows the greeting for Italy:

18.   Click the Quit button to stop the program.

      The program stops, and the development environment returns.

You've finished working with If...Then and Select Case decision structures in this chapter. You'll have several additional opportunities to work with them in this book, however. If...Then and Select Case are two of the crucial decision-making mechanisms in the Visual Basic programming language, and you'll find that you use them in almost every program that you write.

One Step Further: Detecting Mouse Events

I began this chapter by discussing a few of the events that Visual Basic programs can respond to, and as the chapter progressed, you learned how to manage different types of events by using the If...Then and Select Case decision structures. In this section, you'll add an event handler to the Select Case program that detects when the pointer "hovers" over the Country list box for a moment or two. You'll write the special routine, or *event handler*, by building a list box event procedure for the *MouseHover* event, one of several mouse-related activities that Visual Basic can monitor and process. This event procedure will display the message "Please click the country name" if the user holds the mouse over the country list box for a moment or two but doesn't make a selection, perhaps because he or she doesn't know how to make a selection or has become engrossed in another task.

Add a mouse event handler

1. Open the Code Editor if it isn't already open.

2. At the top of the Code Editor, click the Class Name arrow, and then click the *lstCountry-Box* object.

   You can use the ScreenTip feature to help identify elements like the Class Name list box in Visual Studio, which is another example of the *MouseHover* event within the IDE.

3. Click the Method Name arrow, and then click the *MouseHover* event.

   Visual Basic opens the *lstCountryBox_MouseHover* event procedure in the Code Editor, as shown here:

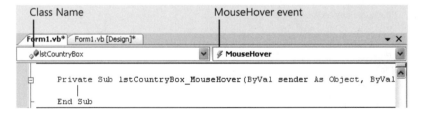

Each object on the form has one event procedure that opens automatically when you double-click the object on the form. You need to open the remaining event procedures by using the Method Name list box.

4. Type the following program statements in the *lstCountryBox_MouseHover* event procedure:

```
If lstCountryBox.SelectedIndex < 0 Or _
  lstCountryBox.SelectedIndex > 4 Then
    lblGreeting.Text = "Please click the country name"
End If
```

This *If* statement evaluates the *SelectedIndex* property of the list box object by using two conditional statements and the *Or* operator. The event handler assumes that if there's a value between 1 and 4 in the *SelectedIndex* property, the user doesn't need help picking the country name (he or she has already selected a country). But if the *SelectedIndex* property is outside that range, the event handler displays the message "Please click the country name" in the greeting label at the bottom of the form. This message appears when the user holds the pointer over the list box and disappears when a country name is selected.

5. Click the Start Debugging button to run the program.

6. Hold the pointer over the country list box, and wait a few moments.

    The message "Please click the country name" appears in red text in the label, as shown here:

7. Click a country name in the list box.

    The translated greeting appears in the label, and the help message disappears.

8. Click the Quit button to stop the program.

You've learned how to process mouse events in a program, and you've also learned that writing event handlers is quite simple. Try writing additional event handlers on your own as you continue reading this book—it will help you learn more about the events available to Visual Studio objects, and it will give you more practice with If...Then and Select Case decision structures.

Chapter 6 Quick Reference

To	Do this
Write a conditional expression	Use one of the following comparison operators between two values: =, < >, >, <, > =, or < =.

Use an If…Then decision structure	Use the following syntax:
	
	```If condition1 Then```
	``` statements executed if condition1 True```
	```ElseIf condition2 Then```
	``` statements executed if condition2 True```
	```Else```
	``` statements executed if none are True```
	```End If```

Receive input from the user in a specific format	Add a *MaskedTextBox* control to your form, and specify the input format by configuring the *Mask* property.

Use a Select Case decision structure	Use the following syntax:
	
	```Select Case variable```
	```Case value1```
	``` statements executed if value1 matches```
	```Case value2```
	``` statements executed if value2 matches```
	```Case Else```
	``` statements executed if none match```
	```End Select```

Rename an object in a program	Select the object that you want to rename, and then modify the object's *Name* property by using the Properties window. If you give the object a three-character prefix that identifies its object type (btn, lbl, lst, etc.), the object is easier to spot in program code.
Make two comparisons in a conditional expression	Use a logical operator between comparisons (*And*, *Or*, *Not*, or *Xor*).
Short-circuit an *If…Then* statement	*If…Then* statements can be short-circuited when the *AndAlso* and *OrElse* operators are used and two or more conditional expressions are given. Depending on the result of the first condition, Visual Basic might not evaluate the additional conditions, and the statement is short-circuited.
Write an event handler	In the Code Editor, click an object name in the Class Name list box, and then click an event name in the Method Name list box. Add program statements to the event procedure (called an *event handler*) that respond to the event you are customizing.

Chapter 7

Using Loops and Timers

After completing this chapter, you will be able to:

- Use a For...Next loop to execute statements a set number of times.

- Display output in a multiline text box by using string concatenation.

- Use a Do loop to execute statements until a specific condition is met.

- Use the *Timer* control to execute code at specific times.

- Create your own digital clock and timed password utility.

- Use the new Insert Snippet command to insert ready-made code templates or snippets into the Code Editor.

In Chapter 6, "Using Decision Structures," you learned how to use the If...Then and Select Case decision structures to choose which statements to execute in a program. You also learned how to process user input and evaluate different conditions in a program, and how to determine which block of program statements to execute based on changing conditions. Now you'll continue learning about program execution and *flow control* by using *loops* to execute a block of statements over and over again. You'll also create a digital clock and other interesting utilities that perform actions at set times or in relation to intervals on your computer's system clock.

In this chapter, you'll use a For...Next loop to execute statements a set number of times, and you'll use a Do loop to execute statements until a conditional expression is met. You'll also learn how to display more than one line of text in a text box object by using the string concatenation (&) operator, and you'll learn how to use the Visual Studio *Timer* control to execute code at specific intervals in your program. Finally, you'll learn how to use the Insert Snippet command to insert code templates into your programs—a handy new feature of the Microsoft Visual Studio 2005 IDE.

Upgrade Notes: Migrating Visual Basic 6 Code to Visual Basic 2005

If you're experienced with Microsoft Visual Basic 6, you'll notice some new features in Visual Basic 2005, including the following:

■ In Visual Basic 6, you can display text directly on your form by using the *Print* method, a holdover from the *Print* statement in GW-BASIC and Microsoft Quick-Basic. In Visual Basic 2005, the *Print* method can be used only to send data to a file on disk. This chapter shows you an alternative method for displaying large amounts of text on a form—appending text in a multiline text box object by using the string concatenation operator (*&*).

■ In Visual Basic 6, a While loop is specified with the *While...Wend* syntax. In Visual Basic 2005, the closing statement is *While...End While* to parallel other similar structures.

■ The *Timer* control in Visual Studio 2005 is similar but not identical to the *Timer* control in Visual Basic 6. For example, the *Timer1_Timer* event procedure (which is executed at each pre-set timer interval) is called *Timer1_Tick* in Visual Studio 2005. In addition, you can no longer disable a timer by setting the *Interval* property to 0.

Writing For...Next Loops

With a For...Next loop, you can execute a specific group of program statements a set number of times in an event procedure or a code module. This approach can be useful if you're performing several related calculations, working with elements on the screen, or processing several pieces of user input. A For...Next loop is really just a shorthand way of writing out a long list of program statements. Because each group of statements in such a list does essentially the same thing, you can define just one group of statements and request that it be executed as many times as you want.

The syntax for a For...Next loop looks like this:

```
For variable = start To end
    statements to be repeated
Next [variable]
```

In this syntax statement, *For*, *To*, and *Next* are required keywords, as is the equal to operator (=). You replace *variable* with the name of a numeric variable that keeps track of the current loop count (the variable after *Next* is optional), and you replace *start* and *end* with numeric values representing the starting and stopping points for the loop. (Note that you must declare *variable* before it's used in the *For...Next* statement.) The line or lines between the *For* and *Next* statements are the instructions that are repeated each time the loop is executed.

For example, the following For...Next loop sounds four beeps in rapid succession from the computer's speaker (although the result might be difficult to hear):

```
Dim i As Integer
For i = 1 To 4
    Beep()
Next i
```

This loop is the functional equivalent of writing the *Beep* statement four times in a procedure. The compiler treats it the same as

```
Beep()
Beep()
Beep()
Beep()
```

The variable used in the loop is *i*, a single letter that, by convention, stands for the first integer counter in a For...Next loop and is declared as an *Integer* type. Each time the loop is executed, the counter variable is incremented by one. (The first time through the loop, the variable contains a value of 1, the value of *start*; the last time through, it contains a value of 4, the value of *end*.) As you'll see in the following examples, you can use this counter variable to great advantage in your loops.

Displaying a Counter Variable in a *TextBox* Control

A counter variable is just like any other variable in an event procedure. It can be assigned to properties, used in calculations, or displayed in a program. One of the practical uses for a counter variable is to display output in a *TextBox* control. You used the *TextBox* control earlier in this book to display a single line of output, but in this chapter, you'll display many lines of text by using a *TextBox* control. The trick to displaying more than one line is simply to set the *Multiline* property of the *TextBox* control to True and to set the *ScrollBars* property to Vertical. Using these simple settings, the one-line text box object becomes a multiline text box object with scroll bars for easy access.

Display information by using a For...Next loop

1. Start Visual Studio, and create a new Visual Basic Windows Application project named **My For Loop**.

   A blank form appears in the Designer. Your first programming step is to add a *Button* control to the form, but this time you'll do it in a new way.

2. Double-click the *Button* control in the Toolbox.

   Visual Studio places a button object in the upper-left corner of the form. With the *Button* control and many others, double-clicking is a quick way to create a standard-sized object on the form. Now you can drag the button object where you want it and customize it with property settings.

3. Drag the button object to the right, and center it near the top of the form.

4. Open the Properties window, and then set the *Text* property of the button to "Loop".

5. Double-click the *TextBox* control in the Toolbox.

   Visual Studio creates a small text box object on the form.

6. Set the *Multiline* property of the text box object to True, and then set the *ScrollBars* property of the text box object to Vertical.

   These settings prepare the text box for displaying more than one line of text.

7. Move the text box below the button, and enlarge it so that it takes up two-thirds of the form.

8. Double-click the *Loop* button on the form.

   The *Button1_Click* event procedure appears in the Code Editor.

9. Type the following program statements in the procedure:

```
Dim i As Integer
Dim Wrap As String
Wrap = Chr(13) & Chr(10)
For i = 1 To 10
    TextBox1.Text = TextBox1.Text & "Line " & i & Wrap
Next i
```

This event procedure declares two variables, one of type *Integer* (*i*) and one of type *String* (*Wrap*). It then assigns a string value representing the carriage return character to the second variable.

> **Tip**   In programmer terms, a carriage return character is the equivalent of pressing the Enter key on the keyboard. I created a special variable for this character in the program code, which is made up of return and linefeed elements, to make coding a carriage return less cumbersome. The return element, Chr(13) moves the I-beam to the beginning of the line. The linefeed element, Chr(10), reminiscent of an older style typewriter, moves the I-beam to the next line.

After the variable declaration and assignment, I use a For...Next loop to display Line *X* 10 times in the text box object, where *X* is the current value of the counter variable (in other words, Line 1 through Line 10). The string concatenation characters (*&*) join together the component parts of each line in the text box. First, the entire value of the text box, which is stored in the *Text* property, is added to the object so that previous lines aren't discarded when new ones are added. Next, the "Line" string, the current line number, and the carriage return character (*Wrap*) are combined to display a new line and move the I-beam to the left margin and down one line. The *Next* statement completes the loop.

Note that Visual Studio automatically adds the *Next* statement to the bottom of the loop when you type *For* to begin the loop. In this case, I edited the *Next* statement to include the *i* variable name—this is an optional syntax clarification that I like to use. (The variable name makes it clear which variable is being updated, especially in nested For...Next loops.)

10. Click the Save All button on the Standard toolbar to save your changes, and specify the c:\vb05sbs\chap07 folder as the location.

Now you're ready to run the program.

> **Tip** The complete For Loop program is available in the c:\vb05sbs\chap07\for loop folder.

11. Click the Start Debugging button on the Standard toolbar.

12. Click the Loop button.

The For...Next loop displays 10 lines in the text box, as shown here:

13. Click the Loop button again.

The For...Next loop displays another 10 lines on the form. (You can see any nonvisible lines by using the vertical scroll bar to scroll down.) Each time the loop is repeated, it adds 10 more lines to the text box object.

> **Tip** Worried about running out of room in the text box object? It will take a while if you're displaying only simple text lines. A multiline text box object has a practical limit of 32 KB of text! If you want even more space and formatting options, you can use the *RichTextBox* control in the Toolbox—a similar but even more capable control for displaying and manipulating text.

14.   Click the Close button on the form to stop the program.

As you can see, a For...Next loop can considerably simplify your code and reduce the total number of statements that you need to type. In the previous example, a loop three lines long processed the equivalent of 10 program statements each time you clicked the Loop button.

Creating Complex For...Next Loops

The counter variable in a For...Next loop can be a powerful tool in your programs. With a little imagination, you can use it to create several useful sequences of numbers in your loops. To create a loop with a counter pattern other than 1, 2, 3, 4, and so on, you can specify a different value for *start* in the loop and then use the *Step* keyword to increment the counter at different intervals. For example, the code

```
Dim i As Integer
Dim Wrap As String
Wrap = Chr(13) & Chr(10)

For i = 5 To 25 Step 5
    TextBox1.Text = TextBox1.Text & "Line " & i & Wrap
Next i
```

displays the following sequence of line numbers in a text box:

```
Line 5
Line 10
Line 15
Line 20
Line 25
```

You can also specify decimal values in a loop if you declare *i* as a single-precision or double-precision type. For example, the For...Next loop

```
Dim i As Single
Dim Wrap As String
Wrap = Chr(13) & Chr(10)

For i = 1 To 2.5 Step 0.5
    TextBox1.Text = TextBox1.Text & "Line " & i & Wrap
Next i
```

displays the following line numbers in a text box:

```
Line 1
Line 1.5
Line 2
Line 2.5
```

In addition to displaying the counter variable, you can use the counter to set properties, calculate values, or process files. The following exercise shows how you can use the counter to open Visual Basic icons that are stored on your hard disk in files that have numbers in their names. You'll find many icons, bitmaps, and animation files in the c:\program files\microsoft visual studio 8\common7\vs2005imagelibrary folder.

Open files by using a For...Next loop

1. On the File menu, click the New Project command.

   The New Project dialog box appears.

2. Create a new project named **My For Loop Icons**.

   Your new project starts, and a blank form appears in the Designer.

3. Click the *PictureBox* control in the Toolbox, and then draw a medium-sized picture box object centered on the top half of the form.

4. Click the *Button* control, and then draw a very wide button below the picture box. (You'll put a longer than usual label on the button.)

5. Set the following properties for the two objects:

Object	Property	Setting
PictureBox1	*BorderStyle*	Fixed3D
	SizeMode	StretchImage
Button1	*Text*	"Display four faces"

6. Double-click the Display Four Faces button on the form to display the event procedure for the button object.

   The *Button1_Click* event procedure appears in the Code Editor.

7. Type the following For...Next loop:

```
Dim i As Integer
For i = 1 To 4
    PictureBox1.Image = System.Drawing.Image.FromFile _
        ("c:\vb05sbs\chap07\face0" & i & ".ico")
    MsgBox("Click here for next face.")
Next
```

> **Tip** The *FromFile* method in this event procedure is too long to fit on one line in this book, so I broke it into two lines by using a space and the line continuation character (_). You can use this character anywhere in your program code except within a string expression.

The loop uses the *FromFile* method to load four icon files from the c:\vb05sbs\chap07 folder on your hard disk. The filename is created by using the counter variable and the concatenation operator you used earlier in this chapter. The code

```
PictureBox1.Image = System.Drawing.Image.FromFile _
  ("c:\vb05sbs\chap07\face0" & i & ".ico")
```

combines a path, a file name, and the .ico extension to create four valid filenames of icons on your hard disk. In this example, you're loading face01.ico, face02.ico, face03.ico, and face04.ico into the picture box. This statement works because several files in the c:\vb05sbs\chap07 folder have the file name pattern facexx.ico. By recognizing the pattern, you can build a For...Next loop around the file names.

> **Note**   The message box function (*MsgBox*) is used primarily to slow the action down so that you can see what's happening in the For...Next loop. In a normal application, you probably wouldn't use such a function (but you're welcome to).

8. Click the Save All button on the Standard toolbar to save your changes. Specify the c:\vb05sbs\chap07 folder as the location.

9. Click the Start Debugging button to run the program, and then click the Display Four Faces button.

The For...Next loop loads the first face into the picture box, and then displays this message box:

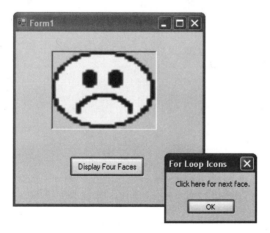

> **Note** If Visual Basic displays an error message, ensure that your program code has no typos, and then verify that the icon files are in the path you specified in the program. If you installed the *Step by Step* practice files in a folder other than the default folder, or if you moved your icon files after installation, the path in the event procedure might not be correct.

10. Click OK to display the next face.

Your screen looks something like this:

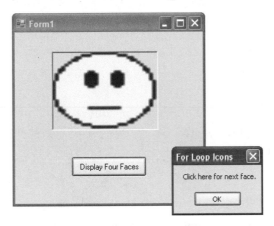

11. Click OK three more times to see the entire face collection.

You can repeat the sequence if you want.

12. When you're finished, click the Close button on the form.

The program stops, and the development environment returns.

Opening Files by Using a Counter That Has Greater Scope

Are there times when using a For...Next loop isn't that efficient or elegant? Sure. In fact, the preceding example, although useful as a demonstration, was a little hampered by the intrusive behavior of the message box, which opened four times in the For...Next loop and distracted the user from the form, where we want his or her attention to be. Is there a way we can do away with that intrusive message box?

One solution is to remove both the *MsgBox* function and the For...Next loop, and substitute in their place a counter variable that has greater scope throughout the form. As you learned in Chapter 5, "Visual Basic Variables and Formulas, and the .NET Framework," you can declare a variable that has scope (or maintains its value) throughout the entire form by placing a *Dim* statement for the variable at the top of the form in the Code Editor—a special location above the event procedures. In the following exercise, you'll use an *Integer* variable named *Counter* that maintains its value between calls to the *Button1_Click* event procedure, and you'll use that variable to open the same icon files without using the *MsgBox* function to pause the action.

Use a global counter

1. Open the Code Editor for the My For Loop Icons project.

2. Move the insertion point above the *Button1_Click* event procedure, and directly below the Public Class Form1 statement, declare an *Integer* variable named *Counter* by using this syntax:

```
Dim Counter As Integer = 1
```

Notice that Visual Studio separates the declaration that you've just entered from the event procedure with a solid line and displays the word "Declarations" in the Method Name list box. You've also done something unusual here—in addition to declaring the *Counter* variable, you've also assigned the variable a value of 1. This is a recent syntax option in Visual Studio (it arrived with Microsoft Visual Studio .NET 2002), and now and then you'll find it very handy to use. (Declaring and assigning at the same time isn't permitted in Visual Basic 6.)

3. Within the *Button1_Click* event procedure, change the code so that it precisely matches the following group of program statements. (Delete any statements that aren't here.)

```
PictureBox1.Image = System.Drawing.Image.FromFile _
   ("c:\vb05sbs\chap07\face0" & Counter & ".ico")
Counter += 1
If Counter = 5 Then Counter = 1
```

As you can see, I've deleted the declaration for the *i* integer, the *For* and *Next* statements, and the *MsgBox* function, and I've changed the way the *FromFile* method works. (I've replaced the *i* variable with the *Counter* variable.) I've also added two new statements that use the *Counter* variable. The first statement adds 1 to *Counter* (`Counter += 1`), and the second statement resets the *Counter* variable if the value has been incremented to 5. (Resetting the variable in this way allows the list of icon files to cycle indefinitely.) The `Counter += 1` syntax is a shortcut feature in Visual Basic 2005—the functional equivalent of the statement

```
Counter = Counter + 1
```

Now you'll run the program.

> **Tip**   The modified For Loop Icons program is available in the c:\vb05sbs\chap07\for loop icons folder.

4. Click the Start Debugging button on the Standard toolbar to run the program.

   The program runs in the development environment.

5. Click the Display Four Faces button several times. (Notice how the mood of the faces develops from glum to cheery.)

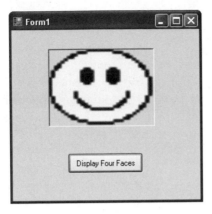

6. When you're finished, click the Close button on the form to stop the program.

As you can see, this solution is a little more elegant than the previous example because the user can click just one button, not a form button *and* a message box button. The shortcoming of the interface in the first program wasn't the fault of the For...Next loop, however, but rather the limitation I imposed that the *Button1_Click* event procedure use only local variables (in other words, variables that were declared within the event procedure itself). Between button clicks, these local variables lost their value, and the only way I could increment the counter was to build a loop. By using an *Integer* variable with a greater scope, I can preserve the value of the *Counter* variable between clicks and use that numeric information to display files within the *Button1_Click* event procedure.

The *Exit For* Statement

Most For...Next loops run to completion without incident, but now and then you'll find it useful to end the computation of a For...Next loop if a particular "exit condition" occurs. Visual Basic allows for this possibility by providing the *Exit For* statement, which you can use to terminate the execution of a For...Next loop early and move execution to the first statement after the loop.

For example, the following For...Next loop prompts the user for 10 names and displays them one by one in a text box unless the user enters the word "Done":

```
Dim i As Integer
Dim InpName As String
For i = 1 To 10
    InpName = InputBox("Enter your name or type Done to quit.")
    If InpName = "Done" Then Exit For
    TextBox1.Text = InpName
Next i
```

If the user does enter "Done", the *Exit For* statement terminates the loop, and execution picks up with the statement after *Next*.

Writing Do Loops

As an alternative to a For...Next loop, you can write a Do loop that executes a group of statements until a certain condition is True. Do loops are valuable because often you can't know in advance how many times a loop should repeat. For example, you might want to let the user enter names in a database until the user types the word "Done" in an input box. In that case, you can use a Do loop to cycle indefinitely until the "Done" text string is entered.

A Do loop has several formats, depending on where and how the loop condition is evaluated. The most common syntax is

```
Do While condition
    block of statements to be executed
Loop
```

For example, the following Do loop prompts the user for input and displays that input in a text box until the word "Done" is typed in the input box:

```
Dim InpName As String
Do While InpName <> "Done"
    InpName = InputBox("Enter your name or type Done to quit.")
    If InpName <> "Done" Then TextBox1.Text = InpName
Loop
```

The conditional statement in this loop is `InpName <> "Done"`, which the Visual Basic compiler translates to mean "loop as long as the *InpName* variable doesn't contain exactly the word 'Done'." This brings up an interesting fact about Do loops: if the condition at the top of the loop isn't True when the *Do* statement is first evaluated, the Do loop is never executed. Here, if the *InpName* string variable did contain the "Done" value before the loop started (perhaps from an earlier assignment in the event procedure), Visual Basic would skip the loop altogether and continue with the line below the *Loop* keyword.

If you always want the loop to run at least once in a program, put the conditional test at the bottom of the loop. For example, the loop

```
Dim InpName As String
Do
    InpName = InputBox("Enter your name or type Done to quit.")
    If InpName <> "Done" Then TextBox1.Text = InpName
Loop While InpName <> "Done"
```

is essentially the same as the previous Do loop, but here the loop condition is tested after a name is received from the *InputBox* function. This has the advantage of updating the *InpName* variable before the conditional test in the loop so that a preexisting "Done" value won't cause the loop to be skipped. Testing the loop condition at the bottom ensures that your loop is executed at least once, but often it forces you to add a few extra statements to process the data.

> **Note** The previous code samples asked the user to type "Done" to quit. Note that the test of the entered text is case sensitive, which means that typing "done" or "DONE" doesn't end the program. You can make the test case-insensitive by using the *StrComp* function, which I'll discuss in Chapter 13, "Exploring Text Files and String Processing."

Avoiding an Endless Loop

Because of the relentless nature of Do loops, it's very important to design your test conditions so that each loop has a true exit point. If a loop test never evaluates to False, the loop executes endlessly, and your program might not respond to input. Consider the following example:

```
Dim Number as Double
Do
    Number = InputBox("Enter a number to square. Type -1 to quit.")
    Number = Number * Number
    TextBox1.Text = Number
Loop While Number >= 0
```

In this loop, the user enters number after number, and the program squares each number and displays it in the text box. Unfortunately, when the user has had enough, he or she can't quit because the advertised exit condition doesn't work. When the user enters -1, the program squares it, and the *Number* variable is assigned the value 1. (The problem can be fixed by setting a different exit condition.) Watching for endless loops is essential when you're writing Do loops. Fortunately, they're pretty easy to spot if you test your programs thoroughly.

> **Important** Be sure that each loop has a legitimate exit condition.

The following exercise shows how you can use a Do loop to convert Fahrenheit temperatures to Celsius temperatures. The simple program prompts the user for input by using the *InputBox* function, converts the temperature, and displays the output in a message box.

Convert temperatures by using a Do loop

1. On the File menu, click New Project.

    The New Project dialog box appears.

2. Create a new Visual Basic Windows Application project named **My Celsius Conversion**.

    The new project is created, and a blank form appears in the Designer. This time, you'll place all the code for your program in the *Form1_Load* event procedure so that Visual Basic immediately prompts you for the Fahrenheit temperature when you start the application. You'll use an *InputBox* function to request the Fahrenheit data, and you'll use a *MsgBox* function to display the converted value.

3. Double-click the form.

The *Form1_Load* event procedure appears in the Code Editor.

4. Type the following program statements in the *Form1_Load* event procedure:

```
Dim FTemp, Celsius As Single
Dim strFTemp As String
Dim Prompt As String = "Enter a Fahrenheit temperature."
Do
    strFTemp = InputBox(Prompt, "Fahrenheit to Celsius")
    If strFTemp <> "" Then
        FTemp = CSng(strFTemp)
        Celsius = Int((FTemp + 40) * 5 / 9 - 40)
        MsgBox(Celsius, , "Temperature in Celsius")
    End If
Loop While strFTemp <> ""
End
```

> **Tip**   Be sure to include the *End* statement at the bottom of the *Form1_Load* event procedure.

This code handles the calculations for the project. The first line declares two single-precision variables, *FTemp* and *Celsius*, to hold the Fahrenheit and Celsius temperatures, respectively. The second line declares a string variable named *strFTemp* that holds a string version of the Fahrenheit temperature. The third line declares a string variable named *Prompt*, which will be used in the *InputBox* function, and assigns it an initial value. The Do loop repeatedly prompts the user for a Fahrenheit temperature, converts the number to Celsius, and then displays it on the screen by using the *MsgBox* function.

The value that the user enters in the input box is stored in the *strFTemp* variable. The *InputBox* function always returns a value of type string, even if the user enters numbers. Because we want to perform mathematical calculations on the entered value, *strFTemp* must be converted to a number. The *CSng* function is used to convert a string into the *Single* data type. *CSng* is one of many conversion functions to convert a string to a different data type. The converted single value is then stored in the *FTemp* variable.

The loop executes until the user clicks the Cancel button or until the user presses Enter or clicks OK with no value in the input box. Clicking the Cancel button or entering no value returns an empty string (""). The loop checks for the empty string by using a *While* conditional test at the bottom of the loop. The program statement

```
Celsius = Int((FTemp + 40) * 5 / 9 - 40)
```

handles the conversion from Fahrenheit to Celsius in the program. This statement employs a standard conversion formula, but it uses the *Int* function to return a value that contains no decimal places to the Celsius variable. (Everything to the right of the decimal point is discarded.) This cutting sacrifices accuracy, but it helps you avoid long, unsightly numbers such as 21.11111, the Celsius value for 70 degrees Fahrenheit.

5. Click the Save All button on the Standard toolbar to save your changes. Specify the c:\vb05sbs\chap07 folder as the location.

Now you'll try running the program.

> **Tip** The complete Celsius Conversion program is available in the c:\vb05sbs\chap07\celsius conversion folder.

6. Click the Start Debugging button on the Standard toolbar.

The program starts, and the *InputBox* function prompts you for a Fahrenheit temperature.

7. Type **212**.

Your screen looks like this:

8. Click OK.

The temperature 212 degrees Fahrenheit is converted to 100 degrees Celsius, as shown in this message box:

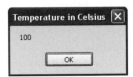

9. Click OK. Then type **72** in the input box, and click OK again.

The temperature 72 degrees Fahrenheit is converted to 22 degrees Celsius.

10. Click OK, and then click Cancel in the input box.

The program closes, and the development environment returns.

Using the *Until* Keyword in Do Loops

The Do loops you've worked with so far have used the *While* keyword to execute a group of statements as long as the loop condition remains True. With Visual Basic, you can also use the *Until* keyword in Do loops to cycle *until* a certain condition is True. You can use the *Until* keyword at the top or bottom of a Do loop to test a condition, just like the *While* keyword. For example, the following Do loop uses the *Until* keyword to loop repeatedly until the user enters the word "Done" in the input box:

```
Dim InpName As String
Do
    InpName = InputBox("Enter your name or type Done to quit.")
    If InpName <> "Done" Then TextBox1.Text = InpName
Loop Until InpName = "Done"
```

As you can see, a loop that uses the *Until* keyword is similar to a loop that uses the *While* keyword, except that the test condition usually contains the opposite operator—the = (equal to) operator versus the <> (not equal to) operator, in this case. If using the *Until* keyword makes sense to you, feel free to use it with test conditions in your Do loops.

The *Timer* Control

As we wrap up our consideration of flow control tools and techniques in this chapter, you should also consider the benefits of using the Visual Studio *Timer* control, which you can use to execute a group of statements for a specific period of *time* or at specific *intervals*. The *Timer* control is essentially an invisible stopwatch that gives you access to the system clock in your programs. The *Timer* control can be used like an egg timer to count down from a preset time, to cause a delay in a program, or to repeat an action at prescribed intervals.

Although timer objects aren't visible at run time, each timer is associated with an event procedure that runs every time the timer's preset interval has elapsed. You set a timer's interval by using the *Interval* property, and you activate a timer by setting the timer's *Enabled* property to True. Once a timer is enabled, it runs constantly—executing its event procedure at the prescribed interval—until the user stops the program or the timer object is disabled.

Creating a Digital Clock by Using a *Timer* Control

One of the most straightforward uses for a *Timer* control is creating a custom digital clock. In the following exercise, you'll create a simple digital clock that keeps track of the current time down to the second. In the example, you'll set the *Interval* property for the timer to 1000, directing Visual Studio to update the clock time every 1000 milliseconds, or once a second. Because the Microsoft Windows operating system is a multitasking environment and other programs also require processing time, Visual Studio might not update the clock every second, but it always catches up if it falls behind. To keep track of the time at other intervals, such as once every tenth of a second, you simply adjust the number in the *Interval* property.

Create the Digital Clock program

1. On the File menu, click the New Project command, and create a new project named **My Digital Clock**.

   The new project is created and a blank form appears in the Designer.

2. Resize the form to a small rectangular window (one that's wider than it is tall).

   You don't want the clock to take up much room.

3. Double-click the *Timer* control on the Components tab of the Toolbox.

   This is the first time that you have used the Components tab and the *Timer* control in this book. (The Components tab provides a number of interesting controls that work "behind the scenes" in your programs.) Visual Studio creates a small timer object in the component tray beneath your form, as shown here:

   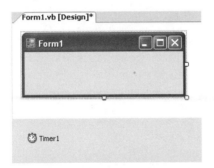

   Recall from Chapter 4, "Working with Menus, Toolbars, and Dialog Boxes," that certain Visual Studio controls don't have a visual representation on the form, and when objects for these controls are created, they appear in the component tray beneath the form. (This was the case for the *MenuStrip* and *ToolStrip* controls that you used in Chapter 4.) However, you can still select controls in this special pane and set properties for them, as you'll do for the timer object in this exercise.

4. Click the *Label* control in the Toolbox, and then draw a very large label object on the form—a label that's almost the size of the entire form itself.

   You'll use the label to display the time in the clock, and you want to create a very big label to hold the 24-point type you'll be using.

> **Note**   When you first create the label object, it resizes automatically to hold the text "Label1" in the default size. But when you set the *AutoSize* property to False in the next step, the label object is restored to the size you originally created.

5. Open the Properties window, and set the following properties for the form and the two objects in your program:

Object	Property	Setting
Label1	AutoSize	False
	Font	Times New Roman, Bold, 24-point
	Text	(empty)
	TextAlign	MiddleCenter
Timer1	Enabled	True
	Interval	1000
Form1	Text	"Digital Clock"

> **Tip**   If you'd like to put some artwork in the background of your clock, set the *BackgroundImage* property of the *Form1* object to the path of a graphics file.

Now you'll write the program code for the timer.

6. Double-click the timer object in the component tray.

The *Timer1_Tick* event procedure appears in the Code Editor. Experienced Visual Basic 6 programmers will notice that this event procedure has been renamed from *Timer1_Timer* to *Timer1_Tick*, clarifying what this event procedure does in the program (that is, the event procedure runs each time that the timer clock ticks).

7. Type the following statement:

```
Label1.Text = TimeString
```

This statement gets the current time from the system clock and assigns it to the *Text* property of the *Label1* object. (If you'd like to have the date displayed in the clock as well as the time, use the *System.DateTime.Now* property instead of the *TimeString* property.) Only one statement is required in this program because you set the *Interval* property for the timer by using the Properties window. The timer object handles the rest.

8. Click the Save All button on the Standard toolbar to save your changes. Specify c:\vb05sbs\chap07 as the folder location.

> **Tip**   The complete Digital Clock program is available in the c:\vb05sbs\chap07\digital clock folder.

9. Click the Start Debugging button on the Standard toolbar to run the clock.

The clock appears, as shown in the following illustration. (Your time will be different, of course.)

If you used the *System.DateTime.Now* property, you'll see the date in the clock also, as shown here:

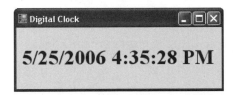

I needed to enlarge the label object and the form a little here to get the data and time to appear on one line. If your system clock information also wrapped, close the program, and resize your label and form.

10.   Watch the clock for a few moments.

Visual Basic updates the time every second.

11.   Click the Close button in the title bar to stop the clock.

The Digital Clock program is so handy that you might want to compile it into an executable file and use it now and then on your computer. Feel free to customize it by using your own artwork, text, and colors.

Using a Timer Object to Set a Time Limit

Another interesting use of a timer object is to set it to wait for a given period of time before either permitting or prohibiting an action. You can also use this timer technique to display a welcome message or a copyright message on the screen or to repeat an event at a set interval, such as saving a file every 10 minutes. Again, this is a little like setting an egg timer in your program. You set the *Interval* property with the delay you want, and then you start the clock ticking by setting the *Enabled* property to True.

The following exercise shows how you can use this approach to set a time limit for entering a password. (The password for this program is "secret.") The program uses a timer to close its own program if a valid password isn't entered in 15 seconds. (Normally, a program like this would be part of a larger application.)

Set a password time limit

1. On the File menu, click the New Project command, and create a new project named **My Timed Password**.

    The new project is created, and a blank form appears in the Designer.

2. Resize the form to a small rectangular window about the size of an input box.

3. Click the *TextBox* control in the Toolbox, and then draw a text box for the password in the middle of the form.

4. Click the *Label* control in the Toolbox, and then draw a long label above the text box.

5. Click the *Button* control in the Toolbox, and then draw a button below the text box.

6. Double-click the *Timer* control on the Components tab of the Toolbox.

    Visual Studio adds a timer object to the component tray below the form.

7. Set the properties in the following table for the program:

Object	Property	Setting
Label1	Text	"Enter your password within 15 seconds"
TextBox1	PasswordChar	"*"
Button1	Text	"Try Password"
Timer1	Enabled	True
	Interval	15000
Form1	Text	"Password"

The *PasswordChar* setting displays asterisk (*) characters in the text box as the user enters a password. Setting the timer *Interval* property to 15000 gives the user 15 seconds to enter a password and click the Try Password button. Setting the *Enabled* property to True starts the timer running when the program starts. (If the timer wasn't needed until later in the program, you could disable this property and then enable it in an event procedure.)

Your form looks like this:

8. Double-click the timer object in the component tray, and then type the following statements in the *Timer1_Tick* event procedure:

```
MsgBox("Sorry, your time is up.")
End
```

The first statement displays a message indicating that the time has expired, and the second statement stops the program. Visual Basic executes this event procedure if the timer interval reaches 15 seconds and a valid password hasn't been entered.

9. Display the form, double-click the button object, and then type the following statements in the *Button1_Click* event procedure:

```
If TextBox1.Text = "secret" Then
    Timer1.Enabled = False
    MsgBox("Welcome to the system!")
    End
Else
    MsgBox("Sorry, friend, I don't know you.")
End If
```

This program code tests whether the password entered in the text box is "secret." If it is, the timer is disabled, a welcome message is displayed, and the program ends. (A more useful program would continue working rather than ending here.) If the password entered isn't a match, the user is notified with a message box and is given another chance to enter the password. But the user has only 15 seconds to do so!

10. Click the Save All button on the Standard toolbar to save your changes. Specify the c:\vb05sbs\chap07 folder as the location.

Test the Timed Password program

> **Tip**   The complete Timed Password program is available in the c:\vb05sbs\chap07\timed password folder.

1. Click the Start Debugging button to run the program.

    The program starts, and the 15-second clock starts ticking.

2. Type **open** in the text box.

    The asterisk characters hide your input, as shown here:

3. Click the Try Password button.

The following message box appears on the screen, noting your incorrect response:

4. Click OK, and then wait patiently until the sign-on period expires.

    The program displays the time-up message shown in this message box:

5. Click OK to end the program.

6. Run the program again, type **secret** (the correct password) in the text box, and then click Try Password.

    The program displays this message:

7. Click OK to end the program.

    The Visual Basic development environment appears.

As you can imagine, there are many practical uses for timer objects. As with For...Next loops and Do loops, you can use timer objects to repeat commands and procedures as many times as you need in a program. Combined with what you learned about the If...Then and Select Case decision structures in Chapter 6, you now have several statements, controls, and techniques that can help you organize your programs and make them respond to user input and data processing tasks in innovative ways. Learning to pick the best tool for the flow-control situation at hand takes some practice, of course, but you'll have ample opportunity to try these tools and techniques as you continue working in the following chapters, and as you construct interesting applications on your own. In fact, you might take the opportunity right now to create a simple project or two from scratch before you tackle the next chapter, which discusses debugging. How about creating a digital clock that displays a different piece of art in a picture box object every 30 seconds?

One Step Further: Inserting Code Snippets

If you enjoyed using the system clock and other Windows resources in this chapter, you might enjoy one additional example that uses the *Computer.Info* namespace to display useful information about the operating system you're currently using. This example also demonstrates an interesting new feature of Visual Studio 2005 called the Insert Snippet command, which lets you insert ready-made code templates or *snippets* into the Code Editor from a list of common programming tasks. Visual Studio 2005 comes automatically configured with a library of useful code snippets, and you can add additional snippets from your own programs or from online resources such as MSDN. The following exercise shows you how to use this useful feature.

Insert the Current Windows Version Snippet

1. On the File menu, click the New Project command, and create a new project named **My Windows Version Snippet**.

   The new project is created, and a blank form appears in the Designer.

2. Create a new button object in the middle of the form, and set the *Text* property of the button to "Display Windows Version".

3. Double-click the button object to display the *Button1_Click* event procedure.

   Now you'll use the Insert Snippet command to insert a code template that automatically returns information about the version of Windows installed on your computer. Note that this particular snippet is just one example from a list of dozens of useful code templates.

4. Click the Edit menu, point to the IntelliSense submenu, and then click the Insert Snippet command.

   The Insert Snippet list box appears in the Code Editor, as shown in the following illustration:

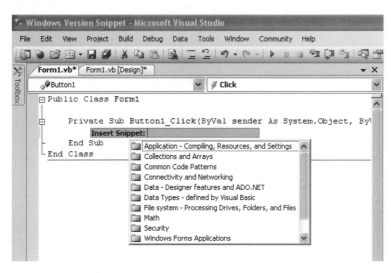

The Insert Snippet list box is a navigation tool that you can use to explore the snippet library and insert snippets into your program at the insertion point. To open a folder in the list box, double click the folder name. To return to the previous folder in the folder hierarchy, press the Backspace key.

5. Scroll to the bottom of the list box, and then double click the Windows Operating System folder.

   In this folder you'll find snippets related to querying and setting operating system settings.

6. Double click the System Information folder.

   A list of system information snippets appears. Now you'll select the snippet that returns information about the current version of Windows.

7. Double click the snippet entitled "Determine the Current Windows Version."

   Visual Studio inserts the following two lines of code into the *Button1_Click* event procedure at the insertion point:

```
Dim osVersion As String
osVersion = My.Computer.Info.OSVersion
```

These statements declare the string variable *osVersion* to hold version information about the operating system, and then use the *Computer.Info* namespace to fill the variable with current information. The snippet also uses the *My* object to gather information about your computer. The *My* object is a new "speed-dial" feature of Visual Studio 2005 designed to reduce the time it takes to code common tasks, and I will introduce it more fully in Chapter 13, "Exploring Text Files and String Processing."

This code snippet is called a template because it supplies the majority of the code that you need to insert for a particular task, but the code is not fully integrated into your project yet. In this case, we should add a second variable to hold the name of the operating system (because there are different Windows versions), and we'll add a *MsgBox* function to display the results for the user. (In other cases, you might need to add controls to your form, create new variables or data structures, or write additional program statements that use the snippet.)

8. Press the Enter key twice to add a blank line below the snippet.

9. Type the following program statements:

```
Dim osName As String
osName = My.Computer.Info.OSFullName
MsgBox(osName & vbCr & osVersion)
```

These statements declare a second variable named *osName* that will hold the Windows version retrieved by the *OSFullName* method of the *Computer.Info* namespace. There is also a *MsgBox* function that displays the two returned values: the operating system name (*osName*) and the operating system version number (*osVersion*). As you probably know, the operating system version number has now become quite detailed in Microsoft Windows, because Windows has the ability to be updated automatically over the Web each time a new security update or improvement is released. Examining the version number is therefore a handy way to see whether your system is up-to-date and safe. Your screen looks like this:

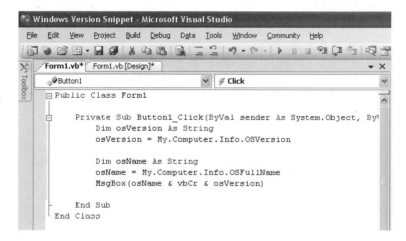

10. Click Save All to save your changes, and specify the c:\vb05sbs\chap07 folder as the location.

11. Click Start Debugging to run the program.

    Visual Studio runs the program in the IDE.

12. Click the Display Windows Version button to display the version information returned by the snippet.

    Your dialog box looks similar to the following:

13. Click OK to close the dialog box, and then click the Close button to end the program.

You've learned a handy skill that will allow you to insert a variety of useful code templates into your own programs.

> **Tip** To insert new snippets or reorganize the snippets you have, click the Code Snippets Manager command on the Tools menu. The Code Snippets Manager dialog box gives you complete control over the contents of the Insert Snippet list box, and also contains a mechanism for gathering new snippets online.

Chapter 7 Quick Reference

To	Do this
Execute a group of program statements a specific number of times	Insert the statements between *For* and *Next* statements in a loop. For example: ```\nDim i As Integer\nFor i = 1 To 10\n MsgBox("Press OK already!")\nNext i\n```
Use a specific sequence of numbers with statements	Insert the statements in a For...Next loop, and use the *To* and *Step* keywords to define the sequence of numbers. For example: ```\nDim i As Integer\nFor i = 2 To 8 Step 2\n TextBox1.Text = TextBox1.Text & i\nNext i\n```
Avoid an endless Do loop	Be sure the loop has a test condition that can evaluate to False.
Exit a For...Next loop prematurely	Use the *Exit For* statement. For example: ```\nDim InpName As String\nDim i As Integer\nFor i = 1 To 10\n InpName = InputBox("Name?")\n If InpName = "Trotsky" Then Exit For\n TextBox1.Text = InpName\nNext i\n```
Execute a group of program statements until a specific condition is met	Insert the statements between *Do* and *Loop* statements. For example: ```\nDim Query As String = ""\nDo While Query <> "Yes"\n Query = InputBox("Trotsky?")\n If Query = "Yes" Then MsgBox("Hi")\nLoop\n```
Loop until a specific condition is True	Use a Do loop with the *Until* keyword. For example: ```\nDim GiveIn As String\nDo\n GiveIn = InputBox("Say 'Uncle'")\nLoop Until GiveIn = "Uncle"\n```
Loop for a specific period of time in your program	Use the *Timer* control.
Insert a code snippet into your program	In the Code Editor, position the insertion point (I-beam) at the location where you want to insert the snippet. On the Edit menu, click IntelliSense, and then click Insert Snippet. Browse to the snippet that you want to use, and then double click the snippet name.
Add or reorganize snippets in the Insert Snippet list box	Click the Code Snippet Manager command on the Tools menu.

Chapter 8
Debugging Visual Basic Programs

After completing this chapter, you will be able to:

- Identify different types of errors in your programs.

- Use Microsoft Visual Studio debugging tools to set breakpoints and correct mistakes.

- Use the Autos and Watch windows to examine variables during program execution.

- Use a visualizer to examine string data types and complex data types within the IDE.

- Use the Immediate and Command windows to change the value of variables and execute commands in Visual Studio.

In the past few chapters, you've had plenty of opportunity to make programming mistakes in your code. Unlike human conversation, which usually works well despite occasional grammatical mistakes and mispronunciations, communication between a software developer and the Microsoft Visual Basic compiler is successful only when the precise rules and regulations of the Visual Basic programming language are followed.

In this chapter, you'll learn more about the software defects, or *bugs*, that stop Visual Basic programs from running. You'll learn about the different types of errors that turn up in programs and how to use the Visual Studio debugging tools to detect and correct these defects. What you learn will be useful as you experiment with the programs in this book and when you write longer programs in the future.

Why focus on debugging now? Some programming books skip this topic altogether or place it near the end of the book (*after* you've learned all the language features of a particular product). There is a certain logic to postponing the discussion, but I think it makes the most sense to master debugging techniques *while* you learn to program so that detecting and correcting errors becomes part of your standard approach to writing programs and solving problems. At this point in *Microsoft Visual Basic 2005 Step by Step*, you know just enough about objects, decision structures, and statement syntax to create interesting programs but also enough to get yourself into a little bit of trouble! As you'll soon see, however, Microsoft Visual Studio 2005 makes it easy to uncover your mistakes and get back on the straight and narrow.

> **Upgrade Notes: Migrating Visual Basic 6 Code to Visual Basic 2005**
>
> If you're experienced with Microsoft Visual Basic 6, you'll notice some new features in Microsoft Visual Basic 2005, including the following:
>
> ■ Visual Studio includes several new tools for finding and correcting errors. A few of the familiar Visual Basic 6 debugging commands are still a part of Visual Studio (Break All, Step Into, Step Over), but there are also new debugging tools and commands, including revised Standard and Debug toolbars and a menu command that manages exceptions.
>
> ■ Several new debugging windows have been added to the Visual Studio IDE, including Autos, Command, Call Stack, Threads, Memory, Script Explorer, Disassembly, and Registers. You won't use these tools for every debugging session, but you might find them useful in more sophisticated applications.
>
> ■ In Visual Studio 2005, you can use a new visualizer feature (a magnifying glass icon) to examine the content of complex variables and objects within the IDE, so you can now view HTML, XML, and sophisticated datasets during a debugging session.

Finding and Correcting Errors

The defects you've encountered in your programs so far have probably been simple typing mistakes or syntax errors. But what if you discover a nastier problem in your program—one you can't find and correct by a simple review of the objects, properties, and statements you've used? The Visual Studio IDE contains several tools that help you track down and fix errors in your programs. These tools won't stop you from making mistakes, but they often ease the pain when you encounter one.

Three Types of Errors

Three types of errors can occur in a Visual Basic program: syntax errors, run-time errors, and logic errors.

■ A *syntax error* (or *compiler error*) is a programming mistake (such as a misspelled property or keyword) that violates the rules of Visual Basic. Visual Basic points out several types of syntax errors in your programs while you type program statements and won't let you run a program until you fix each syntax error.

■ A *run-time error* is a mistake that causes a program to stop unexpectedly during execution. Run-time errors occur when an outside event or an undiscovered syntax error forces a program to stop while it's running. For instance, if you misspell a file name when you use the *System.Drawing.Image.FromFile* method, or if you try to read the floppy drive and it doesn't contain a disk, your code will generate a run-time error.

■ A *logic error* is a human error—a programming mistake that makes the program code produce the wrong results. Most debugging efforts are focused on tracking down logic errors introduced by the programmer.

If you encounter a syntax error, you often can solve the problem by using Visual Basic online Help to learn more about the error message, and you can fix the mistake by paying close attention to the exact syntax of the functions, objects, methods, and properties that you have used. In the Code Editor, incorrect statements are underlined with a blue, jagged line, and you can learn more about the error by holding the mouse pointer over the statement. The following illustration shows the error message that appears in Visual Studio when I type the keyword *Case* incorrectly as "Csae" and then hold the mouse pointer over the error. This error message appears as a ScreenTip.

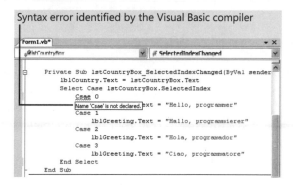

If you encounter a run-time error, you often can address the problem by correcting your typing. For example, if a bitmap loads incorrectly into a picture box object, the problem might simply be a misspelled path. However, many run-time errors require a more thorough solution. You can add a *structured error handler*—a special block of program code that recognizes a run-time error when it happens, suppresses any error messages, and adjusts program conditions to handle the problem—to your programs. I discuss the new syntax for structured error handlers in Chapter 9, "Trapping Errors by Using Structured Error Handling."

Identifying Logic Errors

Logic errors in your programs are often the most difficult to fix. They're the result of faulty reasoning and planning, not a misunderstanding about Visual Basic syntax. Consider the If...Then decision structure on the next page, which evaluates two conditional expressions and then displays one of two messages based on the result.

```
If Age > 13 And Age < 20 Then
    TextBox2.Text = "You're a teenager"
Else
    TextBox2.Text = "You're not a teenager"
End If
```

Can you spot the problem with this decision structure? A teenager is a person who is between 13 and 19 years old, inclusive, but the structure fails to identify the person who's exactly 13. (For this age, the structure erroneously displays the message "You're not a teenager.") This type of mistake isn't a syntax error (because the statements follow the rules of Visual Basic); it's a mental mistake, or logic error. The correct decision structure contains a greater than or equal to operator (>=) in the first comparison after the *If...Then* statement, as shown here:

```
If Age >= 13 And Age < 20 Then
```

Believe it or not, this type of mistake is the most common problem in a Visual Basic program. Code that produces the expected results most of the time—but not all of the time—is the hardest to test and to fix.

Debugging 101: Using Debugging Mode

One way to identify a logic error is to execute your program code one line at a time and examine the content of one or more variables or properties as they change. To do this, you can enter *debugging mode* (or break mode) while your program is running and then view your code in the Code Editor. Debugging mode gives you a close-up look at your program while the Visual Basic compiler is executing it. It's kind of like pulling up a chair behind the pilot and copilot and watching them fly the airplane. But in this case, you can touch the controls.

While you're debugging your application, you'll use buttons on the Standard toolbar and the Debug toolbar, as well as commands on the Debug menu and special buttons and windows in the IDE. The following illustration shows the debugging buttons on the Standard and Debug toolbars, which you can open by pointing to the Toolbars command on the View menu and then clicking Standard or Debug.

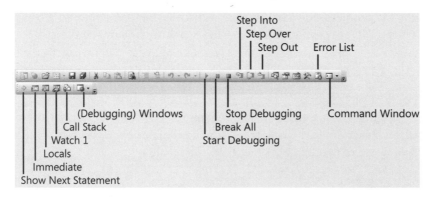

In the following exercise, you'll set a breakpoint—a place in a program where execution stops. You'll then use debugging mode to find and correct the logic error you discovered earlier in the If...Then structure. (The error is part of an actual program.) To isolate the problem, you'll use the Step Into button on the Standard toolbar to execute program instructions one at a time, and you'll use the Autos window to examine the value of key program variables and properties. Pay close attention to this debugging strategy. You can use it to correct many types of glitches in your own programs.

Debug the Debug Test program

1. Start Visual Studio.

2. On the File menu, click Open Project.

    The Open Project dialog box appears.

3. Open the Debug Test project in the c:\vb05sbs\chap08\debug test folder.

    The project opens in the development environment.

4. If the form isn't visible, display it now.

    The Debug Test program prompts the user for his or her age. When the user clicks the Test button, the program informs the user whether he or she is a teenager. The program still has the problem with 13-year-olds that we identified earlier in the chapter, however. You'll open the Debug toolbar now, and set a breakpoint to find the problem.

5. If the Debug toolbar isn't visible, click the View menu, point to the Toolbars, and then click Debug.

    The Debug toolbar appears below the Standard toolbar.

6. Click the Start Debugging button on the Standard toolbar.

    The program runs and displays the Debug Test form.

7. Remove the 0 from the Age text box, type **14**, and then click the Test button.

    The program displays the message "You're a teenager." So far, the program displays the correct result.

8. Type **13** in the Age text box, and then click the Test button.

    The program displays the message "You're not a teenager," as shown on the next page.

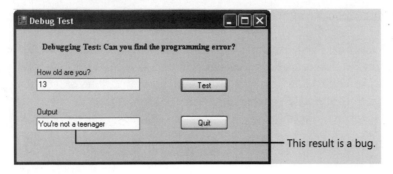

This result is a bug.

This answer is incorrect, and you need to look at the program code to fix the problem.

9.   Click the Quit button on the form, and then open the Code Editor.

10.   Move the mouse pointer to the Margin Indicator bar (the gray bar just beyond the left margin of the Code Editor window), next to the statement `Age = TextBox1.Text` in the *Button1_Click* event procedure, and then click the bar to set a breakpoint.

The breakpoint immediately appears in red. See the following illustration for the breakpoint's location and shape:

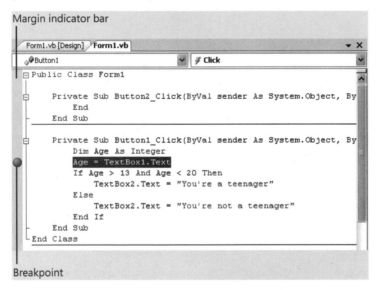

Margin indicator bar

Breakpoint

11.   Click the Start Debugging button to run the program again.

The form appears just like before, and you can continue your tests.

12.   Type **13** in the Age text box, and then click Test.

Visual Basic opens the Code Editor again and displays the *Button1_Click* event procedure—the program code currently being executed by the compiler. The statement that you selected as a breakpoint is highlighted in yellow, and an arrow appears in the Margin Indicator bar, as shown in the following illustration:

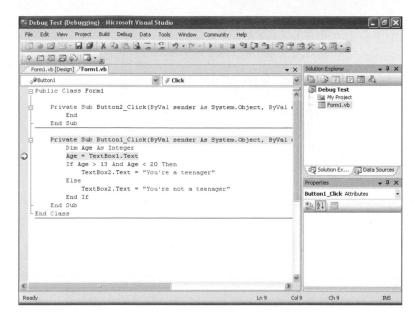

You can tell that Visual Studio is now in debugging mode because the word "Debugging" appears in its title bar. In debugging mode you have an opportunity to see how the logic in your program is evaluated.

> **Note**   You can also enter debugging mode in a Visual Basic program by placing the *Stop* statement in your program code where you'd like to pause execution. This is an older, but still reliable, method for entering debugging mode in a Visual Basic program.

13.   Place the pointer over the *Age* variable in the Code Editor.

Visual Studio displays the message "Age = 0." While you're in debugging mode, you can display the value of variables or properties by simply holding the mouse pointer over the value in the program code. *Age* currently holds a value of 0 because it hasn't yet been filled by the *TextBox1* text box—that statement is the next statement the compiler will evaluate.

14.   Click the Step Into button on the Debug toolbar to execute the next program statement.

The Step Into button executes the next program statement in the event procedure (the line that's currently highlighted). By clicking the Step Into button, you can see how the program state changes when just one more program statement is evaluated. If you hold the pointer over the *Age* variable now, you'll see that it contains a value of 13.

15.   On the Debug menu, point to Windows, and then click Autos.

The Windows submenu provides access to the entire set of debugging windows in Visual Studio. The Autos window shows the state of variables and properties currently being used. As you can see in the following illustration, the *Age* variable holds a value of 13, the *TextBox1.Text* property holds a string of "13", and the *TextBox2.Text* property currently holds an empty string ("").

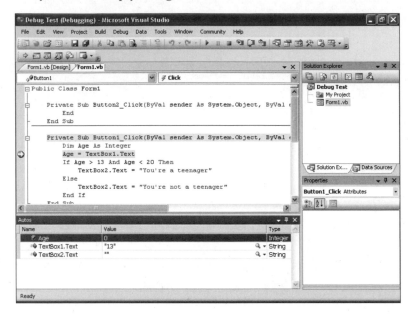

16. Click the Step Into button twice more.

The *If* statement evaluates the conditional expression to False, and the compiler moves to the *Else* statement in the decision structure. Here's our bug—the decision structure logic is incorrect because a 13-year-old *is* a teenager.

17. Select the conditional test `Age > 13`, and then hold the pointer over the selected text.

Visual Studio evaluates the condition and displays the message "Age > 13 = False."

18. Select the conditional test `Age < 20`, and then hold the pointer over the selected text.

Visual Studio displays the message "Age < 20 = True." The pointer has given us an additional clue—only the first conditional test is producing an incorrect result! Because a 13-year-old is a teenager, Visual Basic should evaluate the test to True, but the `Age > 13` condition returns a False value. And this forces the *Else* clause in the decision structure to be executed. Do you recognize the problem? The first comparison needs the >= operator to specifically test for this boundary case of 13. You'll stop debugging now so that you can fix this logic error.

19. Click the Stop Debugging button on the Standard toolbar.

20. In the Code Editor, add the = operator to the first condition in the *If* statement so that it reads

```
If Age >= 13 And Age < 20 Then
```

21. Run the program again and test your solution, paying particular attention to the numbers 12, 13, 19, and 20–the boundary, or "fringe," cases that are likely to cause problems.

Use the Step In button to watch the program flow around the crucial *If* statement, and use the Autos window to track the value of your variables as you complete the tests. When the form appears, enter a new value and try the test again. In addition, you might find that selecting certain expressions, such as the conditional tests, and holding the pointer over them gives you a better understanding of how they're being evaluated.

22. When you're finished experimenting with debugging mode, click the Stop Debugging button on the Standard toolbar to end the program.

Congratulations! You've successfully used debugging mode to find and correct a logic error in a program.

Tracking Variables by Using a Watch Window

The Autos window is useful for examining the state of certain variables and properties as they're evaluated by the compiler, but items in the Autos window *persist*, or maintain their values, only for the current statement (the statement highlighted in the debugger) and the previous statement (the statement just executed). When your program goes on to execute code that doesn't use the variables, they disappear from the Autos window.

To view the contents of variables and properties *throughout* the execution of a program, you need to use a Watch window, a special Visual Studio tool that tracks important values for you as long as you're working in debugging mode. In Visual Basic 6, you can open one Watch window to examine variables as they change. In Visual Studio, you can open up to four Watch windows, numbered Watch 1, Watch 2, Watch 3, and Watch 4. You can open these windows, by pointing to the Windows command on the Debug menu, pointing to Watch, and then clicking the window you want on the Watch submenu. You can also add expressions, such as `Age >= 13`, to a Watch window.

Open a Watch window

> **Tip**   The Debug Test project is located in the c:\vb05sbs\chap08\debug test folder.

1. Click the Start Debugging button on the Standard toolbar to run the Debug Test program again.

I'm assuming that the breakpoint you set on the line `Age = TextBox1.Text` in the previous exercise is still present. If that breakpoint isn't set, stop the program now, and set the breakpoint by clicking in the Margin Indicator bar next to the statement, as shown in step 10 of the previous exercise, and then start the program again.

2.   Type **20** in the Age text box, and then click Test.

The program stops at the breakpoint, and Visual Studio enters debugging mode, which is where you need to be if you want to add variables, properties, or expressions to a Watch window. One way to add an item is to select its value in the Code Editor, right click the selection, and then click the Add Watch command.

3.   Select the *Age* variable, right click it, and then click the Add Watch command.

Visual Studio opens the Watch 1 window and adds the *Age* variable to it. The value for the variable is currently 0, and the Type column in the window identifies the *Age* variable as an *Integer* type.

Another way to add an item is to drag the item from the Code Editor into the Watch window.

4.   Select the *TextBox2.Text* property, and drag it to the empty row in the Watch 1 window.

When you release the mouse button, Visual Studio adds the property and displays its value. (Right now, the property is an empty string.)

5.   Select the expression `Age < 20`, and add it to the Watch window.

`Age < 20` is a conditional expression, and you can use the Watch window to display its logical, or Boolean, value, much as you did by holding the pointer over a condition earlier in this chapter. Your Watch window looks like this:

Now step through the program code to see how the values in the Watch 1 window change.

6.   Click the Step Into button on the Debug toolbar.

> **Tip**   Instead of clicking the Step Into button on the Debug toolbar, you can press the F11 key on the keyboard.

The *Age* variable is set to 20, and the `Age < 20` condition evaluates to False. These values are displayed in red type in the Watch window because they've just been updated.

7.   Click the Step Into button three more times.

The *Else* clause is executed in the decision structure, and the value of the *TextBox2.Text* property in the Watch window changes to "You're not a teenager." This conditional test is operating correctly. Because you're satisfied with this condition, you can remove the test from the Watch window.

8. Click the Age < 20 row in the Watch window, and then press Delete.

   Visual Studio removes the value from the Watch window. As you can see, adding and removing values from the Watch window is a speedy process.

Leave Visual Studio running in debugging mode for now. You'll continue using the Watch window in the next section.

Visualizers: New Debugging Tools That Display Data

Although you can use the Watch, Autos, and Locals windows to examine simple data types such as Integer and String in the IDE, you'll eventually be faced with more complex data in your programs. For example, you might be examining a variable or property containing structured information from a database (a dataset) or a string containing HTML or XML formatting information from a Web page. So that you can examine this type of item more closely in a debugging session, Visual Studio 2005 has added a new set of tools to the IDE called visualizers (small magnifying glasses).

The Visual Studio 2005 IDE offers four standard visualizers: the text, HTML, and XML visualizers (which work on string objects), and the dataset visualizer (which works for *DataSet*, *DataView*, and *DataTable* objects). Microsoft has implied that it will offer additional visualizers as downloads at some point in the future, and they have designed Visual Studio so that third-party developers can write their own visualizers and install them into the Visual Studio debugger. In the following exercise, you'll see how the text visualizer works. (For this exercise, I assume that you are still in debugging mode and that the Watch window is open with a few expressions in it from the Debug Test program.)

Open a text visualizer in the debugger

1. Look on the right side of the Watch window for a small magnifying glass icon.

   A magnifying glass icon indicates that a visualizer is available for the variable or property that you are examining in a Watch window, an Autos window, or a Locals window. If you completed the previous exercise, the *TextBox2.Text* property shows a visualizer now.

2. Click the visualizer arrow.

   When the property you are examining is a text (string) property, Visual Studio offers three visualizers: a simple text visualizer that displays the selected string expression as readable text, an HTML visualizer that converts HTML code to a Web page, and an XML visualizer that converts XML code to a viewable document. Your screen looks like the graphic on the next page.

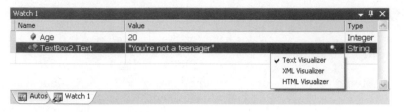

3. Click the Text Visualizer option.

Visual Studio opens a dialog box and displays the contents of the *TextBox2.Text* property. Your screen looks like this:

Although this particular result offers little more than the Watch window did, the benefits of the visualizer tool become immediately obvious when the *Text* property of a multiline textbox object is displayed, or when you examine variables or properties containing database information or Web documents. You'll experiment with these more sophisticated data types later in the book.

4. Click Close to close the Text Visualizer dialog box.

Leave Visual Studio running in debugging mode. You'll continue using the Watch window in the next section, too.

Tip   In debugging mode, visualizers also appear within pop-up windows called *DataTips* in the Code Editor. When you point to a variable or property within the Code Editor during a debugging session, a DataTip appears, and you can click the visualizer icon for more information as you did in the previous exercise.

Using the Immediate and Command Windows

So far, you've used the Visual Studio debugging tools that allow you to enter debugging mode, execute code one statement at a time, and examine the value of important variables, properties, and expressions in your program. Now you'll learn how to change the value of a variable by using the Immediate window, and you'll learn how to run commands, such as Save All or Print, within the Visual Studio IDE by using the Command window. (An improvement in Visual Studio 2005 is that these two windows are more distinct than they were in Microsoft Visual Basic .NET 2003.) The windows contain scroll bars, so you can execute more than one command and view the results by using the arrow keys.

The following exercises demonstrate how the Immediate and Command windows work. I discuss these windows together because, with the following special commands, you can switch between them:

- In the Immediate window, the >cmd command switches to the Command window.

- In the Command window, the immed command switches to the Immediate window.

The exercises assume that you're debugging the Debug Test program in debugging mode.

Use the Immediate window to modify a variable

1. On the Debug menu, point to Windows, and then click Immediate.

   When you select the command, Visual Studio opens the Immediate window and prepares the compiler to receive commands from you *while the Debug Test program is running*. This is a very handy feature, because you can test program conditions on the fly, without stopping the program and inserting program statements in the Code Editor.

2. In the Immediate window, type **Age = 17**, and then press Enter.

   You've just used the Immediate window to change the value of a variable. The value of the *Age* variable in the Watch window immediately changes to 17, and the next time the *If* statement is executed, the value in the *TextBox2.Text* property will change to "You're a teenager." Your Immediate window looks like this:

3. Type the following statement in the Immediate window, and then press Enter:

```
TextBox2.Text = "You're a great age!"
```

The *Text* property of the *TextBox2* object is immediately changed to "You're a great age!" In the Immediate window, you can change the value of properties, as well as variables.

4. Display the Watch 1 window if it is not currently visible. (Click the Watch 1 tab in the Visual Studio IDE.)

   The Watch window looks like this:

As you can see, both items now contain new values, and this gives you the opportunity to test the program further.

5. Click the Step Into button two times to display the Debug Test form again.

   Notice that the *Text* property of the *TextBox2* object has been changed, as you directed, but the *Text* property of the *TextBox1* object still holds a value of 20 (not 17). This is because you changed the *Age* variable in the program, not the property that assigned a value to *Age*. Your screen looks like this:

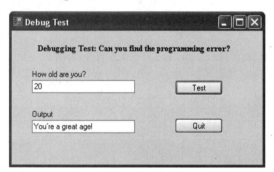

The Immediate window has many uses—it provides an excellent companion to the Watch window, and it can help you experiment with specific test cases that might otherwise be very difficult to enter into your program.

Switching to the Command Window

The text-based Command window offers a complement to the Visual Studio Immediate window. Reminiscent of the MS-DOS command prompt, it can be used to run interface commands in the Visual Studio IDE. For example, entering the File.SaveAll command in the Command window saves all the files in the current project. (This command is the equivalent of the Save All command on the File menu.) If you already have the Immediate window open, you can switch between the Immediate and the Command windows by entering the >cmd and immed commands, respectively. You can also click the Command Window button on the right side of the Standard toolbar to open the Command window. You'll practice using the Command window in the following exercise.

Run the File.SaveAll command

1. In the Immediate window, type **>cmd**, and then press Enter to switch to the Command window.

   The Command window appears, and the Immediate or Watch window might now be partially (or totally) hidden. (You can return to the Immediate window by clicking its tab or typing immed in the Command window.) The > prompt appears, a visual clue that you are now working in the Command window.

2. Type **File.SaveAll** in the Command window, and then press Enter.

   As you begin typing File, all the Visual Studio commands associate with the File menu and file operations appear in a pop-up list box. This "command completion" feature offers a useful way to learn about the many commands that can be executed within the Command window. After you type File.SaveAll and press Enter, Visual Studio saves the current project, and the command prompt returns, as shown in the following illustration.

3. Experiment with other commands now if you like. (Begin your commands with menu names to discover the different commands available.) When you're finished, click the Close button in both the Command and Immediate windows. You're finished with them for now.

One Step Further: Removing Breakpoints

If you've been following the instructions in this chapter carefully, the Debug Test program is still running and has a breakpoint in it. Follow these steps to remove the breakpoint and end the program. You're finished debugging the Debug Test program.

Remove a breakpoint

1. In the Code Editor, click the red circle associated with the breakpoint in the Margin Indicator bar.

The breakpoint disappears. That's all there is to it! But note that if you have more than one breakpoint in a program, you can remove them all by clicking the Delete All Breakpoints command on the Debug menu. Visual Studio saves breakpoints with your project, so it's important to know how to remove them; otherwise, they'll still be in your program, even if you close Visual Studio and restart it!

2. Click the Stop Debugging button on the Standard toolbar.

    The Debug Test program ends.

3. On the View menu, point to Toolbars, and then click Debug.

    The Debug toolbar closes.

You've learned the fundamental techniques of debugging Visual Basic programs with Visual Studio. Place a bookmark in this chapter so that you can return to it as you encounter problems later in the book. In the next chapter, you'll learn how to handle run-time errors by using structured error handling techniques.

Chapter 8 Quick Reference

To	Do this
Display the Debug toolbar	On the View menu, point to Toolbars, and then click Debug.
Set a breakpoint	In the Code Editor, click in the Margin Indicator bar next to the statement where you want to stop program execution. When the compiler reaches the breakpoint, it will enter debugging mode.
	or
	Place a *Stop* statement in the program code where you want to enter debugging mode.
Execute one line of code in the Code Editor	Click the Step Into button on the Standard toolbar.
Examine a variable, a property, or an expression in the Code Editor	In debugging mode, select the value in the Code Editor, and then hold the pointer over it.
Use the Autos window to examine a variable on the current or previous line	In debugging mode, click the Debug menu, point to Windows, and then click Autos.
Add a variable, a property, or an expression to a Watch window	In debugging mode, select the value in the Code Editor, right click the value, and then click Add Watch.
Display a Watch window	In debugging mode, click the Debug menu, point to Windows, point to Watch, and then click the window.
Display HTML, XML, or dataset information during a debugging session	Click the visualizer icon in an Autos, a Watch, a Locals, or a DataTip window during a debugging session
Open the Immediate window	Click the Debug menu, point to Windows, and then click Immediate.

To	Do this
Run a command in the Visual Studio IDE from the Command window	At the > prompt, type the name of the command, and then press Enter. For example, to save the current project, type File.SaveAll, and then press Enter.
Switch to the Command window from the Immediate window	Type >cmd, and then press Enter. To switch back to the Immediate window, type immed, and then press Enter.
Remove one or more breakpoints	Click the breakpoint in the Margin Indicator bar of the Code Editor. *or* Click the Delete All Breakpoints command on the Debug menu.
Stop debugging	Click the Stop Debugging button on the Standard toolbar.

Chapter 9
Trapping Errors by Using Structured Error Handling

After completing this chapter, you will be able to:

- Manage run-time errors by using the Try...Catch error handler.

- Create a disc drive error handler that tests specific error conditions by using the *Catch When* statement.

- Write complex error handlers that use the *Err* object and *Err.Number* and *Err.Description* properties to identify exceptions.

- Build nested *Try...Catch* statements.

- Use error handlers in combination with defensive programming techniques.

- Leave error handlers prematurely by using the *Exit Try* statement.

In Chapter 8, "Debugging Visual Basic Programs," you learned how to recognize run-time errors in a Microsoft Visual Basic program and how to locate logic errors and other defects in your program code by using the Microsoft Visual Studio 2005 debugging tools. In this chapter, you'll learn how to build blocks of code that handle run-time errors, also referred to as *exceptions*, which occur as a result of normal operating conditions—for example, errors due to a CD not being in a drive, a lost Internet connection, or an offline printer. These routines are called *structured error handlers* (or *structured exception handlers*), and you can use them to recognize run-time errors as they occur in a program, suppress unwanted error messages, and adjust program conditions so that your application can regain control and run again.

Fortunately, Visual Basic offers the powerful Try...Catch code block for handling errors. In this chapter, you'll learn how to trap run-time errors by using Try...Catch code blocks, and you'll learn how to use the *Err.Number* and *Err.Description* properties to identify specific run-time errors. You'll also learn how to use multiple *Catch* statements to write more flexible error handlers, build nested Try...Catch code blocks, and use the *Exit Try* statement to exit a Try...Catch code block prematurely. The programming techniques you'll learn were added to Visual Basic with Microsoft Visual Studio .NET versions 2002 and 2003, and they are similar to the structured error handlers provided by the most advanced programming languages, such as Java and C++. The most reliable, or *robust*, Visual Basic programs make use of several error handlers to manage unforeseen circumstances and provide users with consistent and trouble-free computing experiences.

> **Upgrade Notes: Migrating Visual Basic 6 Code to Visual Basic 2005**
>
> If you're experienced with Microsoft Visual Basic 6, you'll notice some new features in Microsoft Visual Basic 2005, including the following:
>
> - The Try...Catch code block is a new mechanism for writing structured error handlers. Although you can still use Visual Basic 6 error-handling keywords, including *On Error Goto*, *Resume*, and *Resume Next*, the Try...Catch syntax avoids the potential complications of Goto constructions and offers a very efficient way to manage run-time errors.
>
> - The *Catch When* statement can be used to test specific program conditions and handle more than one run-time error in a Try...Catch code block.
>
> - The *Exit Try* statement offers a new way to exit structured error handlers.
>
> - Visual Studio 2005 continues to provide the *Err.Number* and *Err.Description* properties to identify run-time errors. In addition, you can use the new *Err.GetException* method to return information about the underlying error condition, or *exception*, that halted program execution.

Processing Errors by Using Try...Catch

A *program crash* is an unexpected problem in a Visual Basic program from which the program can't recover. You might have experienced your first program crash when Visual Basic couldn't load artwork from a file or in the previous chapter, when you *intentionally* introduced errors into your program code during debugging. It's not that Visual Basic isn't smart enough to handle the glitch; it's just that Visual Basic hasn't been "told" what to do when something goes wrong.

Fortunately, you don't have to live with occasional errors that cause your programs to crash. You can write special Visual Basic routines, called structured error handlers, to manage and respond to run-time errors before they force the Visual Basic compiler to terminate your program. An error handler handles a run-time error by telling the program how to continue when one of its statements doesn't work. Error handlers can be placed in each event procedure where there is potential for trouble, or in generic functions or subprograms that receive control after an error has occurred and handle the problem systematically. (You'll learn more about writing functions and subprograms in Chapter 10, "Creating Modules and Procedures.")

Error handlers handle, or *trap*, a problem by using a Try...Catch code block and a special error handling object named *Err*. The *Err* object has a *Number* property that identifies the error number and a *Description* property that you can use to display a description of the error. For example, if the run-time error is associated with loading a file from a CD-ROM drive, your error handler might display a custom error message that identifies the problem and prompts the user to insert a CD, rather than allowing the failed operation to crash the program.

When to Use Error Handlers

You can use error handlers in any situation where an action (either expected or unexpected) has the potential to produce an error that stops program execution. Typically, error handlers are used to manage external events that influence a program—for example, events caused by a failed network or Internet connection, a CD or disk not being inserted correctly in the drive, or an offline printer or scanner. The following table lists potential problems that can be addressed by error handlers.

Problem	Description
Network/Internet problems	Network servers, Internet connections, and other resources that fail, or *go down*, unexpectedly.
Disc drive problems	Unformatted or incorrectly formatted CDs or disks, media that isn't properly inserted, bad sectors, CDs or disks that are full, problems with a CD-ROM drive, and so on.
Path problems	A path to a necessary file that is missing or incorrect.
Printer problems	Printers that are off line, out of paper, out of memory, or otherwise unavailable.
Software not installed	A file or component that your application relies on but that is not installed on the user's computer, or an operating system incompatibility.
Permissions problems	User permissions that are not appropriate for performing a task.
Overflow errors	An activity that exceed the allocated storage space.
Out-of-memory errors	Insufficient application or resource space available in the Microsoft Windows memory management scheme.
Clipboard problems	Problems with data transfer or the Windows Clipboard.
Logic errors	Syntax or logic errors undetected by the compiler and previous tests (such as an incorrectly spelled file name).

Setting the Trap: The Try...Catch Code Block

The code block used to handle a run-time error is called *Try...Catch*. You place the *Try* statement in an event procedure right before the statement you're worried about, and the *Catch* statement follows immediately with a list of the statements that you want to run if a run-time error actually occurs. A number of optional statements, such as *Catch When*, *Finally*, *Exit Try*, and nested Try...Catch code blocks can also be included, as the examples in this chapter will demonstrate. However, the basic syntax for a Try...Catch exception handler is simply the following:

```
Try
    Statements that might produce a run-time error
Catch
    Statements to run if a run-time error occurs
Finally
    Optional statements to run whether an error occurs or not
End Try
```

The *Try* statement identifies the beginning of an error handler in which *Try*, *Catch*, and *End Try* are required keywords, and *Finally* and the statements that follow are optional. Note that programmers sometimes call the statements between the *Try* and *Catch* keywords *protected code* because any run-time errors resulting from these statements won't cause the program to crash. (Instead, Visual Basic executes the error handling statements in the Catch code block.)

Path and Disc Drive Errors

The following example demonstrates a common run-time error situation—a problem with a path, disc drive, or attached peripheral device. To complete this exercise, you'll load a sample Visual Basic project that I created to show how artwork files are opened in a picture box object on a Windows form.

To prepare for the exercise, insert a blank CD into drive D (or equivalent), and use Windows Explorer or your CD creation software to copy or *burn* the fileopen.bmp file to it. Alternatively, you can copy the .bmp file to a disk in drive A or another type of removable storage media, such as an attached digital camera, memory stick, or Iomega Zip Drive.

> **Tip** You'll find the fileopen.bmp file, along with the Disc Drive Error project, in the c:\vb05sbs\chap09 folder.

To complete the exercise, you'll need to be able to remove the CD, or connect and disconnect your external storage device, as test conditions dictate, and you'll need to modify the program code below with the drive letter you're using. You'll use the CD and CD drive (or equivalent media) throughout the chapter to force run-time errors and recover from them.

Experiment with disc drive errors

1. Insert a blank CD in drive D (or the drive in which you create CDs), and copy the fileopen.bmp file to it.

   Use Windows Explorer or a third-party CD creation program to copy the file and burn the disc. If you're using a different external storage device, connect the device or insert a blank disk, copy fileopen.bmp to it, and make a note of the drive letter Windows assigns to the device.

2. Start Visual Studio, and then open the Disc Drive Error project, which is located in the c:\vb05sbs\chap09\disc drive error folder.

   The Disc Drive Error project opens in the IDE.

3. If the project's form isn't visible, display it now.

   The Disc Drive Error project is a skeleton program that displays the fileopen.bmp file in a picture box when the user clicks the Check Drive button. I designed the project as a convenient way to create and trap run-time errors, and you can use it throughout this chapter to build error handlers by using the Try...Catch code block.

4. Double-click the Check Drive button on the form to display the *Button1_Click* event procedure.

   You'll see the following line of program code between the *Private Sub* and *End Sub* statements:

```
PictureBox1.Image = _
  System.Drawing.Bitmap.FromFile("d:\fileopen.bmp")
```

As you've learned in earlier chapters, the *FromFile* method opens the specified file. This particular use of *FromFile* opens the fileopen.bmp file on drive D and displays it in a picture box. However, if the CD is missing, the CD tray is open, the file is not on the CD, or there is another problem with the path or drive letter specified in the code, the statement produces a "File Not Found" error in Visual Basic. This is the run-time error we want to trap.

> **Note**   If your CD drive or attached peripheral device is using a drive letter other than "D" now, change the drive letter in this program statement to match the letter you're using. For example, a floppy disk drive typically requires the letter "A." Memory sticks, digital cameras, and other detachable media typically use "E," "F," or higher letters for the drive.

5. With your CD still in drive D or equivalent, click the Start Debugging button on the Standard toolbar to run the program.

   The form for the project appears, as shown here:

6. Click the Check Drive button on the form.

   The program loads the fileopen.bmp file from the CD and displays it in the picture box, as shown on the next page.

The *SizeMode* property of the picture box object is set to StretchImage, so the file fills the entire picture box object. Now see what happens when the CD isn't in the drive when the program attempts to load the file.

7. Remove the CD from the drive.

   If you are using a different media type, remove it now. If you are testing with a removable storage device, follow your usual procedure to safely turn it off, and remove the media containing fileopen.bmp.

8. Click the Check Drive button again on the form.

   The program can't find the file, and Visual Basic issues a run-time error, or *unhandled exception*, which causes the program to crash. Visual Studio enters debugging mode, highlights the problem statement, and displays the following dialog box:

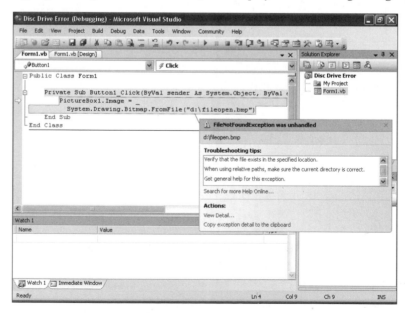

9. Click the Stop Debugging button on the Standard toolbar to close the program.

   The development environment returns.

An excellent addition to the Visual Studio 2005 software is the very detailed help information (including troubleshooting tips) about the unhandled exception that has stopped our program. But we still need to modify the code to handle this very plausible error scenario in the future.

Writing a Disc Drive Error Handler

The problem with the Disc Drive Error program isn't that it somehow defies the inherent capabilities of Visual Basic to process errors. We just haven't specified what Visual Basic should do when it encounters an exception that it doesn't know how to handle. The solution to this problem is to write a Try...Catch code block that recognizes the error and tells Visual Basic what to do about it. You'll add this error handler now.

Use Try...Catch to trap the error

1. Display the *Button1_Click* event procedure if it isn't visible in the Code Editor.

   You need to add an error handler to the event procedure that's causing the problems. As you'll see in this example, you actually build the Try...Catch code block around the code that's the potential source of trouble, protecting the rest of the program from the run-time errors it might produce.

2. Modify the event procedure so that the existing *FromFile* statement fits between *Try* and *Catch* statements, as shown in the following code block:

```
Try
    PictureBox1.Image = _
        System.Drawing.Bitmap.FromFile("d:\fileopen.bmp")
Catch
    MsgBox("Please insert the disc in drive D!")
End Try
```

   You don't need to retype the *FromFile* statement—just type the *Try*, *Catch*, *MsgBox*, and *End Try* statements above and below it. If Visual Studio adds *Catch*, variable declaration, or *End Try* statements in the wrong place, simply delete the statements and retype them as shown in the book. (The Code Editor tries to be helpful, but its auto complete feature sometimes gets in the way.)

This program code demonstrates the most basic use of a Try...Catch code block. It places the problematic *FromFile* statement in a Try code block so that if the program code produces an error, the statements in the Catch code block are executed. The Catch code block simply displays a message box asking the user to insert the required disc in drive D so that the program can continue. This Try...Catch code block contains no *Finally* statement, so the error handler ends with the keywords *End Try*.

Again, if you are using a removable storage device or media associated with a different drive letter, you would make those changes in the statements that you just typed.

1. Remove the CD from drive D, and click the Start Debugging button to run the program.

2. Click the Check Drive button.

    Instead of stopping program execution, Visual Basic invokes the *Catch* statement, which displays the following message box:

3. Click OK, and then click the Check Drive button again.

    The program displays the message box again, asking you to insert the disc properly in drive D. Each time there's a problem loading the file, this message box appears.

4. Insert the disc in drive D, wait a moment for the system to recognize the CD (close any windows that appear when you insert the disc), click OK, and then click the Check Drive button again.

    The bitmap graphic appears in the picture box, as expected. The error handler has completed its work effectively—rather than the program crashing inadvertently, it's told you how to correct your mistake, and you can now continue working with the application.

5. Click Close on the form to stop the program.

It's time to learn some of the variations of the Try...Catch error handler.

Using the *Finally* Clause to Perform Cleanup Tasks

As the syntax description for Try...Catch noted earlier in the chapter, you can use the optional *Finally* clause with Try...Catch to execute a block of statements regardless of how the compiler executes the Try or Catch blocks. In other words, whether or not the *Try* statements produced a run-time error, there might be some code that you need to run each time an error handler is finished. For example, you might want to update variables or properties, display the results of a computation by using a message box or other mechanism, or perform "cleanup" operations by clearing variables or disabling unneeded objects on a form.

The following exercise demonstrates how the *Finally* clause works, by displaying a second message box whether or not the *FromFile* method produces a run-time error.

Use *Finally* to display a message box

1. Display the *Button1_Click* event procedure, and then edit the Try...Catch code block so that it contains two additional lines of code above the *End Try* statement. The complete error handler should look like this:

```
Try
    PictureBox1.Image = _
        System.Drawing.Bitmap.FromFile("d:\fileopen.bmp")
Catch
    MsgBox("Please insert the disc in drive D!")
Finally
    MsgBox("Error handler complete")
End Try
```

The *Finally* statement indicates to the compiler that a final block of code should be executed whether or not a run-time error is processed. To help you learn exactly how this feature works, I've inserted a *MsgBox* function to display a test message below the *Finally* statement. Although this simple use of the *Finally* statement is helpful for testing purposes, in a real program you'll probably want to use the Finally code block to update important variables or properties, display data, or perform other cleanup operations.

2. Remove the CD from drive D, and then click the Start Debugging button to run the program.

3. Click the Check Drive button.

   The error handler displays a dialog box asking you to insert the disc in drive D.

4. Click OK.

   The program executes the *Finally* clause in the error handler, and the following message box appears:

5. Click OK, insert the disc in drive D, and then click the Check Drive button again.

   The file appears in the picture box as expected. In addition, the *Finally* clause is executed, and the "Error handler complete" message box appears again. As I noted earlier, *Finally* statements are executed at the end of a Try...Catch block whether or not there's an error.

6. Click OK, and then click the Close button on the form to stop the program.

More Complex Try...Catch Error Handlers

As your programs become more sophisticated, you might find it useful to write more complex Try...Catch error handlers that manage a variety of run-time errors and unusual error-handling situations. Try...Catch provides for this complexity by:

- Permitting multiple lines of code in each Try, Catch, or Finally code block.

- Offering the *Catch When* syntax, which tests specific error conditions.

- Allowing nested Try...Catch code blocks, which can be used to build sophisticated and robust error handlers.

In addition, by using a special error-handling object named *Err*, you can identify and process specific run-time errors and conditions in your program. You'll investigate each of these error-handling features in the following section.

The *Err* Object

Err is a special Visual Basic object that's assigned detailed error-handling information each time a run-time error occurs. The most useful *Err* properties for identifying run-time errors are *Err.Number* and *Err.Description*. *Err.Number* contains the number of the most recent run-time error, and *Err.Description* contains a short error message that matches the run-time error number. By using the *Err.Number* and *Err.Description* properties together in an error handler, you can recognize specific errors and respond to them, and you can give the user helpful information about how he or she should respond.

The *Err.Number* and *Err.Description* properties contain information about the most recent run-time error.

You can clear the *Err* object by using the *Err.Clear* method (which discards previous error information), but if you use the *Err* object within a Catch code block, clearing the *Err* object isn't usually necessary because Catch blocks are entered only when a run-time error has just occurred in a neighboring Try code block.

The following table lists many of the run-time errors that Visual Basic applications can encounter. In addition to these error codes, you'll find that some Visual Basic libraries and other components (such as database and system components) provide their own unique error messages, which often can be discovered by using the online Help. Note that despite the error message descriptions, some errors don't appear as you might expect them to, so you'll need to specifically test the error numbers (when possible) by observing how the *Err.Number* property changes during program execution. Unused error numbers in the range 1–1000 are reserved for future use by Visual Basic.

Error number	Default error message
5	Procedure call or argument is not valid
6	Overflow

Error number	Default error message
7	Out of memory
9	Subscript out of range
11	Division by zero
13	Type mismatch
48	Error in loading DLL
51	Internal error
52	Bad file name or number
53	File not found
55	File already open
57	Device I/O error
58	File already exists
61	Disk full
62	Input past end of file
67	Too many files
68	Device unavailable
70	Permission denied
71	Disk not ready
74	Can't rename with different drive
75	Path/File access error
76	Path not found
91	Object variable or With block variable not set
321	File format is not valid
322	Cannot create necessary temporary file
380	Property value is not valid
381	Property array index is not valid
422	Property not found
423	Property or method not found
424	Object required
429	Cannot create Microsoft ActiveX component
430	Class does not support Automation or does not support expected interface
438	Object does not support this property or method
440	Automation error
460	Clipboard format is not valid
461	Method or data member not found
462	The remote server machine does not exist or is unavailable
463	Class not registered on local machine
481	Picture is not valid
482	Printer error

The following exercise uses the *Err.Number* and *Err.Description* properties in a Try...Catch error handler to test for more than one run-time error condition. This capability is made possible by the *Catch When* syntax, which you'll use to test for specific error conditions in a Try...Catch code block.

Test for multiple run-time error conditions

1.   In the *Button1_Click* event procedure, edit the Try...Catch error handler so that it looks like the following code block. (The original *FromFile* statement is the same as the code you used in the previous exercises, but the *Catch* statements are all new.)

```
Try
    PictureBox1.Image = _
       System.Drawing.Bitmap.FromFile("d:\fileopen.bmp")
Catch When Err.Number = 53 'if File Not Found error
    MsgBox("Check pathname and disc drive")
Catch When Err.Number = 7  'if Out Of Memory error
    MsgBox("Is this really a bitmap?", , Err.Description)
Catch
    MsgBox("Problem loading file", , Err.Description)
End Try
```

The *Catch When* syntax is used twice in the error handler, and each time the syntax is used with the *Err.Number* property to test whether the Try code block produced a particular type of run-time error. If the *Err.Number* property equals the number 53, the File Not Found run-time error has occurred during the file open procedure, and the message "Check pathname and disc drive" is displayed in a message box. If the *Err.Number* property is equal to the number 7, an Out of Memory error has occurred—probably the result of loading a file that doesn't actually contain artwork. (I get this error if I accidentally try to open a Microsoft Word document in a picture box object by using the *FromFile* method.)

The final *Catch* statement handles all other run-time errors that could potentially occur during a file-opening process—it's a general "catch-all" code block that prints a general error message inside a message box and a specific error message from the *Err.Description* property in the title bar of the message box.

2.   Click the Start Debugging button to run the program.

3.   Remove the CD from drive D.

4.   Click the Check Drive button.

The error handler displays the error message "Check pathname and disc drive" in a message box. The first *Check When* statement works.

5.   Click OK, and then click Close on the form to end the program.

6.   Insert the CD again, and use Windows Explorer or another tool to copy a second file to the CD that isn't an artwork file. For example, copy a Word document or a Microsoft Excel spreadsheet to the CD.

You won't open this file in Word or Excel, but you will try to open it (unsuccessfully, we hope) in your program's picture box object. (If your CD-ROM software or drive doesn't allow you to add additional files to a CD after you have burned it, you might need to create a second CD with the two files.)

7. In the Code Editor, change the name of the fileopen.bmp file in the *FromFile* program statement to the name of the file (Word, Excel, or other) you copied to the CD in drive D.

    Using a file with a different format gives you an opportunity to test a second type of run-time error—an Out of Memory exception, which occurs when Visual Basic attempts to load a file that isn't a graphic or has too much information for a picture box.

8. Run the program again, and click the Check Drive button.

    The error handler displays the following error message:

    Notice that I have used the *Err.Description* property to display a short description of the problem ("Out of memory.") in the message box title bar. Using this property in your error handler can give the user a clearer idea of what has happened.

9. Click OK, and click Close on the form to stop the program.

10. Change the file name back to fileopen.bmp in the *FromFile* method. (You'll use it in the next exercise.)

The *Catch When* statement is very powerful. By using *Catch When* in combination with the *Err.Number* and *Err.Description* properties, you can write sophisticated error handlers that recognize and respond to several types of exceptions.

Raising Your Own Errors

For testing purposes and other specialized uses, you can artificially generate your own run-time errors in a program with a technique called *throwing*, or *raising*, exceptions. To accomplish this, you use the *Err.Raise* method with one of the error numbers in the table presented earlier. For example, the following syntax uses the *Raise* method to produce a Disc Full run-time error and then handles the error by using a *Catch When* statement:

```
Try
    Err.Raise(61) 'raise Disc Full error
Catch When Err.Number = 61
    MsgBox("Error: Disc is full")
End Try
```

When you learn how to write your own procedures, with this technique you can generate your own errors and return them to the calling routine.

Specifying a Retry Period

Another strategy you can use in an error handler is to try an operation a few times and then disable it if the problem isn't resolved. For example, in the following exercise, a Try...Catch block employs a counter variable named *Retries* to track the number of times the message "Please insert the disc in drive D!" is displayed, and after the second time, the error handler disables the Check Drive button. The trick to this technique is declaring the *Retries* variable at the top of the form's program code so that it has scope throughout all of the form's event procedures. The *Retries* variable is then incremented and tested in the Catch code block. The number of retries can be modified by simply changing the "2" in the statement, as shown here:

```
If Retries <= 2
```

Use a variable to track run-time errors

1. In the Code Editor, scroll to the top of the form's program code, and directly below the `Public Class Form1` statement, type the following variable declaration:

```
Dim Retries As Short = 0
```

   Retries is declared as a *Short* integer variable because it won't contain very big numbers. It's assigned an initial value of 0 so that it resets properly each time the program runs.

2. In the *Button1_Click* event procedure, edit the Try...Catch error handler so that it looks like the following code block:

```
Try
    PictureBox1.Image = _
      System.Drawing.Bitmap.FromFile("d:\fileopen.bmp")
Catch
    Retries += 1
    If Retries <= 2 Then
        MsgBox("Please insert the disc in drive D!")
    Else
        MsgBox("File Load feature disabled")
        Button1.Enabled = False
    End If
End Try
```

   The Try block tests the same file-opening procedure, but this time, if an error occurs, the Catch block increments the *Retries* variable and tests the variable to be sure that it's less than or equal to 2. The number 2 can be changed to allow any number of retries—currently it allows only two run-time errors. After two errors, the *Else* clause is executed, and a message box appears indicating that the file-loading feature has been disabled. The Check Drive button is then disabled—in other words, grayed out and rendered unusable for the remainder of the program.

> **Tip**   This revised version of the error handler that you have been building has been renamed Disc Drive Handler and is stored in the c:\vb05sbs\chap09\disc drive handler folder.

3. Click the Start Debugging button to run the program.

4. Remove the CD from drive D.

5. Click the Check Drive button.

    The error handler displays the error message "Please insert the disc in drive D!" in a message box, as shown here. Behind the scenes, the *Retries* variable is also incremented to 1.

6. Click OK, and then click the Check Drive button again.

    The *Retries* variable is set to 2, and the message "Please insert the disc in drive D!" appears again.

7. Click OK, and then click the Check Drive button a third time.

    The *Retries* variable is incremented to 3, and the *Else* clause is executed. The message "File Load feature disabled" appears, as shown here:

8. Click OK in the message box.

    The Check Drive button is disabled on the form, as shown here:

The error handler has responded to the disc drive problem by allowing the user a few tries to fix the problem, and then it has disabled the problematic button. (In other words, the user can no longer click the button.) This disabling action stops future run-time errors, although the program might no longer function exactly as it was originally designed.

9. Click the Close button to stop the program.

Using Nested Try...Catch Blocks

You can also use nested Try...Catch code blocks in your error handlers. For example, the following disc drive error handler uses a second Try...Catch block to retry the file open operation a single time if the first attempt fails and generates a run-time error:

```
Try
    PictureBox1.Image = _
      System.Drawing.Bitmap.FromFile("d:\fileopen.bmp")
Catch
    MsgBox("Insert the disc in drive D, then click OK!")
    Try
        PictureBox1.Image = _
          System.Drawing.Bitmap.FromFile("d:\fileopen.bmp")
    Catch
        MsgBox("File Load feature disabled")
        Button1.Enabled = False
    End Try
End Try
```

If the user inserts the disc in the drive as a result of the message prompt, the second Try block opens the file without error. However, if a file-related run-time error still appears, the second Catch block displays a message saying that the file load feature is being disabled, and the button is disabled.

In general, nested Try...Catch error handlers work well as long as you don't have too many tests or retries to manage. If you do need to retry a problematic operation many times, use a variable to track your retries, or develop a function containing an error handler that can be called repeatedly from your event procedures. (See Chapter 10, "Creating Modules and Procedures," for more information about creating functions.)

Comparing Error Handlers with Defensive Programming Techniques

Error handlers aren't the only mechanism for protecting a program against run-time errors. For example, the following program code uses the *File.Exists* method in the *System.IO* namespace of the .NET Framework class library to check whether a file exists on CD before it's opened:

```
If File.Exists("d:\fileopen.bmp") Then
    PictureBox1.Image = _
        System.Drawing.Bitmap.FromFile("d:\fileopen.bmp")
Else
    MsgBox("Cannot find fileopen.bmp on drive D.")
End If
```

This *If...Then* statement isn't an actual error handler because it doesn't prevent a run-time error from halting a program. Instead, it's a validation technique that some programmers call *defensive programming*. It uses a handy method in the .NET Framework class library to verify the intended file operation *before* it's actually attempted in the program code. And in this particular case, testing to see whether the file exists with the .NET Framework method is actually faster than waiting for Visual Basic to issue an exception and recover from a run-time error using an error handler.

> **Note**   To get this particular program logic to work, the following statement must be included in the declarations section at the very top of the form's program code to make reference to the .NET Framework class library that's being invoked:
>
> ```
> Imports System.IO
> ```
>
> For more information about utilizing the *Imports* statement to use the objects, properties, and methods in the .NET Framework class libraries, see Chapter 5, "Visual Basic Variables and Formulas, and the .NET Framework."

When should you use defensive programming techniques, and when should you use error handlers? The answer depends on how often you think a problem will occur with the statements that you plan to use. If an exception or run-time error will occur somewhat infrequently—say less than 25 percent of the time a particular piece of code is executed—using an error handler is probably the most efficient way to go. Error handlers are also essential if you have more than one condition to test and if you want to provide the user with numerous options for responding to the error. However, if there's a real likelihood that a piece of code will produce a run-time error more than 25 percent of the time, defensive programming logic is usually the most efficient way to manage potential problems. As I mentioned earlier when discussing the If...Then code block, the *File.Exists* method is actually faster than using a

Try...Catch error handler, so it also makes sense to use a defensive programming technique if performance issues are involved. In the end, it probably makes the most sense to use a combination of defensive programming and structured error handling techniques in your code.

One Step Further: The *Exit Try* Statement

You've learned a lot about error handlers in this chapter; now you're ready to put them to work in your own programs. But before you move on to the next chapter, here's one more syntax option for Try...Catch code blocks that you might find useful: the *Exit Try* statement. *Exit Try* is a quick and slightly abrupt technique for exiting a Try...Catch code block prematurely. If you've written Visual Basic programs before, you might notice its similarity to the *Exit For* and *Exit Sub* statements, which you can use to leave a structured routine early. Using the *Exit Try* syntax, you can jump completely out of the current Try or Catch code block. If there's a Finally code block, this code will be executed, but *Exit Try* lets you jump over any remaining *Try* or *Catch* statements you don't want to execute.

The following sample routine shows how the *Exit Try* statement works. It first checks to see whether the *Enabled* property of the *PictureBox1* object is set to False, a flag that might indicate that the picture box isn't ready to receive input. If the picture box isn't yet enabled, the *Exit Try* statement skips to the end of the Catch code block, and the file load operation isn't attempted.

```
Try
    If PictureBox1.Enabled = False Then Exit Try
    PictureBox1.Image = _
        System.Drawing.Bitmap.FromFile("d:\fileopen.bmp")
Catch
    Retries += 1
    If Retries <= 2 Then
        MsgBox("Please insert the disc in drive D!")
    Else
        MsgBox("File Load feature disabled")
        Button1.Enabled = False
    End If
End Try
```

The example builds on the last error handler you experimented with in this chapter (the Disc Drive Handler project). If you'd like to test the *Exit Try* statement in the context of that program, load the Disc Drive Handler project again and enter the *If* statement that contains the *Exit Try* in the Code Editor. You'll also need to use the Properties window to disable the picture box object on the form (in other words, set its *Enabled* property to False).

Congratulations! You've learned a number of important fundamental programming techniques in Visual Basic, including how to write error handlers. Now you're ready to increase your programming efficiency by learning to write Visual Basic modules and procedures.

Chapter 9 Quick Reference

To	Do this

Detect and process run-time errors	Build an error handler by using one or more Try...Catch code blocks. For example, the following error handler code tests for path or disc drive problems:
	
	``
	Try
	    PictureBox1.Image = _
	      System.Drawing.Bitmap.FromFile _
	      ("d:\fileopen.bmp")
	Catch
	    MsgBox("Check path or insert disc")
	Finally
	    MsgBox("Error handler complete")
	End Try
	``

Test for specific error conditions in an event handler	Use the *Catch When* syntax and the *Err.Number* property. For example:
	
	``
	Try
	    PictureBox1.Image = _
	      System.Drawing.Bitmap.FromFile _
	      ("d:\fileopen.bmp")
	Catch When Err.Number = 53 'if File Not Found
	    MsgBox("Check pathname and disc drive")
	Catch When Err.Number = 7 'if Out Of Memory
	    MsgBox("Is this really a bitmap?", , _
	      Err.Description)
	Catch
	    MsgBox("Problem loading file", , _
	      Err.Description)
	End Try
	``

Create your own errors in a program	Use the *Err.Raise* method. For example, the following code generates a Disc Full error and handles it:
	
	``
	Try
	    Err.Raise(61) 'raise Disc Full error
	Catch When Err.Number = 61
	    MsgBox("Error: Disc is full")
	End Try
	``

To	Do this
Write nested Try...Catch error handlers	Place one Try...Catch code block within another. For example:

```
Try
    PictureBox1.Image = _
      System.Drawing.Bitmap.FromFile _
      ("d:\fileopen.bmp")
Catch
    MsgBox("Insert the disc in drive D!")
    Try
        PictureBox1.Image = _
          System.Drawing.Bitmap.FromFile _
          ("d:\fileopen.bmp")
    Catch
        MsgBox("File Load feature disabled")
        Button1.Enabled = False
    End Try
End Try
```

To	Do this
Exit the current Try or Catch code block	Use the *Exit Try* statement in the Try or the Catch code block. For example:

```
If PictureBox1.Enabled = False Then Exit Try
```

Chapter 10

Creating Modules and Procedures

After completing this chapter, you will be able to:

- Employ structured programming techniques and create modules containing public variables and procedure definitions.

- Practice using public variables that have a global scope.

- Increase programming efficiency by creating user-defined functions and Sub procedures.

- Master the syntax for calling and using user-defined procedures.

- Pass arguments to procedures by value and by reference.

In the first nine chapters of this book, you have used event procedures such as *Button1_Click*, *Timer1_Tick*, and *Form1_Load* to manage events and organize the flow of your programs. In Visual Basic programming, all executable statements must be placed inside some procedure; only general declarations and instructions to the compiler can be placed outside a procedure's scope. In this chapter, you'll continue to organize your programs according to *structured programming techniques* by developing a hierarchical structure within your application and by breaking computing tasks into discrete logical units.

You'll start by learning how to create *modules*, which are separate areas within a program that contain global, or *public*, variables and Function and Sub procedures. You'll learn how to declare and use public variables, and you'll learn how to build general-purpose procedures that save coding time and can be used in more than one project. The skills you'll learn will be especially applicable to larger programming projects and team development efforts.

Upgrade Notes: Migrating Visual Basic 6 Code to Visual Basic 2005

If you're experienced with Microsoft Visual Basic 6, you'll notice some new features in Microsoft Visual Basic 2005, including the following:

- Earlier versions of Visual Basic distinguished between standard modules and class modules. In Microsoft Visual Studio 2005, the terms are simply *modules* and *classes*.

- Modules are still supported in Visual Basic 2005, but since Microsoft Visual Basic .NET 2002, it has been necessary to wrap the module content with the keywords *Module* and *End Module* in the Code Editor. Public variables are declared in modules as they are in Visual Basic 6.

- Visual Basic 2005 continues to support the *Function* and *Sub* keywords, with which you can create your own procedures. However, the syntax for declaring and calling procedures has changed a little.

- If you're using the default Option Explicit setting to control variable declaration, a specific type declaration is recommended for functions when you declare them. It's also recommended that you specifically declare all types in your procedure argument lists. If you don't assign a type by using the *As* keyword, Visual Basic uses the default *Object* type for the parameter, which is often less efficient than a specific data type.

- Visual Basic .NET 2002 changed the way that arguments are passed to procedures. In Visual Basic 6, the default mechanism for passing arguments is by reference (*ByRef*), meaning that changes to arguments in the procedure are passed back to the calling routine. Beginning with Visual Basic .NET 2002 (and continuing in Visual Basic 2005), the default way to pass arguments is by value (*ByVal*), meaning that changes to arguments within a procedure aren't passed back to the calling routine. You can explicitly specify the behavior for argument passing by using the *ByRef* and *ByVal* keyword in your argument declarations. If necessary, you can specify *ByRef* to achieve the same functionality you have in Visual Basic 6.

- When you call procedures in Visual Basic 2005, parentheses are required around all argument lists. The Visual Studio IDE adds these for you—even if your procedures don't require any arguments. (If no arguments are required, empty parentheses are inserted.)

- Programmers now have the option of using the *Return* statement to send the result of a function calculation back to the calling routine. The older method—assigning a value to the function name—is also supported.

Working with Modules

As you write longer programs, you're likely to have several forms and event procedures that use some of the same variables and routines. By default, variables are *local* to an event procedure—they can be read or changed only within the event procedure in which they were created. You can also declare variables at the top of a form's program code and give the variables a greater scope throughout the form. However, if you create multiple forms in a project, the variables declared at the top of a form are valid only in the form in which they were declared. Likewise, event procedures are by default declared as private and are only local to the form in which they are created. For example, you can't call the *Button1_Click* event procedure from a second form named Form2 if the event procedure is declared to be private to Form1. (You'll learn how to add additional forms to your project in Chapter 14, "Managing Windows Forms and Controls at Run Time.")

To share variables and procedures among all the forms and event procedures in a project, you can declare them in one or more modules included in the project. A module is a special file that has a .vb file name extension and contains variable declarations and procedures that can be used anywhere in the program. (In Visual Basic 6, standard modules have a .bas extension.)

Like forms, modules are listed separately in Solution Explorer and can be saved to disk by using the Save *ModuleName.vb* As command on the File menu. (*ModuleName.vb* will match your project.) Unlike forms, modules contain only code and don't have a user interface. And although modules have some similarities with classes (formerly called class modules), they are unlike classes in that they are not object-oriented, do not define the structure and characteristics of objects, and cannot be inherited. (You'll learn more about creating classes in Chapter 16, "Inheriting Forms and Creating Base Classes.")

Creating a Module

To create a new module in a program, you click the Add New Item button on the Standard toolbar or click the Add New Item command on the Project menu. You can also click the Add Module command on the Project menu.) A dialog box opens, in which you select the Module template and specify the name of the module. A new, blank module then appears in the Code Editor. The first module in a program is named Module1.vb by default, but you can change the name by right-clicking the module in Solution Explorer and typing a new name or by using the Save Module1.vb As command on the File menu. Try creating an empty module in a project now.

Create and save a module

1. Start Visual Studio, and create a new Visual Basic Windows Application project named **My Module Test**.

    The new project is created, and a blank form appears in the Designer.

2. Click the Add New Item command on the Project menu.

    The Add New Item dialog box appears.

3. Select the Module template.

    The default name, Module1.vb, appears in the Name text box.

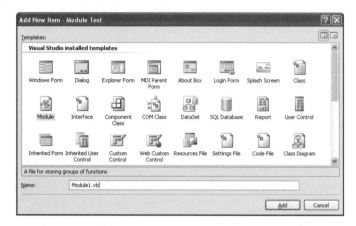

> **Tip**   The Add New Item dialog box offers several templates that you can use in your projects. Each template has different characteristics and includes starter code to help you use them. Visual Studio 2005 includes many new and updated Microsoft Windows forms templates, including Explorer Form, Splash Screen, and Login Form, plus numerous class-related templates. You'll use these templates after you read the introductory material about object-oriented programming in Chapter 16.

4. Click the Add button.

    Visual Basic adds Module1 to your project. The module appears in the Code Editor, as shown here:

The Method Name list box indicates that the general declarations section of the module is open. Variables and procedures declared in this section are available to the entire project. (You'll try declaring variables and procedures later.)

5. Double-click the Solution Explorer title bar to see the entire Solution Explorer window, and then select Module1.vb.

Solution Explorer appears, as shown here:

Solution Explorer lists the module you added to the program in the list of components for the project. The name Module1 identifies the default file name of the module. You'll change this file name in the following steps.

6. Double-click the Properties window title bar to see the window full size.

The Properties window displays the properties for Module1.vb, as shown here:

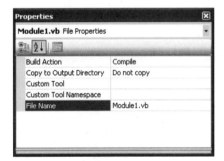

Because a module contains just code, it has only a few properties. By using the most significant property, *File Name*, you can create a custom file name for the module to describe its purpose. Give this identifying label some thought because later you might want to incorporate your module into another solution. The remaining properties for the module are useful for more sophisticated projects—you don't need to worry about them now.

7. Change the *File Name* property to **Math Functions.vb** or another file name that sounds impressive, and then press Enter. (I'm granting you considerable leeway here because this project is simply for testing purposes—you won't actually create math functions or any other "content" for the module, and later you'll discard it.)

   The filename for your module is updated in the Properties window, Solution Explorer, and the Code Editor.

8. Return the Properties window and Solution Explorer to their regular docked positions by double-clicking their title bars.

As you can see, working with modules in a project is a lot like working with forms. In the next exercise, you'll add a public variable to a module.

> **Tip**   To remove a module from a project, click the module in Solution Explorer, and then click the Exclude From Project command on the Project menu. Exclude From Project doesn't delete the module from your hard disk, but it does remove the link between the specified module and the current project. You can reverse the effects of this command by clicking the Add Existing Item command on the File menu, selecting the file that you want to add to the project, and then clicking Open.

Working with Public Variables

Declaring a global, or public, variable in a module is simple—you type the keyword *Public* followed by the variable name and a type declaration. After you declare the variable, you can read it, change it, or display it in any procedure in your program. For example, the program statement

```
Public RunningTotal As Integer
```

declares a public variable named *RunningTotal* of type *Integer*.

The following exercises demonstrate how you can use a public variable named *Wins* in a module. You'll revisit Lucky Seven, the first program you wrote in this book, and you'll use the *Wins* variable to record how many spins you win as the slot machine runs.

> **Note**   Lucky Seven is the slot machine program from Chapter 2, "Writing Your First Program."

Revisit the Lucky Seven project

1. Click the Close Project command on the File menu to close the Module Test project.

Because you haven't saved the project yet, you see the following dialog box:

You don't need to keep this project on your hard disk; it was only for testing purposes. To demonstrate the new "close without saving" feature in Visual Studio 2005, you'll discard the project now.

2. Click the Discard button.

Visual Studio discards the entire project, removing any temporary files associated with the module from your computer's memory and hard disk. It seems like a rather obvious feature, but I wanted to demonstrate that the ability to close a project without saving it is a welcome improvement to the software and just the thing for this type of test. Now you'll open a more substantial project and modify it.

3. Open the TrackWins project in the c:\vb05sbs\chap10\trackwins\lucky7 folder.

The project opens in the IDE.

4. If the form isn't visible, display it now.

You see the following user interface:

The Track Wins project is the same slot machine program that you created in Chapter 2. With this program, the user can click a spin button to display "random" numbers in three number boxes, and if the number 7 appears in one of the boxes, the computer beeps and displays a bitmap showing an enticing, though quite dated, cash payout. I've simply renamed the Lucky7 solution in this chapter so that you won't confuse this new version with the original.

5. Click the Start Debugging button on the Standard toolbar to run the program.

6. Click the Spin button six or seven times, and then click the End button.

    As you might recall, the program uses the *Rnd* function to generate three random numbers each time you click the Spin button. If one of the numbers is a 7, the event procedure for the Spin button (*Button1_Click*) displays a cash payout picture and beeps.

Now you'll edit the form and add a module to enhance the program.

Add a module

1. Click the *Label* control in the Toolbox, and then create a new rectangular label on the form below the Lucky Seven label.

2. Set the properties shown in the following table for the new label. To help identify the new label in the program code, you'll change the new label object's name to lblWins.

Object	Property	Setting
Label5	*Font*	Arial, Bold Italic, 12-point
	ForeColor	Green (on Custom tab)
	Name	lblWins
	Text	"Wins: 0"
	TextAlign	MiddleCenter

When you've finished, your form looks similar to this:

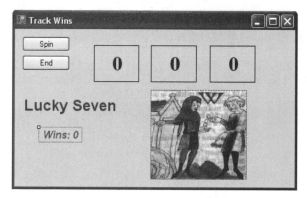

Now you'll add a new module to the project.

3. Click the Add New Item command on the Project menu, select the Module template, and then click Add.

    A module named Module1.vb appears in the Code Editor.

4. Move the insertion point to the blank line between the *Module Module1* and *End Module* statements, type **Public Wins As Short**, and then press Enter.

This program statement declares a public variable of the *Short* integer type in your program. It's identical to a normal variable declaration you might make in your program code, except the *Public* keyword has been substituted for the *Dim* keyword. When your program runs, each event procedure in the program will have access to this variable. Your module looks like this:

5. In Solution Explorer, click TrackWins.vb, click the View Designer button, and then double-click the Spin button.

    The *Button1_Click* event procedure for the Spin button appears in the Code Editor.

6. Type the following statements below the *Beep()* statement in the event procedure:

```
Wins = Wins + 1
lblWins.Text = "Wins. " & Wins
```

This part of the program code increments the *Wins* public variable if a 7 appears during a spin. The second statement uses the concatenation operator (&) to assign a string to the *lblWins* object in the format *Wins: X*, in which *X* is the number of wins. The completed event procedure looks like this:

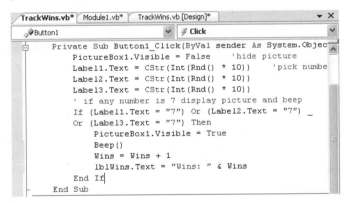

7. Click the Save All button on the Standard toolbar to save all your changes to disk.

    Save All saves your module changes as well as the changes on your form and in your event procedures.

8. Click the Start Debugging button to run the program.

9. Click the Spin button until you have won a few times.

The Wins label keeps track of your jackpots. Each time you win, it increments the total by 1. After 10 spins, I had the output shown below.

> **Note**   The exact number of wins will be different each time you run the program, due to the *Randomize* statement in the *Form1_Load* event procedure.

10.   Click End to exit the program.

The public variable *Wins* was useful in the previous procedure because it maintained its value through several calls to the *Button1_Click* event procedure. If you had declared *Wins* locally in the *Button1_Click* event procedure, the variable would have reset each time, just as the trip odometer in your car does when you reset it. By using a public variable in a module, you can avoid "hitting the reset button."

Public Variables vs. Form Variables

In the preceding exercise, you used a public variable to track the number of wins in the slot machine program. Alternatively, you could have declared the *Wins* variable at the top of the form's program code. Both techniques produce the same result because both a public variable and a variable declared in the general declarations area of a form have scope throughout the entire form. Public variables are unique, however, because they maintain their values in *all* the forms and modules you use in a project—in other words, in all the components that share the same project *namespace*. The project namespace keyword is set automatically when you first save your project. You can view or change the namespace text by selecting the project in Solution Explorer, clicking the TrackWins Properties command on the Project menu, and then examining or changing the text in the Root Namespace text box.

Creating Procedures

Procedures provide a way to group a set of related statements to perform a task. Visual Basic includes two primary types of procedures:

- *Function procedures* are called by name from event procedures or other procedures. Often used for calculations, function procedures can receive arguments and always return a value in the function name.

- *Sub procedures* are called by name from event procedures or other procedures. They can receive arguments and also pass back modified values in an argument list. Unlike functions, however, Sub procedures don't return values associated with their particular Sub procedure names. Sub procedures are typically used to receive or process input, display output, or set properties.

Function procedures and Sub procedures can be defined in a form's program code, but for many users, creating procedures in a module is more useful because then the procedures have scope throughout the entire project. This is especially true for procedures that might be called *general-purpose procedures*—blocks of code that are flexible and useful enough to serve in a variety of programming contexts.

Advantages of General-Purpose Procedures

General-purpose procedures provide the following benefits:

- They enable you to associate an often-used group of program statements with a familiar name.

- They eliminate repeated lines. You can define a procedure once and have your program execute it any number of times.

- They make programs easier to read. A program divided into a collection of small parts is easier to take apart and understand than a program made up of one large part.

- They simplify program development. Programs separated into logical units are easier to design, write, and debug. Plus, if you're writing a program in a group setting, you can exchange procedures and modules instead of entire programs.

- They can be reused in other projects and solutions. You can easily incorporate standard-module procedures into other programming projects.

- They extend the Visual Basic language. Procedures often can perform tasks that can't be accomplished by individual Visual Basic keywords or Microsoft .NET Framework methods.

For example, imagine a program that has three mechanisms for printing a bitmap on different forms: a menu command named Print, a Print toolbar button, and a drag-and-drop printer icon. You could place the same printing statements in each of the three event procedures, or you could handle printing requests from all three sources by using one procedure in a module. General-purpose procedures save you typing time, reduce the possibility of errors, make programs smaller and easier to handle, and make event procedures easier to read.

Writing Function Procedures

A Function procedure is a group of statements located between a *Function* statement and an *End Function* statement. The statements in the function do the meaningful work—typically processing text, handling input, or calculating a numeric value. You execute, or *call*, a function in a program by placing the function name in a program statement along with any required arguments.

Arguments are the data used to make functions work, and they must be included between parentheses and be separated by commas. Basically, using a Function procedure is exactly like using a built-in function or method such as *Int*, *Rnd*, or *FromFile*.

> **Tip**   Functions declared in modules are public by default. As a result, you can use them in any event procedure within the project.

Function Syntax

The basic syntax of a function is as follows:

```
Function FunctionName([arguments]) As Type
    function statements
    [Return value]
End Function
```

The following syntax items are important:

- *FunctionName* is the name of the function you're creating.

- *As Type* is a pair of keywords that specifies the function return type. (In Visual Basic 6, a specific type declaration is optional, but it's strongly recommended in Visual Basic 2005. If you don't provide a type, the return type defaults to Object.)

- *arguments* is a list of optional arguments (separated by commas) to be used in the function. Each argument should also be declared as a specific type. (By default, Visual Basic adds the *ByVal* keyword to each argument, indicating that a copy of the data is passed to the function through this argument but that any changes to the arguments won't be returned to the calling routine.)

- *function statements* is a block of statements that accomplishes the work of the function. The first statements in a function typically declare local variables that will be used in the function, and the remaining statements perform the work of the function.

- *Return* is a newer statement that is not offered in Visual Basic 6—with it, you can indicate when in the function code block you want to return a value to the calling procedure and what that value is. When a *Return* statement is executed, the function is exited, so if there are any function statements after the *Return* statement, these won't be executed. (Alternatively, you can use the Visual Basic 6 syntax and return a value to the calling routine by assigning the value to *FunctionName*.)

- Brackets ([]) enclose optional syntax items. Visual Basic requires those syntax items not enclosed by brackets.

Functions always return a value to the calling procedure in the function's name (*Function-Name*). For this reason, the last statement in a function is often an assignment statement that places the final calculation of the function in *FunctionName*. For example, the Function procedure *TotalTax* computes the state and city taxes for an item and then assigns the result to the *TotalTax* name, as shown here:

```
Function TotalTax(ByVal Cost as Single) As Single
    Dim StateTax, CityTax As Single
    StateTax = Cost * 0.05  'State tax is 5%
    CityTax = Cost * 0.015  'City tax is 1.5%
    TotalTax = StateTax + CityTax
End Function
```

Alternatively, you can use the Visual Basic 2005 syntax and return a value to the calling procedure by using the *Return* statement, as shown in the following function declaration:

```
Function TotalTax(ByVal Cost as Single) As Single
    Dim StateTax, CityTax As Single
    StateTax = Cost * 0.05  'State tax is 5%
    CityTax = Cost * 0.015  'City tax is 1.5%
    Return StateTax + CityTax
End Function
```

I'll use the Return syntax most often in this book, but you can use either mechanism for returning data from a function.

Calling a Function Procedure

To call the *TotalTax* function in an event procedure, you use a statement similar to the following:

```
lblTaxes.Text = TotalTax(500)
```

This statement computes the total taxes required for a $500 item and then assigns the result to the *Text* property of the *lblTaxes* object. The *TotalTax* function can also take a variable as an argument, as shown in the following statements:

```
Dim TotalCost, SalesPrice As Single
SalesPrice = 500
TotalCost = SalesPrice + TotalTax(SalesPrice)
```

The last statement uses the *TotalTax* function to determine the taxes for the number in the *SalesPrice* variable and then adds the computed tax to *SalesPrice* to get the total cost of an item. See how much clearer the code is when a function is used?

Using a Function to Perform a Calculation

In the following exercise, you'll add a function to the Track Wins program to calculate the win rate in the game—in other words, the percentage of spins in which one or more 7s appear. To perform the calculation, you'll add a function named *HitRate* and a public variable named *Spins* to the module. Then you'll call the *HitRate* function every time the Spin button is clicked. You'll display the results in a new label that you'll create on the form.

Create a win rate function

1. Display the form for the Track Wins program that you've been modifying.

   The user interface for the slot machine game appears.

2. Use the *Label* control to create a new label below the Wins label. Set the following properties for the label:

Object	Property	Setting
Label5	Font	Arial, Bold Italic, 12-point
	ForeColor	Red (on Custom tab)
	Name	lblRate
	Text	"0.0%"
	TextAlign	MiddleCenter

Your form looks similar to this:

ZZ =.

. z.-,.=====-=.==.,==.==..-==.===.=.=..====.======..===

3. In Solution Explorer, click the Module1.vb module, and then click the View Code button.

   The Module1 module appears in the Code Editor.

4. Type the following public variable declaration below the `Public Wins As Short` statement:

   ```
   Public Spins As Short
   ```

   The module now includes two public variables, *Wins* and *Spins*, that will be available to all the procedures in the project. You'll use *Spins* as a counter to keep track of the number of spins you make.

5. Insert a blank line in the module, and then type the following function declaration:

   ```
   Function HitRate(ByVal Hits As Short, ByVal Tries As Short) As String
       Dim Percent As Single
       Percent = Hits / Tries
       Return Format(Percent, "0.0%")
   End Function
   ```

   After you type the first line of the function code, Visual Basic automatically adds an *End Function* statement. After you type the remainder of the function's code, your screen looks identical to this:

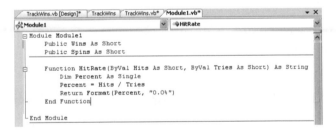

   The *HitRate* function determines the percentage of wins by dividing the *Hits* argument by the *Tries* argument and then adjusts the appearance of the result by using the *Format* function. The *HitRate* function is declared as a string because the *Format* function returns a string value. The *Hits* and the *Tries* arguments are placeholders for the two short integer variables that will be passed to the function during the function call. The *HitRate* function is general-purpose enough to be used with any shorter integer numbers or variables, not only with *Wins* and *Spins*.

6. Display the form again, and then double-click the Spin button on the TrackWins form to bring up the *Button1_Click* event procedure.

7. Below the fourth line of the event procedure (`Label3.Text = CStr(Int(Rnd() * 10))`), type the following statement:

   ```
   Spins = Spins + 1
   ```

This statement increments the *Spins* variable each time the user clicks Spin, and new numbers are placed in the spin windows.

8. Scroll down in the Code Editor, and then, between the *End If* and the *End Sub* statements, type the following statement as the last line in the *Button1_Click* event procedure:

```
lblRate.Text = HitRate(Wins, Spins)
```

As you type the *HitRate* function, notice how Visual Studio automatically displays the names and types of the arguments for the *HitRate* function you just built (a nice touch).

The purpose of this statement is to call the *HitRate* function by using the *Wins* and the *Spins* variables as arguments. The result returned is a percentage in string format, and this value is assigned to the *Text* property of the *lblRate* label on the form after each spin. Now remove the *Randomize* function from the *Form1_Load* event procedure, so that while you test the project, your results will follow a familiar pattern.

9. Scroll down in the Code Editor to the *Form1_Load* event procedure, and remove or "comment out" (place a comment character before) the *Randomize* function.

Now, each time that you run this program, the random numbers generated will follow a predictable pattern. This helps you test your code, but when you're finished testing, you'll want to add the function back again so that your results are truly random.

Now you'll run the program.

Run the Track Wins program

1. Click the Start Debugging button to run the modified Track Wins program.

2. Click the Spin button 10 times.

The first five times you click Spin, the win rate stays at 100.0%. You're hitting the jackpot every time. As you continue to click, however, the win rate adjusts to 83.3%, 71.4%, 75.0% (another win), 66.7%, and 60.0% (a total of 6 for 10). After 10 spins, your screen looks like this:

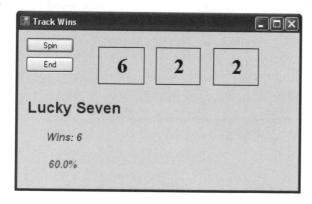

If you continue to spin, you'll notice that the win rate drops to about 28%. The *HitRate* function shows that you were really pretty lucky when you started spinning, but after a while reality sets in.

3. When you're finished with the program, click the End button.

    The program stops, and the development environment returns. You can add the *Randomize* function to the *Form1_Load* event procedure again to see how the program works with "true" randomness. After about 100 spins (enough iterations for statistical variation to even out a little), you should be close to the 28% win-rate each time that you run the program. If you like numbers, it is an interesting experiment.

4. Click the Save All button on the Standard toolbar to save your changes.

Writing Sub Procedures

A Sub procedure is similar to a Function procedure, except that a Sub procedure doesn't return a value associated with its name. Sub procedures are typically used to get input from the user, display or print information, or manipulate several properties associated with a condition. Sub procedures can also be used to process and update variables received in an argument list during a procedure call, and pass back one or more of these values to the calling program.

Sub Procedure Syntax

The basic syntax for a Sub procedure is

```
Sub ProcedureName([arguments])
    procedure statements
End Sub
```

The following syntax items are important:

- *ProcedureName* is the name of the Sub procedure you're creating.

- *arguments* is a list of optional arguments (separated by commas if there's more than one) to be used in the Sub procedure. Each argument should also be declared as a specific type. (Visual Studio adds the *ByVal* keyword by default to each argument, indicating that a copy of the data is passed to the function through this argument but that any changes to the arguments won't be returned to the calling routine.)

- *procedure statements* is a block of statements that accomplishes the work of the procedure.

In the Sub procedure call, the number and type of arguments sent to the procedure must match the number and type of arguments in the Sub procedure declaration, and the entire group must be enclosed in parentheses. If variables passed to a Sub procedure are modified during the procedure, the updated variables aren't passed back to the program unless the procedure defined the arguments by using the *ByRef* keyword. Sub procedures declared in a module are public by default, so they can be called by any event procedure in a project.

> **Important** In Visual Basic 2005, all calls to a Sub procedure must include parentheses after the procedure name. A set of empty parentheses is required if there are no arguments being passed to the procedure. This is a change from Visual Basic 6, where parentheses are required only when an argument is being passed by value to a Sub procedure. You'll learn more about passing variables by reference and by value later in this chapter.

For example, the following Sub procedure receives a string argument representing a person's name and uses a text box to wish that person happy birthday. If this Sub procedure is declared in a module, it can be called from any event procedure in the program.

```
Sub BirthdayGreeting (ByVal Person As String)
    Dim Msg As String
    If Person <> "" Then
        Msg = "Happy birthday " & Person & "!"
    Else
        Msg = "Name not specified."
    End If
    MsgBox(Msg, , "Best Wishes")
End Sub
```

The *BirthdayGreeting* procedure receives the name to be greeted by using the *Person* argument, a string variable received by value during the procedure call. If the value of *Person* isn't empty, or *null*, the specified name is used to build a message string that will be displayed with a *MsgBox* function. If the argument is null, the procedure displays the message "Name not specified."

Calling a Sub Procedure

To call a Sub procedure in a program, you specify the name of the procedure, and then list the arguments required by the Sub procedure. For example, to call the *BirthdayGreeting* procedure, you could type the following statement:

```
BirthdayGreeting("Robert")
```

In this example, the *BirthdayGreeting* procedure would insert the name "Robert" into a message string, and the routine would display the following message box:

The space-saving advantages of a procedure become clear when you call the procedure many times using a variable, as shown in the example below:

```
Dim NewName As String
Do
    NewName = InputBox("Enter a name for greeting.", "Birthday List")
    BirthdayGreeting(NewName)
Loop Until NewName = ""
```

Here the user can enter as many names for birthday greetings as he or she likes. The next exercise gives you a chance to practice using a Sub procedure to handle another type of input in a program.

Using a Sub Procedure to Manage Input

Sub procedures are often used to handle input in a program when information comes from two or more sources and needs to be in the same format. In the following exercise, you'll create a Sub procedure named *AddName* that prompts the user for input and formats the text so that it can be displayed on multiple lines in a text box. The procedure will save you programming time because you'll use it in two event procedures, each associated with a different text box. Because the procedure will be declared in a module, you'll need to type it in only one place. If you add additional forms to the project, the procedure will be available to them as well.

Create a text box Sub procedure

1. On the File menu, click the Close Project command.

    Visual Studio closes the current project (the Track Wins slot machine).

2. Create a new project named **My Text Box Sub**.

    The new project is created, and a blank form appears in the Designer.

3. Use the *TextBox* control to create two text boxes, side by side, in the middle of the form.

    Today you'll make some personnel decisions, and you'll use these text boxes to hold the names of employees you'll be assigning to two departments.

4. Use the *Label* control to create two labels above the text boxes.

    These labels will hold the names of the departments.

5. Use the *Button* control to create three buttons: one under each text box and one at the bottom of the form.

    You'll use the first two buttons to assign employees to their departments and the last button to quit the program.

6. Set the properties shown in the following table for the objects on the form.

    Because the text boxes will contain more than one line, you'll set their *Multiline* properties to True and their *ScrollBars* properties to Vertical. These settings are typically used when multiple lines are displayed in text boxes. You'll also set their *TabStop* properties to False and their *ReadOnly* properties to True so that the information can't be modified.

Object	Property	Setting
TextBox1	Multiline	True
	Name	txtSales
	ReadOnly	True
	ScrollBars	Vertical
	TabStop	False
TextBox2	Multiline	True
	Name	txtMkt
	ReadOnly	True
	ScrollBars	Vertical
	TabStop	False
Label1	Font	Bold
	Name	lblSales
	Text	"Sales"
Label2	Font	Bold
	Name	lblMkt
	Text	"Marketing"
Button1	Name	btnSales
	Text	"Add Name"
Button2	Name	btnMkt
	Text	"Add Name"
Button3	Name	btnQuit
	Text	"Quit"
Form1	Text	"Assign Department Teams"

7. Resize and position the objects so that your form looks similar to this:

Now you'll add a module and create the general-purpose *AddName* Sub procedure.

8. On the Project menu, click the Add New Item command, select the Module template, and then click Add.

A new module appears in the Code Editor.

9. Type the following *AddName* procedure between the *Module Module1* and *End Module* statements:

```
Sub AddName(ByVal Team As String, ByRef ReturnString As String)
    Dim Prompt, Nm, WrapCharacter As String
    Prompt = "Enter a " & Team & " employee."
    Nm = InputBox(Prompt, "Input Box")
    WrapCharacter = Chr(13) + Chr(10)
    ReturnString = Nm & WrapCharacter
End Sub
```

This general-purpose Sub procedure uses the *InputBox* function to prompt the user for an employee name. It receives two arguments during the procedure call: *Team*, a string containing the department name; and *ReturnString*, an empty string variable that will contain the formatted employee name. *ReturnString* is declared with the *ByRef* keyword so that any changes made to this argument in the procedure will be passed back to the calling routine through the argument.

Before the employee name is returned, carriage return and linefeed characters are appended to the string so that each name in the text box will appear on its own line. You can use this general technique in any string to create a new line.

Your Code Editor looks like this:

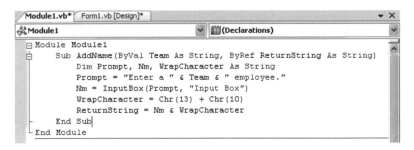

10. Display the form again, and then double-click the first Add Name button on the form (the button below the Sales text box). Type the following statements in the *btnSales_Click* event procedure:

```
Dim SalesPosition As String = ""
AddName("Sales", SalesPosition)
txtSales.Text = txtSales.Text & SalesPosition
```

The call to the *AddName* Sub procedure includes one argument passed by value (*"Sales"*) and one argument passed by reference (*SalesPosition*). The last line uses the argument passed by reference to add text to the *txtSales* text box. The concatenation operator (&) adds the new name to the end of the text in the text box.

11. In the Code Editor, click the Class Name arrow, and click the *btnMkt* object in the list. Then click the Method Name arrow, and click the Click event.

   The *btnMkt_Click* event procedure appears in the Code Editor.

12. Type the following statements in the event procedure:

```
Dim MktPosition As String = ""
AddName("Marketing", MktPosition)
txtMkt.Text = txtMkt.Text & MktPosition
```

   This event procedure is identical to *btnSales_Click*, except that it sends "*Marketing*" to the *AddName* procedure and updates the *txtMkt* text box. (The name of the local return variable *MktPosition* was renamed to make it more intuitive.)

13. Click the Class Name arrow, and click the *btnQuit* object in the list. Then click the Method Name arrow, and click the Click event.

   The *btnQuit_Click* event procedure appears in the Code Editor.

14. Type **End** in the *btnQuit_Click* event procedure.

15. Click the Save All button on the Standard toolbar, and then specify the c:\vb05sbs\chap10 folder as the location.

That's it! Now you'll run the Text Box Sub program.

Run the Text Box Sub program

> **Tip** The complete Text Box Sub program is located in the c:\vb05sbs\chap10\text box sub folder.

1. Click the Start Debugging button on the Standard toolbar to run the program.

2. Click the Add Name button under the Sales text box, and then type **Maria Palermo** in the input box. (Feel free to type a different name.)

   Your input box looks like this:

3. Click the OK button to add the name to the Sales text box.

    The name appears in the first text box.

4. Click the Add Name button under the Marketing text box, type **Abraham Asante** in the Marketing input box, and then press Enter.

    The name appears in the Marketing text box. Your screen looks like this:

5. Enter a few more names in each of the text boxes. This is your chance to create your own dream departments.

    Each name appears on its own line in the text boxes. The text boxes don't scroll automatically, so you won't see every name you've entered if you enter more names than can fit in a text box. You can use the scroll bars to access names that aren't visible.

6. When you've finished, click the Quit button to stop the program.

You've demonstrated that one Sub procedure can manage input tasks from two or more event procedures. Using this basic concept as a starting point, you can now create more sophisticated programs that use Sub and Function procedures as organizing tools and that place common tasks in logical units that can be called over and over again.

One Step Further: Passing Arguments by Value and by Reference

In the discussion of Sub and Function procedures, you learned that arguments are passed to procedures by value or by reference. Using the *ByVal* keyword indicates that variables should be passed to a procedure by value (the default). Any changes made to a variable passed in by value aren't passed back to the calling procedure. However, as you learned in the Text Box Sub program, using the *ByRef* keyword indicates that variables should be passed to a procedure by reference, meaning that any changes made to the variable in the procedure are passed back to the calling routine. Passing by reference can have significant advantages, as long as you're careful not to change a variable unintentionally in a procedure. For example, consider the following Sub procedure declaration and call:

```
Sub CostPlusInterest(ByRef Cost As Single, ByRef Total As Single)
    Cost = Cost * 1.05   'add 5% to cost...
    Total = Int(Cost)    'then make integer and return
End Sub
.
.
.
Dim Price, TotalPrice As Single
Price = 100
TotalPrice = 0
CostPlusInterest(Price, TotalPrice)
MsgBox(Price & " at 5% interest is " & TotalPrice)
```

In this example, the programmer passes two single-precision variables by reference to the *CostPlusInterest* procedure: *Price* and *TotalPrice*. The programmer plans to use the updated *TotalPrice* variable in the subsequent *MsgBox* call but has unfortunately forgotten that the *Price* variable was also updated in an intermediate step in the *CostPlusInterest* procedure. (Because *Price* was passed by reference, changes to *Cost* automatically result in the same changes to *Price*.) This produces the following erroneous result when the program is run:

However, the programmer probably wanted to show the following message:

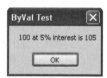

So how should the *CostPlusInterest* procedure be fixed to produce the desired result? The easiest way is to declare the *Cost* argument by using the *ByVal* keyword, as shown in the following program statement:

```
Sub CostPlusInterest(ByVal Cost As Single, ByRef Total As Single)
```

By declaring *Cost* using *ByVal*, you can safely modify *Cost* in the *CostPlusInterest* procedure without sending the changes back to the calling procedure. By keeping *Total* declared using *ByRef*, you can modify the variable that's being passed, and only those changes will be passed back to the calling procedure. In general, if you use *ByRef* only when it's needed, your programs will be freer of defects.

Here are some guidelines on when to use *ByVal* and when to use *ByRef*:

- Use *ByVal* when you don't want a procedure to modify a variable that's passed to the procedure through an argument.

- Use *ByRef* when you want to allow a procedure to modify a variable that's passed to the procedure.

- When in doubt, use the *ByVal* keyword.

Chapter 10 Quick Reference

To	Do this
Create a new module	Click the Add New Item button on the Standard toolbar, and then select the Module template. *or* Click the Add New Item command on the Project menu, and then select the Module template.
Save a module with a new name	Select the module in Solution Explorer, click the Save *Module1.vb* As command on the File menu, and then specify a new name.
Remove a module from a program	Select the module in Solution Explorer, and then click the Exclude From Project command on the Project menu.
Add an existing module to a project	On the Project menu, click the Add Existing Item command.
Create a public variable	Declare the variable by using the *Public* keyword between the *Module* and *End Module* keywords in a module. For example: `Public TotalSales As Integer`

Create a public function	Place the function statements between the *Function* and *End Function* keywords in a module. Functions are public by default. For example:
	
	`Function HitRate(ByVal Hits As Short, ByVal _`
	`   Tries As Short) As String`
	`      Dim Percent As Single`
	`      Percent = Hits / Tries`
	`      Return Format(Percent, "0.0%")`
	`End Function`

Call a Function procedure	Type the function name and any necessary arguments in a program statement, and assign it to a variable or property of the appropriate return type. For example: `lblRate.Text = HitRate(Wins, Spins)`

To	Do this
| Create a public Sub procedure | Place the procedure statements between the *Sub* and *End Sub* keywords in a module. Sub procedures are public by default. For example:<br><br>```
Sub CostPlusInterest(ByVal Cost As Single, _
  ByRef Total As Single)
    Cost = Cost * 1.05
    Total = Int(Cost)
End Sub
``` |
| Call a Sub procedure | Type the procedure name and any necessary arguments in a program statement. For example:<br><br>```
CostPlusInterest(Price, TotalPrice)
``` |
| Pass an argument by value | Use the *ByVal* keyword in the procedure declaration. For example:<br><br>```
Sub GreetPerson(ByVal Name As String)
``` |
| Pass an argument by reference | Use the *ByRef* keyword in the procedure declaration. For example:<br><br>```
Sub GreetPerson(ByRef Name As String)
``` |

Chapter 11

Using Arrays to Manage Numeric and String Data

After completing this chapter, you will be able to:

- Organize information in fixed-size and dynamic arrays.

- Use arrays in your code to manage large amounts of data.

- Preserve array data when you redimension arrays.

- Use the *Sort* and *Reverse* methods in the *Array* class to reorder arrays.

- Use the *ProgressBar* control in your programs to show how long a task is taking.

Managing information in a Microsoft Visual Basic application is an important task, and as your programs become more substantial, you'll need additional tools to store and process data. Of course, storing information in a database is the most comprehensive approach to data management in a program, and you'll start learning how to integrate Visual Basic programs with databases in Chapter 18, "Database and Web Programming." Another classic approach to data management in programs is to store and retrieve information in auxiliary text files, as you'll see in Chapter 13, "Exploring Text Files and String Processing."

In this chapter, you'll learn how to organize variables and other information into useful containers called *arrays*. You'll learn how to streamline data-management tasks with fixed-size and dynamic arrays, and how to use arrays in your code to manage large amounts of data. You'll learn how to redimension arrays and preserve the data in arrays when you decide to change an array's size. To demonstrate how large arrays can be processed, you'll use the *Sort* and *Reverse* methods in the Microsoft .NET Framework *Array* class to reorder an array containing random six-digit integer values. Finally, you'll learn to use the *ProgressBar* control to give your users an indication of how long a process (array-related or otherwise) is taking. The techniques you'll learn provide a solid introduction to the database programming techniques that you'll explore later in the book.

Upgrade Notes: Migrating Visual Basic 6 Code to Visual Basic 2005

If you're experienced with Microsoft Visual Basic 6, you'll notice some new features in Microsoft Visual Basic 2005, including the following:

- Arrays in Visual Basic 2005 are always zero-based, as they were in Microsoft Visual Studio .NET 2002 and 2003, meaning that the lowest array element is always 0. In Visual Basic 6, programmers can use the *Option Base* statement, which is no longer supported, to set the base of arrays to either 0 or 1.

- An obvious side effect of zero-bound arrays is that the *LBound* statement always returns a value of 0 because the lower bound for an array is always 0. (The *UBound* statement, however, continues to return the highest index in an array, which is the number of elements minus 1.)

- Arrays can now be declared and assigned data by using the same program statement. For example, the syntax to declare an array named *myList()* and add four elements to it is

```
Dim myList() as Integer = {5, 10, 15, 20}
```

- The *ReDim* statement is still valid in Visual Basic 2005, although you can't use the *ReDim* statement for an initial array declaration. Visual Basic 6 and Visual Basic 2005 also have something in common in regards to *ReDim*: You can use this statement to change the bounds of an array, but not the number of dimensions.

Working with Arrays of Variables

In this section, you'll learn about arrays, a useful method for storing almost any amount of data during program execution. Arrays are a powerful and time-tested mechanism for storing logically related values in a program. The developers of BASIC, Pascal, C, and other popular programming languages incorporated arrays into the earliest versions of these products to refer to a group of values by using one name and to process those values individually or collectively.

Arrays can help you track a small set of values in ways that are impractical using traditional variables. For example, imagine creating a nine-inning baseball scoreboard in a program. To save and recall the scores for each inning of the game, you might be tempted to create two groups of nine variables (a total of 18 variables) in the program. You'd probably name them something like *Inning1HomeTeam*, *Inning1VisitingTeam*, and so on, to keep them straight. Working with these variables individually would take considerable time and space in your program. Fortunately, with Visual Basic you can organize groups of similar variables into an array that has one common name and an easy-to-use index. For example, you can create a two-dimensional (2-by-9) array named *Scoreboard* to contain the scores for the baseball game. Let's see how this works.

Creating an Array

You create, or *declare*, arrays in program code just as you declare simple variables. As usual, the place in which you declare the array determines where it can be used, or its *scope*, as follows:

- If an array is declared locally in a procedure, it can be used only in that procedure.
- If an array is declared at the top of a form, it can be used throughout the form.
- If an array is declared publicly in a module, it can be used anywhere in the project.

When you declare an array, you typically include the information shown in the following table in your declaration statement.

Information in an array declaration statement	Description
Array name	The name you'll use to represent your array in the program. In general, array names follow the same rules as variable names. (See Chapter 5, "Visual Basic Variables and Formulas, and the .NET Framework," for more information about variables.)
Data type	The type of data you'll store in the array. In most cases, all the variables in an array are the same type. You can specify one of the fundamental data types, or if you're not yet sure which type of data will be stored in the array or whether you'll store more than one type, you can specify the *Object* type.
Number of dimensions	The number of dimensions your array will contain. Most arrays are one-dimensional (a list of values) or two-dimensional (a table of values), but you can specify additional dimensions if you're working with a complex mathematical model, such as a three-dimensional shape.
Number of elements	The number of elements your array will contain. The elements in your array correspond directly to the array index. In Visual Basic 2005, the first array index is always 0 (zero).

> **Tip** Arrays that contain a set number of elements are called *fixed-size arrays*. Arrays that contain a variable number of elements (arrays that can expand during the execution of the program) are called *dynamic arrays*.

Declaring a Fixed-Size Array

The basic syntax for a public fixed-size array is

```
Dim ArrayName(Dim1Index, Dim2Index, ...) As DataType
```

The following arguments are important:

- *Dim* is the keyword that declares the array. Use *Public* instead if you place the array in a module.

- *ArrayName* is the variable name of the array.

- *Dim1Index* is the upper bound of the first dimension of the array, which is the number of elements minus 1.

- *Dim2Index* is the upper bound of the second dimension of the array, which is the number of elements minus 1. (Additional dimensions can be included if they're separated by commas.)

- *DataType* is a keyword corresponding to the type of data that will be included in the array.

For example, to declare a one-dimensional string array named *Employees* that has room for 10 employee names (numbered 0 through 9), you can type the following in an event procedure:

```
Dim Employees(9) As String
```

In a module, the same array declaration looks like this:

```
Public Employees(9) As String
```

Using new syntax supported by Visual Basic 2005 (but not Microsoft Visual Basic .NET 2002 or 2003), you can also explicitly specify the zero lower bound of the array with the following code in an event procedure:

```
Dim Employees(0 To 9) As String
```

This "0 to 9" syntax is included to make your code more readable—newcomers to your program will understand immediately that the *Employees* array has 10 elements numbered 0 through 9. However, the lower bound of the array must always be zero. You cannot use this syntax to create a different lower bound for the array.

Setting Aside Memory

When you create an array, Visual Basic sets aside room for it in memory. The following illustration shows conceptually how the 10-element *Employees* array is organized. The elements are numbered 0 through 9 rather than 1 through 10 because array indexes always start with 0. (Again, the *Option Base* statement in Visual Basic 6, which allows you to index arrays beginning with the number 1, is no longer supported.)

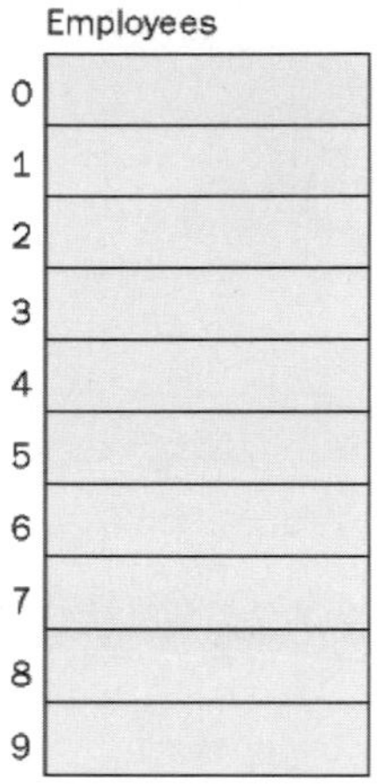

Employees

```
0 │                    │
1 │                    │
2 │                    │
3 │                    │
4 │                    │
5 │                    │
6 │                    │
7 │                    │
8 │                    │
9 │                    │
```

To declare a public two-dimensional array named *Scoreboard* that has room for two rows and nine columns of *Short* integer data, you can type this statement in an event procedure or at the top of the form:

```
Dim Scoreboard(1, 8) As Short
```

Using the new Visual Basic 2005 syntax that emphasizes the lower (zero) bound, you can also declare the array as follows:

```
Dim Scoreboard(0 To 1, 0 To 8) As Short
```

After you declare such a two-dimensional array and Visual Basic sets aside room for it in memory, you can use the array in your program as if it were a table of values, as shown in the following illustration. (In this case, the array elements are numbered 0 through 1 and 0 through 8.)

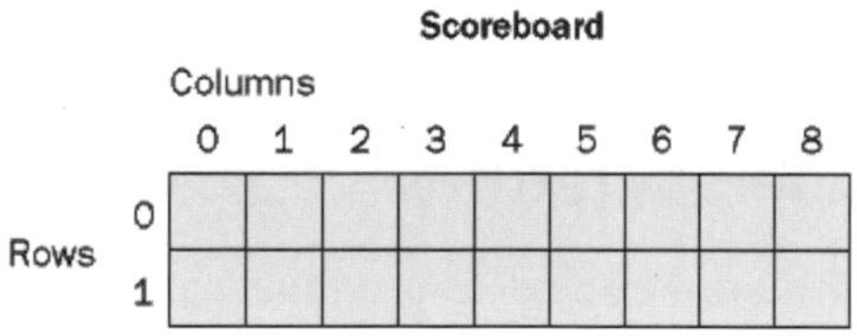

Scoreboard

```
       Columns
       0  1  2  3  4  5  6  7  8
     0 │  │  │  │  │  │  │  │  │  │
Rows
     1 │  │  │  │  │  │  │  │  │  │
```

Working with Array Elements

To refer to an element of an array, you use the array name and an array index enclosed in parentheses. The index must be an integer or an expression that results in an integer. For example, the index could be a number such as 5, an integer variable such as *num*, or an expression such as "num-1". (The counter variable of a For...Next loop is often used.) For example, the following statement assigns the value "Leslie" to the element with an index of 5 in the *Employees* array example in the previous section:

```
Employees(5) = "Leslie"
```

This statement produces the following result in our *Employees* array:

Employees

0	
1	
2	
3	
4	
5	Leslie
6	
7	
8	
9	

Similarly, the following statement assigns the number 4 to row 0, column 2 (the top of the third inning) in the *Scoreboard* array example in the previous section:

```
Scoreboard(0, 2) = 4
```

This statement produces the following result in our *Scoreboard* array:

Scoreboard

	Columns								
	0	1	2	3	4	5	6	7	8
Rows 0			4						
1									

You can use these indexing techniques to assign or retrieve any array element.

Creating a Fixed-Size Array to Hold Temperatures

The following exercise uses a one-dimensional array named *Temperatures* to record the daily high temperatures for a seven-day week. The program demonstrates how you can use an array to store and process a group of related values on a form. The *Temperatures* array variable is declared at the top of the form, and then temperatures are assigned to the array by using an *InputBox* function and a For...Next loop, which you learned about in Chapter 7, "Using Loops and Timers." The loop counter is used to reference each element in the array. The array contents are then displayed on the form by using a For...Next loop and a text box object. The average high temperature is also calculated and displayed.

The *LBound* and *UBound* Functions

To simplify working with the array, the Fixed Array program uses the *UBound* function to check for the upper bound, or top index value, of the array. *UBound* is an earlier Visual Basic keyword that's still quite useful. With it you can process arrays without referring to the declaration statements that defined exactly how many values the array would hold. The closely related *LBound* function, which confirms the lower bound of an array, is still valid in Visual Basic, but because all Visual Basic arrays now have a lower bound of zero (0), the function simply returns a value of 0. The *UBound* and *LBound* functions have the syntax

```
LBound(ArrayName)
UBound(ArrayName)
```

where *ArrayName* is the name of an array that's been declared in the project.

Use a fixed-size array

1. Start Microsoft Visual Studio, and create a new Visual Basic Windows Application project named **My Fixed Array**.

2. Draw a text box object on the form.

3. Set the *Multiline* property of the *TextBox1* object to True so that you can resize the object.

4. Resize the text box object so that it fills up most of the form.

5. Draw two wide button objects on the form below the text box object, oriented one beside the other.

6. Set the following properties for the form and its objects:

Object	Property	Setting
TextBox1	ScrollBars	Vertical
Button1	Text	"Enter Temps"
Button2	Text	"Display Temps"
Form1	Text	"Fixed Array Temps"

Your form looks like the one shown on the next page.

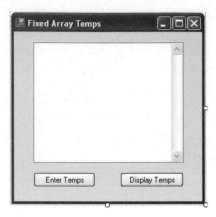

7. In Solution Explorer, click the View Code button to display the Code Editor.

8. Scroll to the top of the form's program code, and directly below the `Public Class Form1` statement, type the following array declaration:

```
Dim Temperatures(0 To 6) As Single
```

This statement creates an array named *Temperatures* (of the type *Single*) that contains seven elements numbered 0 through 6. Because the array has been declared at the top of the form, it is available in all the event procedures in the form.

9. Display the form again, and then double-click the Enter Temps button (*Button1*).

The *Button1_Click* event procedure appears in the Code Editor.

10. Type the following program statements to prompt the user for temperatures and to load the input into the array:

```
Dim Prompt, Title As String
Dim i As Short
Prompt = "Enter the day's high temperature."
For i = 0 To UBound(Temperatures)
    Title = "Day " & (i + 1)
    Temperatures(i) = InputBox(Prompt, Title)
Next
```

The For...Next loop uses the short integer counter variable *i* as an array index to load temperatures into array elements 0 through 6. Rather than using the simplified For loop syntax

```
For i = 0 to 6
```

to process the array, I chose a slightly more complex syntax involving the *UBound* function for future flexibility. The For loop construction

```
For i = 0 To UBound(Temperatures)
```

determines the upper bound of the array by using the *UBound* statement. This technique is more flexible because if the array is expanded or reduced later, the For loop automatically adjusts itself to the new array size.

To fill the array with temperatures, the event procedure uses an *InputBox* function, which displays the current day by using the For loop counter.

11. Display the form again, and then double-click the Display Temps button (*Button2*).

12. Type the following statements in the *Button2_Click* event procedure:

```
Dim Result As String
Dim i As Short
Dim Total As Single = 0
Result = "High temperatures for the week:" & vbCrLf & vbCrLf
For i = 0 To UBound(Temperatures)
    Result = Result & "Day " & (i + 1) & vbTab & _
      Temperatures(i) & vbCrLf
    Total = Total + Temperatures(i)
Next
Result = Result & vbCrLf & _
  "Average temperature:  " & Format(Total / 7, "0.0")
TextBox1.Text = Result
```

This event procedure uses a For...Next loop to cycle through the elements in the array, and it adds each element in the array to a string variable named *Result*, which is declared at the top of the event procedure. I've used several literal strings, constants, and string concatenation operators (&) to pad and format the string by using carriage returns (*vbCrLf*), tab characters (*vbTab*), and headings. The *vbCrLf* constant, used here for the first time, contains the carriage return and linefeed characters and is an efficient way to create new lines. The *vbTab* constant is also used here for the first time to put some distance between the day and temperature values in the *Result* string. At the end of the event procedure, an average for the temperatures is determined, and the final string is assigned to the *Text* property of the text box object, as shown in this statement:

```
TextBox1.Text = Result
```

13. Click the Save All button on the Standard toolbar to save the project. Specify the c:\vb05sbs\chap11 folder as the location.

Now you'll run the program.

> **Tip**   The complete Fixed Array program is located in the c:\vb05sbs\chap11\fixed array folder.

14. Click the Start Debugging button on the Standard toolbar to run the program.

15. Click the Enter Temps button, and when prompted by the *InputBox* function, enter seven different temperatures. (How about using the temperatures from your last vacation?)

The *InputBox* function dialog box looks like this:

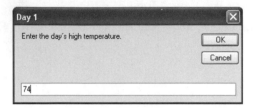

16. After you've entered the temperatures, click the Display Temps button.

Using the array, Visual Basic displays each of the temperatures in the text box and prints an average at the bottom. Your screen looks similar to this:

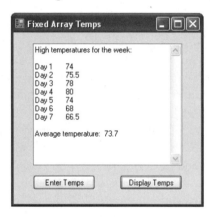

17. Click the Close button on the form to end the program.

Creating a Dynamic Array

As you can see, arrays are quite handy for working with lists of numbers, especially if you process them by using For...Next loops. But what if you're not sure how much array space you'll need before you run your program? For example, what if you want to let the user choose how many temperatures are entered into the Fixed Array program?

Visual Basic handles this problem efficiently with a special elastic container called a *dynamic array*. Dynamic arrays are dimensioned at run time, either when the user specifies the size of the array or when logic you add to the program determines an array size based on specific conditions. Dimensioning a dynamic array takes several steps because although the size of the array isn't specified until the program is running, you need to make "reservations" for the array at design time. To create a dynamic array, you follow these basic steps:

■ Specify the name and type of the array in the program at design time, omitting the number of elements in the array. For example, to create a dynamic array named *Temperatures*, you type

```
Dim Temperatures() As Single
```

■ Add code to determine the number of elements that should be in the array at run time. You can prompt the user by using an *InputBox* function or a text box object, or you can calculate the storage needs of the program by using properties or other logic. For example, the following statements get the array size from the user and assign it to the *Days* variable of type *Short*:

```
Dim Days As Short
Days = InputBox("How many days?", "Create Array")
```

■ Use the variable in a *ReDim* statement to dimension the array, subtracting 1 because arrays are zero-based. For example, the following statement sets the size of the *Temperatures* array at run time by using the *Days* variable:

```
ReDim Temperatures(Days - 1)
```

> **Important**   With *ReDim*, you should not try to change the number of dimensions in an array that you've previously declared.

■ Use the *UBound* function to determine the upper bound in a For...Next loop, and process the array elements as necessary, as shown here:

```
For i = 0 to UBound(Temperatures)
    Temperatures(i) = InputBox(Prompt, Title)
Next
```

In the following exercise, you'll use these steps to revise the Fixed Array program so that it can process any number of temperatures by using a dynamic array.

Use a dynamic array to hold temperatures

1. Open the Code Editor to display the program code for the Fixed Array project.

2. Scroll to the top of the form's code, in which you originally declared the *Temperatures* fixed array.

3. Remove 0 To 6 from the *Temperatures* array declaration so that the array is now a dynamic array.

   The statement looks like the following:

```
Dim Temperatures() As Single
```

4. Add the following variable declaration just below the *Temperatures* array declaration:

```
Dim Days As Integer
```

The integer variable *Days* will be used to receive input from the user and to dimension the dynamic array at run time.

5. Scroll down in the Code Editor to display the *Button1_Click* event procedure, and modify the code so that it looks like the following. (The changed or added elements appear in bold italic.)

```
Dim Prompt, Title As String
Dim i As Short
Prompt = "Enter the day's high temperature."
Days = InputBox("How many days?", "Create Array")
If Days > 0 Then ReDim Temperatures(Days - 1)
For i = 0 To UBound(Temperatures)
    Title = "Day " & (i + 1)
    Temperatures(i) = InputBox(Prompt, Title)
Next
```

The fourth and fifth lines prompt the user for the number of temperatures he or she wants to save, and then the user's input is used to dimension a dynamic array. The If...Then decision structure is used to verify that the number of days is greater than 0. (Dimensioning an array with a number less than 0 or equal to zero generates an error.) Because index 0 of the array is used to store the temperature for the first day, the *Days* variable is decremented by 1 when dimensioning the array. The *Days* variable isn't needed to determine the upper bound of the For...Next loop—as in the previous example, the *UBound* function is used instead.

6. Scroll down in the Code Editor to display the *Button2_Click* event procedure. Modify the code so that it looks like the following routine. (The changed elements appear in bold italic.)

```
Dim Result As String
Dim i As Short
Dim Total As Single = 0
Result = "High temperatures:" & vbCrLf & vbCrLf
For i = 0 To UBound(Temperatures)
    Result = Result & "Day " & (i + 1) & vbTab & _
      Temperatures(i) & vbCrLf
    Total = Total + Temperatures(i)
Next
Result = Result & vbCrLf & _
  "Average temperature:  " & Format(Total / Days, "0.0")
TextBox1.Text = Result
```

The *Days* variable replaces the number 7 in the average temperature calculation at the bottom of the event procedure. I also edited the "High temperatures" heading that will be displayed in the text box.

7. Change the *Form1.Text* property to Dynamic Array.

8. Save your changes to disk.

> **Tip**   On the companion CD-ROM, I gave this project a separate name to keep it distinct from the Fixed Array project. The complete Dynamic Array project is located in the c:\vb05sbs\chap11\dynamic array folder.

9. Click the Start Debugging button to run the program.

10. Click the Enter Temps button.

11. Type **5** when you're prompted for the number of days you want to record, and then click OK.

12. Enter five temperatures when prompted.

13. When you've finished entering temperatures, click the Display Temps button.

    The program displays the five temperatures on the form along with their average. Your screen looks similar to this:

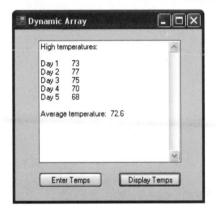

14. Click the Close button on the form to end the program.

You've practiced using the two most common array types in Visual Basic programming. When you write your own programs, you'll soon use much larger arrays, but the concepts are the same, and you'll be amazed at how fast Visual Basic can complete array-related computations.

Preserving Array Contents by Using *ReDim Preserve*

In the previous exercise, you used the *ReDim* statement to specify the size of a dynamic array at run time. However, one potential shortcoming associated with the *ReDim* statement is that if you redimension an array that already has data in it, all the existing data is irretrievably lost. After the *ReDim* statement is executed, the contents of a dynamic array are set to their default value, such as zero or *null*. Depending on your outlook, this can be considered a useful feature for emptying the contents of arrays, or it can be an irksome feature that requires a workaround.

Fortunately, Visual Basic 2005 provides the same useful feature that Visual Basic 6 provides for array redimensioning, the *Preserve* keyword, which you use to preserve the data in an array when you change its dimensions. The syntax for the *Preserve* keyword is as follows:

```
ReDim Preserve ArrayName(Dim1Elements, Dim2Elements, ...)
```

In such a *ReDim* statement, the array must continue to have the same number of dimensions and contain the same type of data. In addition, there's a caveat that you can resize only the last array dimension. For example, if your array has two or more dimensions, you can change the size of only the last dimension and still preserve the contents of the array. (Single-dimension arrays automatically pass this test, so you can freely expand the size of dynamic arrays by using the *Preserve* keyword.)

The following examples show how you can use *Preserve* to increase the size of the last dimension in a dynamic array without erasing any existing data contained in the array.

If you originally declared a dynamic string array named *Philosophers* by using the syntax

```
Dim Philosophers() As String
```

you can redimension the array and add data to it by using code similar to the following:

```
ReDim Philosophers(200)
Philosophers(200) = "Steve Harrison"
```

You can expand the size of the *Philosophers* array to 301 elements (0–300) and preserve the existing contents, by using the following syntax:

```
ReDim Preserve Philosophers(300)
```

A more complex example involving a three-dimensional array uses a similar syntax. Imagine that you want to use a three-dimensional, single-precision, floating-point array named *myCube* in your program. You can declare the *myCube* array by using the following syntax:

```
Dim myCube(,,) As Single
```

You can then redimension the array and add data to it by using the following code:

```
ReDim myCube(25, 25, 25)
myCube(10, 1, 1) = 150.46
```

after which you can expand the size of the third dimension in the array (while preserving the array's contents) by using this syntax:

```
ReDim Preserve myCube(25, 25, 50)
```

In this example, however, only the third dimension can be expanded—the first and second dimensions cannot be changed if you redimension the array by using the *Preserve* keyword.

Attempting to change the size of the first or second dimension in this example produces a run-time error when the *ReDim Preserve* statement is executed.

Experiment a little with *ReDim Preserve*, and see how you can use it to make your own arrays flexible and robust.

One Step Further: Processing Large Arrays by Using Methods in the *Array* Class

In previous sections, you learned about using arrays to store information during program execution. In this section, you'll learn about using methods in the *Array* class of the Microsoft .NET Framework, which you can use to quickly sort, search, and reverse the elements in an array, as well as perform other functions. The sample program I've created demonstrates how these features work especially well with very large arrays. You'll also learn how to use the *ProgressBar* control.

The *Array* Class

When you create arrays in Visual Basic, you are using a base class that is defined by Visual Basic for implementing arrays within user-created programs. This *Array* class also provides a collection of methods that you can use to manipulate arrays while they are active in programs. The most useful methods include *Array.Sort*, *Array.Find*, *Array.Reverse*, *Array.Copy*, and *Array.Clear*. You can locate other interesting methods by experimenting with the *Array* class in the Code Editor (by using Microsoft IntelliSense) and by checking the online help. The *Array* class methods function much like the .NET Framework methods you have already used in this book; that is, they are called by name and (in this case) require a valid array name as an argument. For example, to sort an array of temperatures (such as the *Temperatures* array that you created in the last exercise), you would use the following syntax:

```
Array.Sort(Temperatures)
```

You would make such a call after the *Temperatures* array had been declared and filled with data in the program. When Visual Basic executes the *Array.Sort* method, it creates a temporary storage location for the array in memory and uses a sorting routine to reorganize the array in alphanumeric order. After the sort is complete, the original array is shuffled in ascending order, with the smallest value in array location 0 and the largest value in the last array location. With the *Temperatures* example above, the sort would produce an array of daily temperatures organized from coolest to hottest.

In the following exercise, you'll see how the *Array.Sort* and *Array.Reverse* methods can be used to quickly reorder a large array containing six-digit numbers randomly selected between 0 and 1,000,000. You'll also learn how to use the *ProgressBar* control, an interesting user interface tool that provides useful visual feedback for the user during long sorts. (The *ProgressBar* control is located on the Common Controls tab of the Toolbox, and we're using it now for the first time.)

Use *Array* methods to sort an array of 3000 elements

1. On the File menu, click Open Project, and then open the Array Class Sorts project located in the c:\vb05sbs\chap11 folder.

2. Display the form if it is not already visible.

    Your screen looks like this:

This form looks similar to the earlier projects in this chapter and features a test box for displaying array data. However, it also contains three buttons for manipulating large arrays and a progress bar object that gives the user feedback during longer array operations. (Visual feedback is useful when computations take longer than a few seconds to complete, and if you use this code to sort an array of 3000 array elements, a slight delay is inevitable.)

3. Click the progress bar on the form.

    The *ProgressBar1* object is selected on the form and is listed in the Properties window. I created the progress bar object by using the *ProgressBar* control on the Common Controls tab in the Toolbox. A progress bar is designed to display the progress of a computation by displaying an appropriate number of colored rectangles arranged in a horizontal progress bar. When the computation is complete, the bar is filled with rectangles. You've probably seen this bar many times while you downloaded files or installed programs within Microsoft Windows. Now you can create one in your own programs!

    The important properties that make a progress bar work are the *Minimum*, *Maximum*, and *Value* properties, and these are typically manipulated using program code. (The other progress bar properties, which you can examine in the Properties window, control how the progress bar looks and functions.) You can examine how the *Minimum* and *Maximum* properties are set by looking at this program's *Form1_Load* event procedure.

4. Double-click the form to display the *Form1_Load* event procedure.

You see the following code:

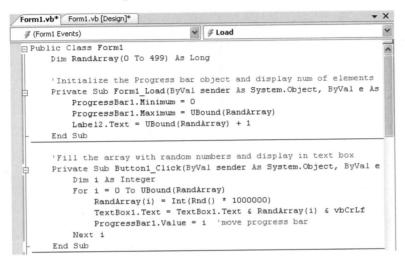

```vb
Form1.vb*   Form1.vb [Design]*                                    ▾ ✕
  ⚡ (Form1 Events)                          ∨   ⚡ Load              ∨
⊟ Public Class Form1
       Dim RandArray(0 To 499) As Long

       'Initialize the Progress bar object and display num of elements
⊟      Private Sub Form1_Load(ByVal sender As System.Object, ByVal e As
           ProgressBar1.Minimum = 0
           ProgressBar1.Maximum = UBound(RandArray)
           Label2.Text = UBound(RandArray) + 1
       End Sub

       'Fill the array with random numbers and display in text box
⊟      Private Sub Button1_Click(ByVal sender As System.Object, ByVal e
           Dim i As Integer
           For i = 0 To UBound(RandArray)
               RandArray(i) = Int(Rnd() * 1000000)
               TextBox1.Text = TextBox1.Text & RandArray(i) & vbCrLf
               ProgressBar1.Value = i  'move progress bar
           Next i
       End Sub
```

For a progress bar to display an accurate indication of how long a computing task will take to complete, you need to set relative measurements for the beginning and the end of the bar. This is accomplished with the *Minimum* and *Maximum* properties, which are set to match the first and the last elements in the array that we are building. As I have noted, the first array element is always 0 but the last array element depends on the size of the array, so I have used the *UBound* function to return that number and set the progress bar *Maximum* property accordingly. The array that we are manipulating in this exercise is *RandArray*, a *Long* integer array declared initially to hold 500 elements (0 to 499).

5. Click the Start Debugging button to run the program.

The program runs, and the Array Class Sorts form appears on the screen. In its *Form1_Load* event procedure, the program declared an array named *RandArray* and dimensioned it with 500 elements. A progress bar object was calibrated to track a calculation of 500 units (the array size), and the number 500 appears to the right of the progress bar (the work of a label object and the *UBound* function).

6. Click the Fill Array button.

The program loads *RandArray* with 500 random numbers (derived by the *Rnd* function), and displays the numbers in the text box. As the program processes the array and fills the text box object with data, the progress bar is slowly filled with green rectangles. Your screen looks like this when the process is finished:

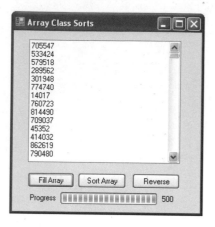

The code that produced this result is the *Button1_Click* event procedure, which contains the following program statements:

```
'Fill the array with random numbers and display in text box
Private Sub Button1_Click(ByVal sender As System.Object, _
ByVal e As System.EventArgs) Handles Button1.Click
    Dim i As Integer
    For i = 0 To UBound(RandArray)
        RandArray(i) = Int(Rnd() * 1000000)
        TextBox1.Text = TextBox1.Text & RandArray(i) & vbCrLf
        ProgressBar1.Value = i  'move progress bar
    Next i
End Sub
```

To get random numbers that are integers, I used the *Int* and *Rnd* functions together as I did in Chapter 2, "Writing Your First Program," and I multiplied the random number produced by *Rnd* by 1,000,000 to get whole numbers that are six digits or less. Assigning these numbers to the array is facilitated by using a For...Next loop with an array index that matches the loop counter (*i*). Filling the array is an extremely fast operation; the slow-down (and the need for the progress bar) is caused by the assignment of array elements to the text box object one at a time. This involves updating a user interface component on the form 500 times, and the process takes a few seconds to complete. It is instructional, however—the delay provides a way for me to show off the *ProgressBar* control. Since the progress bar object has been calibrated to use the number of array elements as its maximum, assigning the loop counter (*i*) to the progress bar's *Value* property allows the bar to display exactly how much of the calculation has been completed.

7. Click the Sort Array button.

The program follows a similar process to sort *RandArray*, this time using the *Array.Sort* method to reorder the array in ascending order. (The 500 elements are listed from lowest to highest.) Your screen looks like this:

The code that produced this result is the *Button2_Click* event procedure, which contains the following program statements:

```
'Sort the array using the Array.Sort method and display
Private Sub Button2_Click(ByVal sender As System.Object, _
ByVal e As System.EventArgs) Handles Button2.Click
    Dim i As Integer
    TextBox1.Text = ""
    Array.Sort(RandArray)
    For i = 0 To UBound(RandArray)
        TextBox1.Text = TextBox1.Text & RandArray(i) & vbCrLf
        ProgressBar1.Value = i  'move progress bar
    Next i
End Sub
```

This event procedure clears the text box object when the user clicks the Sort Array button, and then sorts the array by using the *Array.Sort* method described earlier. The sorting process is very quick. Again, the only slow down is rebuilding the text box object one line at a time in the For...Next loop, a process that is reported by the *ProgressBar1* object and its *Value* property. See how simple it is to use the *Array.Sort* method?

8. Click the Reverse button.

The program uses the *Array.Reverse* method to manipulate *RandArray*, reordering the array in backward or reverse order; that is, the first element becomes last and the last element becomes first.

> **Note**   This method does not always produce a sorted list; the array elements are in descending order only because *RandArray* had been sorted previously in ascending order by the *Array.Sort* method. (To examine the list more closely, use the scroll bars or the arrow keys.)

Your screen looks like this:

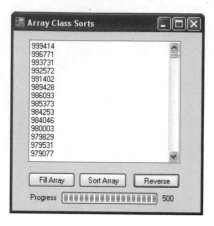

The code that produced this result is the *Button3_Click* event procedure, which contains the following program statements:

```
'Reverse the order of array elements using Array.Reverse
Private Sub Button3_Click(ByVal sender As System.Object, _
ByVal e As System.EventArgs) Handles Button3.Click
    Dim i As Integer
    TextBox1.Text = ""
    Array.Reverse(RandArray)
    For i = 0 To UBound(RandArray)
        TextBox1.Text = TextBox1.Text & RandArray(i) & vbCrLf
        ProgressBar1.Value = i   'move progress bar
    Next i
End Sub
```

This event procedure is identical to the *Button2_Click* event procedure, with the following exception:

```
Array.Sort(RandArray)
```

has become

```
Array.Reverse(RandArray)
```

9. Click the Stop Debugging button to end the program.

10. Scroll to the top of the Code Editor, and locate the program statement that declares the *RandArray* array:

```
Dim RandArray(0 To 499) As Long
```

11. Replace 499 in the array declaration statement with 2999.

    The statement now looks like this:

```
Dim RandArray(0 To 2999) As Long
```

12. Run the program again to see how declaring and filling an array with 3000 elements affects program performance.

    Because processing 3000 elements is much more work, Visual Basic takes a little while to update the text box object again and again as you fill, sort, and reverse *RandArray*. However, the progress bar keeps you posted, and you can see that with just a small change, you can adapt what you've learned in this chapter to different situations. (The secret was using the *UBound* function to report the size of the array to the program's event procedures, rather than "hard coding" the upper bound at 499.)

You can further experiment with this program by adding a *Randomize* statement to the *Form1_Load* event procedure (to make the results truly random each time that you run the program), or by trying additional array sizes and array types. (Try an array size of 100, 800, 2000, or 5000 elements, for example.) If you try larger numbers, you'll eventually exceed the amount of data that the text box object can display, but it takes you a while before you exceed the maximum array size allowed by Visual Basic.

If you want to focus on array operations without displaying the results, place a comment character (') before each line of code that manipulates a text box object to "comment out" the text box (but not the progress bar) portions of the program. You'll be amazed at how fast array operations run when the results do not need to be displayed on the form. (An array of 100,000 elements loads in just a few seconds.)

Chapter 11 Quick Reference

To	Do this
Create an array	Dimension the array by using the *Dim* keyword. For example: `Dim Employees(9) As String`
Create a public array	Dimension the array by using the *Public* keyword in a module. For example: `Public Employees(9) As String`
Create a public array specifying upper and lower bounds	Dimension the array as above, but also use the *To* keyword. For example: `Public Employees(0 To 9) As String` Note: The lower bound of the array must always be zero (0). As a result, this syntax is primarily useful for code readability (and is not supported in Visual Basic .NET 2002 and 2003).
Assign a value to an array	Specify the array name, the index of the array element, and the value. For example: `Employees(5) = "Leslie"`
Format text strings with carriage return and tab characters	Use the *vbCrLf* and *vbTab* constants within your program code. (To add these values to strings, use the & operator.)
Create a dynamic array	Specify the name and type of the array at design time, but omit the number of elements. (If the array has multiple dimensions, insert commas but no numbers between the dimensions.) While your program is running, specify the size of the array by using the *ReDim* statement. For example: `ReDim Temperatures(10)`

Process the elements in an array	Write a For...Next loop that uses the loop counter variable to address each element in the array. For example:
	
	`Dim i As Short`
	`Dim Total As Single`
	`For i = 0 To UBound(Temperatures)`
	`  Total = Total + Temperatures(i)`
	`Next`

Redimension an array while preserving the data in it	Use the *Preserve* keyword in your *ReDim* statement. For example: `ReDim Preserve myCube(25, 25, 50)`

To	Do this

Reorder the contents of an array	Use methods in the *Array* class of the .NET Framework. To sort an array named *RandArray* in ascending order, use the *Array.Sort* method as follows:
	
	`Array.Sort(RandArray)`
	
	To reverse the order of an array named *RandArray*, use the *Array.Reverse* method as follows:
	
	`Array.Reverse(RandArray)`

To give the user visual feedback during long cal-culations	Add a *ProgressBar* control to your form. (You can find the *ProgressBar* control on the Common Controls tab of the Toolbox.) Set the *Minimum*, *Maximum*, and *Value* properties for the control by using program code. The counter variable in a For...Next loop often offers a good way to set the *Value* property.

Chapter 12

Working with Collections and the *System.Collections* Namespace

After completing this chapter, you will be able to:

- Manipulate the *Controls* collection on a form.
- Use a For Each...Next loop to cycle through objects in a collection.
- Create your own collections for managing Web site URLs and other information.
- Use Microsoft Visual Basic for Applications collections within Microsoft Office.

In this chapter, you'll learn how to use groups of objects called *collections* in a Visual Basic program. You'll learn how to manage information with collections, process collection objects by using For Each...Next loops, and explore new objects within the *System.Collections* namespace. When you combine collection-processing skills with what you learned about arrays in Chapter 11, "Using Arrays to Manage Numeric and String Data," you'll have much of what you need to know about managing data effectively in a program, and you'll have taken your first steps in manipulating the object collections exposed by Microsoft Visual Studio 2005 and popular Microsoft Windows applications.

Upgrade Notes: Migrating Visual Basic 6 Code to Visual Basic 2005

If you're experienced with Microsoft Visual Basic 6, you'll notice some new features in Microsoft Visual Basic 2005, including the following:

- Visual Basic no longer has a single *Collection* data type. Instead, the functionality for collections is provided through the *System.Collections* namespace of the Microsoft .NET Framework class library. Using *System.Collections*, you can access several useful collection types, such as *Stack*, *Queue*, *Dictionary*, and *Hashtable*.

- Visual Basic no longer supports *control arrays* (collections of controls that share the same name and are processed as a group), and you cannot group controls by using the Clipboard as you can in Visual Basic 6. However, you can continue to store controls in an array if the array is declared in the object type.

Working with Object Collections

In this section, you'll learn about collections, a powerful mechanism for controlling objects and other data in a Visual Basic program. You already know that objects on a form are stored together in the same file. But did you also know that Visual Basic considers the objects to be members of the same group? In Visual Studio terminology, the entire set of objects on a form is called the *Controls collection*, which is part of the *System.Collections* namespace provided by the .NET Framework. The *Controls* collection is created automatically when you open a new form, and when you add objects to the form, they become part of that collection. In addition, Visual Studio maintains several standard object collections that you can use when you write your programs. In the rest of this chapter, you'll learn the basic skills you need to work with any collection you encounter.

Each collection in a program has its own name so that you can reference it as a distinct unit in the program code. For example, as you just learned, the collection containing all the objects on a form is called the *Controls* collection. This grouping method is similar to the way arrays group a list of elements together under one name, and like Visual Basic arrays, the *Controls* collection is zero-based.

If you have more than one form in a project, you can create public variables associated with the form names and use those variables to differentiate one *Controls* collection from another. (You'll learn more about using public variables to store form data in Chapter 14, "Managing Windows Forms and Controls at Run Time.") You can even add controls programmatically to the *Controls* collection in a form.

In addition to working with collections and objects in your own programs, you can use Visual Studio to browse your system for other application objects and use them in your programs.

Referencing Objects in a Collection

You can reference the objects in a collection, or the individual members of the collection, by specifying the *index position* of the object in the group. Visual Basic stores collection objects in the reverse order of that in which they were created, so you can use an object's "birth order" to reference the object individually, or you can use a loop to step through several objects. For example, to identify the last object created on a form, you can specify the 0 (zero) index, as shown in this example:

```
Controls(0).Text = "Business"
```

This statement sets the *Text* property of the last object on the form to "Business". (The second-to-the-last object created has an index of 1, the third-to-the-last object created has an index of 2, and so on.) Considering this logic, it's important that you don't always associate a particular object on the form with an index value, because if a new object is added to the collection, the new object takes the 0 index spot, and the remaining object indexes are incremented by 1.

The following For...Next loop uses a message box to display the names of the last four controls added to a form:

```
Dim i As Integer
For i = 0 To 3
    MsgBox(Controls(i).Name)
Next i
```

Note that I've directed this loop to cycle from 0 to 3 because the last control object added to a form is in the 0 position. In the following section, you'll learn a more efficient method for writing such a loop.

Writing For Each...Next Loops

Although you can reference the members of a collection individually, the most useful way to work with objects in a collection is to process them as a group. In fact, the reason collections exist is so that you can process groups of objects efficiently. For example, you might want to display, move, sort, rename, or resize an entire collection of objects at once.

To handle this kind of task, you can use a special loop called For Each...Next to cycle through objects in a collection one at a time. A For Each...Next loop is similar to a For...Next loop. When a For Each...Next loop is used with the *Controls* collection, it looks like this:

```
Dim CtrlVar As Control
...
For Each CtrlVar In Controls
    process object
Next CtrlVar
```

The *CtrlVar* variable is declared as a *Control* type and represents the current object in the For Each...Next loop. *Controls* (note the "s") is the collection class I introduced earlier that represents all the control objects on the current form. The body of the loop is used to process the individual objects of the collection. For example, you might want to change the *Enabled*, *Left*, *Top*, *Text*, or *Visible* properties of the objects in the collection, or you might want to list the name of each object in a list box.

Experimenting with Objects in the *Controls* Collection

In the following exercises, you'll use program code to manipulate the objects on a form by using the *Controls* collection. The project you'll create will have three button objects, and you'll create event procedures that change the *Text* properties of each object, move objects to the right, and give one object in the group special treatment. The program will use three For Each...Next loops to manipulate the objects each time the user clicks one of the buttons.

Use a For Each...Next loop to change *Text* properties

1. Create a new Visual Basic Windows Application project named **My Controls Collection**.

2. Use the *Button* control to draw three button objects on the left side of the form, as shown here:

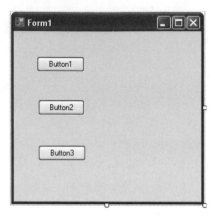

3. Use the Properties window to set the *Name* property of the third button object (*Button3*) to "btnMoveObjects".

4. Double-click the first button object (*Button1*) on the form.

   The *Button1_Click* event procedure appears in the Code Editor.

5. Type the following program statements:

```
For Each ctrl In Controls
    ctrl.Text = "Click Me!"
Next
```

   This For Each...Next loop steps through the *Controls* collection on the form one control at a time and sets each control's *Text* property to "Click Me!" The loop uses *ctrl* as an object variable in the loop, which you'll declare in the following step.

6. Scroll to the top of the form's program code, and directly below the statement `Public Class Form1`, type the following comment and variable declaration:

```
'Declare a variable of type Control to represent form controls
Dim ctrl As Control
```

   This global variable declaration creates a variable in the *Control* class type that represents the current form's controls in the program. You're declaring this variable in the general declarations area of the form so that it is valid throughout all of the form's event procedures.

   Now you're ready to run the program and change the *Text* property for each button on the form.

7. Click the Start Debugging button on the Standard toolbar to run the program.

8. Click the first button on the form (*Button1*).

The *Button1_Click* event procedure changes the *Text* property for each control in the *Controls* collection. Your form looks like this:

9. Click the Close button on the form.

    The program ends.

> **Note**   The *Text* property changes made by the program have not been replicated on the form within the Designer. Changes made at run time do not change the program's core property settings.

10. Click the Save All button on the Standard toolbar to save your changes. Specify the c:\vb05sbs\chap12 folder as the location.

Now you're ready to try a different experiment with the *Controls* collection: using the *Left* property to move each control in the *Controls* collection to the right.

Use a For Each...Next loop to move controls

1. Display the form again, and then double-click the second button object (*Button2*).

2. Type the following program code in the *Button2_Click* event procedure:

```
For Each ctrl In Controls
    ctrl.Left = ctrl.Left + 25
Next
```

Each time the user clicks the second button, this For Each...Next loop steps through the objects in the *Controls* collection one by one and moves them 25 pixels to the right. (To move objects 25 pixels to the left, you would subtract 25 instead.) A *pixel* is a device-independent measuring unit with which you can precisely place objects on a form.

> **Tip**   In Visual Basic 6, you normally use twips instead of pixels to specify measurements.

As in the previous event procedure you typed, the *ctrl* variable is a "stand-in" for the current object in the collection and contains the same property settings as the object it represents. In this loop, you adjust the *Left* property, which determines an object's position relative to the left side of the form.

3. Click the Start Debugging button.

    The program runs, and three buttons appear on the left side of the form.

4. Click the second button several times.

    Each time you click the button, the objects on the form gradually move to the right. Your screen looks like this after five clicks:

5. Click the Close button on the form to stop the program.

6. Click the Save All button to save your changes.

You won't always want to move all the objects on a form as a group. With Visual Basic, you can process collection members individually. In the next exercise, you'll learn how to keep the third button object in one place while the other two buttons move to the right.

Using the *Name* Property in a For Each...Next Loop

If you want to process one or more members of a collection differently than you process the others, you can use the *Name* property, which uniquely identifies each object on the form. You've set the *Name* property periodically in this book to make your program code more readable, but *Name* also can be used programmatically to identify specific objects in your program.

To use the *Name* property programmatically, single out the objects to which you want to give special treatment, and then note their *Name* properties. Then as you loop through the objects on the form by using a For Each...Next loop, you can use one or more *If* statements to test for the important *Name* properties and handle those objects differently. For example, let's say you want to construct a For Each...Next loop that moves one object more slowly across the form than the other objects. You could use an *If...Then* statement to spot the *Name* property of the slower object and then move that object a shorter distance, by not incrementing its *Left* property as much as those of the other objects.

> **Tip**   If you plan to give several objects special treatment in a For Each...Next loop, you can use *ElseIf* statements with the *If...Then* statement, or you can use a Select Case decision structure.

In the following exercise, you'll test the *Name* property of the third button object (*btnMove Objects*) to give that button special treatment in a For Each...Next loop. The result will be an event procedure that moves the top two buttons to the right but keeps the bottom button stationary.

> **Tip**   In addition to the *Name* property, most objects support the *Tag* property. Similar to the *Name* property, the *Tag* property is a location in which you can store string data about the object. The *Tag* property is empty by default, but you can assign information to it and test it to uniquely identify objects in your program that you want to process differently.

Use the *Name* property to give an object in the *Controls* collection special treatment

1. Display the form, and then double-click the third button object.

    The *btnMoveObjects_Click* event procedure appears in the Code Editor. Remember that you changed the *Name* property of this object from "Button1" to "btnMoveObjects" in an earlier exercise.

2. Type the following program code in the event procedure:

    ```
    For Each ctrl In Controls
        If ctrl.Name <> "btnMoveObjects" Then
            ctrl.Left = ctrl.Left + 25
        End If
    Next
    ```

    The new feature of this For Each...Next loop is the *If...Then* statement that checks each collection member to see whether it has a *Name* property called "btnMoveObjects". If the loop encounters this marker, it passes over the object without moving it. Note that, as in the previous examples, the *ctrl* variable was declared at the top of the form as a variable of the *Control* type with scope throughout the form.

3. Click the Save All button to save your edits.

> **Tip** The complete Controls Collection program is located in the
> c:\vb05sbs\chap12\controls collection folder.

4. Click the Start Debugging button.

    The program runs, and the three button objects appear on the form.

5. Click the third button object six or seven times.

    As you click the button, the top two button objects move across the screen. The third
    button stays in the same place, however, as shown here:

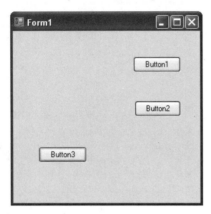

6. Click the Close button on the form to stop the program.

Giving one object in a collection special treatment can be very useful. In this case, using the
Name property in the For Each...Next loop improved the readability of the program code, sug-
gesting numerous potential uses for a game or graphics program. As you use other types of
collections in Visual Basic, be sure to keep the *Name* property in mind.

Creating Your Own Collections

With Visual Basic, you can also create your own collections to track data in a program and
manipulate it systematically. Although collections are often created to hold objects, such as
user interface controls, you can also use collections to store numeric or string values while
a program is running. In this way, collections nicely complement the capabilities of arrays,
which you learned about in the last chapter.

Declaring New Collections

New collections are declared as variables in a program, and the location in which you declare
them determines their scope, or the extent to which their assigned values persist. Because collections are so useful, I usually declare them at the top of a form or in a module.

New collection declarations require the syntax

```
Dim CollectionName As New Collection()
```

where *CollectionName* is the name of your collection. If you place the collection declaration in a module, you use the *Public* keyword instead of the *Dim* keyword. After you create a collection, you can add members to it by using the *Add* method, and you can examine the individual members by using a For Each...Next loop.

The following exercise shows you how to create a collection that holds string data representing the Internet addresses (Uniform Resource Locators, or URLs) you've recently used while surfing the Web. To connect to the Web, the program will use the Visual Basic *System.Diagnostics.Process.Start* method and your default Web browser, a technique that I first introduced in Chapter 3, "Working with Toolbox Controls."

Track Internet addresses by using a new collection

1. Click the Close Project command on the File menu.

2. Create a new project named **My URL Collection**.

3. Draw a wide text box object at the top of the form, centered within the form.

4. Draw two wide button objects below the text box object on the form, one button below the other.

5. Set the following properties for the form and its objects:

Object	Property	Setting
TextBox1	Text	"http://www.microsoft.com/learning/books/"
Button1	Text	"Visit Site"
Button2	Text	"List Recent Sites"
Form1	Text	"URL Collection"

6. Your form looks like this:

7. Click the View Code button in Solution Explorer to display the Code Editor.

8. Move the insertion point at near the top of the form's program code, and directly below the statement `Public Class Form1`, type the following variable declaration, and then press Enter:

```
Dim URLsVisited As New Collection()
```

This statement creates a new collection and assigns it the variable name *URLsVisited*. Because you're placing the declaration in the declaration area for the form, the collection has scope throughout all of the form's event procedures.

9. Display the form again, double-click the Visit Site button, and then type the following code in the *Button1_Click* event procedure:

```
URLsVisited.Add(TextBox1.Text)
System.Diagnostics.Process.Start(TextBox1.Text)
```

This program code uses the *Add* method to fill up, or *populate*, the collection with members. When the user clicks the *Button1* object, the program assumes that a valid Internet address has been placed in the *TextBox1* object. Every time the *Button1* object is clicked, the current URL in *TextBox1* is copied to the *URLsVisited* collection as a string. Next, the *System.Diagnostics.Process.Start* method is called with the URL as a parameter. Because the parameter is a URL, the *Start* method attempts to open the URL by using the default Web browser on the system. (If the URL is invalid or an Internet connection cannot be established, the Web browser handles the error.)

> **Note**   The only URLs this program adds to the *URLsVisited* collection are those you've specified in the *TextBox1* object. If you browse to additional Web sites by using your Web browser, those sites won't be added to the collection.

10. Display the form again, and then double-click the List Recent Sites button.

11. Type the following program code using the Code Editor:

```
Dim URLName As String = "", AllURLs As String = ""
For Each URLName In URLsVisited
    AllURLs = AllURLs & URLName & vbCrLf
Next URLName
MsgBox(AllURLs, MsgBoxStyle.Information, "Web sites visited")
```

This event procedure prints the entire collection by using a For Each...Next loop and a *MsgBox* function. The routine declares a string variable named *URLName* to hold each member of the collection as it's processed and initializes the variable to empty (""). The value is added to a string named *AllURLs* by using the concatenation operator (&), and the *vbCrLf* string constant is used to place each URL on its own line.

Finally, the *AllURLs* string, which represents the entire contents of the *URLsVisited* collection, is displayed in a message box. I added the *MsgBoxStyle.Information* argument in the *MsgBox* function to emphasize that the text being displayed is general information and not a warning. (*MsgBoxStyle.Information* is also a built-in Visual Basic constant.)

12. Click the Save All button to save your changes. Specify the c:\vb05sbs\chap12 folder as the location.

> **Note**   To run the URL Collection program, your computer must establish a connection to the Internet and be equipped with a Web browser, such as Microsoft Internet Explorer or Netscape Navigator.

Run the URL Collection program

> **Tip**   The complete URL Collection program is located in the c:\vb05sbs\chap12\url collection folder.

1. Click the Start Debugging button to run the program.

   The program displays a default Web site in the URL box, so it isn't necessary to type your own Internet address at first.

2. Click the Visit Site button.

   Visual Basic adds the Microsoft Press Web site (*http://www.microsoft.com/learning /books/*) to the *URLsVisited* collection, opens the default Web browser on your system, and loads the requested Web page, as shown here. (You can explore the Web site if you're interested.)

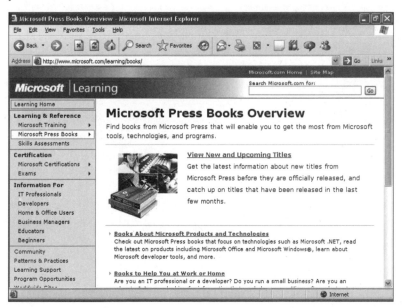

3. Click the form again. (You might need to click the form's icon on the Windows taskbar.)

4. Click the List Recent Sites button.

    Visual Basic executes the event procedure for the *Button2* object. You see a message box that looks like this:

5. Click OK in the message box, type a different Web site in the form's text box, and then click the Visit Site button.

    You might want to visit the Microsoft Visual Basic Developer Center site located at *msdn.microsoft.com/vbasic/* to learn more about Visual Basic.

6. Visit a few more Web sites by using the URL Collection form, and then click the List Recent Sites button.

    Each time you click List Recent Sites, the *MsgBox* function expands to show the growing URL history list, as shown here:

    If you visit more than a few dozen Web sites, you'll need to replace the *MsgBox* function with a multiline text box on the form. (Can you figure out how to write the code?)

7. When you're finished, click the Close button on the form, and then close your Web browser.

Congratulations! You've learned how to use the *Controls* collection and how to process collections by using a For Each...Next loop. These skills will be useful whenever you work with collections in the *System.Collections* namespace. As you become more familiar with classic computer science data structures and algorithms related to list management (stacks, queues, dictionaries, hash tables, and other structured lists), you'll find that *System.Collections* provides Visual Studio equivalents to help you manage information in extremely innovative ways. (For a few book ideas related to data structures and algorithms, see "General Books about Programming and Computer Science" in Appendix A.)

One Step Further: Visual Basic for Applications Collections

If you decide to write Visual Basic macros for Microsoft Office applications in the future, you'll find that collections play a big role in the object models of Microsoft Word, Microsoft Excel, Microsoft Access, Microsoft PowerPoint, and several other applications that support the Visual Basic for Applications programming language. In Word, for example, all the open documents are stored in the *Documents* collection, and each paragraph in the current document is stored in the *Paragraphs* collection. You can manipulate these collections with a For Each...Next loop just as you did the collections in the preceding exercises.

For example, the following sample code comes from a Word 2003 Visual Basic for Applications macro that uses a For Each...Next loop to search each open document in the *Documents* collection for a file named *MyLetter.doc*. If the file is found in the collection, the macro saves the file by using the *Save* method. If the file isn't found in the collection, the macro attempts to open the file from the c:\vb05sbs\chap12 folder.

```
Dim aDoc As Document
Dim docFound As Boolean
Dim docLocation As String
docFound = False
docLocation = "c:\vb05sbs\chap12\myletter.doc"
For Each aDoc In Documents
    If InStr(1, aDoc.Name, "myletter.doc", 1) Then
        docFound = True
        aDoc.Save
        Exit For
    End If
Next aDoc
If docFound = False Then
    Documents.Open FileName:=docLocation
End If
```

The macro begins by declaring three variables. The *aDoc* object variable represents the current collection element in the For Each...Next loop. The *docFound* Boolean variable assigns a Boolean value of True if the document is found in the *Documents* collection. The *docLocation* string variable contains the path of the MyLetter.doc file on disk. (This routine assumes that the MyLetter.doc file is with your book sample files in c:\vb05sbs\chap12.)

The For Each...Next loop cycles through each document in the *Documents* collection, searching for the MyLetter file. If the file is detected by the *InStr* function (which detects one string in another), the file is saved. If the file isn't found, the macro attempts to open it by using the *Open* method of the *Documents* object.

Also note the *Exit For* statement, which I use to exit the For Each...Next loop when the My Letter file has been found and saved. *Exit For* is a special program statement that you can use to exit a For...Next loop or a For Each...Next loop when continuing will cause unwanted results. In this example, if the MyLetter.doc file is located in the collection, continuing the search is fruitless, and the *Exit For* statement affords a graceful way to stop the loop as soon as its task is completed.

Entering the Sample Code

I've included this sample Word 2003 macro to show you how you can use collections in Visual Basic for Applications, but the source code is designed for Word, not the Visual Studio IDE. To try it, you'll need to start Word, click the Macros command on the Macro submenu of the Tools menu, create a new name for the macro (I used OpenMyDoc), and then enter the code by using the Word Visual Basic Editor. (If you aren't working in Word, the *Documents* collection won't have any meaning to the compiler.)

The completed macro looks as shown in the following Word screen, and you can run it by clicking the Run Sub/UserForm button on the toolbar, just as you would run a program in the Visual Studio IDE.

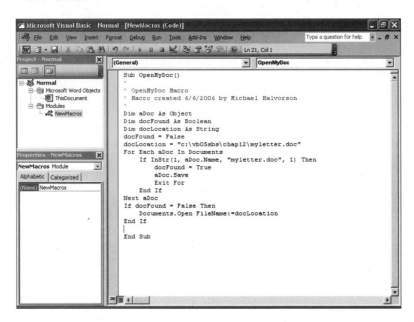

```
Sub OpenMyDoc()
'
' OpenMyDoc Macro
' Macro created 6/6/2006 by Michael Halvorson
'
Dim aDoc As Object
Dim docFound As Boolean
Dim docLocation As String
docFound = False
docLocation = "c:\vb05sbs\chap12\myletter.doc"
For Each aDoc In Documents
    If InStr(1, aDoc.Name, "myletter.doc", 1) Then
        docFound = True
        aDoc.Save
        Exit For
    End If
Next aDoc
If docFound = False Then
    Documents.Open FileName:=docLocation
End If

End Sub
```

Chapter 12 Quick Reference

To	Do this
Process objects in a collection	Write a For Each...Next loop that addresses each member of the collection individually. For example: ```\nDim ctrl As Control\nFor Each ctrl In Controls\n ctrl.Text = "Click Me!"\nNext\n```
Move objects in the *Controls* collection from left to right across the screen	Modify the *Control.Left* property of each collection object in a For Each...Next loop. For example: ```\nDim ctrl As Control\nFor Each ctrl In Controls\n Ctrl.Left = Ctrl.Left + 25\nNext Ctrl\n```
Give special treatment to an object in a collection	Test the *Name* property of the objects in the collection by using a For Each...Next loop. For example: ```\nDim ctrl As Control\nFor Each ctrl In Controls\n If ctrl.Name <> "btnMoveObjects" Then\n ctrl.Left = ctrl.Left + 25\n End If\nNext\n```
Create a new collection and add members to it	Declare a variable by using the New Collection syntax. Use the *Add* method to add members. For example: ```\nDim URLsVisited As New Collection()\nURLsVisited.Add(TextBox1.Text)\n```
Use Visual Basic for Applications collections in Office applications	Open Word or another Office application (Excel, Access, PowerPoint, and so on). Click the Macros command on the Macro submenu of the Tools menu, give the macro a name, click Create, and then enter VBA macro code by using the Visual Basic Editor. Word exposes many useful collections, including *Documents* and *Paragraphs*.

Chapter 13

Exploring Text Files and String Processing

After completing this chapter, you will be able to:

- Display a text file by using a text box object, the *LineInput* function, and the *Stream-Reader* class.

- Use the *My* object, a new "speed dial" feature within Microsoft Visual Studio 2005.

- Save notes in a text file by using the *PrintLine* function and the *SaveFileDialog* control.

- Use string processing techniques to compare, combine, and sort strings.

Managing electronic documents is an important function in any modern business, and Microsoft Visual Basic 2005 provides numerous mechanisms for working with different document types and manipulating the information in documents. The most basic document type is the *text file*, which is made up of non-formatted words and paragraphs, letters, numbers, and a variety of special-purpose characters and symbols.

In this chapter, you'll learn how to work with information stored in text files on your system. You'll learn how to open a text file and display its contents in a text box object, and you'll learn how to create a new text file on disk. You'll also learn more about managing strings in your programs, and you'll use methods in the Microsoft .NET Framework *String* and *Stream-Reader* classes to combine, sort, and display words, lines, and entire text files.

Upgrade Notes: Migrating Visual Basic 6 Code to Visual Basic 2005

If you're experienced with Microsoft Visual Basic 6, you'll notice some new features in Visual Basic 2005, including the following:

- In Visual Basic 6, you open and manipulate text files by using the *Open*, *Line Input #*, *Print #*, *EOF*, and *Close* keywords. Beginning with Microsoft Visual Basic .NET 2002, there's a new set of functions that manage text file operations. These functions are provided by the *FileSystem* object in the *Microsoft.VisualBasic* namespace and include *FileOpen*, *LineInput*, *PrintLine*, and *FileClose*.

- In addition to the *FileSystem* object functions just mentioned, you can use the *My* object and objects in the *System.IO* namespace to open and manipulate files, browse drives and folders, copy and delete files, process text streams, and complete other file-management tasks. These objects have the advantage of being available in all Visual Studio languages, so if you plan to try Microsoft Visual C++ programming eventually (for example), you might prefer using them. *System.IO* objects are very efficient and easy to use, so I'll teach them along with the "Visual Basic only" file operation techniques.

- In terms of string processing, several of the older Visual Basic text functions have been supplemented and replaced by new methods in the .NET Framework *String* class. For example, the new *SubString* method provides functionality similar to the Visual Basic *Mid* function, and the *ToUpper* method is similar to the Visual Basic *UCase* function. You can use either method to manipulate text strings, but the newer .NET Framework methods are recommended.

- By using the new *My* object, you can quickly query the system for useful information and perform common programming tasks, such as opening text files.

Displaying Text Files by Using a Text Box Object

The simplest way to display a text file in a program is to use a text box object. As you have learned, you can create text box objects in any size. If the contents of the text file don't fit neatly in the text box, you can also add scroll bars to the text box so that the user can examine the entire file. To use the Visual Basic language to load the contents of a text file into a text box, you need to use four functions. These functions are described in the following table and are demonstrated in the first exercise in this chapter. As I noted earlier, several of these functions replace older keywords in the Visual Basic language.

Function	Description
FileOpen	Opens a text file for input or output
LineInput	Reads a line of input from the text file

Function	Description
EOF	Checks for the end of the text file
FileClose	Closes the text file

Opening a Text File for Input

A *text file* consists of one or more lines of numbers, words, or characters. Text files are distinct from *document files* and *Web pages*, which contain formatting codes, and from *executable files*, which contain instructions for the operating system. Typical text files on your system are identified by Microsoft Windows Explorer as "Text Documents" or have the file name extension .txt, .ini, .log, or .inf. Because text files contain only ordinary, recognizable characters, you can display them easily by using text box objects.

By using an *OpenFileDialog* control to prompt the user for the file's path, you can let the user choose which text file to open in a program. This control contains the *Filter* property, which controls the type of files displayed; the *ShowDialog* method, which displays the Open dialog box; and the *FileName* property, which returns the path specified by the user. The *OpenFile Dialog* control doesn't open the file; it just gets the path.

The *FileOpen* Function

After you get the path from the user, you open the file in the program by using the *FileOpen* function. The abbreviated syntax for the *FileOpen* function is

```
FileOpen(filenumber, pathname, mode)
```

You can find the complete list of arguments in the Visual Basic online Help. These are the most important:

- *filenumber* is an integer from 1 through 255.
- *pathname* is a valid Microsoft Windows path.
- *mode* is a keyword indicating how the file will be used. (You'll use the *OpenMode.Input* and *OpenMode.Output* modes in this chapter.)

The file number is associated with the file when it's opened. You then use this file number in your code whenever you need to refer to the open file. Aside from this association, there's nothing special about file numbers; Visual Basic simply uses them to keep track of the different files you open in your program.

A typical *FileOpen* function using an *OpenFileDialog* object looks like this:

```
FileOpen(1, OpenFileDialog1.FileName, OpenMode.Input)
```

Here the *OpenFileDialog1.FileName* property represents the path, *OpenMode.Input* is the mode, and 1 is the file number.

> **Tip** Text files that are opened by using this syntax are called *sequential files* because you must work with their contents in sequential order. In contrast, you can access the information in a database file in any order. (You'll learn more about databases in Chapter 18, "Getting Started with ADO.NET.")

The following exercise demonstrates how you can use an *OpenFileDialog* control and the *File-Open* function to open a text file. The exercise also demonstrates how you can use the *Line-Input* and *EOF* functions to display the contents of a text file in a text box and how you can use the *FileClose* function to close a file. (For more information about using controls on the Dialogs tab of the Toolbox to create standard dialog boxes, see Chapter 4, "Working with Menus, Toolbars, and Dialog Boxes.")

Run the Text Browser program

1. Start Microsoft Visual Studio, and open the Text Browser project in the c:\vb05sbs\chap13\text browser folder.

   The project opens in the IDE.

2. If the project's form isn't visible, display it now.

   The Text Browser form appears, as shown here:

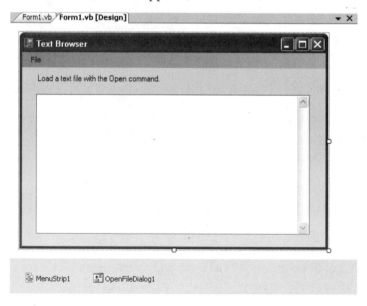

The form contains a large text box object that has scroll bars. It also contains a menu strip object that places Open, Close, and Exit commands on the File menu; an open file dialog object; and a label providing operating instructions. I also created the property settings shown in the following table. (Note especially the text box settings.)

Object	Property	Setting
txtNote	*Enabled*	False
	Multiline	True
	Name	txtNote
	ScrollBars	Both
CloseToolStrip-MenuItem	*Enabled*	False
lblNote	*Text*	"Load a text file with the Open command."
	Name	lblNote
Form1	*Text*	"Text Browser"

3. Click the Start Debugging button on the Standard toolbar.

   The Text Browser program runs.

4. On the Text Browser File menu, click the Open command.

   The Open dialog box appears.

5. Open the c:\vb05sbs\chap13\text browser folder.

   The contents of the Text Browser folder are shown here:

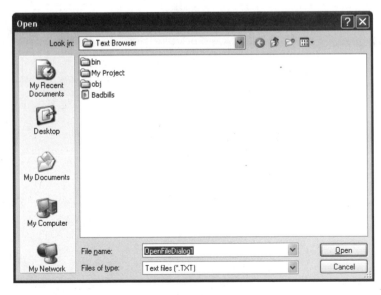

6. Double-click the Badbills.txt file name.

Badbills, a text file containing an article written in 1951 in the United States about the dangers of counterfeit money, appears in the text box, as shown here:

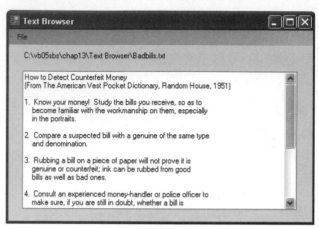

7. Use the scroll bars to view the entire document. Memorize number 5.

8. When you're finished, click the Close command on the File menu to close the file, and then click the Exit command to quit the program.

The program stops, and the IDE returns.

Now you'll take a look at two important event procedures in the program.

Examine the Text Browser program code

1. On the Text Browser form File menu, double-click the Open command.

The *OpenToolStripMenuItem_Click* event procedure appears in the Code Editor.

2. Resize the Code Editor to see more of the program code, if necessary.

The *OpenToolStripMenuItem_Click* event procedure contains the following program code:

```
Dim AllText As String = "", LineOfText As String = ""
OpenFileDialog1.Filter = "Text files (*.TXT)|*.TXT"
OpenFileDialog1.ShowDialog() 'display Open dialog box
If OpenFileDialog1.FileName <> "" Then
    Try 'open file and trap any errors using handler
        FileOpen(1, OpenFileDialog1.FileName, OpenMode.Input)
        Do Until EOF(1) 'read lines from file
            LineOfText = LineInput(1)
            'add each line to the AllText variable
            AllText = AllText & LineOfText & vbCrLf
        Loop
        lblNote.Text = OpenFileDialog1.FileName  'update label
        txtNote.Text = AllText 'display file
        txtNote.Enabled = True 'allow text cursor
        CloseToolStripMenuItem.Enabled = True  'enable Close command
        OpenToolStripMenuItem.Enabled = False  'disable Open command
```

```
    Catch
        MsgBox("Error opening file.")
    Finally
        FileClose(1) 'close file
    End Try
End If
```

This event procedure performs the following actions:

- Declares variables and assigns a value to the *Filter* property of the open file dialog object.

- Prompts the user for a path by using the *OpenFileDialog1* object.

- Traps errors by using a Try...Catch code block.

- Opens the specified file for input by using the *FileOpen* function.

- Uses the *LineInput* function to copy one line at a time from the file into a string named *AllText*.

- Copies lines until the end of the file (EOF) is reached or until there's no more room in the string. The *AllText* string has room for a very large file, but if an error occurs during the copying process, the *Catch* clause displays the error.

- Displays the *AllText* string in the text box, and enables the scroll bars and text cursor.

- Updates the File menu commands, and closes the file by using the *FileClose* function.

Take a moment to see how the statements in the *OpenToolStripMenuItem_Click* event procedure work—especially the *FileOpen*, *LineInput*, *EOF*, and *FileClose* functions. The error handler in the procedure displays a message and aborts the loading process if an error occurs.

> **Tip**   For more information about the statements and functions, highlight the keyword you're interested in, and press F1 to see a discussion of it in the Visual Basic online Help.

3. Display the *CloseToolStripMenuItem_Click* event procedure, which is executed when the Close menu command is clicked.

The event procedure looks like this:

```
txtNote.Text = ""                  'clear text box
lblNote.Text = "Load a text file with the Open command."
CloseToolStripMenuItem.Enabled = False   'disable Close command
OpenToolStripMenuItem.Enabled = True     'enable Open command
```

The procedure clears the text box, updates the *lblNote* label, disables the Close command, and enables the Open command.

Now you can use this simple program as a template for more advanced programs that process text files. In the next section, you'll learn how to type your own text into a text box and how to save the text in the text box to a file on disk.

Using the *StreamReader* Class and *My.Computer.FileSystem* to Open Text Files

In addition to the Visual Basic commands that open and display text files, there are two additional techniques that you can use to open text files in a Visual Studio program: the *Stream-Reader* class and the *My* object. Because these techniques use .NET Framework objects that are available in all Visual Studio programming languages, I prefer them over the "Visual Basic only" functions. However, Microsoft has been careful to preserve multiple file operation mechanisms for aesthetic and compatibility reasons, so the choice is ultimately up to you.

The *StreamReader* Class

The *StreamReader* class in the .NET Framework library allows you to open and display text files in your programs. I'll use this technique several times in this book when I work with text files (for example, in Chapter 16, "Inheriting Forms and Creating Base Classes"). To use the *StreamReader* class, you add the following *Imports* statement to the top of your code, which provides access to the *StreamReader* class:

```
Imports System.IO
```

Then, if your program contains a text box object, you can display a text file inside the text box by using the following program code. (The text file opened in this example is Badbills.txt, and the code assumes an object named *TextBox1* has been created on your form.)

```
Dim StreamToDisplay As StreamReader
StreamToDisplay = New StreamReader("C:\vb05sbs\chap13\text browser\badbills.txt")
TextBox1.Text = StreamToDisplay.ReadToEnd
StreamToDisplay.Close()
TextBox1.Select(0, 0)
```

StreamReader is a .NET Framework alternative to opening a text file by using the Visual Basic *FileOpen* function. In this *StreamReader* example, I declare a variable named *StreamToDisplay* of the type *StreamReader* to hold the contents of the text file, and then I specify a valid path for the file I want to open. Next I read the contents of the text file into the *StreamToDisplay* variable by using the *ReadToEnd* method, which retrieves all the text in the file from the current location (the beginning of the text file) to the end of the text file and assigns it to the *Text* property of the text box object. The final statements close the text file and use the *Select* method to remove the selection in the text box.

The *My* Object

The second alternative to opening text files in a program is a new feature of Visual Studio 2005 that uses the *My* object. The *My* object is a "speed dial" or rapid access feature designed to simplify accessing the .NET Framework to perform common tasks, such as manipulating forms, exploring the host computer and its file system, displaying information about the current application or its user, and accessing Web services. Most of these capabilities were previously available through the .NET Framework Base Class Library, but due to its complexity, many programmers found the features difficult to locate and use.

The *My* object is organized into several categories of functionality, as shown in the following table.

Object	Description
My.Application	Information related to the current application, including the title, directory, and version number.
My.Computer	Information about the hardware, software, and files located on the current (local) computer. *My.Computer* includes *My.Computer.FileSystem*, which you can use to open text files and encoded files on the system.
My.Forms	Information about the forms in your current Visual Studio project. Chapter 16 shows how to use *My.Forms* to switch back and forth between forms at run time.
My.User	Information about the current user active on *My.Computer*.
My.WebServices	Information about Web services active on *My.Computer*, and a mechanism to access new Web services.

The *My* Object is truly a "speed dial" feature, fully explorable via the Microsoft IntelliSense feature of the Code Editor. For example, to use a message box to display the name of the current computer followed by the name of the current user in a program, you can simply type:

```
MsgBox(My.User.Name)
```

This produces output similar to the following:

The *My.Computer* object can display many categories of information about your computer and its files. For example, the following statement displays the current system time (the local date and time) maintained by the computer:

```
MsgBox(My.Computer.Clock.LocalTime)
```

You can use the *My.Computer.FileSystem* object along with the *ReadAllText* method to open a text file and display its contents within a text box object. Here's the syntax you can use if you have a text box object on your form named *txtNote* (as in the last sample program) and you plan to use an open file dialog object named *OpenFileDialog1* to get the name of the text file from the user:

```
Dim AllText As String = ""
OpenFileDialog1.Filter = "Text files (*.TXT)|*.TXT"
OpenFileDialog1.ShowDialog() 'display Open dialog box
If OpenFileDialog1.FileName <> "" Then
    AllText = My.Computer.FileSystem.ReadAllText(OpenFileDialog1.FileName)
    txtNote.Text = AllText 'display file
End If
```

The *ReadAllText* method copies the entire contents of the given text file to a string variable or object (in this case, a string variable named *AllText*), so in terms of performance and coding time, *ReadAllText* is faster than reading the file one line at a time with the *LineInput* function.

Because of this speed factor, the *My* object provides an excellent shortcut to many common programming tasks and is one of the brighter features of Visual Basic 2005. It is important to take note of this new feature and its possible uses, but the *My* object is useful here because we are reading the entire text file. The *LineInput* function and *StreamReader* class offer more features than the current implementation of the *My* object, and especially the ability to process files one line at a time (a crucial capability for sorting and parsing tasks, as we shall soon see). So it is best to master each of the three methods for opening text files discussed in this chapter. The one you use in actual programming practice will depend on the task at hand, and the way you plan to use your code in the future.

Creating a New Text File on Disk

To create a new text file on disk by using Visual Basic, you can use many of the functions and keywords used in the last example. Creating new files on disk and saving data to them is useful if you plan to generate custom reports or logs, save important calculations or values, or create a special-purpose word processor or text editor. Here's an overview of the steps you'll need to follow in the program:

1. Get input from the user or perform mathematical calculations, or do both.

2. Assign the results of your processing to one or more variables. For example, you could assign the contents of a text box to a string variable named *InputForFile*.

3. Prompt the user for a path by using a *SaveFileDialog* control. You use the *ShowDialog* method to display the dialog box.

4. Use the path received in the dialog box to open the file for output.

5. Use the *PrintLine* function to save one or more values to the open file.

6. Close the file when you're finished by using the *FileClose* function.

The following exercise demonstrates how you can use *TextBox* and *SaveFileDialog* controls to create a simple note-taking utility. The program uses the *FileOpen* function to open a file, the *PrintLine* function to store string data in it, and the *FileClose* function to close the file. You can use this program to take notes at home or at work and then to stamp them with the current date and time.

Run the Quick Note program

1. Click the Close Solution command on the File menu.

2. Open the Quick Note project in the c:\vb05sbs\chap13\quick note folder.

   The project opens in the IDE.

3. If the project's form isn't visible, display it now.

   The Quick Note form appears, as shown in the following illustration. It looks similar to the Text Browser form. However, I replaced the *OpenFileDialog* control with the *SaveFileDialog* control on the form. The File menu contains the Save As, Insert Date, and Exit commands.

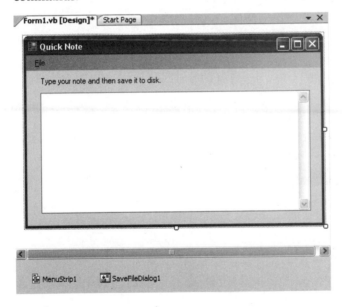

I set the following properties in the project:

Object	Property	Setting
txtNote	*Multiline*	True
	Name	txtNote
	ScrollBars	Vertical
lblNote	*Text*	"Type your note and then save it to disk."
Form1	*Text*	"Quick Note"

4. Click the Start Debugging button.

5. Type the following text, or some text of your own, in the text box:

How to Detect Counterfeit Coins

1) *Drop coins on a hard surface. Genuine coins have a bell-like ring; most counterfeit coins sound dull.*

2) *Feel all coins. Most counterfeit coins feel greasy.*

3) *Cut edges of questionable coins. Genuine coins are not easily cut.*

When you're finished, your screen looks similar to this:

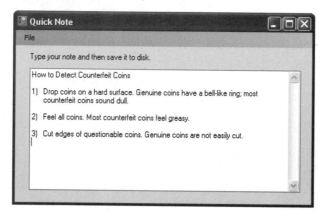

Tip   To paste text from the Windows Clipboard into the text box, press Ctrl+V or Shift+Insert. To copy text from the text box to the Windows Clipboard, select the text, and then press Ctrl+C.

Now try using the commands on the File menu.

6. On the File menu, click the Insert Date command.

The current date and time appears as the first line in the text box, as shown here:

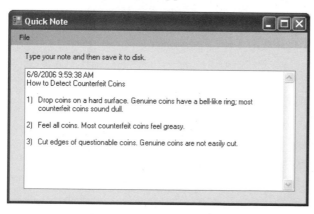

The Insert Date command provides a handy way to include the current time stamp in a file, which is useful if you're creating a diary or a logbook.

7. On the File menu, click the Save As command.

The program displays a Save As dialog box with all the expected features. The default file type is set to .txt. Your screen looks like this:

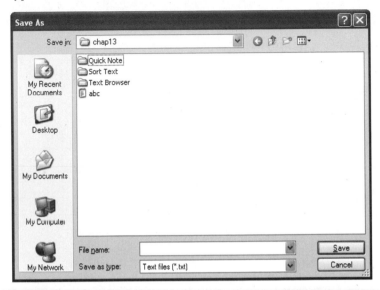

8. In the Save As dialog box, open the c:\vb05sbs\chap13\quick note folder if it isn't already open. Then type **Badcoins.txt** in the File Name text box, and click Save.

The text of your document is saved in the new Badcoins.txt text file.

9. On the File menu, click the Exit command.

The program stops, and the development environment returns.

Now you'll take a look at the event procedures in the program.

Examine the Quick Note program code

1. On the Quick Note form File menu, double-click the Insert Date command.

The *InsertDateToolStripMenuItem_Click* event procedure appears in the Code Editor. You see the following program code:

```
txtNote.Text = My.Computer.Clock.LocalTime & vbCrLf & txtNote.Text
txtNote.Select(1, 0)   'remove selection
```

This event procedure adds the current date and time to the text box by linking together, or *concatenating*, the current date (generated by the *My* object and the *LocalTime* method), a carriage return (added by the *vbCrLf* constant), and the *Text* property. You could use a similar technique to add just the current date (by using *DateString*) or any other information to the text in the text box.

2. Take a moment to see how the concatenation statements work, and then examine the *SaveAsToolStripMenuItem_Click* event procedure in the Code Editor.

    You see the following program code:

    ```
    SaveFileDialog1.Filter = "Text files (*.txt)|*.txt"
    SaveFileDialog1.ShowDialog()
    If SaveFileDialog1.FileName <> "" Then
        FileOpen(1, SaveFileDialog1.FileName, OpenMode.Output)
        PrintLine(1, txtNote.Text)  'copy text to disk
        FileClose(1)
    End If
    ```

    This block of statements uses a save file dialog object to display a Save As dialog box, verifies whether the user selected a file, opens the file for output as file number 1, writes the value in the *txtNote.Text* property to disk by using the *PrintLine* function, and then closes the text file. Note especially the statement

    ```
    PrintLine(1, txtNote.Text)  'copy text to disk
    ```

    which assigns the entire contents of the text box to the open file. *PrintLine* is similar to the older Visual Basic *Print* and *Print #* statements; it directs output to the specified file rather than to the screen or the printer. The important point to note here is that the entire file is stored in the *txtNote.Text* property.

3. Review the *FileOpen*, *PrintLine*, and *FileClose* functions, and then close the program by using the Close Solution command on the File menu.

You're finished with the Quick Note program.

Processing Text Strings with Program Code

As you learned in the preceding exercises, you can quickly open, edit, and save text files to disk with the *TextBox* control and a handful of well-chosen program statements. Visual Basic also provides a number of powerful statements and functions specifically designed for processing the textual elements in your programs. In this section, you'll learn how to extract useful information from a text string, copy a list of strings into an array, and sort a list of strings.

An extremely useful skill to develop when working with textual elements is the ability to sort a list of strings. The basic concepts in sorting are simple. You draw up a list of items to sort, and then compare the items one by one until the list is sorted in ascending or descending alphabetical order.

In Visual Basic, you compare one item with another by using the same relational operators that you use to compare numeric values. The tricky part (which sometimes provokes long-winded discussion among computer scientists) is the specific sorting algorithm you use to compare elements in a list. We won't get into the advantages and disadvantages of different sorting algorithms in this chapter. (The bone of contention is usually speed, which makes a difference only when several thousand items are sorted.) Instead, we'll explore how the basic string comparisons are made in a sort. Along the way, you'll learn the skills necessary to sort your own text boxes, list boxes, files, and databases.

Processing Strings by Using Methods and Keywords

The most common task you've accomplished so far with strings is concatenating them by using the concatenation operator (&). For example, the following program statement concatenates three literal string expressions and assigns the result "Bring on the circus!" to the string variable *Slogan*:

```
Dim Slogan As String
Slogan = "Bring" & " on the " & "circus!"
```

You can also concatenate and manipulate strings by using methods in the *String* class of the .NET Framework library. For example, the *String.Concat* method allows equivalent string concatenation by using this syntax:

```
Dim Slogan As String
Slogan = String.Concat("Bring", " on the ", "circus!")
```

Visual Basic 2005 features two methods for string concatenation and many other string-processing tasks: You can use operators and functions from earlier versions of Visual Basic (*Mid*, *UCase*, *LCase*, and so on), or you can use newer methods from the .NET Framework (*Substring*, *ToUpper*, *ToLower*, and so on). There's no real "penalty" for using either string-processing technique, although the older methods exist primarily for compatibility purposes. (By providing both methods, Microsoft hopes to welcome upgraders and let them learn new features at their own pace.) In the rest of this chapter, I'll focus on the newer string-processing functions from the .NET Framework *String* class. However, you can use either string-processing method or a combination of both.

The table on the next page lists several of the .NET Framework methods that appear in subsequent exercises and their close equivalents in the Visual Basic programming language. The fourth column in the table provides sample code for the methods in the *String* class of the .NET Framework.

.NET Framework method	Visual Basic function	Description	.NET Framework example

ToUpper	UCase	Changes letters in a string to uppercase.	`Dim Name, NewName As String`
			`Name = "Kim"`
			`NewName = Name.ToUpper`
			`'NewName = "KIM"`

ToLower	LCase	Changes letters in a string to lowercase.	`Dim Name, NewName As String`
			`Name = "Kim"`
			`NewName = Name.ToLower`
			`'NewName = "kim"`

Length	Len	Determines the number of characters in a string.	`Dim River As String`
			`Dim Size As Short`
			`River = "Mississippi"`
			`Size = River.Length`
			`'Size = 11`

Substring	Mid	Returns a fixed number of characters in a string from a given starting point. (Note: The first element in a string has an index of 0.)	`Dim Cols, Middle As String`
			`Cols = "First Second Third"`
			`Middle = Cols.Substring(6, 6)`
			`'Middle = "Second"`

IndexOf	InStr	Finds the starting point of one string within a larger string.	`Dim Name As String`
			`Dim Start As Short`
			`Name = "Abraham"`
			`Start = Name.IndexOf("h")`
			`'Start = 4`

Trim	Trim	Removes leading and following spaces from a string.	`Dim Spacey, Trimmed As String`
			`Spacey = "   Hello   "`
			`Trimmed = Spacey.Trim`
			`'Trimmed = "Hello"`

Remove		Removes characters from the middle of a string.	`Dim RawStr, CleanStr As String`
			`RawStr = "Hello333 there!"`
			`CleanStr = RawStr.Remove(5, 3)`
			`'CleanStr = "Hello there!"`

Insert		Adds characters to the middle of a string.	`Dim Oldstr, Newstr As String`
			`Oldstr = "Hi Felix"`
			`Newstr = Oldstr.Insert(3, "there ")`
			`'Newstr = "Hi there Felix"`

StrComp		Compares strings and disregards case differences.	`Dim str1 As String = "Soccer"`
			`Dim str2 As String = "SOCCER"`
			`Dim Match As Short`
			`Match = StrComp(str1, _`
			`   str2, CompareMethod.Text)`
			`'Match = 0 [strings match]`

Sorting Text

Before Visual Basic can compare one character with another in a sort, it must convert each character into a number by using a translation table called the *ASCII character set* (also called the *ANSI character set*). ASCII is an acronym for American Standard Code for Information Interchange. Each of the basic symbols that you can display on your computer has a different ASCII code. These codes include the basic set of "typewriter" characters (codes 32 through 127) and special "control" characters, such as tab, linefeed, and carriage return (codes 0 through 31). For example, the lowercase letter "a" corresponds to the ASCII code 97, and the uppercase letter "A" corresponds to the ASCII code 65. As a result, Visual Basic treats these two characters quite differently when sorting or performing other comparisons.

In the 1980s, IBM extended ASCII with codes 128 through 255, which represent accented, Greek, and graphic characters, as well as miscellaneous symbols. ASCII and these additional characters and symbols are typically known as the *IBM extended character set.*

> **Tip**   To see a table of the codes in the ASCII character set, search for "Chr, ChrW functions" in the Visual Studio online Help, and then click ASCII Character Codes in the Other Resources section near the end of the article.

The ASCII character set is still the most important numeric code for beginning programmers to learn, but it isn't the only character set. As the market for computers and application software has become more global, a more comprehensive standard for character representation called *Unicode* has emerged. Unicode can hold up to 65,536 symbols—plenty of space to represent the traditional symbols in the ASCII character set plus most (written) international languages and symbols. A standards body maintains the Unicode character set and adds symbols to it periodically. Microsoft Windows NT, Microsoft Windows 2000, Microsoft Windows XP, Microsoft Windows Server 2003, and Visual Studio have been specifically designed to manage ASCII and Unicode character sets. (For more information about the relationship between Unicode, ASCII, and Visual Basic data types, see "Working with Specific Data Types" in Chapter 5, "Visual Basic Variables and Formulas, and the .NET Framework.")

In the following sections, you'll learn more about using the ASCII character set to process strings in your programs. As your applications become more sophisticated and you start planning for the global distribution of your software, you'll need to learn more about Unicode and other international settings.

Working with ASCII Codes

To determine the ASCII code of a particular letter, you can use the Visual Basic *Asc* function. For example, the following program statement assigns the number 122 (the ASCII code for the lowercase letter "z") to the *AscCode* short integer variable:

```
Dim AscCode As Short
AscCode = Asc("z")
```

Conversely, you can convert an ASCII code to a letter with the *Chr* function. For example, this program statement assigns the letter "z" to the letter character variable:

```
Dim letter As Char
letter = Chr(122)
```

The same result could also be achieved if you used the *AscCode* variable just declared as shown here:

```
letter = Chr(AscCode)
```

How can you compare one text string or ASCII code with another? You simply use one of the six relational operators Visual Basic supplies for working with textual and numeric elements. These relational operators are shown in the following table.

Operator	Meaning
< >	Not equal
=	Equal
<	Less than
>	Greater than
< =	Less than or equal to
> =	Greater than or equal to

A character is "greater than" another character if its ASCII code is higher. For example, the ASCII value of the letter "B" is greater than the ASCII value of the letter "A," so the expression

```
"A" < "B"
```

is true, and the expression

```
"A" > "B"
```

is false.

When comparing two strings that each contain more than one character, Visual Basic begins by comparing the first character in the first string with the first character in the second string and then proceeds character by character through the strings until it finds a difference. For example, the strings Mike and Michael are the same up to the third characters ("k" and "c"). Because the ASCII value of "k" is greater than that of "c," the expression

```
"Mike" > "Michael"
```

is true.

If no differences are found between the strings, they are equal. If two strings are equal through several characters but one of the strings continues and the other one ends, the longer string is greater than the shorter string. For example, the expression

```
"AAAAA" > "AAA"
```

is true.

Sorting Strings in a Text Box

The following exercise demonstrates how you can use relational operators and several string methods and functions to sort lines of text in a text box. The program is a revision of the Quick Note utility and features an Open command that opens an existing file and a Close command that closes the file. There's also a Sort Text command on the File menu that you can use to sort the text currently displayed in the text box.

Because the entire contents of a text box are stored in one string, the program must first break that long string into smaller individual strings. These strings can then be sorted by using the *ShellSort* Sub procedure, a sorting routine based on an algorithm created by Donald Shell in 1959. To simplify these tasks, I created a module that defines a dynamic string array to hold each of the lines in the text box. I also placed the *ShellSort* Sub procedure in the module so that I can call it from any event procedure in the project. (For more about using modules, see Chapter 10, "Creating Modules and Procedures.") Although you learned how to use the powerful *Array.Sort* method in Chapter 11, "Using Arrays to Manage Numeric and String Data," the *ShellSort* procedure is a more flexible and customizable tool. Building the routine from scratch also gives you a little more experience with processing textual values—an important learning goal of this chapter.

Another interesting aspect of this program is the routine that determines the number of lines in the text box object. No existing Visual Basic function computes this value automatically. I wanted the program to be able to sort a text box of any size line by line. To accomplish this, I created the code that follows. It uses the *Substring* method to examine one letter at a time in the text box object and then uses the *Chr* function to search for the carriage return character, ASCII code 13, at the end of each line. (Note in particular how the *Substring* method is used as part of the *Text* property of the *txtNote* object. The *String* class automatically provides this method, and many others, for any properties or variables that are declared in the *String* type.)

```
Dim ln, curline, letter As String
Dim i, charsInFile, lineCount As Short

'determine number of lines in text box object (txtNote)
lineCount = 0 'this variable holds total number of lines
charsInFile = txtNote.Text.Length 'get total characters
```

```
For i = 0 To charsInFile - 1 'move one char at a time
    letter = txtNote.Text.Substring(i, 1) 'get letter
    If letter = Chr(13) Then 'if carriage ret found
        lineCount += 1 'go to next line (add to count)
        i += 1 'skip linefeed char (typically follows cr on PC)
    End If
Next i
```

The total number of lines in the text box is assigned to the *lineCount* short integer variable. I use this value a little later to dimension a dynamic array in the program to hold each individual text string. The resulting array of strings then gets passed to the *ShellSort* Sub procedure for sorting, and *ShellSort* returns the string array in alphabetical order. After the string array is sorted, I can simply copy it back to the text box by using a For loop.

Run the Sort Text program

1. Open the Sort Text project located in the c:\vb05sbs\chap13\sort text folder.

2. Click the Start Debugging button to run the program.

3. Type the following text, or some text of your own, in the text box:

   Zebra

   Gorilla

   Moon

   Banana

   Apple

   Turtle

   Be sure to press Enter after you type "Turtle" (or your own last line) so that Visual Basic can calculate the number of lines correctly.

4. Click the Sort Text command on the File menu.

   The text you typed is sorted and redisplayed in the text box as follows:

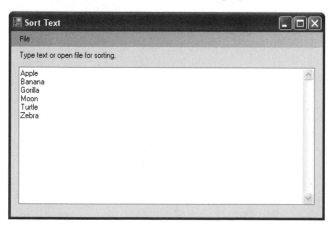

5.   Click the Open command on the File menu, and open the abc.txt file in the
     c:\vb05sbs\chap13 folder, as shown here:

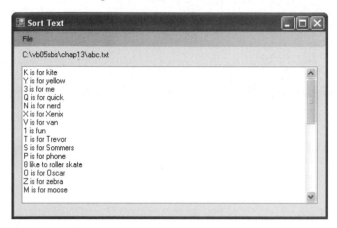

The abc.txt file contains 36 lines of text. Each line begins with either a letter or a number
from 1 through 10.

6.   Click the Sort Text command on the File menu to sort the contents of the abc.txt file.

The Sort Text program sorts the file in ascending order and displays the sorted list of
lines in the text box, as shown here:

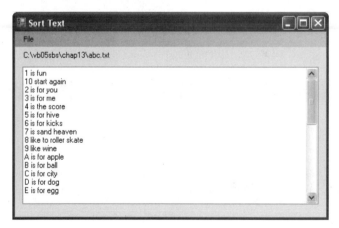

7.   Scroll through the file to see the results of the alphabetical sort.

Notice that although the alphabetical portion of the sort ran perfectly, the sort produced
a strange result for one of the numeric entries—the line beginning with the number 10
appears second in the list rather than tenth. What's happening here is that Visual Basic
read the 1 and the 0 in the number 10 as two independent characters, not as a number.
Because we're comparing the ASCII codes of these strings from left to right, the program
produces a purely alphabetical sort. If you want to sort only numbers with this program,
you need to prohibit textual input, modify the code so that the numeric input is stored
in numeric variables, and then compare the numeric variables instead of strings.

One Step Further: Examining the Sort Text Program Code

To add a few more tools to your programming skill set and review some of the concepts that I have discussed in the last several chapters, in the next exercise you'll take a closer look at the Sort Text program code.

Examine the Sort Text program

1. On the Sort Text program File menu, click the Exit command to stop the program.

2. Open the Code Editor, and display the code for the *SortTextToolStripMenuItem_Click* event procedure.

    We've already discussed the first routine in this event procedure, which counts the number of lines in the text box by using the *Substring* method to search for carriage return codes. The remainder of the event procedure dimensions a string array, copies each line of text into the array, calls a procedure to sort the array, and displays the reordered list in the text box.

    The entire *SortTextToolStripMenuItem_Click* event procedure looks like this:

```
Dim ln, curline, letter As String
Dim i, charsInFile, lineCount As Short

'determine number of lines in text box object (txtNote)
lineCount = 0 'this variable holds total number of lines
charsInFile = txtNote.Text.Length 'get total characters
For i = 0 To charsInFile - 1 'move one char at a time
    letter = txtNote.Text.Substring(i, 1) 'get letter
    If letter = Chr(13) Then 'if carriage ret found
        lineCount += 1 'go to next line (add to count)
        i += 1 'skip linefeed char (typically follows cr on PC)
    End If
Next i

'build an array to hold the text in the text box
ReDim strArray(lineCount) 'create array of proper size
curline = 1
ln = "" 'use ln to build lines one character at a time
For i = 0 To charsInFile - 1 'loop through text again
    letter = txtNote.Text.Substring(i, 1) 'get letter
    If letter = Chr(13) Then 'if carriage return found
        curline = curline + 1 'increment line count
        i += 1 'skip linefeed char
        ln = "" 'clear line and go to next
    Else
        ln = ln & letter 'add letter to line
        strArray(curline) = ln 'and put in array
    End If
Next i

'sort array
ShellSort(strArray, lineCount)
```

```
'then display sorted array in text box
txtNote.Text = ""
curline = 1
For i = 1 To lineCount
    txtNote.Text = txtNote.Text & _
      strArray(curline) & vbCrLf
    curline += 1
Next i
txtNote.Select(1, 0)    'remove text selection
```

The *strArray* array was declared in a module (Module1.vb) that's also part of this program (Chapter 10). By using the *ReDim* statement (Chapter 11), I am dimensioning *strArray* as a dynamic array with the *lineCount* variable. This statement creates an array that has the same number of elements as the text box has lines of text (a re-quirement for the *ShellSort* Sub procedure). Using a For loop (Chapter 7) and the *ln* variable, I scan through the text box again, looking for carriage return characters and copying each complete line found to *strArray*. After the array is full of text, I call the *ShellSort* procedure located in the Module1.vb module, which I created earlier in this chapter.

3. Display the code for the Module1.vb module in the Code Editor.

   This module declares the *strArray* public array variable (Chapter 11) and then defines the content of the *ShellSort* procedure. The *ShellSort* procedure uses an *If* statement and the <= relational operator (Chapters 6, 8, and 13) to compare array elements and swap any that are out of order. The procedure looks like this:

```
Sub ShellSort(ByRef sort() As String, ByVal numOfElements As Short)
    Dim temp As String
    Dim i, j, span As Short
    'The ShellSort procedure sorts the elements of sort()
    'array in descending order and returns it to the calling
    'procedure.

    span = numOfElements \ 2
    Do While span > 0
        For i = span To numOfElements - 1
            For j = (i - span + 1) To 1 Step -span
                If sort(j) <= sort(j + span) Then Exit For
                'swap array elements that are out of order
                temp = sort(j)
                sort(j) = sort(j + span)
                sort(j + span) = temp
            Next j
        Next i
        span = span \ 2
    Loop
End Sub
```

The method of the sort is to continually divide the main list of elements into sublists that are smaller by half. The sort then compares the tops and the bottoms of the sublists to see whether the elements are out of order. If the top and bottom are out of order, they're exchanged. The result is an array named *sort()* that's sorted alphabetically in descending order. To change the direction of the sort, simply reverse the relational operator (change <= to >=).

The remaining event procedures (*OpenToolStripMenuItem_Click*, *CloseToolStripMenuItem_Click*, *SaveAsToolStripMenuItem_Click*, *InsertDateToolStripMenuItem_Click*, and *ExitToolStripMenuItem_Click*) are all similar to the procedures that you studied in the Text Browser and the Quick Note programs. (See my explanations earlier in this chapter for the details.)

4. Click the Close Project command on the File menu.

You're finished working with strings, arrays, and text files for now.

Congratulations! If you've worked through Chapters 5 through 13, you've completed the programming fundamentals portion of this book, and you are now ready to focus specifically on creating professional-quality user interfaces in your programs. You have come a long way in your study of Visual Basic programming skills and in your use of the Visual Studio IDE. Take a short break, and I'll see you again in Part III, "Designing the User Interface"!

Chapter 13 Quick Reference

To	Do this
Open a text file	Use the *FileOpen* function. For example: ```FileOpen(1, OpenFileDialog1.FileName, _ OpenMode.Input)```
Get a line of input from a text file	Use the *LineInput* function. For example: ```Dim LineOfText As String LineOfText = LineInput(1)```

Check for the end of a file	Use the *EOF* function. For example:
	
	``Dim LineOfText, AllText As String
	Do Until EOF(1)
	    LineOfText = LineInput(1)
	    AllText = AllText & LineOfText & _
	        vbCrLf
	Loop```

Close an open file	Use the *FileClose* function. For example: ```FileClose(1)```

To	Do this
Display a text file by using *LineInput*	Use the *LineInput* function to copy text from an open file to a string variable, and then assign the string variable to a text box object. For example:

```
Dim AllText, LineOfText As String
Do Until EOF(1) 'read lines from file
    LineOfText = LineInput(1)
    AllText = AllText & LineOfText & _
      vbCrLf
Loop
txtNote.Text = AllText 'display file
```

To	Do this
Display a text file by using the *StreamReader* class	Add the statement "Imports System.IO" to your form's declaration section, and then use *StreamReader*. For example, to display the file in a text box object named *TextBox1*:

```
Dim StreamToDisplay As StreamReader
StreamToDisplay = _
New StreamReader("c:\vb05sbs\chap13\text browser\badbills.txt")
TextBox1.Text = StreamToDisplay.ReadToEnd
StreamToDisplay.Close()
TextBox1.Select(0, 0)
```

To	Do this
Display a text file by using the *My* object	Use the *My.Computer.FileSystem* object and the *ReadAllText* method. For example, assuming that you are also using an open file dialog object named *ofd* and a text box object named *txtNote*:

```
Dim AllText As String = ""
ofd.Filter = "Text files (*.TXT)|*.TXT"
ofd.ShowDialog()
If ofd.FileName <> "" Then
  AllText = _
  My.Computer.FileSystem.ReadAllText(ofd.FileName)
  txtNote.Text = AllText 'display file
End If
```

To	Do this
Display an Open dialog box	Add an *OpenFileDialog* control to your form, and then use the *ShowDialog* method of the open file dialog object. For example:

```
OpenFileDialog1.ShowDialog()
```

To	Do this
Create a new text file	Use the *FileOpen* function. For example:

```
FileOpen(1, SaveFileDialog1.FileName, _
    OpenMode.Output)
```

To	Do this
Display a Save As dialog box	Add a *SaveFileDialog* control to your form, and then use the *ShowDialog* method of the save file dialog object. For example:

```
SaveFileDialog1.ShowDialog()
```

To	Do this
Save text to a file	Use the *Print* or *PrintLine* function. For example:

```
PrintLine(1, txtNote.Text)
```

To	Do this
Convert text characters to ASCII codes	Use the *Asc* function. For example:

```
Dim Code As Short
Code = Asc("A")  'Code equals 65
```

To	Do this

Convert ASCII codes to text characters	Use the *Chr* function. For example:
	
	 ```Dim Letter As Char```
	```Letter = Chr(65) 'Letter equals "A"```

Extract characters from the middle of a string	Use the *Substring* method or the *Mid* function. For example:
	
	 ```Dim Cols, Middle As String```
	```Cols = "First Second Third"```
	```Middle = Cols.SubString(6, 6)```
	```'Middle = "Second"```

Part III
Designing the User Interface

Chapter 14

Managing Windows Forms and Controls at Run Time

After completing this chapter, you will be able to:

- Add new forms to a program and switch between multiple forms.
- Change the position of a form on the Microsoft Windows desktop.
- Add controls to a form at run time.
- Change the alignment of objects within a form at run time.
- Use the Properties dialog box to specify the startup form.

In Part II, you learned many of the core development skills necessary for writing Microsoft Visual Basic applications. You learned how to use variables, operators, and decision structures; how to manage code flow with loops, timers, procedures, and structured error handlers; how to debug your programs; and how to organize information with arrays, collections, text files, and string processing techniques.

Each exercise you have worked with so far concentrated on one or more of these core skills in a simple, stand-alone program. Real-world programs are rarely so simple. They usually require you to combine the techniques in various ways and with various enhancements. Your programs will quite often require multiple forms, used as dialog boxes, input and output forms, reports, and so on. Because Visual Basic treats each form as a separate object, you can think of them as simple building blocks that you can combine to create powerful programs.

In Part III, you'll focus again on the user interface, and you'll learn how to add multiform projects, animation effects, visual inheritance, and printing support to your Visual Basic applications.

In this chapter, you'll learn how to add additional forms to an application to handle input, output, and special messages. You'll also learn how to use the *Me* and *My.Forms* objects to switch between forms, how to use the *DesktopBounds* property to resize a form, how to add Toolbox controls to a form at run time, how to change the alignment of objects within a form, and how to specify which form runs when a program is started.

Upgrade Notes: Migrating Visual Basic 6 Code to Visual Basic 2005

If you're experienced with Microsoft Visual Basic 6, you'll notice some new features in Microsoft Visual Basic 2005, including the following:

- The *My.Forms* object now offers an easy way to manipulate the forms in a project at run time. (In Microsoft Visual Basic .NET 2003, you cannot set the properties of a second form without declaring an instance variable of the form.)

- In Visual Basic 6, you can set a form's run-time position on the Windows desktop by using the graphical Form Layout window. There's no Form Layout window in Microsoft Visual Studio 2005, but you can use a new form property named *DesktopBounds* to set the size and location of a form at run time.

- In Visual Basic 6, you can add new controls to a form at run time by using program code. Visual Basic 2005 has a similar capability, but with some syntax changes for adding controls at run time, which will be discussed in this chapter.

- With the *Anchor* and *Dock* properties introduced in Microsoft Visual Basic .NET 2002, you can create forms in which the objects are sized as the form is resized. The *Anchor* property for objects on a form specifies which sides should remain at a constant from the edges of the form. The *Dock* property forces an object to remain attached to one edge of the form.

Adding New Forms to a Program

Each program you've written so far has used one form and a series of general-purpose dialog boxes for input and output. In many cases, dialog boxes and a form are sufficient for communicating with the user. But if you need to exchange more information with the user in a more customized manner, you can add additional forms to your program. Each new form is considered an object that inherits its capabilities from the *System.Windows.Forms.Form* class. The first form in a program is named Form1.vb. Subsequent forms are named Form2.vb, Form3.vb, and so on. (You can change the specific name for a form by using the Add New Item dialog box or by using Solution Explorer.) Each new form has a unique name and its own set of objects, properties, methods, and event procedures.

The following table lists several practical uses for additional forms in your programs.

Form or forms	Description
Introductory form	A form that displays a welcome message, artwork, or copyright information when the program starts
Program instructions	A form that displays information and tips about how the program works

Form or forms	Description
Dialog boxes	Custom dialog boxes that accept input and display output in the program
Document contents	A form that displays the contents of one or more files and artwork used in the program

How Forms Are Used

Visual Basic gives you significant flexibility when using forms. You can make all the forms in a program visible at the same time, or you can load and unload forms as the program needs them. If you display more than one form at once, you can allow the user to switch between the forms, or you can control the order in which the forms are used. A form that must be addressed when it's displayed on the screen is called a dialog box. Dialog boxes (called *modal forms* in Visual Basic 6) retain the focus until the user clicks OK, clicks Cancel, or otherwise dispatches them. To display an existing form as a dialog box in Visual Basic 2005, you open it by using the *ShowDialog* method.

If you want to display a form that the user can switch away from, you use the *Show* method instead of the *ShowDialog* method. In Visual Basic 6, forms that can lose the application focus are called *non-modal forms* or *modeless forms*, and you will still see these terms being used. Most Windows applications use regular, non-modal forms when displaying information because they give the user more flexibility, so this style is the default when you create a new form in Visual Studio. Because forms are simply members of the *System.Windows.Forms.Form* class, you can also create and display forms by using program code.

Working with Multiple Forms

The following exercises demonstrate how you can use a second form to display Help information for the Lucky Seven program that you worked with in Chapter 2, "Writing Your First Program," and Chapter 10, "Creating Modules and Procedures." You'll add a second form by using the Add Windows Form command on the Project menu, and you'll display the form in your program code by using the *My* object and the *ShowDialog* method. The second form will display a short Readme.txt file that I created to display help and copyright information for the program (the type of information you typically see in an About or a Help dialog box).

Add a second form

1. Start Visual Studio, and then open the Lucky Seven Help project in the c:\vb05sbs\chap14\lucky seven help folder.

    The Lucky Seven Help project is the same slot machine game that you worked with in Chapter 10. The program uses a module and a function to calculate the win rate as you try to spin one or more 7s.

2. Display the primary form (LuckySeven.vb) in the Designer, if it isn't already visible.

3. Click the Add Windows Form command on the Project menu to add a second form to the project.

You'll see this dialog box:

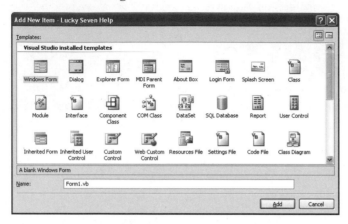

You use the Add New Item dialog box to add forms, classes, modules, and other components to your Visual Basic project. Although you selected the Add Windows Form command, forms aren't the only components listed here. (The Windows Form template is selected by default, however.) The Add New Item dialog box is flexible enough that you can pick other project components if you change your mind.

> **Tip**   I especially recommend that you experiment with the Explorer Form template, which allows you to add a Windows Explorer–style browser to your application, complete with menus, toolbar, and a folder hierarchy pane.

4. Type **HelpInfo.vb** in the Name text box, and then click Add.

A second form named HelpInfo.vb is added to the Lucky Seven Help project, and the form appears in Solution Explorer, as shown here:

> **Tip** You can rename or delete form files by using Solution Explorer. To rename a file, right-click the file, and then click the Rename command. To remove a file from your project, right-click the file, and then click the Exclude From Project command. To remove a file from your project and permanently delete it from your computer, select the file, and then press Delete.

Now you'll add some controls to the HelpInfo.vb form.

5. Use the *Label* control to create a label at the top of the HelpInfo.vb form. Place the label near the left edge of the form, but leave a small indent so that there is room for a descriptive label.

6. Use the *TextBox* control to create a text box object.

7. Set the *Multiline* property for the text box object to True so that you can resize the object easily.

8. Resize the text box object so that it covers most of the form.

9. Use the *Button* control to create a button at the bottom of the form.

10. Set the following properties for the objects on the HelpInfo.vb form:

Object	Property	Setting
Label1	Text	"Operating Instructions for Lucky Seven Slot Machine"
TextBox1	Scrollbars	Vertical
Button1	Text	"OK"
HelpInfo.vb	Text	"Help"

The HelpInfo.vb form looks similar to this:

Now you'll enter a line of program code for the HelpInfo.vb form's *Button1_Click* event procedure.

11. Double-click the OK button to display the *Button1_Click* event procedure in the Code Editor.

12. Type the following program statement:

```
Me.DialogResult = DialogResult.OK
```

The HelpInfo.vb form acts as a dialog box in this project because the Lucky Seven form opens it using the *ShowDialog* method. After the user has read the Help information displayed by the dialog box, he or she will click the OK button, which sets the *DialogResult* property of the current form to DialogResult.OK. (The *Me* keyword is used here to refer to the HelpInfo form, and you'll see this shorthand syntax from time to time when a reference is being made to the current *instance* of a class or structure in which the code is executing.)

DialogResult.OK is a Visual Basic constant that indicates the dialog box has been closed and should return a value of "OK" to the calling procedure. A more sophisticated dialog box might allow for other values to be returned by parallel button event procedures, such as DialogResult.Cancel, DialogResult.No, and DialogResult.Yes. When the *Dialog-Result* property is set, however, the form is automatically closed.

13. At the top of the Code Editor, type the following *Imports* statement above the *Public Class* declaration:

```
Imports System.IO
```

This statement incorporates the class library containing the *StreamReader* class into the project. The *StreamReader* class isn't specifically related to defining or using additional forms—I'm just using it as a quick way to add textual information to the new form I'm creating.

14. Display the HelpInfo.vb form again, and then double-click the form background.

The *HelpInfo_Load* event procedure appears in the Code Editor. This is the event procedure that runs when the form is first loaded into memory and displayed on the screen.

15. Type the following program statements:

```
Dim StreamToDisplay As StreamReader
StreamToDisplay = _
  New StreamReader("c:\vb05sbs\chap14\lucky seven help\readme.txt")
TextBox1.Text = StreamToDisplay.ReadToEnd
StreamToDisplay.Close()
TextBox1.Select(0, 0)
```

Rather than type the contents of the Help file into the *Text* property of the text box object (which would take a long time), I've used the *StreamReader* class to open, read, and display an appropriate Readme.txt file in the text box object. This file contains operating instructions and general contact information.

The *StreamReader* class was introduced in the Chapter 13, "Exploring Text Files and String Processing," but you might not have experimented with it yet. As you learned, *StreamReader* is a Microsoft .NET Framework alternative to opening a text file with the *My.Computer.FileSystem* object or the Visual Basic *FileOpen* function. To use *Stream-Reader*, you include the *System.IO* class library at the top of the code for your form. Next you declare a *StreamToDisplay* variable of the type *StreamReader* to hold the contents of the text file, and open the text file by using a specific path. Finally you read the contents of the text file into the *StreamToDisplay* variable by using the *ReadToEnd* method, which reads all the text in the file from the current location (the beginning of the text file) to the end of the text file and assigns it to the *Text* property of the text box object. The *StreamReader.Close* statement closes the text file, and the *Select* method removes the selection from the text in the text box object.

You're finished with the HelpInfo.vb form. Now you'll add a button object and some code to the first form.

Display the second form by using an event procedure

1. Click LuckySeven.vb in Solution Explorer, and then click the View Designer button.

    The Lucky Seven form appears in the IDE. Now you'll add a Help button to the user interface.

2. Use the *Button* control to draw a small button object in the lower-right corner of the form.

3. Use the Properties window to set the button object's *Text* property to Help.

    Your form looks something like this:

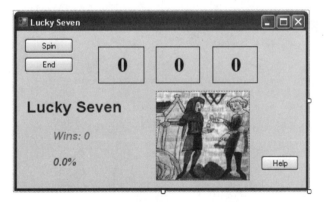

4. Double-click the Help button to display the *Button3_Click* event procedure in the Code Editor.

5. Type the following program statement:

```
My.Forms.HelpInfo.ShowDialog()
```

This statement uses the *My* object (introduced in Chapter 13) to access the forms active within the current project. As you typed the statement, the Visual Studio IntelliSense feature listed the forms available in the *Forms* collection, as shown in the following illustration:

Unlike Visual Basic .NET 2003, which required that you specifically declare a variable of the form's type before you used a second form, the *My* object makes all the forms in your project available without specific declaration.

Note that you can also open and manipulate forms directly (as you can in Visual Basic 6) by using the following syntax:

```
HelpInfo.ShowDialog()
```

This statement opens the HelpInfo form as a dialog box by using the *ShowDialog* method.

Alternatively, you can use the *Show* method to open the form, but in that case, Visual Basic won't consider HelpInfo.vb to be a dialog box; the form is a non-modal form that the user can switch away from and return to as needed. In addition, the *DialogResult* property in the HelpInfo.vb form's *Button1_Click* event procedure won't close the HelpInfo.vb form. Instead, the program statement `Me.Close` is required.

> **Tip** Keep the differences between modal and non-modal forms in mind as you build your own projects. There are differences between each type of form, and you'll find that each style provides a benefit to the user.

Now you'll run the program to see how a multiple-form application works.

Run the program

1. Click the Start Debugging button on the Standard toolbar.

   The first form in the Lucky Seven project appears.

2. Click the Spin button seven or eight times to play the game.

   Your screen looks similar to this:

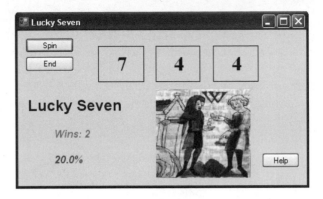

3. Click the Help button.

    Visual Basic opens the second form in the project, HelpInfo.vb, and displays the
    Readme.txt file in the text box object. The form looks like this:

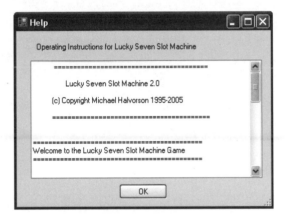

4. Use the vertical scroll bar to view the entire Readme file.

5. Click the OK button to close the HelpInfo.vb form.

    The form closes, and the first form becomes active again.

6. Click the Spin button a few more times, and then click the Help button again.

    The HelpInfo.vb form appears again and is fully functional. Notice that you cannot acti-
    vate the first form while the second form is active. (To test this, try to click Spin on the
    first form while the second form is active.) Because the second form is a dialog box (a
    modal form), you must address it before you can continue with the program.

7. Click the OK button, and then click the End button on the first form.

    The program stops, and the development environment returns.

Using the *DialogResult* Property in the Calling Form

Although I didn't demonstrate it in the sample program, you can use the *DialogResult* property that you assigned to the dialog box to great effect in a Visual Basic program. As I mentioned earlier, a more sophisticated dialog box might provide additional buttons to the user—Cancel, Yes, No, Abort, and so on. Each dialog box button can be associated with a different type of action in the main program. And in each of the dialog box's button event procedures, you can assign the *DialogResult* property for the form that corresponds to the button name, such as the following program statement:

```
Me.DialogResult = DialogResult.Cancel    'user clicked Cancel button
```

In the calling event procedure—in other words, in the *Button3_Click* event procedure of LuckySeven.vb—you can write additional program code to detect which button the user clicked in the dialog box. This information is stored in the form's *DialogResult* property, which can be evaluated using a basic decision structure such as If...Then or Select...Case. For example, the following code can be used in the *Button3_Click* event procedure to verify whether the user clicked OK, Cancel, or another button in the dialog box. (The first line isn't new, but reminds you of the HelpInfo form name that you are using in this example.)

```
My.Forms.HelpInfo.ShowDialog()

If HelpInfo.DialogResult = DialogResult.OK Then
    MsgBox("The user clicked OK")
ElseIf HelpInfo.DialogResult = DialogResult.Cancel Then
    MsgBox("The user clicked Cancel")
Else
    MsgBox("Another button was clicked")
End If
```

By using creative event procedures that declare, open, and process dialog box choices, you can add any number of forms to your programs, and you can create a user interface that looks professional and feels flexible and user friendly.

Positioning Forms on the Windows Desktop

You've learned how to add forms to your Visual Basic project and how to open and close forms by using program code. But which tool or setting determines the placement of forms on the Windows desktop when your program runs? As you might have noticed, the placement of forms on the screen at run time is different from the placement of forms within the Visual Studio development environment at design time. In this section, you'll learn how to position your forms just where you want them at run time so that users see just what you want them to see.

In Visual Basic 6, a graphical tool called the *Form Layout window* controls the placement of forms at run time. You drag a tiny form icon within the Form Layout window to where you want the final form to appear at run time, and Visual Basic records the screen coordinates you specify. In Visual Basic 2005, there's no Form Layout window, but you can still position your forms precisely on the Windows desktop.

The tool you use isn't a graphical layout window but a property named *DesktopBounds* that is maintained for each form in your project. *DesktopBounds* can be read or set only at run time, and it takes the dimensions of a rectangle as an argument—that is, two point pairs that specify the coordinates of the upper-left corner of the window and the lower-right corner of the window. The coordinate points are expressed in pixels, and the distances to the upper-left and lower-right corners are measured from the upper-left corner of the screen. (You'll learn more about the Visual Basic coordinate system in the next chapter.) Because the *DesktopBounds* property takes a rectangle structure as an argument, you can set both the size and the location of the form on the Windows desktop.

In addition to the *DesktopBounds* property, you can use a simpler mechanism with fewer capabilities to set the location of a form at design time. This mechanism, the *StartPosition* property, positions a form on the Windows desktop by using one of the following property settings: Manual, CenterScreen, WindowsDefaultLocation, WindowsDefaultBounds, or CenterParent. The default setting for the *StartPosition* property, WindowsDefaultLocation, lets Windows position the form on the desktop where it chooses—usually the upper-left corner of the screen.

If you set *StartPosition* to Manual, you can manually set the location of the form by using the *Location* property, in which the first number (x) is the distance from the left edge of the screen and the second number (y) is the distance from the top edge of the screen. (You'll learn more about the *Location* property in the next chapter.) If you set *StartPosition* to CenterScreen, the form appears in the middle of the Windows desktop. (This is my preferred *StartPosition* setting.) If you set *StartPosition* to WindowsDefaultBounds, the form is resized to fit the standard window size for a Windows application, and then the form is opened in the default location for a new Windows form. If you set *StartPosition* to CenterParent, the form is centered within the the parent form. This final setting is especially useful in so-called multiple document interface (MDI) applications in which parent and child windows have a special relationship.

The following exercises demonstrate how you can set the *StartPosition* and *DesktopBounds* properties to position a Visual Basic form. You can use either technique to locate your forms on the Windows desktop at run time.

Use the *StartPosition* property to position the form

1. Click the Close Project command on the File menu, and then create a new application project named **My Desktop Bounds**.

2. If the project's form isn't visible, display it now.

3. Click the form to display its properties in the Properties window.

4. Set the *StartPosition* property to CenterScreen.

    Changing the *StartPosition* property to CenterScreen directs Visual Basic to display the form in the center of the Windows desktop when you run the program.

5. Click the Start Debugging button to run the application.

    Visual Basic loads the form and displays it in the middle of the screen, as shown here:

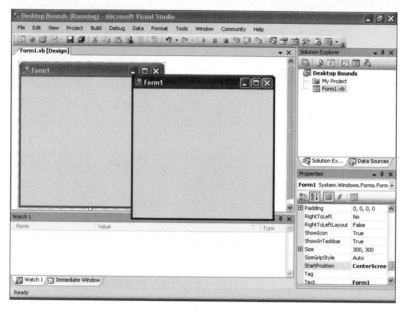

6. Click the Close button on the form to stop the program.

    The IDE returns.

7. Set the *StartPosition* property to Manual.

    The Manual property setting directs Visual Basic to position the form based on the values in the *Location* property.

8. Set the *Location* property to 100, 50.

    The *Location* property specifies the position, in pixels, of the upper-left corner of the form.

9. Click the Start Debugging button to run the application.

    Visual Basic loads the form and then displays it on the Windows desktop 100 pixels from the left and 50 pixels from the top, as shown here:

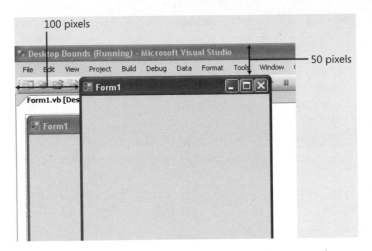

100 pixels

50 pixels

10.   Click the Close button on the form to close the program.

You've experimented with a few basic *StartPosition* settings for positioning a form at run time. Now you'll use the *DesktopBounds* property to size and position a second form window while the program is running. You'll also learn how to create a new form at run time without using the Add Windows Form command on the Project menu.

Set the *DesktopBounds* property

1.   Use the *Button* control to add a button object to the form, and then change the *Text* property of the button object to "Create Form".

2.   Double-click the Create Form button to display the *Button1_Click* event procedure in the Code Editor.

3.   Type the following program code:

```
'Create a second form named form2
Dim form2 As New Form

'Define the Text property and border style of the form
form2.Text = "My New Form"
form2.FormBorderStyle = FormBorderStyle.FixedDialog

'Specify that the position of the form will be set manually
form2.StartPosition = FormStartPosition.Manual

'Declare a Rectangle structure to hold the form dimensions
'Upper left corner of form (200, 100)
'Width and height of form (300, 250)
Dim Form2Rect As New Rectangle(200, 100, 300, 250)

'Set the bounds of the form using the Rectangle object
form2.DesktopBounds = Form2Rect

'Display the form as a modal dialog box
form2.ShowDialog()
```

When the user clicks the Create Form button, this event procedure creates a new form with the title "My New Form" and a fixed border style. To use program code to create a new form, you use the *Dim* statement and specify a variable name for the form and the *Form* class, which is automatically included in projects as part of the *System .Windows.Forms* namespace. You can then set properties such as *Text*, *FormBorderStyle*, *StartPosition*, and *DesktopBounds*. The *StartPosition* property is set to FormStartPosition.Manual to indicate that the position will be set manually. The *DesktopBounds* property sizes and positions the form and requires an argument of type *Rectangle*. The *Rectangle* type is a structure that defines a rectangular region and is automatically included in Visual Basic projects. Using the *Dim* statement, the *Form2Rect* variable is declared of type *Rectangle* and initialized with the form position and size values. At the bottom of the event procedure, the new form is opened as a dialog box using the *Show-Dialog* method.

Although I usually recommend placing your *Dim* statements together at the top of the form, here I have placed one a little lower in the code to make it easier to understand the context and use of the variable.

> **Tip**   The complete Desktop Bounds program is located in the c:\vb05sbs\chap14\desk-top bounds folder.

4. Click the Start Debugging button to run the program.

    Visual Basic displays the first form on the desktop.

5. Click the Create Form button.

    Visual Basic displays the My New Form dialog box with the size and position you specified in the program code, as shown here:

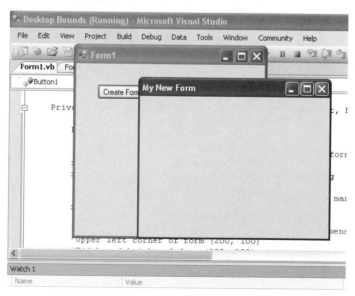

Notice that you can't resize the second form, because the *FormBorderStyle* was set to FixedDialog.

6. Close the second form, and then close the first form.

   Your program stops running, and the IDE returns.

7. Click the Save All button, and specify the c:\vb05sbs\chap14 folder as the location.

Minimizing, Maximizing, and Restoring Windows

In addition to establishing the size and location of a Visual Basic form, you can minimize a form to the Windows taskbar, maximize a form so that it takes up the entire screen, or restore a form to its normal shape. These settings can be changed at design time or at run time based on current program conditions.

To allow a form to be both minimized and maximized, you must first verify that the form's minimize and maximize boxes are available. Using the Properties window or program code, you specify the following settings:

```
MaximizeBox = True
MinimizeBox = True
```

Then, in program code or by using the Properties window, you set the *WindowState* property for the form to Minimized, Maximized, or Normal. (In code, you need to add the *FormWindowState* constant, as shown below.) For example, the following program statement minimizes a form to the Windows taskbar:

```
WindowState = FormWindowState.Minimized
```

If you want to control the maximum or minimum size of a form, set the *MaximumSize* or *MinimumSize* properties at design time by using the Properties window. To set the *MaximumSize* or *MinimumSize* in code, you'll need to use a *Size* structure (which is similar to the *Rectangle* structure used in the previous exercise), as shown here:

```
Dim FormSize As New Size(400, 300)
MaximumSize = FormSize
```

Adding Controls to a Form at Run Time

Throughout this book, you've added objects to forms by using the Toolbox and the Designer. However, as the previous exercise demonstrated, you can also create Visual Basic objects on forms at run time, either to save development time (if you're copying routines you have used before) or to respond to a current need in the program. For example, you might want to generate a simple dialog box containing objects that process input only under certain conditions.

Creating objects is very simple because the fundamental classes that define controls in the Toolbox are available to all programs. Objects are declared and *instantiated* (or brought into being) by using the *Dim* and *New* keywords. The following program statement shows how this process works when a new button object named *button1* is created on a form:

```
Dim button1 As New Button
```

After you create an object at run time, you can also use code to customize it with property settings. In particular, it's useful to specify a name and location for the object because you didn't specify them manually by using the Designer. For example, the following program statements configure the *Text* and *Location* properties for the new *button1* object:

```
button1.Text = "Click Me"
button1.Location = New Point(20, 25)
```

Finally, your code must add the following new object to the *Controls* collection of the form where it will be created. This will make the object visible and active in the program:

```
form2.Controls.Add(button1)
```

If you are adding the new button to the current form (that is, if you are adding a button to Form1 and your code is located inside a Form1 event procedure), you can use the *Me* object instead. For example,

```
Me.Controls.Add(button1)
```

adds the *button1* object to the *Controls* collection of the current form. When you do this, be sure that a *button1* object doesn't already exist on the form you are adding it to. (Each object must have its own, unique name.)

You can use this process to add any control in the Toolbox to a Visual Basic form. The class name you use to declare and instantiate the control is a variation of the name that appears in the *Name* property for each control.

The following exercise demonstrates how you can add a *Label* control and a *Button* control to a new form at run time. The new form will act as a dialog box that displays the current date.

Create new *Label* and *Button* controls

1. Click the Close Project command on the File menu, and then create a new application project named **My Add Controls**.

2. Display the form (Form1.vb).

3. Use the *Button* control to add a button object to the form, and then change the *Text* property of the button object to Display Date.

4. Double-click the Display Date button to display the *Button1_Click* event procedure in the Code Editor.

5. Type the following program code:

```
'Declare new form and control objects
Dim form2 As New Form
Dim lblDate As New Label
Dim btnCancel As New Button

'Set label properties
lblDate.Text = "Current date is: " & DateString
lblDate.Size = New Size(150, 50)
lblDate.Location = New Point(80, 50)

'Set button properties
btnCancel.Text = "Cancel"
btnCancel.Location = New Point(110, 100)

'Set form properties
form2.Text = "Current Date"
form2.CancelButton = btnCancel
form2.StartPosition = FormStartPosition.CenterScreen

'Add new objects to Controls collection
form2.Controls.Add(lblDate)
form2.Controls.Add(btnCancel)

'Display form as a dialog box
form2.ShowDialog()
```

This event procedure displays a new form containing a label object and a button object on the screen. The label object contains the current date as recorded by your computer's system clock (returned through *DateString*). The *Text* property of the button object is set to "Cancel".

As I mentioned earlier, you add controls to a form by declaring a variable to hold the control, setting object properties, and adding the objects to the *Controls* collection. In this exercise, I also demonstrate the *Size* and *CancelButton* properties for the first time. The *Size* property requires a *Size* structure. The *New* keyword is used to immediately create the *Size* structure. The *CancelButton* property allows the user to close the dialog box by pressing Esc or clicking the Cancel button. (The two actions are equivalent.)

6. Click the Save All button, and specify the c:\vb05sbs\chap14 folder as the location.

> **Tip**   The complete Add Controls program is located in the c:\vb05sbs\chap14\add controls folder.

7. Click the Start Debugging button to run the program.

   Visual Basic displays the first form on the desktop.

8. Click the Display Date button.

Visual Basic displays the second form on the desktop. This form contains the label and button objects that you defined by using program code. The label object contains the current date, as shown here:

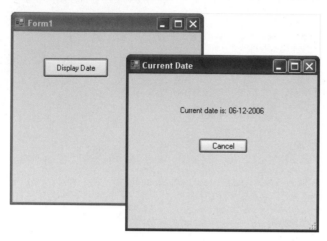

9.   Click the Cancel button to close the new form.

10.   Click the Display Date button again.

The new form appears as it did the first time.

11.   Press Esc to close the form.

Because you set the *CancelButton* property to the *btnCancel* object, clicking Cancel and pressing Esc produce the same result.

12.   Click the Close button on the form to end the program.

The program stops, and the development environment returns.

Organizing Controls on a Form

When you add controls to a form programmatically, it takes a bit of trial and error to position the new objects so that they're aligned properly and look nice. After all, you don't have the Visual Studio Designer to help you—just the (*x*, *y*) coordinates of the *Location* and *Size* properties, which are clumsy values to work with unless you have a knack for two-dimensional thinking or have the time to run the program repeatedly to verify the placement of your objects.

Fortunately, Visual Basic contains several property settings that you can use to organize objects on the form at run time. These include the *Anchor* property, which forces an object on the form to remain at a constant distance from the specified edges of the form, and the *Dock* property, which forces an object to remain attached to one edge of the form. You can use the *Anchor* and *Dock* properties at design time, but I find that they're also very helpful for programmatically aligning objects at run time. The following exercise shows how these properties work.

Anchor and dock objects at run time

1. Click the Close Project command on the File menu, and then create a new application project named **My Anchor and Dock**.

2. Display the form.

3. Click the *PictureBox* control, and add a picture box object in the top middle of the form.

4. Use the *TextBox* control to create a text box object.

5. Set the *Multiline* property for the text box object to True so that you can resize the object appropriately.

6. Resize the text box object so that it covers most of the bottom half of the form.

7. Click the *Button* control, and add a button object to the lower-right corner of the form.

8. Set the following properties for the form and the objects on it. (You'll be using one image file from the next chapter.)

Object	Property	Setting
PictureBox1	Image	"c:\vbnet03sbs\chap15\sun.ico"
	SizeMode	StretchImage
Button1	Text	"Align Now"
TextBox1	Text	"Anchor and Dock Samples"

Your form looks similar to this:

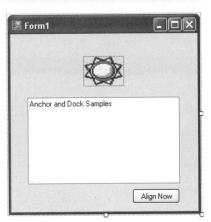

9. Double-click the Align Now button to open the *Button1_Click* event procedure in the Code Editor.

10. Type the following program code:

```
PictureBox1.Dock = DockStyle.Top
TextBox1.Anchor = AnchorStyles.Bottom Or _
  AnchorStyles.Left Or AnchorStyles.Right Or _
  AnchorStyles.Top
Button1.Anchor = AnchorStyles.Bottom Or _
  AnchorStyles.Right
```

When this event procedure is executed, the *Dock* property of the *PictureBox1* object is used to dock the picture box to the top of the form. This forces the top edge of the picture box object to touch and adhere to the top edge of the form—much as the Visual Studio docking feature works in the IDE. The only surprising behavior here is that the picture box object is also resized so that its sides adhere to the left and right edges of the form. You'll see this behavior in the following step.

Next, the *Anchor* property for the *TextBox1* and *Button1* objects is used. The *Anchor* property maintains the current distance from the specified edges of the form, even if the form is resized. Note that the *Anchor* property maintains the object's current distance from the specified edges—it doesn't attach the object to the specified edges unless it's already there. In this example, I specify that the *TextBox1* object should be anchored to all four edges of the form (bottom, left, right, and top). I use the *Or* operator to combine my edge selections. I anchor the *Button1* object to the bottom and right edges of the form.

11. Save the project, and specify the c:\vb05sbs\chap14 folder as the location.

> **Tip**   The complete Anchor and Dock program is located in the
> c:\vb05sbs\chap14\anchor and dock folder.

12. Click the Start Debugging button to run the program.

The form appears, just as you designed it.

13. Move the pointer to the lower-right corner of the form until it changes into a Resize pointer, and then enlarge the form.

Notice that the size and position of the objects on the form do not change.

14. Resize the form to its original size.

15. Click the Align Now button on the form.

The picture box object is now docked at the top edge of the form. The picture box is also resized so that its sides adhere to the left and right edges of the form, as shown here:

Notice that the Sun icon in the picture box is now distorted, which is a result of the docking process.

16. Enlarge the form again.

As you resize the form, the picture box and text box objects are also resized. Because the text box is anchored on all four sides, the distance between the edges of the form and the text box remains constant. During the resizing activity, it also becomes apparent that the button object is being repositioned. Although the distance between the button object and the top and left edges of the form changes, the distance to the bottom and right edges remains constant, as shown here:

17. Experiment with the *Anchor* and *Dock* properties for a while, and try a different bitmap image if you like. When you're finished, click the Close button on the form to end the program.

You now have the skills necessary to add new forms to a project, position them on the Windows desktop, populate them with new controls, and align the controls by using program code. You've gained a number of useful skills for working with Windows forms in a program.

One Step Further: Specifying the Startup Object

If your project contains more than one form, which form is loaded and displayed first when you run the application? Although Visual Basic normally loads the first form that you created in a project (Form1.vb), you can change the form that Visual Basic loads first by adjusting a setting in the Visual Studio Project Designer, a handy tool that I'll introduce now for the first time.

The following exercise shows you how to change the first form, or *startup form*, by using the Visual Studio Project Designer.

Switch the startup form from Form1 to Form2

1. Click the Close Project command on the File menu, and then create a new project named **My Startup Form**.

2. Display Form1.vb, if it isn't already visible.

3. Click the Add Windows Form command on the Project menu.

    You'll add a new form to the project to demonstrate how switching the startup form works.

4. Click Add to add the second form (Form2.vb) to Solution Explorer.

5. Click My Startup Form Properties on the Project menu.

    The Project Designer appears, as shown here:

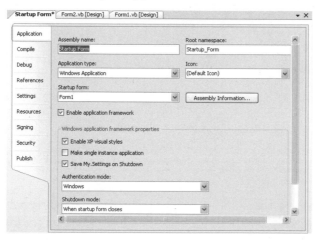

The Project Designer, formerly called a "property pages" dialog box because of its multiple screens of project properties, lets you adjust settings that apply to the entire project in one place. Here you'll use the Application tab and the Startup Form list box to specify a new startup form.

6. Click the Startup Form arrow, and then click Form2.

   Visual Basic changes the startup form in your project from Form1 to Form2. When the program runs, Form2 will be displayed, and Form1 will appear only if it's opened using the *Show* or *ShowDialog* method.

7. Click the Close button to close the Project Designer.

8. Click the Start Debugging button.

   The program runs in the development environment, and Form2 appears.

9. Click the Close button on the form to end the program.

10. Close the project, and discard your changes—it is not necessary to save this simple demonstration project, and you're finished managing forms for now.

Although this demonstration exercise was fairly simple, you can see that Visual Basic offers you some flexibility in how you start your programs. You can specify the startup form, and you can place code within that form's *_Load* event procedure to configure the program or adjust its settings before the first form is actually loaded.

Console Applications

If you want to write a Visual Basic application that displays no graphical user interface at all, consider writing a *console* application. This Visual Studio project type processes input and output by using a command-line console (a character-based window also known as the *command prompt*).

You can specify the console application type when you create your project by using the New Project command on the File menu (select the Console Application template), and you can convert an existing project into a console application by displaying the Project Designer, clicking the Application tab, and then selecting Console Application in the Application Type list box. Console applications begin execution within the *Sub Main* procedure inside a code module, because there are no forms to display. You can find out more about this topic by reviewing "Building Console Applications" in the Contents section of the Visual Studio online Help. (Look for the article under the "Visual Studio" and "Types of Applications and Components" topics.)

Chapter 14 Quick Reference

To	Do this
Add a new form to a program	On the Project menu, click Add Windows Form, and then click Add.
Switch between forms in your project, or open hidden forms by using program code	Use the *Show* or *ShowDialog* method. For example: ``` form2.ShowDialog() ``` You can also use the *My.Forms* object to display a form. For example: ``` My.Forms.HelpInfo.ShowDialog() ``` Hide the current form by using the *Me* object. For example: ``` Me.Visible = False ``` Display a form that is hidden by using the *Me* object. For example: ``` Me.ShowDialog() ``` Note that to use the *Me* object, your program code must be located within the form you are manipulating.
Create a new form with program code and set its properties	Create the form by using the *Dim* and *New* keywords and the *Form* class, and then set any necessary properties. For example: ``` Dim form2 As New Form form2.Text = "My New Form" ```
Position a startup form on the Windows desktop	Set the *StartPosition* property to one of the available options, such as CenterScreen or CenterParent.
Size and position a startup form on the Windows desktop by using code	Set the *StartPosition* to Manual, declare a *Rectangle* structure that defines the form's size and position, and then use the *DesktopBounds* property to size and position the form on the desktop. For example: ``` form2.StartPosition = FormStartPosition.Manual Dim Form2Rect As New Rectangle _ (200, 100, 300, 250) form2.DesktopBounds = Form2Rect ```
Minimize, maximize, or restore a form at run time	Set the *MaximizeBox* and *MinimizeBox* properties for the form to True in design mode to allow for maximize and minimize operations. In the program code, set the form's *WindowState* property to FormWindowState.Minimized, FormWindowState.Maximized, or FormWindowState.Normal when you want to change the window state of the form.
Add controls to a form at run time	Create a control of the desired type, set its properties, and then add it to the form's *Controls* collection. For example: ``` Dim button1 as New Button button1.Text = "Click Me" button1.Location = New Point(20, 25) form2.Controls.Add(button1) ```

To	Do this
Anchor an object a specific distance from specific edges of the form	Set the *Anchor* property of the object, and specify the edges you want to remain a constant distance from. Use the *Or* operator when specifying multiple edges. For example: ```\nButton1.Anchor = AnchorStyles.Bottom Or _\n AnchorStyles.Right\n```
Dock an object to one of the form's edges	Set the *Dock* property of the object, and specify the edge you want the object to be attached to. For example: ```\nPictureBox1.Dock = DockStyle.Top\n```
Specify the startup form in a project	Click the Properties command on the Project menu to open the Project Designer. For a Windows Application project, you can specify any form in your project as the startup form by clicking the form name in the Startup Form list box.
Create a Visual Basic program with no user interface (or only a command line interface)	Create a console application project by clicking the New Project command on the File menu, clicking the Console Application template, and clicking OK. You then add the program code to one or more modules, not forms, and execution begins with a procedure named *Sub Main*.

Chapter 15

Adding Graphics and Animation Effects

After completing this chapter, you will be able to:

- Use the *System.Drawing* namespace to add graphics to your forms.
- Create animation effects on your forms.
- Expand or shrink objects on a form at run time.
- Change the transparency of a form.

For many developers, adding artwork and special effects to an application is the most exciting—and addictive—part of programming. Fortunately, creating impressive and useful graphical effects with Microsoft Visual Basic 2005 is both satisfying and easy.

In this chapter, you'll learn how to add a number of visually interesting features to your programs. You'll learn how to create compelling artwork on a form, how to create simple animation effects by using *PictureBox* and *Timer* controls, and how to expand or shrink objects at run time by using the *Height* and *Width* properties. You'll also learn how to change the transparency of the form. When you've finished, you'll have many of the skills you need to create a visually exciting user interface.

What will you be able to do on your own? This is the point when your imagination takes over. One of my favorite results is from a reader of a previous version of this book who used what he had learned about Visual Basic and graphics to build his own electrocardiograph machine, complete with analog circuitry and a Windows form displaying digital data from the home-made EKG. If this isn't your idea of fun, you might more modestly decide to enhance your application's start page so that it contains custom artwork and visual effects—perhaps in combination with one or more digital photographs loaded into picture box objects on a form.

Even game programmers can have some serious fun using graphics in Visual Basic and Visual Studio. However, if you're planning on creating the next version of Microsoft Zoo Tycoon or Microsoft Halo, you had better plan for much more than visual output. Modern video games contain huge libraries of objects and complex formulas for rendering graphical images that go well beyond the scope of this book. But that still leaves a lot of room for experimentation and fun!

Upgrade Notes: Migrating Visual Basic 6 Code to Visual Basic 2005

If you're experienced with Microsoft Visual Basic 6, you'll notice some new features in Visual Basic 2005, including the following:

- In Visual Basic 6, you use the *Line* and *Shape* controls to create simple lines, rectangles, and circles on your forms. In Visual Basic 2005, no drawing controls are provided in the Toolbox. Instead, you're encouraged to use the GDI+ graphics services directly through the *System.Drawing* namespace.

- The Visual Basic 6 keywords *Circle*, *Line*, and *PSet* have been replaced, respectively, by the *DrawEllipse* method, the *DrawLine* method, and the *Point* structure in the *System.Drawing.Graphics* class.

- The coordinate system in Visual Basic is now pixels rather than twips.

- In Visual Basic 6, many controls can be relocated, or *animated*, on the form by rapidly calling the control's *Move* method. Visual Basic 2005 controls don't have a *Move* method, but they can still be relocated quickly by updating the control's *Left*, *Top*, or *Location* property or by using the *SetBounds* method.

- Visual Basic 2005 controls continue to support drag-and-drop effects, but they handle them in a different way. For example, although Visual Basic 2005 continues to support the *DragDrop* event, the *DragIcon* and *DragMode* properties are no longer available.

- Microsoft Visual Studio 2005 can work with more image formats than Visual Basic 6 can. In particular, the *System.Drawing.Imaging* namespace contains functions to work with the following image formats: BMP, EMF, EXIF, GIF, Icon, JPEG, MemoryBMP, PNG, TIFF, and WMF.

Adding Artwork by Using the *System.Drawing* Namespace

Adding ready-made artwork to your programs is easy in Visual Basic. Throughout this book you've experimented with adding bitmaps and icons to a form by using picture box objects. Now you'll learn how to create original artwork on your forms by using the GDI+ functions in the *System.Drawing* namespace, an application programming interface (API) provided by the Microsoft .NET Framework for creating two-dimensional vector graphics, imaging, and typography within the Microsoft Windows operating system. The effects that you create can add color, shape, and texture to your forms.

Using a Form's Coordinate System

The first thing to learn about creating graphics is the layout of the form's predefined coordinate system. In Visual Basic, each form has its own coordinate system. The coordinate system's starting point, or *origin*, is the upper-left corner of a form. The default coordinate system is made up of rows and columns of device-independent picture elements, or *pixels*, which represent the smallest points that you can locate, or *address*, on a Visual Basic form.

In the Visual Basic coordinate system, rows of pixels are aligned to the *x*-axis (horizontal axis), and columns of pixels are aligned to the *y*-axis (vertical axis). You define locations in the coordinate system by identifying the intersection of a row and a column with the notation (*x*, *y*). The (*x*, *y*) coordinates of the upper-left corner of a form are always (0, 0). The following illustration shows how the location for a picture box object on the form is described in the Visual Basic coordinate system:

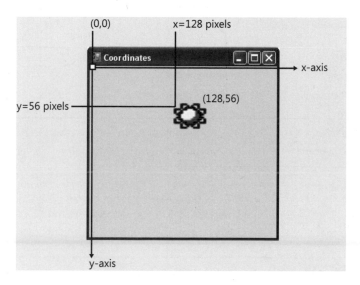

Visual Basic works along with your computer's video display driver software to determine how pixels are displayed on the form and how shapes such as lines, rectangles, curves, and circles are displayed. Occasionally, more than one pixel is turned on to display a particular shape, such as the line drawing shown in the following illustration. The logic that handles this type of rendering isn't your responsibility—it's handled by your display adapter and the drawing routines in the GDI+ graphics library. The following illustration shows a zoomed-in view of the distortion or jagged edges you sometimes see in Visual Basic and Windows applications:

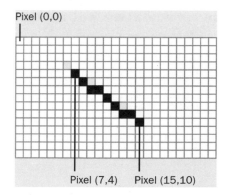

The *System.Drawing.Graphics* Class

The *System.Drawing* namespace includes numerous classes for creating artwork and special effects in your programs. In this section, you'll learn a little about the *System.Drawing.Graphics* class, which provides methods and properties for drawing shapes on your forms. You can learn about the other classes by referring to the Visual Studio online Help.

Whether you're creating simple illustrations or building complex drawings, it's important to be able to render many of the standard geometric shapes in your programs. The following table lists several of the fundamental drawing shapes and the methods you use in the *System .Drawing.Graphics* class to create them.

Shape	Method	Description
Line	*DrawLine*	Simple line connecting two points.
Rectangle	*DrawRectangle*	Rectangle or square connecting four points.
Arc	*DrawArc*	Curved line connecting two points (a portion of an ellipse).
Circle/Ellipse	*DrawEllipse*	Elliptical shape that is "bounded" by a rectangle.
Polygon	*DrawPolygon*	Complex shape with a variable number of points and sides (stored in an array).
Curve	*DrawCurve*	A curved line that passes through a variable number of points (stored in an array); complex curves called *cardinal splines* can also be drawn with this method.
Bézier splines	*DrawBezier*	A curve drawn by using four points. (Points two and three are "control" points.)

In addition to the preceding methods, which create empty or "non-filled" shapes, there are several methods for drawing shapes that are filled with color. These methods usually have a "Fill" prefix, such as *FillRectangle*, *FillEllipse*, and *FillPolygon*.

When you use a graphics method in the *System.Drawing.Graphics* class, you need to create a *Graphics* object in your code to represent the class and either a *Pen* or *Brush* object to indicate the attributes of the shape you want to draw, such as line width and fill color. The *Pen* object is passed as one of the arguments to the methods that aren't filled with color. The *Brush* object is passed as an argument when a fill color is desired. For example, the following call to the *DrawLine* method uses a *Pen* object and four integer values to draw a line that starts at pixel (20, 30) and ends at pixel (100, 80). The *Graphics* object is declared by using the name *GraphicsFun*, and the *Pen* object is declared by using the name *PenColor*.

```
Dim GraphicsFun As System.Drawing.Graphics
Dim PenColor As New System.Drawing.Pen(System.Drawing.Color.Red)
GraphicsFun = Me.CreateGraphics
GraphicsFun.DrawLine(PenColor, 20, 30, 100, 80)
```

The syntax for the *DrawLine* method is important, but also note the three lines above it, which are required to use a method in the *System.Drawing.Graphics* class. You must create variables to represent both the *Graphics* and *Pen* objects, and the *Graphics* variable needs to be instantiated by using the *CreateGraphics* method for the Windows form. Note that the *System .Drawing.Graphics* namespace is included in your project automatically—you don't need to include an *Imports* statement in your code to declare the necessary class.

Using the Form's *Paint* Event

If you test the previous *DrawLine* method in a program, you'll notice that the line you created lasts, or *persists*, on the form only as long as nothing else covers it up. If a dialog box appears on the form momentarily and covers the line, the line is no longer visible when the entire form is visible again. The line also disappears if you minimize the form window and then maximize it again. To address this shortcoming, you need to place your graphics code in the form's *Paint* event procedure so that each time the form is refreshed, the graphics are repainted, too.

In the following exercise, you'll create three shapes on a form by using the form's *Paint* event procedure. The shapes you draw will continue to persist even if the form is covered or minimized.

Create line, rectangle, and ellipse shapes

1. Start Visual Studio, and create a new Windows Application project named **My Draw Shapes**.

2. Resize the form so that it's higher and wider than the default form size.

    You'll need a little extra space to create the graphics shapes. You won't be using any Toolbox controls, however. You'll create the shapes by placing program code in the form's *Form1_Paint* event procedure.

3. Set the *Text* property of Form1 to "Draw Shapes".

4. Click the View Code button in Solution Explorer to display the Code Editor.

5. In the Class Name list box, click Form1 Events.

    Form1 Events is the list of events in your project associated with the *Form1* object.

6. In the Method Name list box, click the *Paint* event.

7. The *Form1_Paint* event procedure appears in the Code Editor.

    This event procedure is where you place code that should be executed when Visual Basic refreshes the form.

8.   Type the following program code:

```
'Prepare GraphicsFun variable for graphics calls
Dim GraphicsFun As System.Drawing.Graphics
GraphicsFun = Me.CreateGraphics

'Use a red pen color to draw a line and an ellipse
Dim PenColor As New System.Drawing.Pen(System.Drawing.Color.Red)
GraphicsFun.DrawLine(PenColor, 20, 30, 100, 80)
GraphicsFun.DrawEllipse(PenColor, 10, 120, 200, 160)

'Use a green brush color to create a filled rectangle
Dim BrushColor As New SolidBrush(Color.Green)
GraphicsFun.FillRectangle(BrushColor, 150, 10, 250, 100)

'Create a blue cardinal spline curve with four points
Dim Points() As Point = {New Point(358, 280), _
New Point(300, 320), New Point(275, 155), New Point(350, 180)}
For tension As Single = 0 To 2.5 Step 0.5
    GraphicsFun.DrawCurve(Pens.DodgerBlue, Points, tension)
Next
```

This sample event procedure draws four graphic shapes on your form: a red line, a red ellipse, a green-filled rectangle, and a blue cardinal spline (a complex curve made up of five lines). To enable graphics programming, the routine declares a variable named *GraphicsFun* in the code and uses the *CreateGraphics* method to activate or instantiate the variable. The *PenColor* variable of type *System.Drawing.Pen* is used to set the drawing color in the line and ellipse, and the *BrushColor* variable of type *SolidBrush* is used to set the fill color in the rectangle. These examples are obviously just the tip of the graphics library iceberg—there are many more shapes, colors, and variations that you can create by using the methods in the *System.Drawing.Graphics* class.

> **Tip**   The complete Draw Shapes program is located in the c:\vb05sbs\chap15\draw shapes folder.

9.   Click the Start Debugging button on the Standard toolbar to run the program.

Visual Basic loads the form and executes the form's *Paint* event. Your form looks like this:

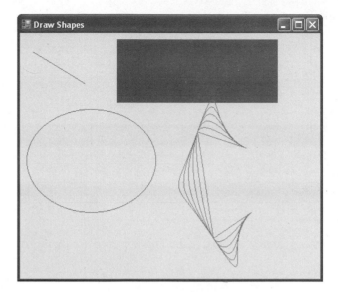

10. Minimize the form, and then restore it again.

     The form's *Paint* event is executed again, and the graphics shapes are refreshed on the form.

11. Click the Close button to end the program.

12. Click the Save All button on the Standard toolbar to save the project, and specify the c:\vb05sbs\chap15 folder as the location.

Now you're ready to move on to some simple animation effects.

Adding Animation to Your Programs

Displaying bitmaps and drawing shapes adds visual interest to a program, but for programmers, the king of graphical effects has always been animation. *Animation* is the simulation of movement produced by rapidly displaying a series of related images on the screen. Real animation involves moving objects programmatically, and it often involves changing the size or shape of the images along the way.

In this section, you'll learn how to add simple animation to your programs. You'll learn how to update the *Top* and *Left* properties of a picture box, control the rate of animation by using a timer object, and sense the edge of your form's window.

Moving Objects on the Form

In Visual Basic 6, a special method named *Move* allows you to move objects in the coordinate system. The *Move* method is no longer supported by Microsoft Visual Basic .NET 2003 or Visual Basic 2005 controls. However, you can use the method and properties shown in the following table instead.

Keyword	Description
Left	This property can be used to move an object horizontally (left or right).
Top	This property can be used to move an object vertically (up or down).
Location	This property can be used to move an object to the specified location.
SetBounds	This method sets the boundaries of an object to the specified location and size.

The following sections discuss how you can use the *Left*, *Top*, and *Location* properties to move objects.

To move an object in a horizontal direction, use the *Left* property, which uses the syntax

```
object.Left = horizontal
```

where *object* is the name of the object on the form that you want to move, and *horizontal* is the new horizontal, or *x*-axis, coordinate of the left edge of the object, measured in pixels. For example, the following program statement moves a picture box object to a location 300 pixels to the right of the left window edge:

```
PictureBox1.Left = 300
```

To move a relative distance to the right or left, you would add or subtract pixels from the current *Left* property setting. For example, to move an object 50 pixels to the right, you add 50 to the *Left* property, as follows:

```
PictureBox1.Left = PictureBox1.Left + 50
```

In a similar way, you can change the vertical location of an object on a form by setting the *Top* property, which takes the syntax

```
object.Top = vertical
```

where *object* is the name of the object on the form that you want to move, and *vertical* is the new vertical, or *y*-axis, coordinate of the top edge of the object, measured in pixels. For example, the following program statement moves a picture box object to a location 150 pixels below the window's title bar:

```
PictureBox1.Top = 150
```

Relative movements down or up are easily made by adding or subtracting pixels from the current *Top* property setting. For example, to move 30 pixels in a downward direction, you add 30 to the current *Top* property, as follows:

```
PictureBox1.Top = PictureBox1.Top + 30
```

The *Location* Property

To move an object in both vertical and horizontal directions, you can use a combination of the *Left* and *Top* property settings. For example, to relocate the upper-left corner of a picture box object to the (x, y) coordinates (300, 200), you enter the following program code:

```
PictureBox1.Left = 300
PictureBox1.Top = 200
```

However, the designers of Visual Studio don't recommend using two program statements to relocate an object if you plan to make numerous object movements in a program (for example, if you plan to move an object hundreds or thousands of times during an elaborate animation effect). Instead, you should use the *Location* property with the syntax

```
object.Location = New Point(horizontal, vertical)
```

where *object* is the name of the object, *horizontal* is the horizontal *x*-axis coordinate, *vertical* is the vertical *y*-axis coordinate, and *Point* is a structure identifying the pixel location for the upper-left corner of the object. For example, the following program statement moves a picture box object to an (x, y) coordinate of (300, 200):

```
PictureBox1.Location = New Point(300, 200)
```

To perform a relative movement using the *Location* property, the *Location.X* and *Location.Y* properties are needed. For example, the program statement

```
PictureBox1.Location = New Point(PictureBox1.Location.X - 50, _
  PictureBox1.Location.Y - 40)
```

moves the picture box object 50 pixels left and 40 pixels up on the form. Although this construction seems a bit unwieldy, it's the recommended way to relocate objects in relative movements on your form at run time.

Creating Animation by Using a *Timer* Object

The trick to creating animation in a program is placing one or more *Location* property updates in a timer event procedure so that at set intervals the timer causes one or more objects to drift across the screen. In Chapter 7, "Using Loops and Timers," you learned how to use a timer object to update a simple clock utility every second so that it displayed the correct time. When you create animation, you set the *Interval* property of the timer to a much faster rate—1/5 second (200 milliseconds), 1/10 second (100 milliseconds), or less. The exact rate you choose depends on how fast you want the animation to run.

Another trick is to use the *Top* and *Left* properties and the size of the form to "sense" the edges of the form. By using these values in an event procedure, you can stop the animation (disable the timer) when an object reaches the edge of the form. And by using the *Top* property, the *Left* property, form size properties, and an If...Then or Select Case decision structure, you can make an object appear to bounce off one or more edges of the form.

The following exercise demonstrates how you can animate a picture box containing a Sun icon (Sun.ico) by using the *Location* property and a timer object. In this exercise, you'll use the *Top* property to detect the top edge of the form, and you'll use the *Size.Height* property to detect the bottom edge. The Sun icon will move back and forth between these extremes each time you click a button.

Animate a Sun icon on your form

1. Click the Close Project command on the File menu, and then create a new project named **My Moving Icon**.

2. Using the *Button* control, draw two button objects in the lower-left corner of the form.

3. Using the *PictureBox* control, draw a small rectangular picture box object in the lower-right corner of the form.

    This is the object that you'll animate in the program.

4. Double-click the *Timer* control on the Components tab of the Toolbox to add it to the component tray below the form.

    The timer object is the mechanism that controls the pace of the animation. Recall that the timer object itself isn't visible on the form, so it's shown below the form in the component tray reserved for non-visible objects.

5. Set the following properties for the button, picture box, timer, and form objects. To set the *PictureBox1* object's *Image* property, select All Files in the Files of Type list box before you browse to the file (files of the .ico type are not displayed by default).

Object	Property	Setting
Button1	*Text*	"Move Up"
Button2	*Text*	"Move Down"
PictureBox1	*Image*	"c:\vb05sbs\chap15\sun.ico"
	SizeMode	StretchImage
Timer1	*Interval*	75
Form1	*Text*	"Basic Animation"

After you set these properties, your form looks similar to this:

6. Double-click the Move Up button to edit its event procedure.

   The *Button1_Click* event procedure appears in the Code Editor.

7. Type the following program code:

```
GoingUp = True
Timer1.Enabled = True
```

   This simple event procedure sets the *GoingUp* variable to True and enables the timer
   object. The actual program code to move the picture box object and sense the correct
   direction is stored in the *Timer1_Tick* event procedure. The *GoingUp* variable is underlined now because you have not declared it yet.

8. Near the top of the form's program code (below the statement `Public Class Form1`),
   type the following variable declaration:

```
Dim GoingUp As Boolean   'GoingUp stores current direction
```

   This variable declaration makes *GoingUp* available to all the event procedures in the
   form, so the underline in the *Button1_Click* event procedure is removed. I've used a
   Boolean variable because there are only two possible directions for movement in this
   program—up and down.

9. Display the form again, double-click the Move Down button, and then enter the following program code in the *Button2_Click* event procedure:

```
GoingUp = False
Timer1.Enabled = True
```

This routine is very similar to the *Button1_Click* event procedure, except that it changes the direction from up to down.

10. Display the form again, double-click the *Timer1* object, and then enter the following program code in the *Timer1_Tick* event procedure:

```
If GoingUp = True Then
    'move picture box toward the top
    If PictureBox1.Top > 10 Then
        PictureBox1.Location = New Point _
          (PictureBox1.Location.X - 10, _
          PictureBox1.Location.Y - 10)
    End If
Else
    'move picture box toward the bottom
    If PictureBox1.Top < (Me.Size.Height - 75) Then
        PictureBox1.Location = New Point _
          (PictureBox1.Location.X + 10, _
          PictureBox1.Location.Y + 10)
    End If
End If
```

As long as the timer is enabled, this If...Then decision structure is executed every 75 milliseconds. The first line in the procedure checks whether the *GoingUp* Boolean variable is set to True, indicating that the icon is moving toward the top of the form. If it's set to True, the procedure moves the picture box object to a relative position 10 pixels closer to both the top and left edges of the form.

If the *GoingUp* variable is currently set to False, the decision structure moves the icon down instead. In this case, the picture box object moves until the edge of the form is detected. The height of the form can be determined by using the *Me.Size.Height* property. (I subtract 75 from the form height so that the icon is still displayed on the form.) The *Me* object in this example represents the form (*Form1*).

As you'll see when you run the program, this movement gives the icon animation a steady drifting quality. To make the icon move faster, you decrease the *Interval* setting for the timer object. To make the icon move slower, you increase the *Interval* setting.

Run the Moving Icon program

> **Tip**   The complete Moving Icon program is located in the c:\vb05sbs\chap15\moving icon folder.

1. Click the Start Debugging button to run the program.

   The Moving Icon program runs in the IDE.

2. Click the Move Up button.

The picture box object moves up the form on a diagonal path, as indicated here:

After a few moments, the button comes to rest at the upper edge of the form.

> **Note**   If you placed the picture box object in the lower-right corner of the form as instructed in step 3 of the previous exercise, you see something similar to this illustration. However, if you placed the picture box object in another location, or created a smaller form, the image might drift off the screen when you click Move Up or Move Down. Can you tell why?

3. Click the Move Down button.

    The picture box moves back down again to the lower-right corner of the screen.

4. Click both buttons again several times, and ponder the animation effects.

    Note that you don't need to wait for one animation effect to end before you click the next button. The *Timer1_Tick* event procedure uses the *GoingUp* variable immediately to manage your direction requests, so it doesn't matter whether the picture box has finished going in one direction. Consider this effect for a moment, and imagine how you could use a similar type of logic to build your own Visual Basic video games. You could increase or decrease the animation rates according to specific conditions or "collisions" on screen, and you could force the animated objects to move in different directions. You could also change the picture displayed by the picture box object based on where the icon is on the screen or what conditions it encounters.

5. When you're finished running the program, click the Close button on the form to stop the demonstration.

6. Click the Save All button to save the project, and specify the c:\vb05sbs\chap15 folder as the location.

Expanding and Shrinking Objects While a Program Is Running

In addition to maintaining a *Top* property and a *Left* property, Visual Basic maintains a *Height* property and a *Width* property for most objects on a form. You can use these properties in clever ways to expand and shrink objects while a program is running. The following exercise shows you how to do it.

Expand a picture box at run time

1. On the File menu, click the Close Project command.

2. Create a new project named **My Zoom In**.

3. Display the form, click the *PictureBox* control in the Toolbox, and then draw a small picture box object near the upper-left corner of the form.

4. Set the following properties for the picture box and the form. When you set the properties for the picture box, note the current values in the *Height* and *Width* properties within the *Size* property. (You can set these at design time, too.)

Object	Property	Setting
PictureBox1	Image	"c:\vb05sbs\chap15\earth.ico"
	SizeMode	StretchImage
Form1	Text	"Approaching Earth"

5. Double-click the *PictureBox1* object on the form.

    The *PictureBox1_Click* event procedure appears in the Code Editor.

6. Type the following program code in the *PictureBox1_Click* event procedure:

    ```
    PictureBox1.Height = PictureBox1.Height + 15
    PictureBox1.Width = PictureBox1.Width + 15
    ```

7. These two lines increase the height and width of the Earth icon by 15 pixels each time the user clicks the picture box. If you stretch your imagination a little, watching the effect makes you feel like you're approaching Earth in a spaceship.

8. Click the Save All button, and then save the project in the c:\vb05sbs\chap15 folder.

> **Tip**   The complete Zoom In program is located in the c:\vb05sbs\chap15\zoom in folder.

9. Click the Start Debugging button to run the program.

The Earth icon appears alone on the form, as shown here:

10. Click the Earth icon several times to expand it on the screen.

    After 10 or 11 clicks, your screen looks similar to this:

11. When you get close enough to establish a standard orbit, click the Close button to quit the program.

    The program stops, and the development environment returns.

One Step Further: Changing Form Transparency

Interested in one last special effect? With GDI+, you can do things that are difficult or even impossible in earlier versions of Visual Basic. For example, you can make a form partially transparent so that you can see through it. Let's say you're designing a photo-display program that includes a separate form with various options to manipulate the photos. You can make the option form partially transparent so that the user can see any photos beneath it while still having access to the options.

In the following exercise, you'll change the transparency of a form by changing the value of the *Opacity* property.

Set the *Opacity* property

1. On the File menu, click the Close Project command.

2. Create a new project named **My Transparent Form**.

3. Display the form, click the *Button* control in the Toolbox, and then draw two buttons on the form.

4. Set the following properties for the two buttons and the form:

Object	Property	Setting
Button1	*Text*	"Set Opacity"
Button2	*Text*	"Restore"
Form1	*Text*	"Transparent Form"

5. Double-click the Set Opacity button on the form.

6. Type the following program code in the *Button1_Click* event procedure:

```
Me.Opacity = 0.75
```

Opacity is specified as a percentage, so it has a range of 0 to 1. This line sets the *Opacity* of Form1 (*Me*) to 75 percent.

7. Display the form again, double-click the Restore button, and then enter the following program code in the *Button2_Click* event procedure:

```
Me.Opacity = 1
```

This line restores the opacity to 100 percent.

8. Click the Save All button, and save the project in the c:\vb05sbs\chap15 folder.

> **Tip** The complete Transparent Form program is located in the c:\vb05sbs\chap15\transparent form folder.

9. Click the Start Debugging button to run the program.

10. Click the Set Opacity button.

Notice how you can see through the form, as shown here:

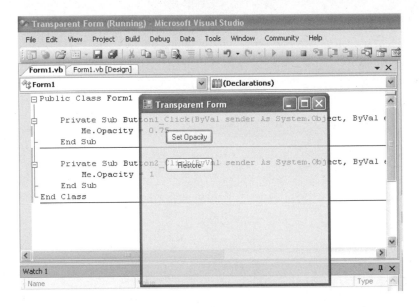

11. Click the Restore button.

    The transparency effect is removed.

12. When you're done testing the transparency effect, click the Close button to quit the program.

    The program stops, and the development environment returns.

Chapter 15 Quick Reference

To	Do this
Create lines or shapes on a form	Use methods in the *System.Drawing.Graphics* namespace. For example, the following program statements draw an ellipse on the form:

	``Dim GraphicsFun As System.Drawing.Graphics
	GraphicsFun = Me.CreateGraphics
	Dim PenColor As New System.Drawing.Pen _
	   (System.Drawing.Color.Red)
	GraphicsFun.DrawEllipse(PenColor, 10, _
	   120, 200, 160)```

Create lines or shapes that persist on the form during window redraws	Place the graphics methods in the *Paint* event procedure for the form.
Move an object on a form	Relocate the object by using the *Location* property, the *New* keyword, and the *Point* structure. For example: ```PictureBox1.Location = New Point(300, 200)```

To	Do this
Animate an object	Use a timer event procedure to modify the *Left*, *Top*, or *Location* properties for an object on the form. The timer's *Interval* property controls animation speed.
Expand or shrink an object at run time	Change the object's *Height* property or *Width* property.
Change the transparency of a form	Change the *Opacity* property.

Chapter 16
Inheriting Forms and Creating Base Classes

After completing this chapter, you will be able to:

- Use the Inheritance Picker to incorporate existing forms in your projects.

- Create your own base classes with custom properties and methods.

- Derive new classes from base classes by using the *Inherits* statement.

An important skill for virtually all professional software developers today is the ability to understand and utilize *object-oriented programming* (OOP) techniques. Although Microsoft Visual Basic 6 offers several object-oriented programming features, experts say that it lags behind the "true" OOP languages, such as Microsoft Visual C++, because it lacks *inheritance*, a mechanism that allows one class to acquire the interface and behavior characteristics of another class.

Beginning with Microsoft Visual Basic .NET 2002, the Visual Basic language and IDE *have* supported inheritance, which means that you can build one form in the development environment and pass its characteristics and functionality on to other forms. In addition, you can build your own classes and inherit properties, methods, and events from them.

In this chapter, you'll experiment with both types of inheritance. You'll learn how to integrate existing forms into your projects by using the Inheritance Picker dialog box that is part of Microsoft Visual Studio 2005, and you'll learn how to create your own classes and derive new ones from them by using the *Inherits* statement. With these skills, you'll be able to utilize many of the forms and coding routines you've already developed, making Visual Basic programming a faster and more flexible endeavor. These improvements will help you design compelling user interfaces rapidly and will extend the work that you have done in other programming projects.

Upgrade Notes: Migrating Visual Basic 6 Code to Visual Basic 2005

If you're experienced with Visual Basic 6, you'll notice some new features in Microsoft Visual Basic 2005, including the following:

- You can inherit forms within the Visual Studio IDE by using the Inheritance Picker dialog box.

- Classes are now defined between the *Public Class* and *End Class* keywords.

- Several user-defined classes can now be stored in a single source file. (In Visual Basic 6, each new class has to be stored in its own file.)

- You can add properties to classes by using a new syntax, first introduced in Visual Basic .NET 2002.

- The *Inherits* keyword allows a new derived class to inherit the interface and behaviors of an existing class.

Inheriting a Form by Using the Inheritance Picker

In object-oriented programming syntax, *inheritance* means having one class receive the objects, properties, methods, and other attributes of another class. As I mentioned in the section "Adding New Forms to a Program" in Chapter 14, "Managing Windows Forms and Controls at Run Time," Visual Basic goes through this process routinely when it creates a new form in the development environment. The first form in a project (*Form1*) relies on the *System.Windows.Forms.Form* class for its definition and default values. In fact, this class is identified in the Properties window when you select a form in the Designer, as shown in the following illustration:

Although you haven't realized it, you've been using inheritance all along to define the Windows forms that you've been using to build Visual Basic applications. Although existing forms can be inherited by using program code as well, the designers of Microsoft Visual Studio considered the task to be so important that they designed a special dialog box in the development environment to facilitate the process. This dialog box is called the Inheritance Picker, and it's accessed through the Add New Item command on the Project menu. In the following exercise, you'll use the Inheritance Picker to create a second copy of a dialog box in a project.

Inherit a simple dialog box

1. Start Visual Studio, and create a new Visual Basic Windows Application project named **My Form Inheritance**.

2. Display the form in the project, and use the *Button* control to add two button objects at the bottom of the form, positioned side by side.

3. Change the *Text* properties of the *Button1* and *Button2* buttons to OK and Cancel, respectively.

4. Double-click the OK button to display the *Button1_Click* event procedure in the Code Editor.

5. Type the following program statement:

```
MsgBox("You clicked OK")
```

6. Display the form again, double-click the Cancel button, and then type the following program statement in the *Button2_Click* event procedure:

```
MsgBox("You clicked Cancel")
```

7. Display the form again, and set the *Text* property of the form to "Dialog Box".

    You now have a simple form that can be used as the basis of a dialog box in a program. With some customization, you can use this basic form to process several tasks—you just need to add the controls that are specific to your individual application.

8. Click the Save All button to save your project, and specify the c:\vb05sbs\chap16 folder as the location.

    Now you'll practice inheriting the form. The first step in this process is building, or *compiling*, the project because you can inherit only from forms that are compiled into .exe or .dll files. Each time the base form is recompiled, changes made to the base form are passed to the derived (inherited) form.

9. Click the Build My Form Inheritance command on the Build menu.

    Visual Basic compiles your project and creates an .exe file.

10. Click the Add New Item command on the Project menu, and then click the Inherited Form template.

    The Add New Item dialog box looks as shown on the next page.

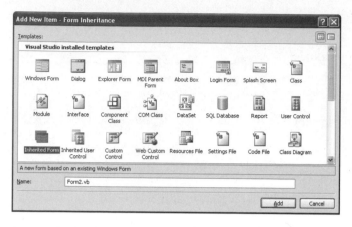

As usual, Visual Studio lists all the possible templates you could include in your projects, not just those related to inheritance. The Inherited Form template gives you access to the Inheritance Picker dialog box.

You can use the Name text box at the bottom of the dialog box to assign a name to your inherited form. This name will appear in Solution Explorer and in the file name of the form on disk.

11. Click Add to accept the default settings for the new, inherited form.

Visual Studio displays the Inheritance Picker dialog box, as shown here:

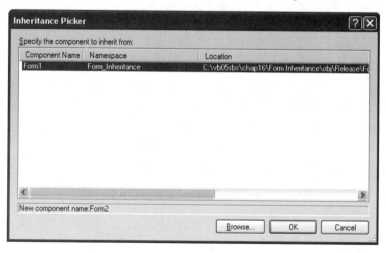

This dialog box lists all the inheritable forms in the current project. If you want to browse for other compiled forms, click the Browse button, and locate the .dll file on your hard disk.

> **Note**   If you want to inherit a form that isn't a component of the current project, the form must be compiled as a .dll file.

12. Click Form1 in the Inheritance Picker dialog box, and then click OK.

    Visual Studio creates the Form2.vb entry in Solution Explorer and displays the inherited form in the Designer. Notice in the following figure that the form looks identical to the Form1 window you created earlier, except that the two buttons contain tiny icons, which indicate that the objects come from an inherited source:

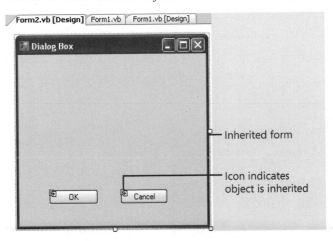

    It can be difficult to tell an inherited form from a base form (the tiny inheritance icons aren't that obvious), but you can also use Solution Explorer and the IDE tabs to distinguish between the forms.

Now you'll add a few new elements to the inherited form.

Customize the inherited form

1. Use the *Button* control to add a third button object to Form2 (the inherited form).

2. Set the *Text* property for the button object to "Click Me!"

3. Double-click the Click Me! button.

4. In the *Button3_Click* event procedure, type the following program statement:

   ```
   MsgBox("This is the inherited form!")
   ```

5. Display Form2 again, and then try double-clicking the OK and Cancel buttons on the form.

   You can't display or edit the event procedures or properties for these inherited objects without taking additional steps that are beyond the scope of this chapter. (Tiny "lock" icons indicate that the inherited objects are read only.) However, you can add new objects to the form to customize it.

6. Enlarge the form.

   You can also change other characteristics of the form, such as its size and location. Notice that if you use the Properties window to customize a form, the Object list box displays the form from which the current form is derived.

   Now set the startup object to Form2.

7. Click the Properties command on the Project menu.

   The Project Designer, first introduced in Chapter 14, "Managing Windows Forms and Controls at Run Time," appears.

8. Click the Startup Form list box, click Form2, and then close the Project Designer.

   Now run the new project.

9. Click the Start Debugging button.

   The inherited form opens, as shown here:

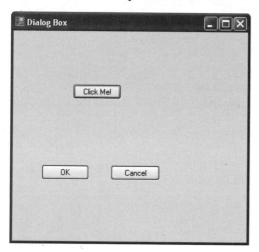

10. Click the OK button.

    The inherited form runs the event procedure it inherited from Form1, and the event procedure displays the following message box:

11. Click OK, and then click the Click Me! button.

Form2 displays the inherited form message.

The inherited form has been customized to include the new object as well as the two inherited button objects. Congratulations! You've taken your first steps with inheritance by using the Inheritance Picker dialog box.

12. Click OK to close the message box, and then click Close on the form to end the program.

The program stops, and the IDE returns.

Creating Your Own Base Classes

The Inheritance Picker managed the inheritance process in the previous exercise by creating a new class in your project named *Form2*. To build the *Form2* class, the Inheritance Picker established a link between the *Form1* class in the My Form Inheritance project and the new form. Here's what the new *Form2* class looks like in the Code Editor:

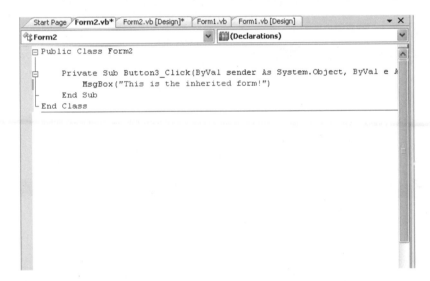

The *Button3_Click* event procedure that you added is also a member of the new class. But recall for a moment that the *Form1* class itself relied on the *System.Windows.Forms.Form* class for its fundamental behavior and characteristics. So the last exercise demonstrates that one derived class (*Form2*) can inherit its functionality from another derived class (*Form1*), which in turn inherited its core functionality from an original base class (*Form*), which is a member of the *System.Windows.Forms* namespace in the Microsoft .NET Framework library.

> **Tip**   In addition to the Inheritance Picker, Visual Studio offers the Inherits statement, which causes the current class to inherit the properties, procedures, and variables of another class. To use the Inherits statement to inherit a form, you must place the Inherits statement at the top of the form as the first statement in the class. Although you might choose to use the Inheritance Picker for this sort of work with forms, it is useful to know about Inherits because it can be used for classes and interfaces other than forms, and you will probably run into it now and then in your colleagues' program code. You'll see an example of the Inherits statement near the end of this chapter.

Recognizing that classes are such a fundamental building block in Visual Basic programs, you might very well ask how new classes are created and how these new classes might be inherited down the road by subsequently derived classes. To ponder these possibilities, I'll devote the remainder of this chapter to discussing the syntax for creating classes in Visual Basic 2005 and introducing how these user-defined classes might be inherited later by still more classes. Along the way, you'll learn how very useful creating your own classes can be.

> **Nerd Alert**
>
> There's a potential danger for terminology overload when discussing class creation and inheritance. A number of very smart computer scientists have been thinking about these object-oriented programming concepts for several years, and there are numerous terms and definitions in use for the concepts that I plan to cover. However, if you stick with me, you'll find that creating classes and inheriting them is quite simple in Visual Basic 2005 and that you can accomplish a lot of useful work by adding just a few lines of program code to your projects.

Adding a New Class to Your Project

Simply stated, a *class* in Visual Basic is a representation or *blueprint* that defines the structure of one or more objects. Creating a class allows you to define your own objects in a program—objects that have properties, methods, fields, and events, just like the objects that the Toolbox controls create on Windows forms. To add a new class to your project, you click the Add Class command on the Project menu, and then you define the class by using program code and a few Visual Basic keywords.

In the following exercise, you'll create a program that prompts a new employee for his or her first name, last name, and date of birth. You'll store this information in the properties of a new class named *Person*, and you'll create a method in the class to compute the current age of the new employee. This project will teach you how to create your own classes and also how to use the classes in the event procedures of your program.

Build the Person Class project

1. Click the Close Project command on the File menu, and then create a new project named **My Person Class**.

2. Use the *Label* control to add a label object to the top of Form1.

3. Use the *TextBox* control to draw two wide text box objects below the label object.

4. Use the *DateTimePicker* control to draw a date time picker object below the text box objects.

   You last used the *DateTimePicker* control to enter dates in Chapter 3, "Working with Toolbox Controls." Go to that chapter if you want to review this control's basic methods and properties.

5. Use the *Button* control to draw a button object below the date time picker object.

6. Set the following properties for the objects on the form:

Object	Property	Setting
Label1	Text	"Enter employee first name, last name, and date of birth."
TextBox1	Text	"First name"
TextBox2	Text	"Last name"
Button1	Text	"Display Record"
Form1	Text	"Person Class"

7. Your form looks something like this:

This is the basic user interface for a form that defines a new employee record for a business. (The form isn't connected to a database, so only one record can be stored at a time.) Now you'll add a class to the project to store the information in the record.

8. Click the Add Class command on the Project menu.

Visual Studio displays the Add New Item dialog box, with the Class template selected, as shown here:

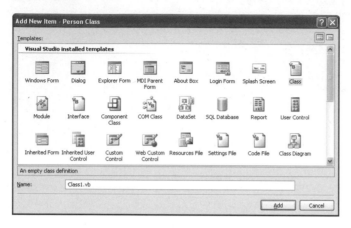

The Add New Item dialog box gives you the opportunity to name your class. Because you can store more than one class in a new class module, you might want to specify a name that is somewhat general.

9. Type **Person.vb** in the Name box, and then click Add.

Visual Studio opens a blank class module in the Code Editor and lists a file named Person.vb in Solution Explorer for your project, as shown here:

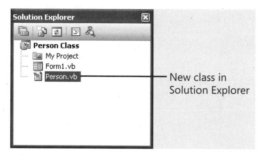

New class in
Solution Explorer

Now you'll type the definition of your class in the class module and learn a few new Visual Basic keywords. You'll follow four steps: declare class variables, create properties, create a method, and finally, create an object based on the new class.

Step 1: Declare class variables

1. Below the *Public Class Person* program statement, type the following variable declarations:

```
Private Name1 As String
Private Name2 As String
```

Here you declare two variables that will be used exclusively within the class module to store the values for two string property settings. I've declared the variables by using the *Private* keyword because, by convention, Visual Basic programmers keep their internal class variables private—in other words, not available for inspection outside the class module itself.

Step 2: Create properties

1. Below the variable declarations, type the following program statement, and press Enter:

```
Public Property FirstName() As String
```

This statement creates a property named *FirstName*, which is of type *String*, in your class. When you press Enter, Visual Studio immediately supplies a code structure for the remaining elements in the property declaration. The required elements are a Get block, which determines what other programmers see when they check the *FirstName* property; a Set block, which determines what happens when the *FirstName* property is set or changed; and an *End Property* statement, which marks the end of the property procedure.

2. Fill out the property procedure structure so that it looks like the code that follows. (The elements you type are in bold italic.)

```
Public Property FirstName() As String
    Get
        Return Name1
    End Get
    Set(ByVal value As String)
        Name1 = value
    End Set
End Property
```

The *Return* keyword specifies that the *Name1* string variable will be returned when the *FirstName* property is referenced. The Set block assigns a string value to the *Name1* variable when the property is set. Notice here especially the *value* variable, which is used in property procedures to stand for the value that's assigned to the class when a property is set. Although this syntax might look strange, trust me for now—this is how you create property settings in controls, although more sophisticated properties would add additional program logic here to test values or make computations.

3. Below the *End Property* statement, type a second property procedure for the *LastName* property in your class. It should look like the code that follows. (The bold italic lines are the ones you type.)

```
Public Property LastName() As String
    Get
        Return Name2
    End Get
    Set(ByVal value As String)
        Name2 = value
    End Set
End Property
```

This property procedure is similar to the first one, except that it uses the second string variable (*Name2*) that you declared at the top of the class.

You're finished defining the two properties in your class. Now let's move on to a method named *Age* that will determine the new employee's current age based on his or her birth date.

Step 3: Create a method

1. Below the *LastName* property procedure, type the following function definition:

```
Public Function Age(ByVal Birthday As Date) As Integer
    Return Int(Now.Subtract(Birthday).Days / 365.25)
End Function
```

To create a method in the class that performs a specific action, you add a function or a Sub procedure to your class. Although many methods don't require arguments to accomplish their work, the *Age* method I'm defining requires a *Birthday* argument of type *Date* to complete its calculation. The method uses the *Subtract* method to subtract the new employee's birth date from the current system time, and it returns the value expressed in days divided by 365.25—the approximate length in days of a single year. The *Int* function converts this value to an integer, and this number is returned to the calling procedure via the *Return* statement—just like a typical function. (For more information about function definitions, see Chapter 10, "Creating Modules and Procedures.")

Your class definition is finished, and in the Code Editor, the Person Class now looks like the following:

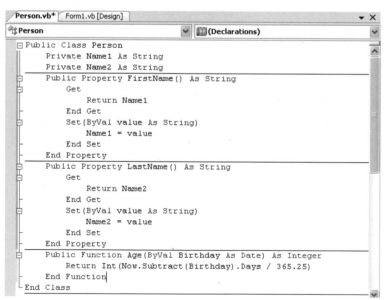

Now you'll return to Form1 and use the new class in an event procedure.

Tip Although you didn't do it for this example, it's usually wise to add some type-checking logic to class modules in actual projects so that properties or methods that are improperly used don't trigger run-time errors that halt the program.

Step 4: Create an object based on the new class

1. Click the Form1.vb icon in Solution Explorer, and then click the View Designer button.

   The Form1 user interface appears.

2. Double-click the Display Record button to open the *Button1_Click* event procedure in the Code Editor.

3. Type the following program statements:

```
Dim Employee As New Person
Dim DOB As Date

Employee.FirstName = TextBox1.Text
Employee.LastName = TextBox2.Text
DOB = DateTimePicker1.Value.Date

MsgBox(Employee.FirstName & " " & Employee.LastName _
  & " is " & Employee.Age(DOB) & " years old.")
```

   This routine stores the values entered by the user in an object named *Employee* that's declared as type *Person*. The *New* keyword indicates that you want to immediately create a new instance of the *Employee* object. You've declared variables often in this book—now you get to declare one based on a class you created yourself! The routine then declares a *Date* variable named *DOB* to store the date entered by the user, and the *FirstName* and *LastName* properties of the *Employee* object are set to the first and last names returned by the two text box objects on the form. The value returned by the date and time picker object is stored in the *DOB* variable, and the final program statement displays a message box containing the *FirstName* and *LastName* properties plus the age of the new employee as determined by the *Age* method, which returns an integer value when the *DOB* variable is passed to it. After you define a class in a class module, it's a simple matter to use it in an event procedure, as this routine demonstrates.

4. Click the Save All button to save your changes, and specify the c:\vb05sbs\chap16 folder as the location.

5. Click the Start Debugging button to run the program.

   The user interface appears in the IDE, ready for your input.

6. Type your first name in the First Name text box and your last name in the Last Name text box.

7. Click the date time picker object's arrow, and scroll in the list box to your birth date (mine is March 1, 1963).

> **Tip** You can scroll faster into the past by clicking the year field when the date time picker dialog box is open. Tiny scroll arrows appear, and you can move one year at a time backward or forward. You can also move quickly to the month you want by clicking the month field and then clicking the month in a pop-up menu.

Your form looks similar to this:

8. Click the Display Record button.

   Your program stores the first name and last name values in property settings and uses the *Age* method to calculate the new employee's current age. A message box displays the result, as shown here:

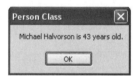

9. Click OK to close the message box, and then experiment with a few different date values, clicking Display Record each time you change the birth date field.

10. When you're finished experimenting with your new class, click the Close button on the form.

    The development environment returns.

One Step Further: Inheriting a Base Class

As promised at the beginning of this chapter, I have one more trick to show you regarding user-defined classes and inheritance. Just as forms can inherit form classes, they can also inherit classes that you've defined by using the Add Class command and a class module. The mechanism for inheriting a base (parent) class is to use the *Inherits* statement to include the previously defined class in a new class. You can then add additional properties or methods to the derived (child) class to distinguish it from the base class.

In the following exercise, you'll modify the My Person Class project so that it stores information about new teachers and the grades they teach. First you'll add a second user-defined class, called *Teacher*, to the *Person* class module. This new class will inherit the *FirstName* property, the *LastName* property, and the *Age* method from the *Person* class and will add an additional property named *Grade* to store the grade in which the new teacher teaches.

Use the *Inherits* keyword

1. Click the Person.vb class in Solution Explorer, and then click the View Code button.

2. Scroll to the bottom of the Code Editor so that the insertion point is below the *End Class* statement.

   As I mentioned earlier, you can include more than one class in a class module, as long as each class is delimited by *Public Class* and *End Class* statements. You'll create a class named *Teacher* in this class module, and you'll use the *Inherits* keyword to incorporate the method and properties you defined in the *Person* class.

3. Type the following class definition in the Code Editor. (Type the statements formatted in bold italic below—Visual Studio adds the remaining statements automatically.)

```
Public Class Teacher
    Inherits Person
    Private Level As Short

    Public Property Grade() As Short
        Get
            Return Level
        End Get
        Set(ByVal value As Short)
            Level = value
        End Set
    End Property
End Class
```

   The *Inherits* statement links the *Person* class to this new class, incorporating all of its variables, properties, and methods. If the *Person* class were located in a separate module or project, you could identify its location by using a namespace designation, just as you identify classes when you use the *Imports* statement at the top of a program that uses classes in the .NET Framework class libraries. Basically, I've defined the *Teacher* class as a special type of *Person* class—in addition to the *FirstName* and *LastName* properties, the *Teacher* class has a *Grade* property that records the level at which the teacher teaches.

   Now you'll use the new class in the *Button1_Click* event procedure.

4. Display the *Button1_Click* event procedure in Form1.

Rather than create a new variable to hold the *Teacher* class, I'll just use the *Employee* variable as it is—the only difference will be that I can now set a *Grade* property for the new employee.

5. Modify the *Button1_Click* event procedure as follows. (You need to change the bold italic lines.)

```
Dim Employee As New Teacher
Dim DOB As Date

Employee.FirstName = TextBox1.Text
Employee.LastName = TextBox2.Text
DOB = DateTimePicker1.Value.Date
Employee.Grade = InputBox("What grade do you teach?")

MsgBox(Employee.FirstName & " " & Employee.LastName _
  & " teaches grade " & Employee.Grade)
```

In this example, I've removed the current age calculation—the *Age* method isn't used—but I did this only to keep information to a minimum in the message box. When you define properties and methods in a class, you aren't required to use them in the program code.

Now you'll run the program.

> **Tip**   The revised Person Class program is located in the c:\vb05sbs\chap16\person class folder.

6. Click the Start Debugging button to run the program.

    The new employee form appears on the screen.

7. Type your first name in the First Name text box and your last name in the Last Name text box.

8. Click the date time picker object, and scroll to your birth date.

9. Click the Display Record button.

    Your program stores the first name and last name values in property settings and then displays the following input box, which prompts the new teacher for the grade he or she teaches:

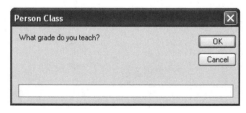

10. Type **3**, and then click OK to close the input box.

    The application stores the number 3 in the new *Grade* property and uses the *FirstName*, *LastName*, and *Grade* properties to display the new employee information in a confirming message box. You see this message:

11. Experiment with a few more values if you like, and then click the Close button on the form.

    The program stops, and the development environment returns. You're finished working with classes and inheritance in this chapter. Nice job!

Further Experiments with Object-Oriented Programming

If you've enjoyed this foray into object-oriented coding techniques, more fun awaits you in Visual Basic 2005, a truly object-oriented programming language. In particular, you might want to add events to your class definitions, create default property values, and experiment with a polymorphic feature called *method overloading*. These and other OOP features can be explored by using the Visual Studio online Help or by perusing an advanced book on Visual Basic programming. (See Appendix A, "Where to Go for More Information," for a reading list.)

Chapter 16 Quick Reference

To	Do this
Inherit an existing form's interface and functionality	Click the Add New Item command on the Project menu, click the Inherited Form template, specify a name for the inherited form, and then click Add. Use the Inheritance Picker to select the form you want to inherit, and then click OK. Note that to be eligible for inheritance, base forms must be compiled as .exe or .dll files. If you want to inherit a form that isn't a component in the current project, the form must be compiled as a .dll file.
Customize an inherited form	Add Toolbox controls to the form, and set property settings. Note that you won't be able to set the properties of inherited objects on the form. These objects are identified by small icons and are inactive.
Create your own base classes	Click the Add Class command on the Project menu, specify the class name, and then click Open. Define the class in a class module by using program code.

To	Do this
Hide declared variables in a class	Use the *Private* keyword to hide class variables from other programmers that examine your class. For example: ``` Private Name1 As String ```

Create a new property in the class	Define a public property procedure in the class. For example:
	
	``
	Public Property FirstName() As String
	    Get
	        Return Name1
	    End Get
	    Set(ByVal value As String)
	        Name1 = value
	    End Set
	End Property
	``

Create a new method in the class	Define a Sub or Function procedure in the class. For example:
	
	``
	Public Function Age(ByVal Birthday As Date) _
	  As Integer
	    Return Int(Now.Subtract(Birthday).Days _
	    / 365.25)
	End Function
	``

Declare an object variable to use the class	Use the *Dim* and *New* keywords, a variable name, and the user-defined class in a program statement. For example: ``` Dim Employee As New Person ```
Set properties for an object variable	Use the regular syntax for setting object properties. For example: ``` Employee.FirstName = TextBox1.Text ```

Inherit a base class in a new class	Create a new class, and use the *Inherits* keyword to incorporate the base class's class definitions. For example:
	
	``
	Public Class Teacher
	    Inherits Person
	    Private Level As Short
	
	    Public Property Grade() As Short
	        Get
	            Return Level
	        End Get
	        Set(ByVal value As Short)
	            Level = value
	        End Set
	    End Property
	End Class
	``

Chapter 17
Working with Printers

After completing this chapter, you will be able to:

- Print graphics from a Microsoft Visual Basic program.

- Print text from a Visual Basic program.

- Print multipage documents.

- Create Print, Page Setup, and Print Preview dialog boxes in your programs.

In the following sections, you'll complete your survey of user interface design and components by learning how to add printer support to your Windows applications. Microsoft Visual Basic 2005 supports printing by offering the *PrintDocument* class and its many objects, methods, and properties, which facilitate printing.

Upgrade Notes: Migrating Visual Basic 6 Code to Visual Basic 2005

If you're experienced with Microsoft Visual Basic 6, you'll notice some new features in Visual Basic 2005, including the following:

- In Visual Basic 6, printing is accomplished by using the methods and properties of the *Printer* object. For example, the *Printer.Print* method sends a string of text to the default printer. In Microsoft Visual Basic .NET 2003 and Visual Basic 2005, printing is accomplished by using the *PrintDocument* class, which provides more functionality than the older method but is also more complex.

- In Visual Basic 6, you have access to one predefined dialog box for printing services—the Print dialog box provided by the *CommonDialog* ActiveX control. In Visual Basic 2005, you have access to several predefined dialog box controls for printing, including *PrintDialog*, *PrintPreviewDialog*, and *PageSetupDialog*.

- To implement multipage printing in Visual Basic 2005, you must create a *PrintPage* event handler that prints each page of your document one at a time. Although managing this printing process can be somewhat involved, it's simplified by services in the *System.Drawing.Printing* namespace.

In this chapter, you'll learn how to print graphics and text from Visual Basic programs, manage multipage printing tasks, and add printing dialog boxes to your user interface. In my opinion, this chapter is one of the most useful in the book, with lots of practical code that you can immediately incorporate into real-world programming projects. Printing support doesn't come automatically in Visual Basic 2005, but the routines in this chapter will help you print longer text documents and display helpful dialog boxes such as Page Setup, Print, and Print Preview from within your programs. I'll start the chapter with two very simple printing routines to show you the basics, and then I'll get considerably more sophisticated.

Using the *PrintDocument* Class

Most Microsoft Windows applications allow users to print documents after they create them, and by now you might be wondering just how printing works in Visual Basic programs. This is one area where Visual Basic 2005 has improved considerably over Visual Basic 6, although the added functionality comes at a little cost. Producing printed output from Visual Basic 2005 programs isn't a trivial process, and the technique you use depends on the type and amount of printed output you want to generate. In all cases, however, the fundamental mechanism that regulates printing in Visual Basic 2005 is the *PrintDocument* class, which you can create in a project in two ways:

- By adding the *PrintDocument* control to a form
- By defining it programmatically with a few lines of Visual Basic code

The *PrintDocument* class provides several useful objects for printing text and graphics, including the *PrinterSettings* object, which contains the default print settings for a printer; the *PageSettings* object, which contains print settings for a particular page; and the *PrintPageEventArgs* object, which contains event information about the page that's about to be printed. The *PrintDocument* class is located in the *System.Drawing.Printing* namespace. If you add a *PrintDocument* control to your form, some of the objects in the *PrintDocument* class are automatically incorporated into your project, but you still need to add the following *Imports* statement to the top of your form:

```
Imports System.Drawing.Printing
```

This defines *PrintPageEventArgs* and other important values.

To learn how to use the *PrintDocument* class in a program, complete the following exercise, which teaches you how to add a *PrintDocument* control to your project and use it to print a graphics file on your system.

Use the *PrintDocument* control

1. Start Microsoft Visual Studio, and create a new Visual Basic Windows Application project named **My Print Graphics**.

    A blank form appears in the Visual Studio IDE.

2. Use the *Label* control to draw a label object near the top of the form.

3. Use the *TextBox* control to draw a text box object below the label object.

    The text box object will be used to type the name of the artwork file that you want to open. A single-line text box will be sufficient.

4. Use the *Button* control to draw a button object below the text box.

    This button object will print the graphics file. Now you'll add a *PrintDocument* control.

5. On the Printing tab of the Toolbox, scroll down until you see the *PrintDocument* control, and then double-click it.

    Like the *Timer* control, the *PrintDocument* control is invisible at run time, so it's placed in the component tray beneath the form when you create it. Your project now has access to the *PrintDocument* class and its useful printing objects.

6. Set the following properties for the objects on your form:

Object	Property	Setting
Label1	Text	"Type the name of a graphic file to print."
TextBox1	Text	"c:\vb05sbs\chap15\sun.ico"
Button1	Text	"Print Graphics"
Form1	Text	"Print Graphics"

Your form looks similar to this:

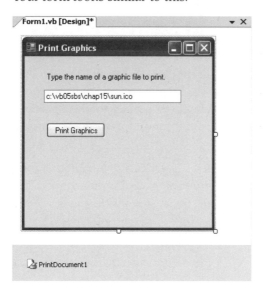

Now add the program code necessary to print a graphic file (bitmap, icon, metafile, JPEG file, and so on).

7. Double-click the Print Graphic button.

    The *Button1_Click* event procedure appears in the Code Editor.

8. Move the insertion point to the top of the form's code, and then type the following program statement:

```
Imports System.Drawing.Printing
```

This *Imports* statement declares the *System.Drawing.Printing* namespace, which is needed to define the *PrintPageEventArgs* object in the *PrintGraphic* procedure. The *Print-Graphic* procedure will be added in a later step. (The other *PrintDocument* objects will receive their definitions from the *PrintDocument* control.)

9. Now move the insertion point down to the *Button1_Click* event procedure, and enter the following program code:

```
' Print using an error handler to catch problems
Try
    AddHandler PrintDocument1.PrintPage, AddressOf Me.PrintGraphic
    PrintDocument1.Print()   'print graphic
Catch ex As Exception  'catch printing exception
    MessageBox.Show("Sorry--there is a problem printing", _
        ex.ToString())
End Try
```

This code uses the *AddHandler* statement, which specifies that the *PrintGraphic* event handler should be called when the *PrintPage* event of the *PrintDocument1* object fires. You've seen *error handlers* in previous chapters—an *event handler* is a closely related mechanism that handles system events that aren't technically errors but that also represent crucial actions in the life cycle of an object.

In this case, the event handler being specified is related to printing services, and the request comes with specific information about the page to be printed, the current printer settings, and other attributes of the *PrintDocument* class. Technically, the *AddressOf* operator is used to identify the *PrintGraphic* event handler by determining its internal address and storing it. The *AddressOf* operator implicitly creates an object known as a *delegate* that forwards calls to the appropriate event handler when an event occurs.

The third line of the code you just entered uses the *Print* method of the *PrintDocument1* object to send a print request to the *PrintGraphic* event procedure, a routine that you'll create in the next step. This print request is located inside a Try code block to catch any printing problems that might occur during the printing activity. Note that the syntax I'm using in the Catch block is slightly different than the syntax I introduced in Chapter 9, "Trapping Errors by Using Structured Error Handling." Here the *ex* variable is being declared of type *Exception* to get a detailed message about any errors that occur. Using the *Exception* type is another way to get at the underlying error condition that created the problem.

10. Scroll above the *Button1_Click* event procedure in the Code Editor to the general declaration space below the `Public Class Form1` statement. Then type the following Sub procedure declaration:

```
'Sub for printing graphic
Private Sub PrintGraphic(ByVal sender As Object, _
  ByVal ev As PrintPageEventArgs)
    ' Create the graphic using DrawImage
    ev.Graphics.DrawImage(Image.FromFile(TextBox1.Text), _
      ev.Graphics.VisibleClipBounds)
    ' Specify that this is the last page to print
    ev.HasMorePages = False
End Sub
```

This routine handles the printing event generated by the *PrintDocument1.Print* method. I've declared the Sub procedure within the form's code, but you can also declare the Sub as a general-purpose procedure in a module. Note the *ev* variable in the argument list for the *PrintGraphic* procedure. This variable is the crucial carrier of information about the current print page, and it's declared of type *PrintPageEventArgs*, an object in the *System.Drawing.Printing* namespace.

To actually print the graphic, the procedure uses the *Graphics.DrawImage* method associated with the current print page to load a graphics file by using the file name stored in the *Text* property of the *TextBox1* object. (By default, I set this property to c:\vb05sbs\chap15\sun.ico—the same Sun icon used in Chapter 15, "Adding Graphics and Animation Effects"—but you can change this value at run time and print any artwork files that you like.) Finally, I set the *ev.HasMorePages* property to False so that Visual Basic understands that the print job doesn't have multiple pages.

11. Click the Save All button on the Standard toolbar to save your changes, and specify the c:\vb05sbs\chap17 folder as the location.

Now you're ready to run the program. Before you do so, you might want to locate a few graphics files on your system that you can print. (Just jot down the paths for now and type them in.)

Run the Print Graphics program

> **Tip**   The complete Print Graphics program is located in the c:\vb05sbs\chap17\print graphics folder.

1. Click the Start Debugging button on the Standard toolbar.

   Your program runs in the IDE. You see this form:

   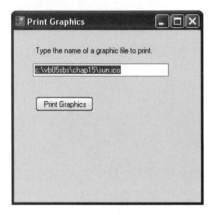

2. Turn on your printer, and verify that it is on line and has paper.

3. If you installed your sample files in the default c:\vb05sbs folder, click the Print Graphic button now to print the Sun.ico icon graphic.

   If you didn't use the default sample file location, or if you want to print a different artwork file, modify the text box path accordingly, and then click the Print Graphic button.

   The *DrawImage* method expands the graphic to the maximum size your printer can produce on one page and then sends the graphic to the printer. (This "expansion feature" fills up the page and gives you a closer look at the image.) Admittedly this might not be that interesting for you, but we'll get more sophisticated in a moment. (If you want to modify the location or size of your output, search the Visual Studio online Help for the "Graphics.DrawImage Method" topic, study the different argument variations available, and then modify your program code.)

   If you look closely, you see the following dialog box appear when Visual Basic sends your print job to the printer:

This status box is also a product of the *PrintDocument* class, and it provides users with a professional-looking print interface, including the page number for each printed page.

4. Type additional paths if you like, and then click the Print Graphic button for more print-outs.

5. When you're finished experimenting with the program, click the Close button on the form.

    The program stops. Not bad for your first attempt at printing from a Visual Basic program!

Printing Text from a Text Box Object

You've had a quick introduction to the *PrintDocument* control and printing graphics. Now try using a similar technique to print the contents of a text box on a Visual Basic form. In the following exercise, you'll build a simple project that prints text by using the *PrintDocument* class, but this time you'll define the class by using program code without adding the *PrintDocument* control to your form. In addition, you'll use the *Graphics.DrawString* method to send the entire contents of a text box object to the default printer.

> **Note**   The following program is designed to print one page or less of text. To print multiple pages, you need to add additional program code, which will be explored later in the chapter. I don't want to introduce too many new printing features at once.

Use the *Graphics.DrawString* method to print text

1. Click the Close Project command on the File menu, and then create a new project named **My Print Text**.

    A blank form appears.

2. Use the *Label* control to draw a label object near the top of the form.

    This label will display a line of instructions for the user.

3. Use the *TextBox* control to draw a text box object below the label object.

    The text box object will contain the text you want to print.

4. Set the *Multiline* property of the text box object to True, and then expand the text box so that it's large enough to enter several lines of text.

5. Use the *Button* control to draw a button object below the text box.

    This button object will print the text file.

6. Set the following properties for the objects on your form:

Object	Property	Setting
Label1	Text	"Type some text in this text box object, then click Print Text."
TextBox1	ScrollBars	Vertical
Button1	Text	"Print Text"
Form1	Text	"Print Text"

Your form looks similar to this:

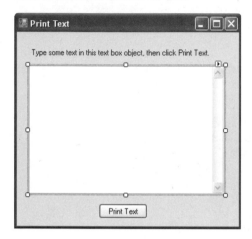

Now add the program code necessary to print the contents of the text box.

7. Double-click the Print Text button.

The *Button1_Click* event procedure appears in the Code Editor.

8. Scroll to the very top of the form's code, and then type the following *Imports* declaration:

```
Imports System.Drawing.Printing
```

This defines the *System.Drawing.Printing* namespace, which is needed to define the *PrintDocument* class and its necessary objects.

9. Now scroll back down to the *Button1_Click* event procedure, and enter the following program code:

```
' Print using an error handler to catch problems
Try
    ' Declare PrintDoc variable of type PrintDocument
    Dim PrintDoc As New PrintDocument
    AddHandler PrintDoc.PrintPage, AddressOf Me.PrintText
    PrintDoc.Print()    'print text
Catch ex As Exception  'catch printing exception
    MessageBox.Show("Sorry--there is a problem printing", _
        ex.ToString())
End Try
```

The lines that are new or changed from the Print Graphics program are highlighted in bold italic. Rather than add a *PrintDocument* control to your form, this time you simply created the *PrintDocument* programmatically by using the *Dim* keyword and the *PrintDocument* type, which is defined in your program when you define the *System.Drawing.Printing* namespace. From this point on, the *PrintDoc* variable represents the *PrintDocument* object, and it is used to declare the error handler and to print the text document. Note that for clarity, I renamed the Sub procedure that will handle the print event *PrintText* (rather than *PrintGraphic*).

10. Scroll above the *Button1_Click* event procedure in the Code Editor to the general declaration area. Type the following Sub procedure declaration:

```
'Sub for printing text
Private Sub PrintText(ByVal sender As Object, _
  ByVal ev As PrintPageEventArgs)
    'Use DrawString to create text in a Graphics object
    ev.Graphics.DrawString(TextBox1.Text, New Font("Arial", _
      11, FontStyle.Regular), Brushes.Black, 120, 120)
    ' Specify that this is the last page to print
    ev.HasMorePages = False
End Sub
```

This routine handles the printing event generated by the *PrintDoc.Print* method. The changes from the *PrintGraphic* procedure in the previous exercises are also highlighted in bold italic. As you can see, when you print text, you need to use a new method. Rather than use *Graphics.DrawImage*, which renders a graphics image, you must use *Graphics.DrawString*, which prints a text string. I've specified the text in the *Text* property of the text box object to print, some basic font formatting (Arial, 11 point, regular style, black color), and an (x, y) coordinate (120, 120) on the page to start drawing. These specifications will give the printed output a default look that's similar to the text box on the screen. Like last time, I've also set the *ev.HasMorePages* property to False to indicate that the print job doesn't have multiple pages.

11. Click the Save All button on the toolbar to save your changes, and specify c:\vb05sbs\chap17 as the folder location.

Now you'll run the program to see how a text box object prints.

Run the Print Text program

> **Tip**   The complete Print Text program is located in the c:\vb05sbs\chap17\print text folder.

1. Click the Start Debugging button on the toolbar.

   Your program runs in the IDE.

2.   Verify that your printer is on.

3.   Type some sample text in the text box. If you type multiple lines, be sure to include a carriage return at the end of each line.

Wrapping isn't supported in this demonstration program—very long lines will potentially extend past the right margin. (Again, we'll solve this problem soon.) Your form looks something like this:

4.   Click the Print Text button.

The program displays a printing dialog box and prints the contents of your text box.

5.   Modify the text box, and try additional printouts, if you like.

6.   When you're finished, click the Close button on the form to stop the program.

Now you know how to print both text and graphics from a program.

Printing Multipage Text Files

The printing techniques that you've just learned are useful for simple text documents, but they have a few important limitations. First, the method I used doesn't allow for long lines—in other words, text that extends beyond the right margin. Unlike the text box object, the *Print-Document* object doesn't automatically wrap lines when they reach the edge of the paper. If you have files that don't contain carriage returns at the end of lines, you'll need to write the code that handles these long lines.

The second limitation is that the Print Text program can't print more than one page of text. Indeed, it doesn't even understand what a page of text *is*—the printing procedure simply sends the text to the default printer. If the text block is too long to fit on a single page, the additional text won't be printed. To handle multipage printouts, you need to create a virtual page of text called the *PrintPage* and then add text to it until the page is full. When the page is full, it is sent to the printer, and this process continues until there is no more text to print. At that point, the print job ends.

If fixing these two limitations sounds complicated, don't despair yet—there are a few handy mechanisms that help you create virtual text pages in Visual Basic and help you print text files with long lines and several pages of text. The first mechanism is the *PrintPage* event, which occurs when a page is printed. *PrintPage* receives an argument of the type *PrintPageEventArgs*, which provides you with the dimensions and characteristics of the current printer page. Another mechanism is the *Graphics.MeasureString* method. The *MeasureString* method can be used to determine how many characters and lines can fit in a rectangular area of the page. By using these mechanisms and others, it's relatively straightforward to construct procedures that process multipage print jobs.

Complete the following steps to build a program named Print File that opens text files of any length and prints them. The Print File program also demonstrates how to use the *RichTextBox*, *PrintDialog*, and *OpenFileDialog* controls. The *RichTextBox* control is a more robust version of the *TextBox* control you just used to display text. The *PrintDialog* control displays a standard Print dialog box so that you can specify various print settings. The *OpenFileDialog* control lets you select a text file for printing. (You used *OpenFileDialog* in Chapter 4, "Working with Menus, Toolbars, and Dialog Boxes.")

Manage print requests with *RichTextBox*, *OpenFileDialog*, and *PrintDialog* controls

1. Click the Close Project command on the File menu, and then create a new project named **My Print File**.

   A blank form appears.

2. Use the *Button* control in the Toolbox to draw two buttons in the upper-left corner of the form.

   This program has a simple user interface, but the printing techniques you'll learn are easily adaptable to much more complex solutions.

3. Click the *RichTextBox* control in the Toolbox, and then draw a rich text box object that covers the bottom half of the form.

4. Double-click the *OpenFileDialog* control on the Dialogs tab to add an open file dialog object to the component tray below your form.

   You'll use the open file dialog object to browse for text files on your system.

5. Double-click the *PrintDocument* control on the Printing tab to add a print document object to the component tray.

   You'll use the print document object to support printing in your application.

6. Double-click the *PrintDialog* control on the Printing tab to add a print dialog object to the component tray.

   You'll use the print dialog object to open a Print dialog box in your program.

7. Now set the following properties for the objects on your form:

Object	Property	Setting
Button1	*Name*	btnOpen
	Text	"Open"
Button2	*Name*	btnPrint
	Enabled	False
	Text	"Print"
Form1	*Text*	"Print File"

Your form looks something like this:

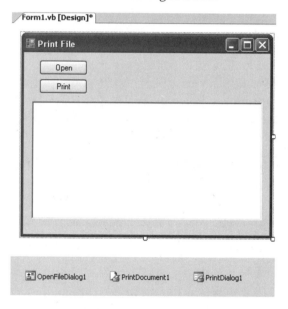

Now add the program code necessary to open the text file and print it.

8. Double-click the Open button.

   The *btnOpen_Click* event procedure appears in the Code Editor.

9. Scroll to the top of the form, and enter the following code:

```
Imports System.IO  'for FileStream class
Imports System.Drawing.Printing
```

These library definitions make available the *FileStream* class and the classes for printing.

10. Move the cursor below the `Public Class Form1` statement, and then enter the following variable declarations:

```
Private PrintPageSettings As New PageSettings
Private StringToPrint As String
Private PrintFont As New Font("Arial", 10)
```

These statements define important information about the pages that will be printed.

11. Scroll to the *btnOpen_Click* event procedure, and then type the following program code:

```
Dim FilePath As String
'Display Open dialog box and select text file
OpenFileDialog1.Filter = "Text files (*.txt)|*.txt"
OpenFileDialog1.ShowDialog()
'If Cancel button not selected, load FilePath variable
If OpenFileDialog1.FileName <> "" Then
    FilePath = OpenFileDialog1.FileName
    Try
        'Read text file and load into RichTextBox1
        Dim MyFileStream As New FileStream(FilePath, FileMode.Open)
        RichTextBox1.LoadFile(MyFileStream, _
          RichTextBoxStreamType.PlainText)
        MyFileStream.Close()
        'Initialize string to print
        StringToPrint = RichTextBox1.Text
        'Enable Print button
        btnPrint.Enabled = True
    Catch ex As Exception
        'display error messages if they appear
        MessageBox.Show(ex.Message)
    End Try
End If
```

When the user clicks the Open button, this event procedure displays an Open dialog box using a filter that displays only text files. When the user selects a file, the file name is assigned to a public string variable named *FilePath*, which is declared at the top of the event procedure. The procedure then uses a Try...Catch error handler to load the text file into the *RichTextBox1* object. To facilitate the loading process, I've used the *FileStream* class and the *Open* file mode, which places the complete contents of the text file into the *MyFileStream* variable. Finally, the event procedure enables the Print button (*btnPrint*) so that the user can print the file. In short, this routine opens the file and enables the print button on the form but doesn't do any printing itself.

Now you'll add the necessary program code to display the Print dialog box and print the file by using logic that monitors the dimensions of the current text page.

Add code for the *btnPrint* and *PrintDocument1* objects

1. Display the form again, and then double-click the Print button (*btnPrint*) to display its event procedure in the Code Editor.

2. Type the following program code:

```
Try
    'Specify current page settings
    PrintDocument1.DefaultPageSettings = PrintPageSettings
    'Specify document for print dialog box and show
    StringToPrint = RichTextBox1.Text
    PrintDialog1.Document = PrintDocument1
    Dim result As DialogResult = PrintDialog1.ShowDialog()
    'If click OK, print document to printer
    If result = DialogResult.OK Then
        PrintDocument1.Print()
    End If
Catch ex As Exception
    'Display error message
    MessageBox.Show(ex.Message)
End Try
```

This event procedure sets the default print settings for the document and assigns the contents of the *RichTextBox1* object to the *StringToPrint* string variable (defined at the top of the form) in case the user changes the text in the rich text box. It then opens the Print dialog box and allows the user to adjust any print settings (printer, number of copies, the print to file option, and so on). If the user clicks the OK button, the event procedure sends this print job to the printer by issuing the following statement:

```
PrintDocument1.Print()
```

3. Display the form again, and then double-click the *PrintDocument1* object in the component tray.

Visual Studio adds the *PrintPage* event procedure for the *PrintDocument1* object.

4. Type the following program code in the *PrintDocument1_PrintPage* event procedure:

```
Dim numChars As Integer
Dim numLines As Integer
Dim stringForPage As String
Dim strFormat As New StringFormat
'Based on page setup, define drawable rectangle on page
Dim rectDraw As New RectangleF( _
   e.MarginBounds.Left, e.MarginBounds.Top, _
   e.MarginBounds.Width, e.MarginBounds.Height)
'Define area to determine how much text can fit on a page
'Make height one line shorter to ensure text doesn't clip
Dim sizeMeasure As New SizeF(e.MarginBounds.Width, _
   e.MarginBounds.Height - PrintFont.GetHeight(e.Graphics))

'When drawing long strings, break between words
strFormat.Trimming = StringTrimming.Word
'Compute how many chars and lines can fit based on sizeMeasure
e.Graphics.MeasureString(StringToPrint, PrintFont, _
   sizeMeasure, strFormat, numChars, numLines)
```

```
'Compute string that will fit on a page
stringForPage = StringToPrint.Substring(0, numChars)
'Print string on current page
e.Graphics.DrawString(stringForPage, PrintFont, _
  Brushes.Black, rectDraw, strFormat)
'If there is more text, indicate there are more pages
If numChars < StringToPrint.Length Then
    'Subtract text from string that has been printed
    StringToPrint = StringToPrint.Substring(numChars)
    e.HasMorePages = True
Else
    e.HasMorePages = False
    'All text has been printed, so restore string
    StringToPrint = RichTextBox1.Text
End If
```

This event procedure handles the actual printing of the text document, and it does so by carefully defining a printing area (or printing rectangle) based on the settings in the Page Setup dialog box. Any text that fits within this area can be printed normally; text that's outside this area needs to be wrapped to the following lines, or pages, as you'd expect to happen in a standard Windows application.

The printing area is defined by the *rectDraw* variable, which is based on the *RectangleF* class. The *strFormat* variable and the *Trimming* method are used to trim strings that extend beyond the edge of the right margin. The actual text strings are printed by the *DrawString* method, which you've already used in this chapter. The *e.HasMorePages* property is used to specify whether there are additional pages to be printed. If no additional pages remain, the *HasMorePage* property is set to False, and the contents of the *StringToPrint* variable are restored to the contents of the *RichTextBox1* object.

5. Click the Save All button on the toolbar to save your changes, and specify the c:\vb05sbs\chap17 folder as the location.

That's a lot of typing! But now you're ready to run the program and see how printing text files on multiple pages works.

Run the Print File program

> **Tip** The complete Print File program is located in the c:\vb05sbs\chap17\print file folder.

1. Click the Start Debugging button on the toolbar.

   Your program runs in the IDE. Notice that the Print button is currently disabled because you haven't selected a file yet.

2. Click the Open button.

   The program displays an Open dialog box.

3. Browse to the c:\vb05sbs\chap17 folder, and then click the longfile.txt file.

    Your Open dialog box looks like this:

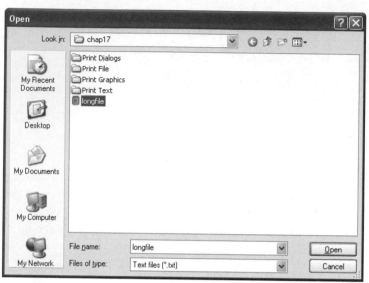

4. Click Open to select the file.

    Your program loads the text file into the rich text box object on the form and then enables the Print button. This file is long and has a few lines that wrap so that you can test the wide margin and multipage printing options. Your form looks like this:

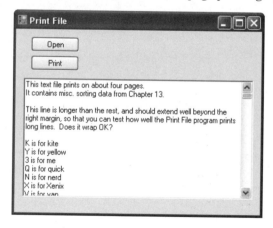

5. Verify that your printer is on, and then click the Print button.

    Visual Basic displays the Print dialog box, customized with the name and settings for your printer, as shown in the following illustration:

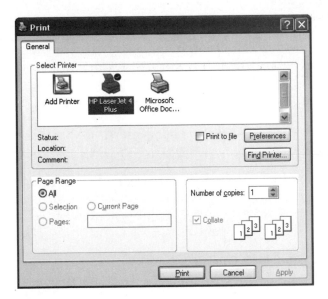

Many of the options in the Print dialog box are active, and you can experiment with them as you would a regular Windows application.

6. Click Print to print the document.

    Your program submits the four-page print job to the Windows print queue. After a moment (and if your printer is ready), the printer begins printing the document. As in previous exercises, a dialog box automatically appears to show you the printing status and give you an indication of how many pages your printed document will be.

7. Click the Close button on the form to stop the program.

You've just created a set of very versatile printing routines which can be added to any Visual Basic application that needs to print multiple pages of text!

One Step Further: Adding Print Preview and Page Setup Dialog Boxes

The Print File application is ready to handle several printing tasks, but its interface isn't as visually compelling as that of a commercial Windows application. You can make your program more flexible and interesting by adding a few extra dialog box options to supplement the Print dialog box that you experimented with in the previous exercise.

Two additional printing controls are available on the Printing tab of the Toolbox, and they work much like the familiar *PrintDialog* and *OpenFileDialog* controls that you've used in this book:

- The *PrintPreviewDialog* control displays a custom Print Preview dialog box.
- The *PageSetupDialog* control displays a custom Page Setup dialog box.

As with other dialog boxes, you can add these printing controls to your form by using the Toolbox, or you can create them programmatically.

In the following exercise, you'll add Print Preview and Page Setup dialog boxes to the Print File program you've been working with. In the completed practice files, I've named this project Print Dialogs so that you can distinguish the code of the two projects, but you can add the dialog box features directly to the Print File project if you want.

Add *PrintPreviewDialog* and *PageSetupDialog* controls

1. If you didn't complete the previous exercise, open the Print File project from the c:\vb05sbs\chap17\print file folder.

   The Print File project is the starting point for this project.

2. Display the form, and then use the *Button* control to add two additional buttons to the top of the form.

3. Double-click the *PrintPreviewDialog* control on the Printing tab of the Toolbox.

   A print preview dialog object is added to the component tray.

4. Double-click the *PageSetupDialog* control on the Printing tab of the Toolbox.

   A page setup dialog object is added to the component tray. If the objects in the component tray obscure one another, you can drag them to a better (more visible) location, or you can right-click the component tray and select Line Up Icons.

5. Set the following properties for the button objects on the form:

Object	Property	Setting
Button1	Name	btnSetup
	Enabled	False
	Text	"Page Setup"
Button2	Name	btnPreview
	Enabled	False
	Text	"Print Preview"

Your form looks like this:

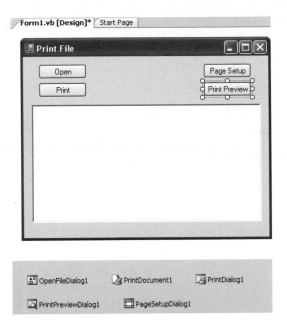

6. Double-click the Page Setup button (*btnSetup*) to display the *btnSetup_Click* event procedure in the Code Editor.

7. Type the following program code:

```
Try
    'Load page settings and display page setup dialog box
    PageSetupDialog1.PageSettings = PrintPageSettings
    PageSetupDialog1.ShowDialog()
Catch ex As Exception
    'Display error message
    MessageBox.Show(ex.Message)
End Try
```

The code for creating a Page Setup dialog box in this program is quite simple because the *PrintPageSettings* variable has already been defined at the top of the form. This variable holds the current page definition information, and when it's assigned to the *PageSettings* property of the *PageSetupDialog1* object, the *ShowDialog* method automatically loads a dialog box that allows the user to modify what the program has selected as the default page orientation, margins, and so on. The Try...Catch error handler simply handles any errors that might occur when the *ShowDialog* method is used.

8. Display the form again, and then double-click the Print Preview button (*btnPreview*) to display the *btnPreview_Click* event procedure.

9.   Type the following program code:

```
Try
    'Specify current page settings
    PrintDocument1.DefaultPageSettings = PrintPageSettings
    'Specify document for print preview dialog box and show
    StringToPrint = RichTextBox1.Text
    PrintPreviewDialog1.Document = PrintDocument1
    PrintPreviewDialog1.ShowDialog()
Catch ex As Exception
    'Display error message
    MessageBox.Show(ex.Message)
End Try
```

In a similar way, the *btnPreview_Click* event procedure assigns the *PrintPageSettings* variable to the *DefaultPageSettings* property of the *PrintDocument1* object, and then it copies the text in the rich text box object to the *StringToPrint* variable and opens the Print Preview dialog box. Print Preview automatically uses the page settings data to display a visual representation of the document as it will be printed—you don't need to display this information manually.

Now you'll make a slight modification to the program code in the *btnOpen_Click* event procedure.

10.   Scroll up to the *btnOpen_Click* event procedure in the Code Editor.

This is the procedure that displays the Open dialog box, opens a text file, and enables the printing buttons. Because you just added the Page Setup and Print Preview buttons, you have to add program code to enable those two printing buttons as well.

11.   Scroll to the bottom of the event procedure, just before the final Catch code block, and locate the following program statement:

```
btnPrint.Enabled = True
```

12.   Below that statement, add the following lines of code:

```
btnSetup.Enabled = True
btnPreview.Enabled = True
```

Now your program will enable the print buttons when there's a document available to print.

13.   Click the Save All button on the toolbar to save your changes.

Test the Page Setup and Print Preview features

> **Tip**   The complete Print Dialogs program is located in the c:\vb05sbs\chap17\print dialogs folder.

1. Click the Start Debugging button on the toolbar.

   The program opens, with only the first button object enabled.

2. Click the Open button, and then open the longfile.txt file in the c:\vb05sbs\chap17 folder.

   The remaining three button objects are now enabled, as shown here:

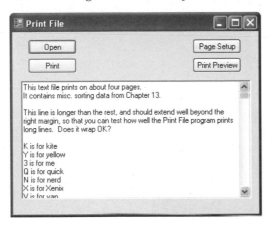

3. Click the Page Setup button.

   Your program displays the Page Setup dialog box, as shown here:

   Page Setup provides numerous useful options, including the ability to change the paper size and source, the orientation of the printing (Portrait or Landscape), and the page margins (Left, Right, Top, and Bottom).

4. Change the Left margin to 2, and then click OK.

The left margin will now be 2 inches.

5. Click the Print Preview button.

Your program displays the Print Preview dialog box, as shown in the following illustration:

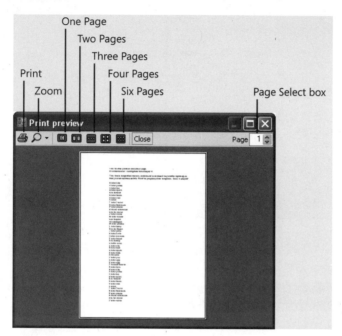

If you've used the Print Preview command in Microsoft Word or Microsoft Excel, you will recognize several of the buttons and preview features in this Print Preview dialog box. The Zoom, One Page, Two Pages, Three Pages, Four Pages, Six Pages, and Page Select Box controls all work automatically in the dialog box. No program code is required to make them operate.

6. Click the Four Pages button to display your document four pages at a time.

7. Click the Maximize button on the Print Preview title bar to make the window full size.

8. Click the Zoom arrow, click 150 percent, and expand the size of the window a little.

Your screen looks like this:

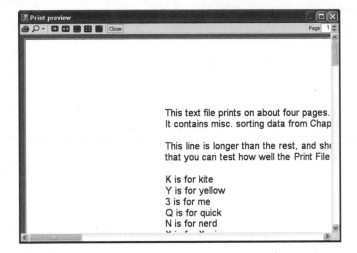

9. Click the One Page button, and then click the Up arrow in the Page Select box to view pages 2 through 4.

   As you can see, this Print Preview window is quite impressive—and you incorporated it into your program with just a few lines of code!

10. If you want to test printing the entire document again, click the Print button.

11. When you're finished experimenting, click the Close button to close the Print Preview dialog box, and then click the Close button to close the program.

You're done working with printers for now.

Chapter 17 Quick Reference

To	Do this
Incorporate the *PrintDocument* class in your projects and prepare for printing	Add the following *Imports* statement to the top of your form: `Imports System.Drawing.Printing`

Create a printing event handler	Use the *AddHandler* statement and the *AddressOf* operator. For example:
	
	`AddHandler PrintDocument1.PrintPage, _`
	`    AddressOf Me.PrintGraphic`

Create a *PrintDocument* object in your project	Double-click the *PrintDocument* control on the Printing tab of the Toolbox. *or* Include the following variable declaration in your program code: `Dim PrintDoc As New PrintDocument`

To	Do this
| Print graphics from a printing event handler | Use the *Graphics.DrawImage* method. For example:<br><br>```vb
ev.Graphics.DrawImage(Image.FromFile _
    (TextBox1.Text), ev.Graphics.VisibleClipBounds)
``` |
| Print text from a printing event handler | Use the *Graphics.DrawString* method in an event handler. For example:<br><br>```vb
ev.Graphics.DrawString(TextBox1.Text, _
    New Font("Arial", 11, FontStyle.Regular), _
    Brushes.Black, 120, 120)
``` |
| Call a printing event handler | Use the *Print* method of an object of type *PrintDocument*. For example:<br><br>```vb
PrintDoc.Print()
``` |
| Print multipage text documents | Write a handler for the *PrintPage* event, which receives an argument of the type *PrintPageEventArgs*. Compute the rectangular area on the page for the text, use the *MeasureString* method to determine how much text will fit on the current page, and use the *DrawString* method to print the text on the page. If additional pages are needed, set the *HasMorePages* property to True. When all text has been printed, set *HasMorePages* to False. |
| Open a text file by using the *FileStream* class, and load it into a *RichTextBox* object | Create a variable of type *FileStream*, specifying the path and file mode, load the stream into a *RichTextBox*, and then close the stream. For example:<br><br>```vb
Imports System.IO  'at the top of the form
...
Dim MyFileStream As New FileStream( _
    FilePath, FileMode.Open)
RichTextBox1.LoadFile(MyFileStream, _
    RichTextBoxStreamType.PlainText)
MyFileStream.Close()
``` |
| Display printing dialog boxes in your programs | Use the *PrintDialog*, *PrintPreviewDialog*, and *PageSetupDialog* controls on the Printing tab of the Toolbox. |

Part IV
Database and Web Programming

Chapter 18
Getting Started with ADO.NET

After completing this chapter, you will be able to:

- Use the Data Source Configuration Wizard to establish a connection to a database and build a dataset.

- Use the Dataset Designer and the Data Sources window to examine dataset members and create bound objects on forms.

- Create datacentric applications using dataset and data navigator objects.

- Use bound *TextBox* and *MaskedTextBox* controls to display database information on a Windows form.

- Write SQL statements to filter and sort dataset information using the Visual Studio Query Builder tool.

In Part IV, you'll learn how to work with information stored in databases and Web sites. First, you'll learn about Microsoft ADO.NET, the newest paradigm for working with database information, and you'll learn how to display, modify, and search for database content by using a combination of program code and Windows Forms controls. Microsoft Visual Studio 2005 was specifically designed to create applications that provide access to a rich variety of data sources. These custom interfaces have traditionally been called database *front ends*, meaning that through your Visual Basic application, the user is given a more useful window into database information than simply manipulating raw database records. However, a more appropriate description in Visual Studio 2005 is that you can build *datacentric* applications, meaning that through your application, the user is invited to explore the full potential of any number of rich data source connections, whether to local or remote locations, and that the application places this data at the center of the user's computing experience.

In this chapter, you'll take your first steps with ADO.NET and with datacentric applications. You'll use the Data Source Configuration Wizard to establish a connection to an Access database on your system, you'll create a dataset that represents a subset of useful fields and records from a database table, and you'll use the Dataset Designer and Data Sources window to examine dataset members and create bound objects on your forms. You'll also learn how to use *TextBox* and *MaskedTextBox* controls to present database information to your user, and you'll learn to write SQL SELECT statements that filter datasets (and therefore what your user sees and uses) in interesting ways.

Upgrade Notes: Migrating Visual Basic 6 Code to Visual Basic 2005

The features in Visual Studio related to database programming have changed significantly in each recent release of the software. Although continually learning new techniques can be a source of frustration, the rapid pace of change can be explained partially by the relative newness of distributed and multiple-tier database application programming in Windows, as well as technical innovations that are beyond the control of the Visual Studio development team. If you're experienced with Microsoft Visual Basic .NET 2003, you'll notice several new windows and tools in Visual Studio 2005, although the underlying dataset model introduced with ADO.NET is still the same. (Microsoft ADO.NET 1.1 has been upgraded to Microsoft ADO.NET 2.0 with this release.) If you're experienced with Microsoft Visual Basic 6, you'll notice many new features in Microsoft Visual Basic 2005, including the following:

- ADO.NET, first introduced in Microsoft Visual Studio .NET 2002, is the standard data model for all programs in Visual Studio 2005, including Microsoft Visual Basic, Microsoft Visual C++, Microsoft Visual J#, and Microsoft Visual C#. This version of ADO.NET offers a wider range of data access possibilities than its predecessors and is based on more recent Microsoft data access technology.

- The Visual Basic 6 Remote Data Objects (RDO) and ActiveX Data Objects (ADO) data access models have been replaced by ADO.NET.

- In Visual Basic 6, database information is represented in a program by the recordset object. In Visual Basic 2005, database information is represented by the dataset object, a disconnected image of the database table you're accessing.

- The Visual Basic 6 *Data* and *ADO Data* controls are no longer available in Visual Studio 2005. To display data on a form, you typically create a dataset by using the Data Source Configuration Wizard and then add bound controls to your form to display information from the dataset. If you use the Data Sources window to do this, a navigation toolbar is added automatically.

- The internal data format of ADO.NET is Extensible Markup Language (XML), making it easier to use existing XML data sources and to use ADO.NET in programs designed for the Web.

Database Programming with ADO.NET

A *database* is an organized collection of information stored in a file. You can create powerful databases by using any of a variety of database products, including Microsoft Access, Microsoft SQL Server, Oracle, and Paradox. You can also store and transmit database information by using XML, a file format designed for exchanging structured data over the Internet and in other settings.

Creating and maintaining databases has become an essential task for all major corporations, government institutions, non-profit agencies, and most small businesses. Rich data resources—for example, customer addresses, manufacturing inventories, account balances, employee records, donor lists, and order histories—have become the lifeblood of the business world.

Visual Studio 2005 isn't designed for creating new databases, but rather for displaying, analyzing, and manipulating the information in existing databases. Although previous versions of Visual Studio and Visual Basic have also provided this capability, Visual Studio 2005 offers an enhanced data model called ADO.NET 2.0 that you can use to work with an even greater number of database formats and access scenarios. In particular, ADO.NET has been designed for Internet use, meaning that it uses the same method for accessing local, client-server, and Internet-based data sources. As a testimony to its goal of making ADO.NET a great technology for manipulating databases over the Internet, Microsoft has made XML—a standard defined by the World Wide Web Consortium—the internal data format of ADO.NET. Using XML in this way makes ADO.NET easier to utilize with existing Internet data sources, and it makes it easier for software vendors to write adapters, or "providers," that convert third-party database formats to be compatible with ADO.NET.

Database Terminology

When working with databases and ADO.NET, it's important to understand some basic database terminology.

A *field* (also called a *column*) is a category of information stored in a database. Typical fields in a customer database might contain customer names, addresses, phone numbers, and comments. All the information about a particular customer or business is called a *record* (less commonly called a *row*). When a database is created, information is entered in a *table* of fields and records. Records correspond to rows in the table, and fields correspond to columns, as shown here:

Instructor ID	Instructor	Phone Number	Extension
1	Delamarco, Stefan	3105551234	
2	McKay, Yvonne	3105556543	
3	Barr, Adam	3105554321	
4	Wilson, Dan	3105550088	
5	Burke, Brian	3105554567	
6	Oviatt, Lori	2065557777	
7	Dyck, Shelley	3605551111	
8	Halvorson, Michael	2065554444	
9	Halvorson, Kim	2065552222	
(AutoNumber)			

A *relational database* can consist of multiple linked tables. In general, most of the databases that you connect to from Visual Studio will probably be relational databases that contain multiple tables of data organized around a particular theme.

In ADO.NET, various objects are used to retrieve and modify information in a database. The following illustration shows an overview of the approach that will be covered in more detail in this chapter:

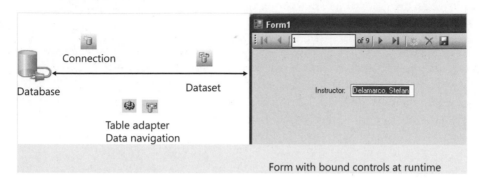

First a *connection* is made, which specifies connection information about the database and creates something for other controls and components to bind to. Next the Data Sources Configuration Wizard creates a *dataset*, which is a representation of one or more database tables you plan to work with in your program. (You don't manipulate the actual data, but rather a copy of it.) The Data Sources Configuration Wizard also adds an *XML schema file* to your project and associates a *table adapter* and *data navigator* with the dataset to handle retrieving data from the database, posting changes, and moving from one record to the next in the dataset. You can then bind information in the dataset to controls on a form by using the Data Sources window or *DataBindings* property settings

Working with an Access Database

In the following sections, you'll learn how to use the ADO.NET 2.0 data access technology in Visual Basic 2005. You'll get started by using the Data Source Configuration Wizard to establish a connection to a database named Students.mdb that I created in Microsoft Access 2002/2003 format. Students.mdb contains various tables of academic information that would be useful for a teacher who is tracking student coursework or a school administrator who is scheduling rooms, assigning classes, or building a time schedule. You'll learn how to create a dataset based on a table of information in the Students database, and you'll display this information on a Windows form. When you've finished, you'll be able to put these skills to work in your own database projects.

> **Tip** Although the sample in this chapter uses a Microsoft Access database, you don't
> have to have Access installed. Visual Studio and ADO.NET include the necessary support to
> understand the Access file format, as well as other formats. If you decide to open the data-
> base in Access, you'll find that Students.mdb is in Access 2002/2003 format. I have also in-
> cluded the file in Access 2000 format (Students_2000format.mdb) and Access 1997 format
> (Students_97format.mdb) so that you can experiment with the sample database in Access
> even if you have an older version.

Establish a connection by using the Data Source Configuration Wizard

1. Start Visual Studio, and create a new Visual Basic Windows Application project named
   My ADO Form.

   A new project appears in the IDE.

2. On the Data menu, click the Add New Data Source command.

   The Data Source Configuration Wizard appears in the development environment, as
   shown here:

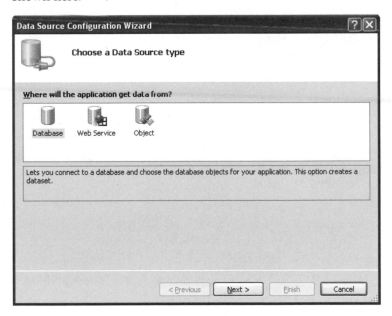

The Data Source Connection Wizard is a new feature within the Visual Studio 2005 IDE
that automatically prepares your Visual Basic program to receive database information.
The wizard prompts you for the type of database that you will be connecting to (a local
or remote database, Web service, or custom data object that you have created), establishes a connection to the data, and then creates a dataset within the program to hold
specific database tables and fields. The end result is that the wizard opens the Data
Sources window and fills it with a visual representation of each database object that you
can use in your program.

3. Click the Database icon in the Data Source Configuration Wizard, and then click Next.

    The wizard displays a screen that helps you establish a connection to your database by building a statement called a *connection string*. A connection string contains the information that Visual Studio needs to open and extract information from a database file. This includes a path name and file name, but also potentially sensitive data such as a username and password. For this reason, the connection string is treated carefully within the Data Source Connection Wizard, and you should take care to protect it from unauthorized access as you copy your source files from place to place.

4. Click the New Connection button.

    The first time that you click the New Connection button, the Choose Data Source dialog box appears, prompting you to select the database format that you plan to use. If you see the Add Connection dialog box instead of the Choose Data Source dialog box, it simply means that your copy of Visual Studio has already been configured to favor a particular database format. No problem; simply click the Change button in the Add Connection dialog box, and you'll see the same thing that first-time wizard users see, except that the title bar reads Change Data Source, as shown in the following illustration:

    The Change/Choose Data Source dialog box is the place where you select your preferred database format, which Visual Studio uses as the default format. In this chapter, you'll select the Microsoft Access format, but note that you can change the database format to one of the other choices at any time. You can also establish more than one database connection—each to a different type of database—within a single project.

5. Click Microsoft Access Database File, and then click OK.

    The Add Connection dialog box appears, as shown in the following illustration:

Now you'll specify the location and connection settings for your database, so that Visual Studio can build a valid connection string.

6. Click Browse.

   The Select Microsoft Access Database File dialog box appears, which functions like an Open dialog box.

7. Browse to the c:\vb05sbs\chap18 folder, click the Students database, and then click Open.

   You have selected the Access database in 2002/2003 format that I built to demonstrate how database fields and records are displayed within a Visual Basic program. The Add Connections dialog box appears again with the path name recorded. I don't restrict access to this file in any way, so a username and password are not necessary with Students.mdb. However, if your database requires a username and/or password for use, you can specify it now in the User Name and Password boxes. These values are then included in the connection string.

8. Click the Test Connection button.

   Visual Studio attempts to open the specified database file with the connection string that the wizard has built for you. If the database is in a recognized format and the user-name and password entries (if any) are correct, you see the following message:

9. Click OK to close the message box, and then click OK to close the Add Connection dialog box.

   Visual Studio displays the Data Source Configuration Wizard again.

10. Click the plus sign (+) next to the Connection String item in the dialog box to display your completed connection string.

   Your wizard page looks similar to the following:

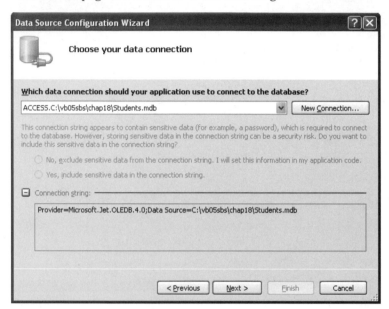

The connection string identifies a *provider* (also called a *managed provider*) named Microsoft.Jet.OLEDB.4.0, which is an underlying database component that understands how to connect to a database and extract data from it. The two most popular providers offered by Visual Studio are Microsoft Jet OLE DB and Microsoft SQL, but third-party providers are available for many of the other popular database formats.

11. Click the Next button.

   The wizard displays an alert message indicating that a new local database has been selected, and you are asked if the database should be copied to your project folders. (This message only appears the first time that you make a connection to a local database file. If you are repeating this exercise, you probably won't see the message.)

12. Click No to avoid making an extra copy of the database at this time.

   You are not commercially distributing this project; it is only a sample program, and an extra copy is not needed.

13. Click the Next button.

The Data Source Configuration Wizard now asks you the following question: "Do you want to save the connection string to the application configuration file?" Saving the connection string is the default selection, and in this example, the recommended string name is "StudentsConnectionString". You usually want to save this string within your application's default configuration file, because then if the location of your database changes, you can edit the string in your configuration file (which is listed in Solution Explorer), as opposed to tracking down the connection string within your program code and recompiling the application.

14. Click Next to save the default connection string.

You are now prompted to select the subset of database objects that you want to use for this particular project, as shown in the following dialog box:

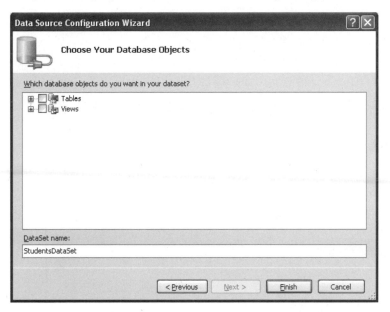

> **Note**   Visual Studio allows you to use just part of a database or to combine different databases—useful features when you're working to build datacentric applications.

The items you select in this dialog box are referred to within the project as *database objects*. Database objects can include tables of fields and records, database views, stored procedures, functions, and other items unique to your database. The collective term for all the database objects that you select is a *dataset*. In this project, the dataset is assigned the default name *StudentsDataSet*, which you can adjust in the DataSet Name box.

> **Tip** Note that the dataset you create now only *represents* the data in your database—if you add, delete, or modify database records in the dataset, you don't actually modify the underlying database tables until you issue a command that writes your changes back to the original database. Database programmers call this kind of arrangement a *disconnected data source*, meaning that there is a layer of abstraction between the actual database and your dataset.

15. Click the plus sign (+) next to the Tables node to expand the list of the tables included in the Students.mdb database.

    The list of the tables that appears in the wizard includes *Assignments*, *Classes*, *Departments*, and *Instructors*. Each table relates to some aspect of academic scheduling. The table we'll use in this example is *Instructors*.

16. Click the plus sign (+) next to the Instructors node, and then select the check boxes for the *Instructor* and *PhoneNumber* fields.

    You'll add these two fields to the *StudentsDataSet* dataset. The wizard page looks like this:

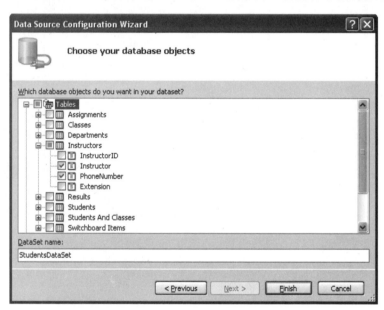

17. Click Finish to complete and close the Data Source Configuration Wizard.

    Visual Studio finishes the tasks of adding a database connection to your project and configuring the dataset with the selected database objects. (Depending on how the Visual Studio IDE has been used and configured, you might or might not see a Data Sources tab or window now.)

18. Click the Save All button on the Standard toolbar to save your changes. Specify the c:\vb05sbs\chap18 folder as the location.

19. If Solution Explorer is not currently visible, open it now to display the major files and components contained in the ADO Form project.

Your screen looks like this:

In addition to the standard Solution Explorer entries for a project, you see a new file named StudentsDataSet.xsd. This file is an XML schema that describes the tables, fields, data types, and other elements in the dataset that you have just created. The presence of the schema file means that you have added a *typed dataset* to your project. (Typed datasets have a schema file associated with them, but un-typed datasets don't.) Typed datasets are advantageous because they enable the statement-completion feature of the Visual Studio Code Editor, and they give you specific information about the fields and tables you're using.

20. Click the schema file in Solution Explorer, and then click the View Designer button.

You see a visual representation of the tables, fields, and data adapter commands related to your new dataset in a visual tool called the *Dataset Designer*. The Dataset Designer contains tools for creating components that communicate between your database and your application—what database programmers call *data access layer components*. You can create and modify table adapters, table adapter queries, data tables, data columns, and data relationships with the Dataset Designer. You can also use the Dataset Designer to review and set important properties related to objects in a dataset, such as the length of database fields and the data types associated with fields.

21. Click the *Instructor* field, and then press F4 to highlight the Properties window.

22. Click the *MaxLength* property.

Your screen looks similar to the graphic on the next page.

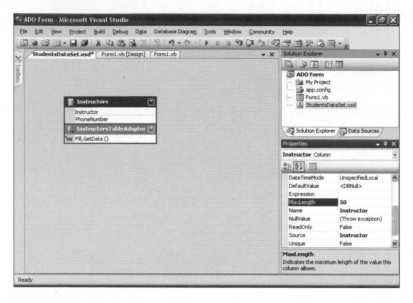

Here the Dataset Designer is shown with an active dataset named *StudentsDataSet*, and the Properties window shows that the *MaxLength* property is set to allow for a maximum of 50 characters in the *Instructor* field. Although this length seems sufficient, you can adjust this property (and others, too) if you find that the underlying database settings are inadequate for your application.

Setting the Dataset Designer aside for a moment, let's continue building the sample database application in the Data Sources window.

The Data Sources Window

The Data Sources window is a new (and hopefully timesaving) feature of the Visual Studio 2005 IDE. Its purpose is to display a visual representation of the datasets that have been configured for use within your project, and to help you bind these datasets to controls on the form. Remember that a dataset is just a temporary representation of database information in your program, and that each dataset contains only a subset of the tables and fields within your entire database file; that is, only the items that you selected while using the Data Source Configuration Wizard. The dataset is displayed in a hierarchical (tree) view in the Data Sources window, with a root node for each of the objects that you selected in the wizard. Each time you run the wizard to create a new dataset, a new dataset tree is added to the Data Sources window, giving you potential access to a wide range of data sources and views within a single program.

If you have been following the instructions for selecting fields in the *Instructors* table of the Students database, you have something interesting to display in the Data Sources window now. To prepare for the following exercises and display the Data Sources window, display the form again (click the Form1.vb tab), and then click the Show Data Sources command on the Data menu. (You can also click the Data Sources tab if it is visible below Solution Explorer.)

When the Data Sources window is open, expand the *Instructors* table so that you can see the two fields that we selected. Your Data Sources window looks like this, with the important features identified:

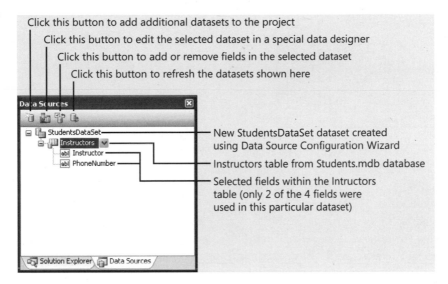

The easiest way to display the information in a dataset on a form (and therefore for your users) is to drag objects from the Data Sources window to the Windows Forms Designer. (This is the Designer you used in earlier chapters, but I am calling it *the Windows Forms Designer* here to distinguish it from the Dataset Designer.)

Chapter 19, "Data Presentation Using the *DataGridView* Control," describes how you can display entire tables of data on a form. In the remainder of this chapter, however, you'll experiment with dragging individual fields of data to the Windows Forms Designer to bind controls to select fields in the Students database. Give it a try now.

Use the Data Sources window to create database objects on a form

1. In the Data Sources window, click the plus sign (+) next to the *Instructors* node to display the available fields in *StudentsDataSet*.

   Your Data Sources window looks like the previous illustration. In Visual Studio 2005, you can display individual fields or an entire table of data by simply dragging the desired database objects onto your form.

2. Click the *Instructor* field, which contains the name of each instructor in the Students database.

   An arrow appears to the right of the *Instructor* field in the Data Sources window. Clicking this arrow displays a list of options related to how a database field is displayed on the form when you drag it.

3. Click the *Instructor* arrow.

   The Data Sources window looks as shown on the next page.

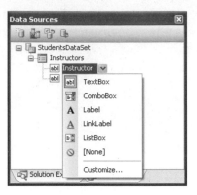

Although I haven't discussed it yet, most of the controls on the Common Controls tab of the Toolbox have the built-in ability to display database information. In Visual Studio terminology, these controls are called *bound controls* when they are connected to data-ready fields in a dataset. The list of controls you see now is a group of popular options for displaying string information from a database, but you can add additional controls to the list (or remove items) by clicking the Customize command. In this case, however, you'll simply use the *TextBox* control, the default bound control for string data.

4. Click *TextBox* in the list, and then drag the *Instructor* field to the middle of the form in the Windows Forms Designer.

As you drag the field over the form, a plus sign below the pointer indicates that adding this database object to a form is a valid operation. When you release the mouse button, Visual Studio creates a data-ready text box object and places a professional-looking navigation bar at the top of the form. The form looks something like this:

Visual Studio has actually created two objects for this *Instructor* field: a descriptive label object containing the name of the field, and a bound text box object that will display the contents of the field when you run the program. Below the form in the component tray, Visual Studio has also created several objects to manage internal aspects of the data access process. These objects include:

- *StudentsDataSet*, the dataset you created with the Data Source Configuration Wizard to represent fields in the Students database

- *InstructorsBindingSource*, an intermediary component that acts as a conduit between the *Instructors* table and bound objects on the form

- *InstructorsTableAdapter*, an intermediary component that moves data between *StudentsDataSet* and tables in the underlying Students database

- *InstructorsBindingNavigator*, which provides navigation services and properties related to the navigation toolbar and the *Instructors* table.

Several of these objects replace Visual Studio .NET 2003 features—for example, the table adapter object is a replacement for one or more data adapter objects in Visual Studio .NET 2003, which can hold data related to only one database table or query at a time. (For this reason, Visual Studio .NET 2003 projects sometimes require multiple data adapter objects, whereas Visual Studio 2005 projects require only one table adapter.)

Now you'll run the program to see how all of these objects work.

5. Click the Start Debugging button on the Standard toolbar.

The ADO Form program runs in the IDE. The text box object is loaded with the first *Instructor* record in the database (Delamarco, Stefan), and a navigation toolbar appears at the top of the form, as shown in the following illustration:

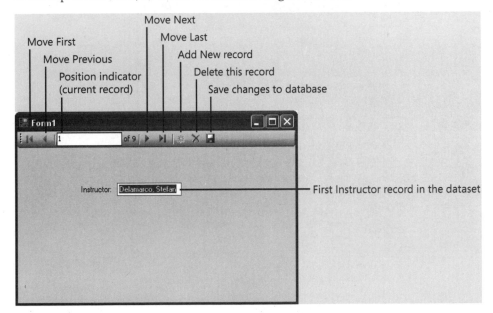

The navigation toolbar is an impressive addition to the Visual Studio 2005 database programming tools. It contains Move First, Move Previous, Move Next, and Move Last buttons, as well as a current position indicator and buttons that (when properly configured) add new records to the dataset, delete unwanted records from the dataset, and save a modified dataset to disk. You can change or delete these toolbar buttons by setting the Items property for the binding navigator object in the Properties window, which displays a visual tool called the Items Collection Editor. You can also enable or disable individual toolbar buttons.

6. Click the Move Next button to scroll to the second instructor name in the dataset.

    The McKay, Yvonne record appears.

7. Continue scrolling through the dataset one record at a time. As you scroll through the list of names, notice that the position indicator keeps track of where you are in the list of records.

8. Click the Move First and Move Last buttons to move to the first and last records of the dataset, respectively.

9. Delete the last record from the dataset (Halvorson, Kim) by clicking the Delete button.

    The record is deleted from the dataset, and the position indicator shows that there are now 8 records remaining. (Halvorson, Michael has become the last and current record.) Your form looks like this:

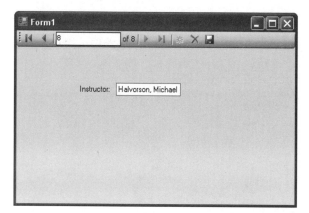

As I mentioned earlier, the dataset represents only the subset of tables from the Students database that have been used in this project—the dataset is a disconnected image of the database, not the database itself. Accordingly, the record that you deleted has been deleted only from the dataset that is loaded in memory while the program is running. However, to verify that the program is actually working with disconnected data and is not modifying the original database, you'll stop and restart the program now.

10. Click the Close button on the form to end the program.

    The program terminates, and the IDE returns.

11. Click Start Debugging to run the program again.

     When the program restarts and the form loads, the navigation toolbar shows that the dataset contains 9 records, as it did originally. In other words, it works as expected.

12. Click the Move Last button to view the last record in the dataset.

     The record for Halvorson, Kim appears again. This final instructor name was deleted only from memory and has reappeared because the underlying database still contains the name.

13. Click the Close button again to close the program.

Congratulations! Without writing any program code, you have built a functioning database application that displays specific information from a database. Setting up a dataset has taken many steps, but the dataset is now ready to be used in many useful ways in the program. Although I selected only one table and two fields from the Students database to reduce screen clutter and focus our attention, you will probably want to select a much wider range of objects from your databases when you build datasets using the Data Source Configuration Wizard. As you can see, it is not necessary to create bound objects for each dataset item on a form—you can decide which database records you want to use and display.

Using Bound Controls to Display Database Information

As I mentioned earlier, Visual Studio can use a variety of the controls in the Visual Studio Toolbox to display database information. You can bind controls to datasets by dragging fields from the Data Sources window (the easiest method), and you can create controls separately on your forms and bind them to dataset objects at a later time. This second option is an important feature, because occasionally you will be adding data sources to a project after the basic user interface has been created. The procedure I'll demonstrate in this section handles that situation, while giving you additional practice with binding data objects to controls within a Visual Basic application. You'll create a masked text box object on your form, configure the object to format database information in a useful way, and then bind the *PhoneNumber* field in *StudentsDataSet* to the object.

Bind a masked text box control to a dataset object

1. Display the form in the Windows Forms Designer, and then open the Toolbox, if it is not already visible.

2. Click the *MaskedTextBox* control on the Common Controls tab, and then create a masked text box object on the form below the *Instructor* label and text box.

    As you might recall from Chapter 6, "Using Decision Structures," the *MaskedTextBox* control is similar to the *TextBox* control, but it gives you more ability to regulate or limit the information entered by the user into a program. The input format for the *Masked-TextBox* control is adjusted by setting the *Mask* property. In this exercise, you'll use *Mask* to prepare the masked text box object to display formatted phone numbers from the

PhoneNumber field. (By default, phone numbers in the Students database are stored without the spacing, parentheses, or dashes of North American phone numbers, but you want to see this formatting in your program.)

3. Click the shortcut arrow in the upper-right corner of the masked text box object, and then click the Set Mask command.

Visual Studio displays the Input Mask dialog box, which lists a number of pre-defined formatting masks. Visual Studio uses these masks to format output in the masked text box object, as well as input received from users.

4. Click the Phone Number input mask, and then click OK.

The masked text box object now appears with input formatting guidelines for the country and language settings stored within Microsoft Windows. (These settings might vary from country to country, but for me it looks like a North American telephone number with area code.)

5. Add a label object in front of the new masked text box object, and set its *Text* property to "Phone number:" (including the colon).

The first descriptive label was added automatically by the Data Sources window, but we need to add this one manually.

6. Adjust the spacing between the two labels and text boxes so that they are aligned consistently. When you're finished, your form looks similar to the following:

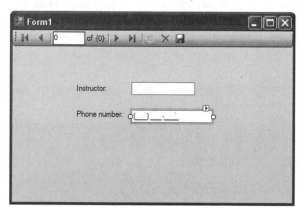

Now you'll bind the *PhoneNumber* field in *StudentsDataSet* to the new masked text box object. In Visual Studio 2005, the process is easier than it was in Visual Basic 6 or Visual Studio .NET 2003—you simply drag the *PhoneNumber* field from the Data Sources window onto the object that you want to bind to the data—in this case, the *MaskedTextBox1* object.

7. Display the Data Sources window if it is not visible, and then drag the *PhoneNumber* field onto the *MaskedTextBox1* object.

When you drag a dataset object onto an object that already exists on the form (what we might call the *target object*), a new bound object is not created. Instead, the *DataBindings* properties for the target object are set to match the dragged dataset object in the Data Sources window. (*DataBindings* properties are also a feature of Visual Studio .NET 2003, so this part of creating bound objects will seem familiar if you're experienced with the previous version of Visual Studio.)

After this drag-and-drop operation, the masked text box object is bound to the *Phone-Number* field, and the masked text box object's *Text* property contains a small database icon (a sign that the object is bound to a dataset).

8. Verify that the *MaskedTextBox1* object is selected on the form, and then press F4 to high-light the Properties window.

9. Scroll to the *DataBindings* category within the Properties window, and then click the plus sign (+) to open it.

   Visual Studio displays the properties typically associated with data access in a masked text box object. Your Properties window looks similar to the following:

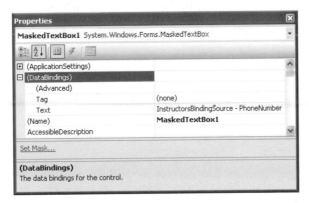

The noteworthy bound property here is the *Text* property, which has been set to "InstructorsBindingSource – PhoneNumber" as a result of the drag-and-drop operation. (Note that the tiny database icon does not appear here, but only in the *Text* property at the bottom of the alphabetical list of properties.) In addition, if you click the arrow in the *Text* property now, you'll see a data sources tree with the bound field highlighted. (This useful visual display allows you to quickly change the data source that the control is bound to, but don't adjust that setting now.)

10. Click the Start Debugging button to run the program.

    Visual Studio runs the program in the IDE. After a moment, the two database fields are loaded into the text box and masked text box objects, as shown in the illustration on the next page.

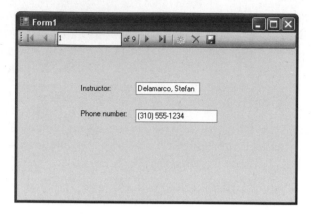

Importantly, the masked text box object correctly formats the phone number information so that it is in the expected format for North American phone numbers.

11.   Click the Move Next button a few times.

Another important feature is also demonstrated here: The two dataset fields scroll together, and the displayed instructor names match the corresponding phone numbers recorded in the Students database. This synchronization is handled by the *Instructors-BindingNavigator* object, which keeps track of the current record for each bound object on the form.

12.   Click the Close button to stop the program, and then click the Save All button to save your changes.

You've learned to display multiple database fields on a form, use the navigation toolbar to browse through a dataset, and format database information with a mask. Before you leave this chapter and move on to the useful *DataGridView* control discussed in Chapter 19, take a moment to see how you can further customize your dataset by using a few SQL statements.

One Step Further: Writing SQL Statements to Filter Data

You have used the Data Source Configuration Wizard to extract just the tables and fields you wanted from the Students database by creating a custom dataset named *StudentsDataSet*. In addition to this filtering, however, you can further organize and fine-tune the data displayed by bound controls by using SQL statements and the Visual Studio Query Builder. This section introduces these tools.

For Visual Basic users who are familiar with Microsoft Access or SQL Server, filtering data with SQL statements is nothing new. But the rest of us need to learn that *SQL statements* are commands that extract, or *filter*, information from one or more structured tables in a database. The reason for this filtering is simple: Just as Web users are routinely confronted with a bewildering amount of data on the Internet (and use clever search keywords in their browsers to locate just the information they need), database programmers are routinely confronted with tables containing tens of thousands of records that need refinement and organization. The SQL SELECT statement is one traditional mechanism for organizing database information. By chaining together a group of these statements, programmers can create complex search directives, or *queries*, that extract just the data that is needed from a database.

Realizing the industry-wide acceptance of SQL statements, previous versions of the Visual Studio and Visual Basic IDEs have included mechanisms for using SQL statements. In addition, Visual Studio 2005 provides a tool called Query Builder for those who have less experience with SQL programming and would prefer to use a visual tool to help them construct the queries. In the following exercise, you'll use Query Builder to further organize your dataset by sorting it alphabetically.

Create SQL statements with Query Builder

1. On the form, click the *InstructorTextBox* object (the first bound object that you created to display the names of instructors in the Students database).

2. Click the Add Query command on the Data menu.

    The Add Query command is available when a bound object, such as *InstructorTextBox*, is selected in the Designer. The Search Criteria dialog box appears, as shown in the following illustration:

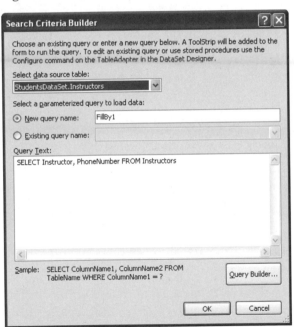

This dialog box helps you organize and view your queries, which are created by the Query Builder and consist of SQL statements. The table that your query will filter and organize by default (*StudentsDataSet.Instructors*) is selected in the Select Data Source Table box near the top of the dialog box. You'll recognize the object hierarchy format used by the table name, which is read as "the *Instructors* table within the *StudentsDataSet* dataset." If you had other tables to choose from, they would be listed in the list box displayed when you click the Select Data Source Table arrow.

3. Type **SortInstructors** in the New Query Name box.

    This text box assigns a name to your query, and forms the basis of toolbar buttons added to the form. (For easy access, the default arrangement is that new queries are assigned to toolbar buttons within the application you are building.)

4. Click the Query Builder button in the dialog box to open the Query Builder tool.

    The Query Builder allows you to create SQL statements by typing them directly into a large SQL statement text box or by clicking list boxes and other visual tools.

5. In the *Instructor* row representing the *Instructor* field in your dataset, click the cell under Sort Type, and then click the arrow to display the Sort Type list box.

    Your screen looks like this:

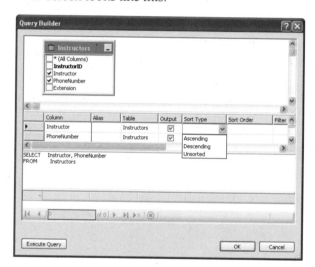

    The SQL ORDER BY statement sorts database records based on a key field and sort order number.

6. To build an SQL ORDER BY statement that sorts records in the *Instructor* field in ascending order, click Ascending in the Sort Type list box.

7. Click the SQL statement text box below the grid pane to update the Query Builder window.

    The new query is added to the SQL statement box, and your screen looks like this:

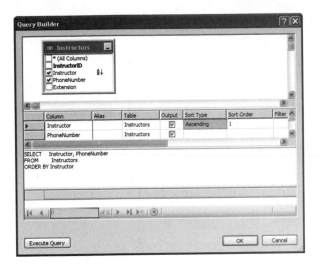

8. Click OK to complete your query.

   Visual Studio closes the Query Builder and displays your new query in the Search Criteria Builder dialog box. The name of the query (*SortInstructors*) is listed, as well as the SQL statements that make up the sort.

9. Click OK to close the dialog box and configure the *InstructorTextBox* object to list names in ascending alphabetical order.

   This particular SQL statement does not filter the data, but organizes dataset records in a more useful order when the user clicks a SortInstructors button on a new toolbar at the top of the form. The process has also created a *SortInstructorsToolStrip* object in the component tray below the form. The Designer and component tray look like this now:

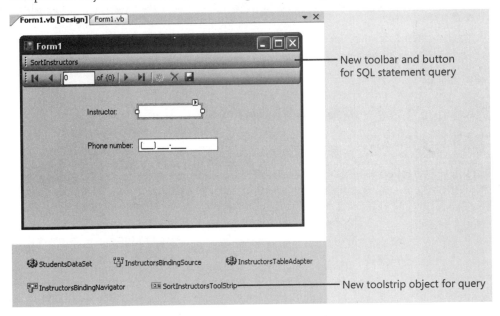

10.   Click Start Debugging to run the program.

Visual Studio loads the form and displays the first record for two dataset objects.

11.   Click the SortInstructors button on the new toolbar.

Your new SQL statement sorts the *Instructor* records in the dataset and displays the records in their new order. The first record is now Barr, Adam, as shown in the following illustration:

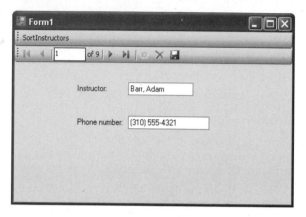

12.   Scroll through the list of records, and verify that it is now in ascending alphabetical order. (The last record should be Wilson, Dan.)

13.   Click the Close button to end the program.

You're on your way with building custom queries by using SQL statements and Query Builder. Database programming is a complex topic, but you have already learned much that will help you build datacentric applications—highly personalized collections of data that benefit *the user* and his or her computing needs—in Visual Basic. You will continue exploring the theme of rich data access in Chapter 19. And in Chapter 20, "Creating Web Sites and Web Pages using Microsoft Visual Web Developer and ASP.NET," your final project will be displaying database records on a Web site.

Chapter 18 Quick Reference

To	Do this
Establish a connection to a database	Click the Add New Data Source command on the Data menu, and then use the Data Source Configuration Wizard to browse to the database for you want to provide access by building a connection string.
Create a dataset	Using the Data Source Configuration Wizard, specify a name for the dataset in the DataSet Name box, expand the Tables node in the tree view of your database presented by the wizard, and then specify the tables and fields that you want to include in your dataset. (A dataset need not include all database tables and fields.)

To	Do this
Create bound objects capable of displaying data from a dataset on a Windows form	After running the Data Source Configuration Wizard, open the Data Sources window, and drag tables and/or fields to the Windows form. To control the type of bound control created by Visual Studio for a table or field, click its arrow and select a control from the list box before dragging it. If you placed a control on the form before adding data sources to the project, bind a database object to the control by the dragging the database objects from the Data Sources window onto the control on the form. Alternatively, set an object's *DataBinding* properties to a valid field (column) in the dataset. (One of the most useful *DataBinding* properties is *Text*.)
Add navigation controls to a Windows form	In Visual Studio 2005, a navigation toolbar is added automatically to Windows forms when a valid database object is dragged from the Data Sources window to the form. To customize the buttons on this toolbar, right-click the *InstructorBindingNavigator* object in the component tray, and then click Edit Items.
Format database information on a form	Use a *MaskedTextBox* control to format the content of string data in the dataset. The *MaskedTextBox* control offers many useful input masks and the ability to create custom string formats.
Filter or sort database information stored in a dataset	Use SQL statements to create custom queries in the Visual Studio Query Builder, and add these queries to a toolbar on a Windows form.

Chapter 19

Data Presentation Using the *DataGridView* Control

After completing this chapter, you will be able to:

- Create a data grid view object on a Windows form, and use it to display a database table.

- Sort database tables by column.

- Change the format and color of cells in a data grid view object.

- Add and remove columns and column headings.

- Display multiple data tables and navigation bars on a form, and switch among them.

- Permit changes in grid cells, and write updates to the underlying database.

In Chapter 18, "Getting Started with ADO.NET," you learned how to use Microsoft ADO.NET database programming techniques to establish a connection to a Microsoft Access database and display columns from the database in a Windows form. You also learned how to add a navigation bar to a form and how to organize database information using SQL statements and the Query Builder tool.

Upgrade Notes: Migrating Visual Basic 6 Code to Visual Basic 2005

If you're experienced with Microsoft Visual Basic 6, you'll notice some new features in Microsoft Visual Basic 2005, including the following:

- In Visual Basic 6, you can use several grid controls to display database information on a form, including *FlexGrid*, *Hierarchical FlexGrid*, and *DataGrid*. In Visual Basic 2005, the *DataGridView* control is the only spreadsheet-style control that's provided to display a database table.

- The *DataGridView* control included with Visual Basic 2005 is somewhat different from the *DataGrid* control included with Microsoft Visual Studio .NET 2003, and quite different from the *DataGrid* control included with Visual Basic 6. One important improvement is that the Visual Basic 2005 *DataGridView* control doesn't require data-specific commands because the underlying data adapter and dataset objects handle all the data access functionality.

In this chapter, you'll continue working with the database programming features of Microsoft Visual Studio 2005 and the useful classes, objects, and design tools in ADO.NET. In particular, you'll learn how to use the *DataGridView* control, which allows you to present an entire table of database information to the user.

Using *DataGridView* to Display Database Records

The *DataGridView* control presents information by establishing a grid of rows and columns on a form to display data as you might see it in a program such as Microsoft Excel or Microsoft Access. A *DataGridView* control can be used to display any type of tabular data: text, numbers, dates, or the contents of an array.

In this chapter, however, you'll focus on the ability of the *DataGridView* control to display the colums (fields) and rows (records) of the Students.mdb database, the file of structured student information that you started working with in Chapter 18. You'll start by filling a simple data grid view object with text records from the database, and then you'll set a few formatting options. Next you'll move on to sorting records in grid objects and learning how to manage multiple grids and navigation bars on a form. Finally, you'll learn how to adjust *DataGridView* properties, including the *ReadOnly* property that allows or prevents a user from saving changes back to the original database.

The *DataGridView* control is connected, or bound, to underlying data access components through the its *BindingSource* property. This property contains useful information only after your program has established a connection to a valid data source by using the Data Source Configuration Wizard and the Data Sources window. (The steps involved in establishing this connection will be reviewed quickly here but are described in greater detail in Chapter 18; if you want more information , read the section entitled "Working with an Access Database" in that chapter.) After a data grid view object is bound to a valid data source, Visual Studio fills, or *populates*, the grid automatically by using the *Fill* method when the form is loaded into memory.

Establish a connection to a database table

1. Start Visual Studio, and create a new Visual Basic Windows Application project named **My DataGridView Sample**.

   A new project appears in the IDE.

2. Click the Add New Data Source command on the Data menu.

   The Data Source Configuration Wizard opens in the development environment. You used this tool Chapter 18 to link the Students.mdb database to your project and fill the

Data Sources window with tables and columns from the database. This time you'll select a broader range of information from the sample Access database.

3. Click the Database icon, and then click Next.

The wizard prompts you to build a connection string, but if you completed the exercises in Chapter 18, the Students.mdb database is automatically offered to you, as shown in the following screen:

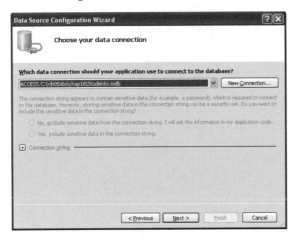

If you don't see the Students database connection, click the New Connection button, and browse to the Students.mdb file, located in the c:\vb05sbs\chap18 folder. (Detailed steps for establishing this connection are given in Chapter 18, if you'd like additional information.)

4. With the Students.mdb connection string highlighted, click the Next button.

The wizard asks whether you want to save your connection string.

5. Click Next to save the string in the default location (your project's configuration file).

You are now prompted to select the database objects you want to use for this particular project. Remember that the Data Source Configuration Wizard allows you to pick and choose database tables and columns at this point—you can select all the objects in the database or just a subset.

6. Expand the Tables node to see the names of the seven tables in the database and an additional entry called Switchboard Items.

7. Click the plus sign (+) next to the Tables node to select all eight items.

You'll add a broader range of database information to this project, because the goal of this chapter is to view large amounts of data by using the DataGridView control. Your wizard page looks as shown on the next page.

8. Click Finish to close the Data Source Configuration Wizard.

   Visual Studio creates a dataset named *StudentsDataSet* to represent the eight database objects you selected. Visual Studio also adds an XML schema file named Students-DataSet.xsd to your project and the Solution Explorer window. You have now established a connection to the Students.mdb database that you can use for the remainder of this chapter.

9. Click the Save All button on the Standard toolbar to save the project. Specify the c:\vb05sbs\chap19 folder as the location.

10. Click the Data Source tab below Solution Explorer to open the Data Sources window. (If the Data Sources tab is not visible, click the Show Data Sources command on the Data menu.)

    The Data Sources window displays the objects in *StudentsDataSet*, as shown in the following illustration:

In Chapter 18, you dragged individual fields from the Data Sources window to a Windows form to bind data objects to controls in the user interface. In the next exercise, you'll follow a similar procedure, but this time you'll drag an entire table to the form, and you'll bind the table to a *DataGridView* control so that all the fields in the table can be displayed at once.

Create a data grid view object

1. Resize the form so that it covers most of the screen.

   Before this chapter is complete, you'll place two data grid view objects side by side on the form, each with four columns and about ten rows of data. Remember that the form can be larger than the room allotted for it within the IDE, and you can close programming tools or use the scroll bars to see portions of the form that are hidden. (However, you'll want to keep the Data Sources window open for the next step.)

2. In the Data Sources window, click the *Instructors* table, and then click the arrow to its right to display the list of controls that can be bound to the *Instructors* table on the form.

   The Data Sources window looks like this:

   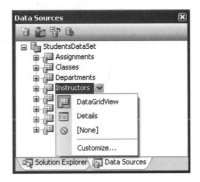

   Because you have selected an entire table, you do not see individual bound controls in this list box. Instead you see the following options:

   - DataGridView, the default selection, which displays a grid of columns and rows representing the fields and records in the *Instructors* table.

   - Details, which configures Visual Basic to automatically create individual controls (with associated labels) for each field in a table that you drag to the form. Although I won't demonstrate Details now, it is a useful option if you want to present tabular data in a slightly more approachable format.

   - None, which removes any association between the table and a user interface element or control. (If you select None for a table, you will not be able to drag the table from the Data Sources window to the form, and a Null icon will appear next to the table name.)

   - Customize, which lets you select a different control that might be suitable for displaying multiple database fields (such as the *ListBox* control).

3. Click the DataGridView option, and then drag the *Instructors* table to the left side of your form.

   Visual Studio creates a navigation bar at the top of the form, adds dataset, binding source, table adapter, and binding navigator components to the component tray, and creates a data grid view object named *InstructorsDataGridView* on the form. Your screen looks similar to the following:

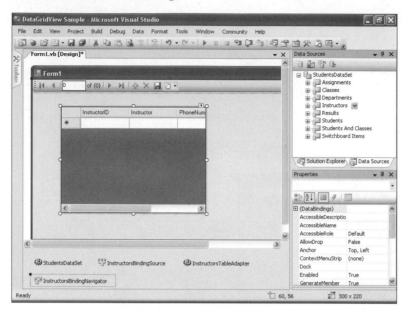

As you can see, the grid does not contain any information at this point, and it is probably not the right size either. (My data grid view object is not wide enough to display all four columns, for example.) However, you can clearly see that Visual Studio has organized the *Instructors* table in the grid so that its fields appear as columns and its rows represent individual records. A blank row is reserved for the first record in the table, and additional rows will be added as soon as the program is run and the grid is filled with data.

4. Move and resize the data grid view object so that all four of its columns are clearly visible and there is ample room for at least ten rows of data.

5. Use the Properties window to set the form's *Text* property to "The Instructors Table".

Your form looks similar to the following:

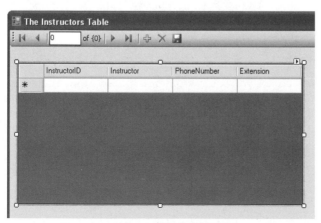

You have completed the basic steps necessary to create a data grid view object on a form and size it appropriately. Next you'll preview the data and customize your table. The ability to preview grid data and adjust basic settings is made easy by the new Visual Studio shortcut arrow feature.

Preview the data bound to a data grid view object

1. Select the data grid view object on the form, and then click the shortcut arrow in the upper-right corner of the object.

    Visual Studio displays *DataGridView* Tasks, a list of common property settings and commands related to the data grid view object. The DataGridView Tasks list looks like this:

    You can use the settings and commands in this list to change the table that is bound to the data grid view object and to enable or disable editing within the grid. (The default setting is to give the user limited abilities to edit information in the table, although you can still control whether the changes he or she makes are written to the underlying database.) You can also adjust the columns shown, dock (attach) the grid to the parent container (in this case, the form), filter records with a query (SQL statement), and preview the data in the table.

2. Click Preview Data to open the Preview Data dialog box.

    You display this dialog box when you want to examine the data in a table before you actually run the program—a handy feature.

3. Click the Preview button.

    Visual Studio loads the *Instructors* table from *StudentsDataSet*, as shown on the next page.

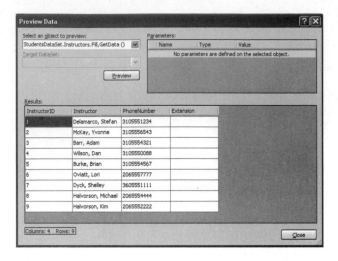

You should be familiar with some of this data from Chapter 18, but you now have an opportunity to see all four columns in the table. Seeing all the columns at once is interesting but also disconcerting—the *Extension* column contains no data at all, something that might confuse or annoy your users. (This column was designed to hold office phone extensions, but no data has been entered in this column in the database.) Visual Studio makes it easy to detect such a shortcoming and tailor the grid's output so that the unused column is not shown.

4. Click the Close button to close the Preview Data dialog box.

Now you'll remove the empty *Extension* column from the grid.

Remove a column from a data grid view object

1. With the DataGridView Tasks list still open, click the Edit Columns command.

   You see the following dialog box:

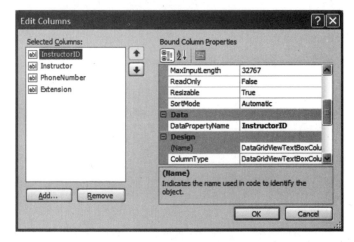

You can use the Edit Columns dialog box to add or remove columns from those displayed by the data grid view object. (As you'll learn later in the chapter, you also use this dialog box to change the properties of the *InstructorsDataGridView* object.) Right now you want to delete the unused *Extension* column.

> **Note**   Although you are removing the *Extension* column from the data grid, it still exists in the underlying Students.mdb database.

2. Click the *Extension* column in the Selected Columns list box.

3. Click the Remove button.

    Visual Studio removes the column from the list.

4. Click OK to confirm your change.

    The *InstructorsDataGridView* object appears again, but without the *Extension* column. You now have more room on the form to display database information.

5. Resize the *InstructorsDataGridView* object so that it takes up less space.

    Your form looks similar to the following:

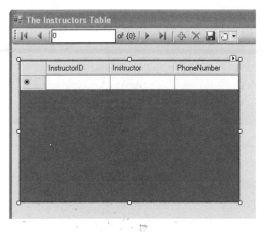

6. Click the Save All button to save your changes.

You've previewed and customized your table using database tools. Now you'll run the program to see what the grid looks like at run time. You'll also learn how to sort records in a data grid view object.

Manage a data grid view object at run time

1. Click the Start Debugging button.

   Visual Studio runs your project in the IDE. The *Instructors* database table appears within the data grid view object, just as you configured it. Your form looks something like this:

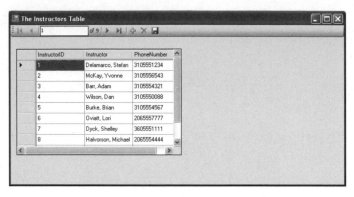

   The program statement in the *Form1_Load* event procedure that populated the grid with information from the *Instructors* table looks like this:

```
Me.InstructorsTableAdapter.Fill(Me.StudentsDataSet.Instructors)
```

   This line was added to your program by Visual Studio when you dragged the *Instructors* table to the form from the Data Sources window.

   Each row in the grid represents a record of data from the *Instructors* table in the database. Scroll bars are provided so that you can view any records or columns that aren't immediately visible. This is a handy ease-of-use feature that comes automatically with the *DataGridView* control.

2. Scroll down the list of records to view all nine rows, which represent instructor data for a college or university.

3. Reduce the size of the InstructorID column by placing the pointer between the InstructorID and Instructor column headings and dragging the column border to the left.

   When you place the pointer between the column headings, it changes to a resizing handle. You can resize columns at run time because the data grid view object's *AllowUserToResizeColumns* property is by default set to True. If you want to prevent resizing, you can set this property to False.

4. Return the InstructorID column to its original width.

   When a data grid view object is filled with data, you can also take advantage of the *DataGridView* control's sorting feature.

5. Click the Instructor column heading.

The grid is sorted alphabetically by instructor name. (Barr, Adam is now first.) Your form looks something like this:

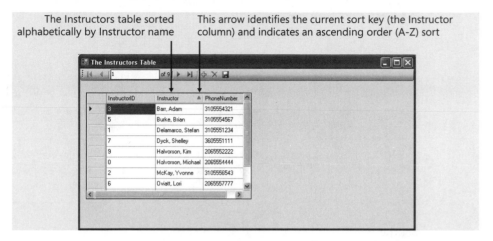

The Instructors table sorted alphabetically by Instructor name

This arrow identifies the current sort key (the Instructor column) and indicates an ascending order (A-Z) sort

When database records are sorted, a sorting column, or *key*, is required—you establish this key by clicking the heading of the column on which you want to base the sort. The *DataGridView* control provides visual identification for the current sort key—a tiny arrow to the right of the column header. If the sort order is currently an ascending alphabetical (A–Z) list, the arrow points up. Clicking the column heading will reverse the sort order to create a descending alphabetical (Z–A) list. The arrow acts like a toggle, so you can switch back and forth between sorting directions.

6. Click the Instructor column several times to see how the sort order can be switched back and forth.

7. Click other column headings such as InstructorID and PhoneNumber to sort the database based on those keys.

8. When you're finished experimenting with the scrolling, resizing, and sorting features of the *DataGridView* control, click the Close button on the form to stop the program.

    The program closes, and the development environment returns.

Formatting *DataGridView* Cells

To customize the appearance of your dataset on a form, you can control the look and orientation of several *DataGridView* characteristics by setting properties at design time. For example, you can change the default width of cells in the grid, add or remove column headers, change the grid or header background colors, and change the color of the gridlines. The exercise on the next page steps you through some of these useful property settings.

Set data grid view properties at design time

1. Display the form, click the data grid view object (if it is not already selected), and then highlight the Properties window.

2. Click the *Columns* property, and then click the ellipsis button to open the *Columns* collection in the Edit Columns dialog box.

   You used this dialog box earlier to delete the *Extension* column from the *Instructors* table. (It is used to set property settings for individual columns.) Now you'll use the Edit Columns dialog box to change the default width of the *InstructorID* column.

> **Note**   Because *InstructorID* is currently selected (it is the highlighted column in the Selected Columns list box), you don't need to click it again. However, always remember to select the desired column before you adjust a column property.

3. Set the *Width* property to 70.

   A width of 70 (measured in pixels) will provide plenty of room for the integer values in the *InstructorID* column.

4. Click OK to close the Edit Columns dialog box.

   Now you'll set properties that control the appearance of all the columns in the table.

> **Note**   You use the Edit Columns dialog box to configure individual columns. To modify properties that apply to all the columns in a table, you adjust property settings for the data grid view object in the Properties window.

5. In the Properties window, set the *ColumnHeadersVisible* property to False.

   Although the column names are somewhat useful in this particular database, sometimes column names don't clearly identify their contents or they contain abbreviations or words that you want to hide from your users. Setting this property removes the column names from the table.

6. Click the *AlternatingRowsDefaultCellStyle* property, and then click the ellipses button.

   The *AlternatingRowsDefaultCellStyle* property controls the color that appears in the background of grid cells in alternating rows. Changing this setting produces an alternating effect (white and the color you select) from row to row in the grid. In my opinion, this effect makes it easy to read records in longer tables.

   Visual Studio displays the CellStyle Builder dialog box, a tool used to set the properties of column cells in data grid view tables.

7. Click the *BackColor* property, click its arrow, then click the Custom tab, and click the light yellow color.

Your dialog box looks like this:

8. Click OK to close the dialog box.

    When you run the program, the rows in the grid will be displayed in alternating white and yellow colors.

> **Note** The color that appears around the edges of the cell grid is controlled by the *BackgroundColor* property. To change the color of all the cells in a grid, you can adjust the *DefaultCellStyle* property. To change the background color used for the header cells (if you display them), you can modify the *ColumnHeadersDefaultCellStyle* property.

9. Click the *GridColor* property, click its arrow, click the Custom tab, and then click Navy (the darkest blue color).

    This property setting controls the color of the gridlines. If you change the background color of the cells, you might also want to modify the gridline color.

    Now you'll run the program to see the effect of your formatting changes.

10. Click the Start Debugging button.

    After a few moments, the grid appears with information from the *Instructors* table. Your screen looks similar to the one shown on the next page.

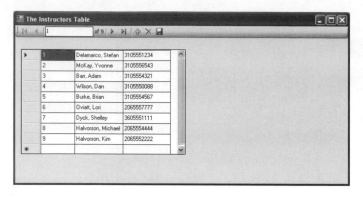

Notice that the column headers are missing now and that the first column is a little narrower. Notice also the alternating white and yellow row pattern and the blue gridlines (not discernible in this book, alas, but on the screen).

11. Click the Close button on the form to stop the program.

You might want to scan the Properties window for additional property settings and customizations. There are several possibilities if you look closely at the list of formatting options. Remember, these property settings affect all the columns in a table, not just individual columns.

Datacentric Focus: Adding a Second Grid and Navigation Control

To provide your users with a data-rich user interface containing multiple database tables, you should consider adding a second data grid view object to your form. After you have established a dataset in the Data Sources window, it is relatively straightforward to add an additional *DataGridView* control bound to a second table within the dataset. The only tricky part is learning how to add a second navigation bar and setting its *BindingSource* property to the underlying binding source object. You'll give it a try in the following exercise.

Bind a second *DataGridView* control to the *Classes* table

1. Open the Data Sources window, if it is not currently visible.

2. Drag the *Classes* table from the Data Sources window to the right side of the form.

    Visual Studio creates a second data grid view object named *ClassesDataGridView* on the form.

3. Right-click the *ClassesDataGridView* object, and then click the Edit Columns command.

    The Edit Columns dialog box opens.

4. Select and remove the *ClassID*, *SectionNumber*, *Term*, *Units*, *Year*, *Location*, and *Notes* columns.

The form is not large enough to display all the columns in the table, so for this example I want you to pare down the list. When you're finished, the *ClassName*, *Department*, *Prof*, and *DaysAndTimes* columns are left, as shown in the following illustration:

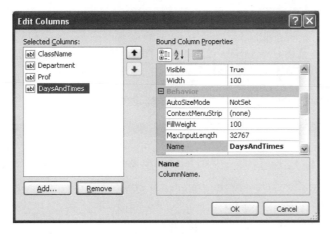

5. Click OK to close the Edit Columns dialog box.

6. Move and resize the *ClassesDataGridView* object on the form so that all four rows are displayed at once. You might need to move and resize the form, and possibly also the *InstructorsDataGridView* object, to be able to display all four rows.

7. Change the form's *Text* property to "The Instructors and Classes Tables".

    Your form looks something like the following illustration. (Because I am running Visual Studio at a screen resolution of 800 x 600, I needed to hide many of the Visual Studio tool windows to show the form.)

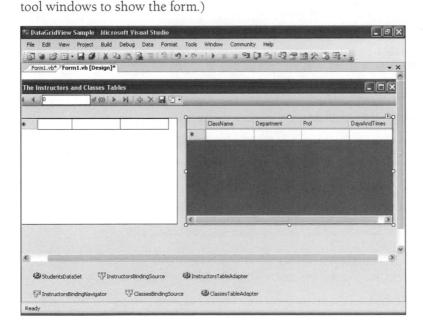

Notice that Visual Studio has also added two new objects to the component tray: a *ClassesBindingSource* object and a *ClassesTableAdapter* object. These two items are intermediary components that move data between the *ClassesDataGridView* object, the *StudentsDataSet* dataset, and the *Classes* table in the underlying Students database.

Now you'll add a second navigation bar to the form to provide navigation services and properties related to the *Classes* table and the second grid. The second bar is necessary because the first (*InstructorsBindingNavigator*) is bound only to the *InstructorsDataGridView* object.

Link a *BindingNavigator* control to the *ClassesDataGridView* object

1. Double-click the *BindingNavigator* control on the Data tab of the Toolbox.

   Visual Studio adds a binding navigator object named *BindingNavigator1* to the component tray, and adds a second navigation bar to the top of your form.

2. In the Properties window, change the *Name* property of the new *BindingNavigator1* object to "ClassesBindingNavigator".

   Using this name will make it clearer which binding source and table adapter your new navigation bar is linked to.

3. Change the *BindingSource* property of the *ClassesBindingNavigator* object to ClassesBindingSource.

   If you click the *BindingSource* arrow, the Properties window shows the names of the two valid binding sources in the program, as shown in the following illustration:

Now that a link has been established between the second navigation bar and the binding source object representing the *Classes* table, your program is ready to run.

4. Click the Save All button to save your changes.

5. Click the Start Debugging button on the toolbar.

   Visual Studio runs the DataGridView Sample program in the IDE. You see two grids and two navigation bars, as shown in the following illustration:

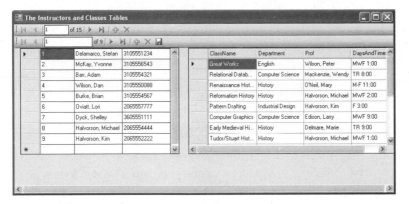

6. Click the Move Last button on the navigation bar that contains 15 records.

   The last class name in the Classes table, Deviant Behavior (Psychology), is highlighted. Your new navigation bar works, and you have complete access to the columns you selected in the Classes table.

7. Use both navigation bars in tandem to highlight different records in the two database tables.

   The two data grid view objects work independently, providing you access to exactly the database records that you want to see. You can appreciate how useful this access might be for a user who needs to compare longer tables containing sets of information that are closely related. If the data is further filtered by SQL SELECT statements, the application quickly becomes quite powerful.

8. When you're finished experimenting with the two tables and navigation bars, click the Close button to close the DataGridView Sample application.

One Step Further: Updating the Original Database

As I mentioned earlier, the dataset object in your program is only a representation of the data in your original database. This is also true of the information stored in the grids on your form—if the user makes a change to this data, the change isn't written back to the original database unless you have set the data grid view object's *ReadOnly* property to False and the user clicks the Save button on the navigation bar. The designers of ADO.NET and Visual Studio created this relationship to protect the original database and to allow your users to manipulate data freely in your programs—whether you plan to save the changes or not.

In the following exercise, you'll examine the first data grid view object's *ReadOnly* property, which enables or disables changes in the *InstructorsDataViewGrid* object. You'll also learn how to use the Save Data button, which writes changes back to the original database tables on disk.

Enable updates to the database

1. Click the first data grid view object on the form (*InstructorsDataViewGrid*), and then highlight the Properties window.

2. Scroll to the *ReadOnly* property, and examine its property setting.

   If the *ReadOnly* property is set to False, the user is free to make changes to the information in grid cells. If you want to allow your users to modify the information and write it back to the database your program is connected to, you should keep this default setting. If you want to disable editing, you should set the *ReadOnly* property to True.

   You'll keep the default setting of False in this case—you want to test updating the underlying Students.mdb database.

> **Tip**   The complete DataGridView Sample program is located in the c:\vb05sbs\chap19\datagridview sample folder.

3. Click the Start Debugging button to test the first grid's Read Only property.

   The two grids appear with data from the *Instructors* table and the *Classes* table of the Students.mdb database.

4. In the first grid, click the cell containing the phone number for Kim Halvorson, type **1234567890**, and then press Enter.

   As you make the change, a tiny pencil icon appears in the row header to the left, indicating that a change is being made. Your screen looks similar to this:

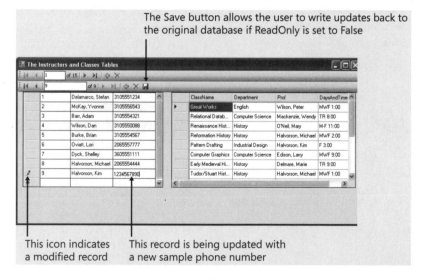

When you press Enter or click a different cell in the grid, the change is stored in the *StudentsDataSet* dataset.

5. Click the Save Data button on the navigation bar.

Visual Studio uses the *Update* method in the grid's table adapter object to write the changed dataset to the underlying database. The program statement used to accomplish this save operation in the *bindingNavigatorSaveItem_Click* event procedure looks like this:

```
Me.InstructorsTableAdapter.Update(Me.StudentsDataSet.Instructors)
```

After the save operation, the *Instructors* table is permanently updated.

6. Click the Close button to end the program.

The program closes and the Visual Studio IDE returns. Now you'll run the program again to see whether the *Instructors* table in the Students.mdb database has indeed been modified. (When you restart the program, it will load data from the database file.)

7. Click the Start Debugging button.

After a moment, the data grid view objects are loaded with data. As you can see, the row in the *Instructors* table containing the name Kim Halvorson has been updated with the changed telephone number. The program works!

8. Click the Close button to end the program.

If you want to continue experimenting with the *ReadOnly* property for one or both of the girds, set *ReadOnly* to True now, and see what happens when you try to modify the database. (You won't be able to save any changes.) You might also experiment with adding new rows of data to the database by using the built-in editing features and toolbar buttons associated with the *DataGridView* and *BindingNavigator* controls. (Before you add new rows, set the *ReadOnly* property back to False.)

Now take stock of your accomplishments. You've learned to display multiple tables and records by using the *DataGridView* and *BindingNavigator* controls, and you've learned how to customize the grid with property settings and how to write table updates from the grid back to the original database. As you can begin to see, database programming with ADO.NET and Visual Studio is straightforward but also somewhat involved. There are many tools, components, and programming techniques related to viewing, manipulating, and updating database records, and we haven't even begun to talk seriously about important issues such as security and what happens when you work with large databases that are being used by many users at the same time. Although you've been able to accomplish a lot with little or no program code, there is still much to learn if you plan to make extensive use of databases within Visual Basic applications. For a list of books I recommend for you to continue your studies, see Appendix A, "Where to Go for More Information."

Data Access in a Web Forms Environment

The data access techniques discussed in Chapter 18 and this chapter were designed for use in the Windows Forms Designer—the Visual Studio environment you've used to build most of the programs in this book. However, you can also use ADO.NET programming techniques in a Web Forms environment, which allows you to share data resources over the Internet and datacentric applications that are accessible through a Web browser such as Internet Explorer. I'll show you how to do this near the end of the next chapter, and you'll learn how to use a few new tools there too, including the *GridView* control, a version of the *DataGridView* control designed for displaying database tables on Web sites.

Chapter 19 Quick Reference

To	Do this
Establish a connection to database tables in a project	Use the Data Source Configuration Wizard to link the project to a database, create a dataset, and fill the Data Sources window with a representation of the selected tables.
Create a data grid view object on a form to display an entire database table	Drag a table icon from the Data Sources window to the form. Then resize the data grid view object so that each column is visible.
Preview data bound to a data grid view object	Click the data grid view object's shortcut arrow to display the DataGridView Tasks list box. Click the Preview Data command, and then click the Preview button in the Preview Data dialog box.
Remove a column from a data grid view object	Click the data grid view object's shortcut arrow to display the DataGridView Tasks list box. Click the Edit Columns command, click the column that you want to remove in the Selected Columns list box, and then click the Remove button.
Sort the records in a grid at run time	Click the column header that you want to sort by. Visual Studio sorts the grid alphabetically based on that column.
Reverse the direction of a grid sort at run time	Click the column header a second time to reverse the direction of the sort (from A–Z to Z–A).
Change the default column width for a column in a data grid view object	In the Properties window, click the *Columns* property and then the ellipses button. In the Edit Columns dialog box, adjust the *Width* property.
Hide column headers in a data grid view object	Set the *ColumnHeadersVisible* property to False.
Create an alternating color scheme for rows within a data grid view object	Pick a color for alternating rows by using the *AlternatingRowsDefaultCellStyle* property. In the CellStyle Builder dialog box, adjust the *BackColor* property. The color that you select will alternate with white.
Change the color of gridlines in a grid	Adjust the *GridColor* property.

To	Do this
Add a second data grid view object to a form	Drag a second table from the Data Sources window to the form. Resize and customize the table, taking care to make the form large enough to display all the database columns and records that your user will want to see. If you want to add a second navigation bar to the form to provide access to the table, create a second *BindingNavigator* control on the form, and set its *BindingSource* property to the binding source representing the new table you created.
Prevent the user from editing or changing the data in a data grid view object	Set the grid's *ReadOnly* property to True.
Write changes made in the grid back to the underlying database	Verify that the data grid view object's *ReadOnly* property has been set to False. Then at run time, use the Save button on the navigation bar to save your changes and update the database. Alternatively, you can use the table adapter's *Update* method within program code.

Creating Web Sites and Web Pages Using Microsoft Visual Web Developer and ASP.NET

After completing this chapter, you will be able to:

- Start Visual Web Developer and create a new Web site.
- Use Visual Web Developer tools and windows, including the Web Page Designer.
- Use the Visual Web Developer Toolbox to add server controls to Web pages.
- Add text, formatting effects, and Visual Basic code to a Web page that calculates loan payments for a car loan.
- Create an HTML page that displays Help information.
- Use the *HyperLink* control to link one Web page to another on a Web site.
- Use the *GridView* control to display a table of database information on a Web page.
- Set the *Document* object's *Title* property and assign a name to a Web page.

In this chapter, you'll learn how to build Web sites and Web pages by using the new Visual Web Developer tool included with Microsoft Visual Studio 2005. Visual Web Developer has the look and feel of the Visual Studio IDE, but it is customized for Web programming and Microsoft ASP.NET 2.0, the Microsoft .NET Framework component designed to provide state-of-the-art Internet functionality. ASP.NET was introduced with Microsoft Visual Studio .NET 2002 and is a replacement for WebClasses and the DHTML Page Designer in Microsoft Visual Basic 6. Although a complete description of Web programming and ASP.NET isn't possible here, there's enough in common between Web programming and Windows programming to allow you to do some useful experimentation—even if you have little or no experience with HTML. Invest a few hours in this chapter, and you'll see how quickly you can build a Web site that calculates loan payments for car loans, create an HTML page with Help information, and display loan prospects from an Access database by using the *GridView* control.

> ## Upgrade Notes: Migrating Visual Basic 6 Code to Visual Basic 2005
>
> If you're experienced with Visual Basic 6, you'll notice some new features in Visual Studio 2005, including the following:
>
> - A new Internet programming model called ASP.NET, and a new IDE called Visual Web Developer. These technologies are a replacement for the Visual Basic 6 Web-Classes and DHTML Page Designer, which were discontinued in Visual Studio .NET 2002.
>
> - Although the Web Page Designer is distinct from the Windows Forms Designer, both IDE tools offer similar controls and support drag-and-drop programming techniques. Because the Web Page Designer is part of Visual Web Developer (a tool accessible to all Visual Studio programming languages), it's available to Microsoft Visual Basic 2005, Microsoft Visual C# 2005, and Microsoft Visual J# 2005.
>
> - Web sites and Web pages are designed to be displayed by Web browsers such as Microsoft Internet Explorer. The controls on Web pages are visible in the client's Web browser (in other words, on the end user's computer), but the functionality for the controls resides on the Web server that hosts the actual Web application.
>
> - Although many of the Web page controls have the same names as the Windows Forms controls, the controls aren't identical. For example, Web page controls have an *ID* property, rather than a *Name* property.

Inside ASP.NET 2.0

ASP.NET 2.0 is Microsoft's latest Web development platform. Although ASP.NET has some similarities with an earlier Web programming technology named Active Server Pages (ASP), ASP.NET has been completely redesigned based on the .NET Framework. The design component of ASP.NET is Visual Web Developer, which you use to create and manage Internet user interfaces, commonly called *Web pages* or (in a more comprehensive sense) *Web sites*.

> **Note** In programming books, you'll sometimes see Web pages referred to as *Web forms* and Web sites referred to as *Web applications*, but those terms are less prevalent in the Visual Studio 2005 documentation.

By using Visual Web Developer, you can create a Web site that displays a user interface, processes data, and provides many of the commands and features that a standard application for Microsoft Windows might offer. However, the Web site you create is viewed in a Web browser such as Internet Explorer or Netscape Navigator, and it is typically stored on one or more *Web servers*, which use Microsoft Internet Information Services to display the correct Web pages and handle most of the computing tasks required by your Web site. (In Visual Studio 2005, Web sites can also be located and run on a local computer that does not require Internet Information Services, giving you more options for development and deployment.) This distributed strategy allows your Web sites to potentially run on a wide range of Internet-based or stand-alone computers—wherever your users and their rich data sources are located.

To create a Web site in Visual Studio 2005, you click the New Web Site command on the File menu, and then use the Visual Web Developer to build one or more Web pages that will collectively represent your Web site. Each Web page consists of two pieces:

- A Web Forms page, which contains HTML and controls to create the user interface.

- A code-behind file, which is a code module that contains program code that "stands behind" the Web Forms page.

(This division is conceptually much like the Windows forms you've been creating in Visual Basic—there's a user interface component and a code module component.) The code for both of these components can be stored in a single .aspx file, but typically the Web Forms page code is stored in an .aspx file, and the code-behind file is stored in an .aspx.vb file. The following illustration shows a conceptual view of how an ASP.NET Web site stored on a server is displayed in a Web browser:

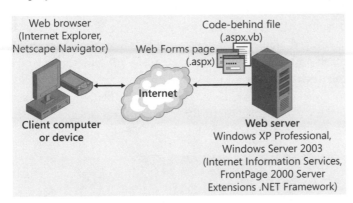

In addition to Web pages, Web sites can contain code modules (.vb files), HTML pages (.htm files), configuration information (a Web.config file), global Web application information (a Global.asax file), and other components. You can use the Web Page Designer and Solution Explorer to switch back and forth between these components quickly and efficiently.

Web Pages vs. Windows Forms

What are the important differences between Web pages and Windows forms? To begin with, Web pages offer a slightly different programming paradigm than Windows forms. Whereas Windows forms use a Windows application window as the primary user interface for a program, a Web site presents information to the user via one or more Web pages with supporting program code. These pages are viewed through a Web browser, and you can create them by using the Web Page Designer.

Like a Windows form, a Web page can include text, graphic images, buttons, list boxes, and other objects that are used to provide information, process input, or display output. However, the basic set of controls you use to create a Web page is not the set on the Common Controls tab of the Toolbox. Instead, ASP.NET Web sites must use controls on one of the tabs in the Visual Web Developer Toolbox, including Standard, Data, HTML, and many others. Each of the Visual Web Developer controls has its own unique methods, properties, and events, and although there are many similarities between these controls and Windows Forms controls, there are also several important differences. For example, Visual Studio *DataGridView* control is called *GridView* in Visual Web Developer and has different properties and methods.

Many Web page controls are *server controls*, meaning that they run on the Web server. Server controls can be identified on a Web page by the small green icon that appears in the upper-left corner of the control at design time. HTML controls (located in the HTML tab of the Visual Web Developer Toolbox) are *client controls* by default, meaning that they run only within the end user's browser. An HTML control can be configured as a server control by right-clicking the control in the Web Page Designer and clicking Run As Server Control, or by setting its *Runat* attribute to Server. For now, however, you simply need to know that you can use server controls, HTML controls, or a combination of both in your Web site projects.

Server Controls

Server controls are more capable than HTML controls and function in many ways like the Windows Forms controls. Indeed, many of the server controls have the same names as the Windows Forms controls and offer many of the same properties, methods, and events. In addition to simple controls such as *Button*, *TextBox*, and *Label*, more sophisticated controls such as *FileUpload*, *LoginView*, and *RequiredFieldValidator* are provided on a number of tabs in the Toolbox (Visual Studio 2005 has added to the list of controls significantly). The following illustration shows some of the server controls in the Visual Web Developer Toolbox:

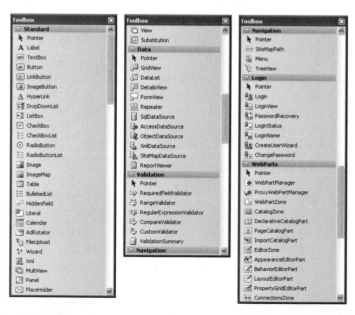

HTML Controls

The HTML controls are a set of older user interface controls that are supported by most Web browsers and conform closely to the early HTML standards developed for managing user interface elements on a typical Web page. They include *Button*, *Text Field*, and *Checkbox*—useful basic controls for managing information on a Web page that can be represented entirely with HTML code. Indeed, you might recognize these controls if you've coded in HTML before or if you've had some experience with the Visual Basic 6 DHTML Page Designer. However, although they're easy to use and have the advantage of being a "common denominator" for most Web browsers, they're limited by the fact that they have no ability to maintain their own state unless they're configured as server controls. (In other words, the data that they contain will be lost between views of a Web page.) The following illustration shows the HTML controls offered on the HTML tab of the Toolbox in Visual Web Developer:

Building a Web Site by Using Visual Web Developer

The best way to learn about Visual Web Developer and ASP.NET is to get some hands-on practice. In the exercises in this chapter, you'll create a simple car loan calculator that determines monthly payments and displays an HTML page containing Help text. Later in the chapter, you'll use the *GridView* control to display a table of data on a Web page in the same Web site. You'll begin by verifying that Visual Studio is properly configured for ASP.NET programming, and then you'll create a new Web site project. Next you'll use the Web Page Designer to create a Web page with text and links on it, and you'll use controls in the Visual Web Developer Toolbox to add controls to the Web page.

Considering Software Requirements for ASP.NET Programming

Before you create your first ASP.NET Web site, you need to consider the type of environment that you want to run your Web site in. A useful improvement in Visual Studio 2005 is that you no longer need to develop your Web site on a computer that is fully configured to act as a Web server. In Visual Studio .NET 2002 and 2003, your development system needed to host or have access to a Web server running Microsoft Windows 2000, Microsoft Windows XP Professional, or Microsoft Windows Server 2003 that also contained an installation of Internet Information Services (IIS), the Microsoft FrontPage 2000 Server Extensions, and the .NET Framework libraries. This meant that if you were running Microsoft Windows XP Home Edition, you were potentially out of luck, because Windows XP Home Edition does not include or support IIS and the FrontPage 2000 Server Extensions. (The only workaround was to access a properly configured remote Web server.)

In Visual Studio 2005, you can create and run your Web site in one of three locations:

- Your own computer (the local file system)
- An HTTP server that contains IIS and related components
- An FTP site (a remote file server)

The first location is the option we'll use in this book, because it requires no additional hardware or software. If you have Visual Studio 2005 and the .NET Framework, you have what you need to create the sample Web sites. In addition, when you develop your Web site on the local file system, all the Web site files are stored in one location. When you're finished testing the application, you can deploy the files to a Web server of your choosing.

> **Note**   If you want to develop your Web site on a Web server, use the Control Panel now to see whether IIS and the FrontPage 2000 Server Extensions are installed on your system. (Click the Add Or Remove Programs category in Control Panel, click Add/Remove Windows Components, and then browse for these programs.) Traditionally, Microsoft has required that you install these Web server components before the .NET Framework and Visual Studio because the .NET Framework registers extensions with IIS. If you install IIS after Visual Studio and run into problems, this could be the reason.

Create a new Web site

1. Start Visual Studio, and click the New Web Site command on the File menu.

   Although you might have seen the New Web Site command before, we haven't used it yet in this book. This command starts Visual Web Developer and prepares Visual Studio to build a Web site. You see a New Web Site dialog box similar to the following:

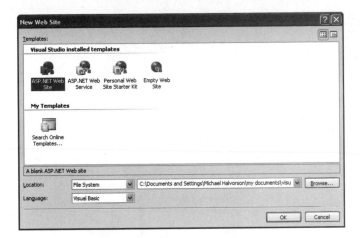

In this dialog box you can select the Web site or application template that you want to use, the location for the Web site (local file system, HTTP server, or FTP site), and the programming language that you want to use (Visual Basic, Visual C#, or Visual J#).

2. In the New Web Site dialog box, verify that ASP.NET Web Site is the selected template, and that Visual Basic is the selected language.

3. Click File System in the Location box, click Browse, and then specify c:\vb05sbs\mychap20 as the folder location.

   You'll notice that the Choose Location dialog box is a little different than the Project Location dialog box you've been using so far. And although you have been specifying the folder location for projects *after* you have built the projects in this book, in Visual Web Developer projects are saved upfront. The "my" prefix in the pathname will avoid a conflict with the solution Web site in the practice files (c:\vb05sbs\chap20) that I've built for you.

4. Click OK to finalize your changes.

   Visual Studio loads Visual Web Developer and creates a Web page (Default.aspx) to contain the user interface and a code-behind file (Default.aspx.vb) that will store the code for your Web page. The HTML source code for the Web page is displayed on the Source tab of the Web Page Designer. (If you don't see the Web Page Designer, double-click Default.aspx in Solution Explorer now.) Your screen looks something like the one shown on the next page.

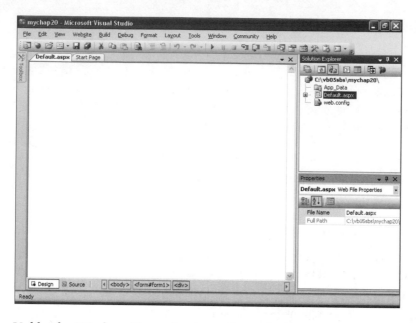

Unlike the Windows Forms Designer, the Web Page Designer displays the Web page in two possible modes in the IDE, and two tabs at the bottom of the designer (Design and Source) allow you to change your view of the Web page. Depending on how your system has been configured and used, you might see either the Design tab or the Source tab now. (The illustration shows the Design tab.)

On the Source tab, you can view and edit the HTML code that's used to display the Web page in a Web browser. If you've used Microsoft Visual InterDev or Microsoft FrontPage, you'll be familiar with these two ways of displaying a Web page and perhaps with some of the HTML formatting tags that control how Web pages are actually displayed.

The Design tab shows you approximately how your Web page will look when a Web browser displays it. When the Design tab is selected, a white page appears in the Designer with the result of source-code formatting, and you can add controls to your Web page and adjust how objects on the page are arranged. (In Visual Studio .NET 2003, a grid appeared on the Web page by default, but that grid has been removed.)

A few additional changes in Visual Web Developer are worth noting at this point. The Toolbox now contains several collections of controls used exclusively for Web programming. (This is a change from Visual Studio .NET 2003, where Web programming controls were located on the Web Forms and HTML tabs of the regular Visual Studio Toolbox.) Solution Explorer also contains a different list of project files for the Web site you're building. In particular, notice the Default.aspx file in Solution Explorer; this file contains the user interface code for the active Web page. A configuration file named Web.config is also listed.

Now you're ready to add some text to the Web page by using the Web Page Designer.

Using the Web Page Designer

Unlike a Windows form, a Web page can have text added directly to it when it is in the Web Page Designer. In Source mode, the text appears within HTML tags somewhat like the Visual Studio Code Editor. In Design mode, the text appears in top-to-bottom fashion as it does in a word processor such as Microsoft Word, and you'll see no HTML (which is not necessary for simple Web sites). In this section, you'll type text in Design mode, edit it, and then make formatting changes by using buttons on the Formatting toolbar. Manipulating text in this way is usually much faster than adding a *Label* control to the Web page to contain the text. You'll practice entering the text for your car loan calculator in the following exercise.

Add text in Design mode

1. Click the Design tab, if it is not currently selected, to view the Web Page Designer in Design mode.

   A blinking I-beam appears at the top of the Web page.

2. Type **Car Loan Calculator**, and then press Enter.

   Visual Studio displays the title of your Web page exactly as it will appear when you open the Web site in your browser.

3. Type the following sentence below the title:

   Enter the required information and click Calculate!

   Now you'll use the Formatting toolbar to format the title with bold formatting and a larger point size.

4. Right-click the Standard toolbar in Visual Web Developer to display the list of toolbars available in the IDE.

5. Click the Formatting toolbar.

   The Formatting toolbar now appears in the IDE. Notice that it contains a few features not usually found on a text formatting toolbar.

6. Select the text "Car Loan Calculator".

   Before you can format text in Visual Web Developer, you must select it.

7. Click the Bold button on the Formatting toolbar, and set the font size to 24 point.

   Your screen looks like this:

Now you'll examine the HTML code for the text and formatting you entered.

View the HTML for a Web page

1. Click the Source tab at the bottom of the Designer.

    The Source tab displays the actual HTML code for your Web page. To see more of the code, you might want to temporarily close a few programming tools. The HTML code looks like this:

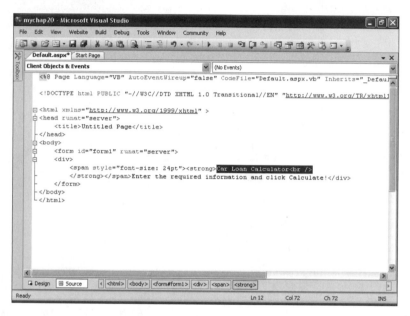

A Web page is made up of file and document information, formatting codes called HTML tags that are enclosed in angle brackets, and the text and objects to be displayed by your Web page. This Web page is still rather short—it contains a header with information about the language you selected when creating the Web application, the name of any code-behind file, and any inherited forms.

HTML tags typically appear in pairs so that you can see clearly where a section begins and ends. For example, the <body> tag identifies the beginning of the document; and the </body> tag identifies the end. Notice that the "Car Loan Calculator" text appears within a line of HTML that formats the text as strong (bold) with a font size of 24 points. Below this text, the second line of text you entered is displayed.

> **Tip**   Remember that the Source tab is an actual editor, so you can change the text you entered by using standard text editing techniques. If you know something about HTML, you can add additional formatting tags and content as well.

2. Click the Design tab to display your Web page in Design mode, and open the Toolbox if it is not visible.

Adding Server Controls to a Web Site

Now you'll add *TextBox*, *Label*, and *Button* controls to the car loan calculator. Although these controls are located in the Visual Web Developer Toolbox, they're very similar to the Windows Forms controls of the same name that you've used throughout this book. (I'll cover a few of the important differences as they come up.) The most important thing to remember is that in the Web Page Designer, controls are inserted at the insertion point if you double-click the control name in the Toolbox. After you add the controls to the Web page, you'll set property settings for the controls.

Use *TextBox*, *Label*, and *Button* controls

1. Display the Standard tab of the Toolbox, if it isn't already visible.

2. Move the insertion point to the end of the second line of text on the Web page, and then press the Enter key three times to create a little blank space for the controls.

    Because controls are placed at the insertion point, you need to use the text editing keys to position the insertion point appropriately before double-clicking a control in the Toolbox. (This is an important difference between the Web Page Designer and the Windows Forms Designer. The Windows Forms Designer allows you to create controls wherever you like on a form.)

3. Double-click the *TextBox* control to create a text box object at the insertion point on the Web page.

    Notice the small green icon that appears in the upper-left corner of the control, which indicates that this control runs on the server.

4. Click the right side of the text box object to place the insertion point at the outside edge, and then press Enter twice.

5. Double-click the *TextBox* control again to add a second text box object to the Web page.

6. Repeat steps 4 and 5 to create a third text box object below the second text box.

    Now you'll use the *Label* control to insert labels that identify the purpose of the text boxes.

7. Click to the right of the first text box object to place the insertion point at the right edge of the text box.

8. Press Spacebar twice to add two blank spaces, and then double-click the *Label* control in the Toolbox to add a label object to the Web page.

9. Repeat steps 7 and 8 to add label objects to the right of the second and third text boxes.

10. Click to the right of the third label object to place the insertion point to the right of the label, and then press Enter twice.

11. Double-click the *Button* control to create a button object at the bottom of the Web page.

The *Button* control, like the *TextBox* and *Label* controls, is very similar to its Windows Forms counterpart. Your screen looks like this:

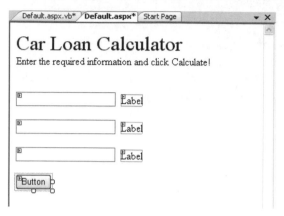

Now you'll set a few properties for the seven new controls you have created on the Web page. As you set the properties, you'll notice one important difference between Web pages and Windows forms—the familiar *Name* property has been changed to *ID* in Visual Web Developer. Despite their different names, the two properties perform the same function.

12. Set the following properties for the objects on the form:

Object	Property	Setting
TextBox1	ID	txtAmount
TextBox2	ID	txtInterest
TextBox3	ID	txtPayment
Label1	ID	lblAmount
	Text	"Loan Amount"
Label2	ID	lblInterest
	Text	"Interest Rate (for example, 0.09)"
Label3	ID	lblPayment
	Text	"Monthly Payment"
Button1	ID	btnCalculate
	Text	"Calculate"

Your Web page looks like this:

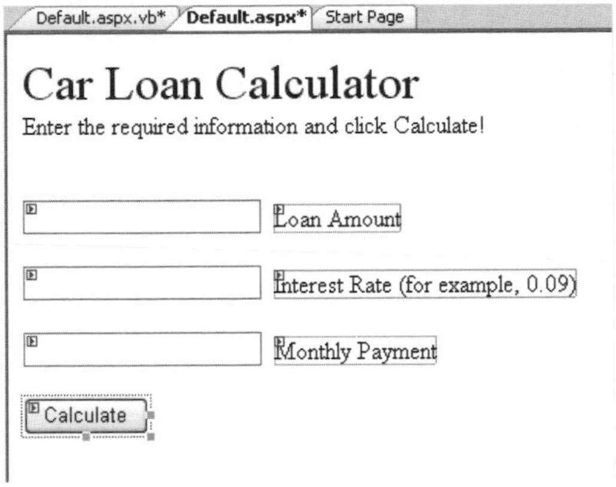

Writing Event Procedures for Web Page Controls

You write event procedures (or event handlers) for controls on a Web page by double-clicking the objects on the Web page and typing the necessary program code in the Code Editor. Although the user will see the controls on the Web page in his or her own Web browser, the actual code that's executed will be located on the local test machine or a Web server, depending on how you configured your project for development and how it is eventually deployed. For example, when the user clicks a button on a Web page that is hosted by a Web server, the browser sends the button click event back to the server, which processes the event and sends a new Web page back to the browser. Although the process seems similar to that of Windows forms, there's actually a lot going on behind the scenes when a control is used on an ASP.NET Web page!

In the following exercise, you'll practice creating an event procedure for the *btnCalculate* object on the Web page.

Create the *btnCalculate_Click* event procedure

1. Double-click the Calculate button on the Web page.

   The code-behind file (Default.aspx.vb) opens in the Code Editor, and the *btnCalculate_Click* event procedure appears.

2. Type the following program code:

```
Dim LoanPayment As Double
'Use Pmt function to determine payment for 36 month loan
LoanPayment = Pmt(CDbl(txtInterest.Text) / 12, 36, CDbl(txtAmount.Text))
txtPayment.Text = Format(Abs(LoanPayment), "$0.00")
```

This event procedure uses the *Pmt* function, a financial function that's part of the Visual Basic language, to determine what the monthly payment for a car loan would be by using the specified interest rate (*txtInterest.Text*), a three-year (36-month) loan period, and the specified principal amount (*txtAmount.Text*). The result is stored in the *Loan-Payment* double-precision variable, and then it is formatted with appropriate monetary formatting and displayed by using the *txtPayment* text box object on the Web page. The two *Text* properties are converted from string format to double-precision format by using the *CDbl* function. The *Abs* (absolute value) function is used to make the loan payment a positive number. (*Abs* is underlined in the Code Editor because it relies on the *System.Math* class, which you'll import below.) Why make the loan payment appear as a positive number? The *Pmt* function returns a negative number by default (reflecting money that's owed), but I think negative formatting looks strange when it isn't part of a balance sheet, so I'm converting it to positive.

Notice that the program statements in the code-behind file are just regular Visual Basic code—the same stuff you've been using throughout this book. Basically, the process feels similar to creating a Windows application.

3. Scroll to the top of the Code Editor, and enter the following program statement as the first line of the file:.

```
Imports System.Math
```

As you learned in Chapter 5, "Visual Basic Variables and Formulas, and the .NET Framework," the *Abs* function isn't included in Visual Basic by default, but it's part of the *System.Math* class in the .NET Framework and can be included in your project via the *Imports* statement. Web applications can make use of the .NET Framework class libraries just as Windows applications can.

4. Click the Save All button on the Standard toolbar.

That's it! You've entered the program code necessary to run the car loan calculator and make your Web page interactive. Now you'll build and run the project and see how it works!

Build and view the Web site

1. Click the Start Debugging button on the Standard toolbar.

   Visual Studio displays the following message about debugging:

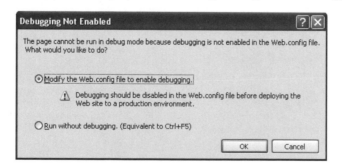

This potentially confusing dialog box is not a major concern. It just indicates that the Web.config file in your project does not currently allow debugging (a standard security feature). Although you can bypass this dialog box each time you test the application within Visual Studio by clicking the Run Without Debugging button, I recommend that you modify the Web.config file now.

2. Click OK to modify the Web.config file.

Visual Studio modifies the file, builds your Web site, and displays the opening Web page in Internet Explorer. The car loan calculator looks like this:

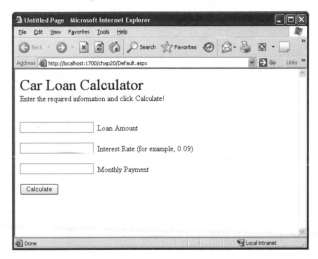

> **Tip** If Internet Explorer displays the message "Warning: Cannot debug script code," you can adjust a security setting within Internet Explorer so that this message does not appear in the future. (We won't be debugging right now.) You can modify the Internet Explorer Disable Script Debugging setting by clicking the Internet Options command on the Tools menu, clicking the Advanced tab, and clicking to clear the Disable Script Debugging option. If you don't see the warning message, however, you have nothing to worry about.

3. Type **18000** in the Loan Amount text box, and then type **0.09** in the Interest Rate text box.

You'll compute the monthly loan payment for an $18,000 loan at 9 percent interest for 36 months.

4. Click the Calculate button.

Visual Basic calculates the payment amount and displays $572.40 in the Monthly Payment text box. Your screen looks like this:

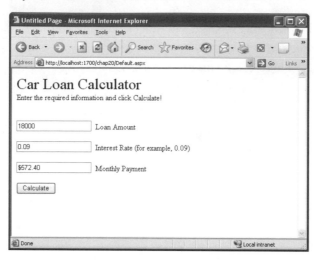

5.   Close Internet Explorer.

You're finished testing your Web site for now. When Internet Explorer closes, your program is effectively ended. As you can see, building and viewing a Web site is basically the same as building and running a Windows application, except that the Web site is executed in the browser. You can even set break points and debug your application just as you can in a Windows application.

Tip   To deploy a Web site created in Visual Web Developer, you can create a setup program or a *ClickOnce* deployment service, just as you prepare deployment options for Windows applications created in Visual Studio. (The basic procedure for Web sites is to copy the .aspx file and any necessary support files for the project to a properly configured virtual directory on a Web server.) For more information, see "Deploying Your Application" in Chapter 2, "Writing Your First Program."

Validating Input Fields on a Web Page

Although this Web page is useful, it runs into problems if the user forgets to enter a principal amount or an interest rate or specifies data in the wrong format. To make this Web site more robust, consider adding one or more *validator controls* that will require user input in the proper format. The validator controls are located on the Validation tab of the Visual Web Developer Toolbox and include controls that require data entry in a field (*RequiredFieldValidator*), require entry in the proper range (*RangeValidator*), and so on. For information on the validator controls, search the Visual Studio online Help.

Adding Additional Web Pages and Resources to a Web Site

Now the fun begins! Only very simple Web sites consist of just one Web page. Using Visual Web Developer you can quickly expand your Web site to include additional information and resources, including HTML pages, XML pages, text files, database records, Web services, site maps, and more. If you want to add an HTML page (a standard Web page containing text and HTML client-side controls), you have two options:

- Create a new HTML page by using the Add New Item command on the Website menu. After you create the HTML page, you add text and HTML objects to the page by using the Web Page Designer.

- Add an HTML page that you have already created by using the Add Existing Item command on the Website menu, and then customize the page in the Web Page Designer. You use this method if you want to include one or more Web pages that you have already created in a tool such as Microsoft FrontPage. (If possible, add pages that don't rely on external style sheets and resources, or you'll need to add those items to the project as well.)

To link pages together, Visual Web Developer provides the *HyperLink* control, which creates a hyperlink label object that the user clicks to jump from the current Web page to a new one. When you use a *HyperLink* control, you set the text that will be displayed on the page by using the *Text* property, and you specify the desired resource to jump to (either a URL or a local path) by using the *NavigateUrl* property.

In the following exercise, you'll create a second Web page by using the Add New Item command, and you'll save it in HTML format along with your other project files. The new page will be a Help file that users of your Web site can access to get operating instructions for the loan calculator. After you create the new page, you'll add a *HyperLink* control to the first page and set the *HyperLink* control's *NavigateUrl* property to the new HTML page.

Create an HTML page

1. Click the Add New Item command on the Website menu.

    The Add New Item dialog box appears, allowing you to add a number of different Internet resources to your Web site.

2. Click the HTML Page icon.

    You'll insert a blank HTML page into the project, which you can use to display formatted text and HTML controls. (You cannot add server controls to this page, because simple HTML pages are controlled by the client's browser, not a Web server.)

3. Type **WebCalculatorHelp.htm** in the Name text box.

Your screen looks like this:

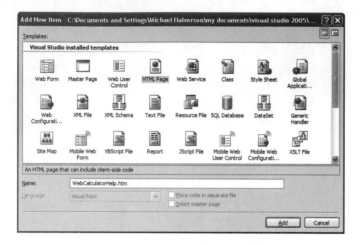

4. Click Add.

    The WebCalculatorHelp.htm file is added to Solution Explorer and is opened in the
    Web Page Designer in Source mode.

    Notice that only HTML controls are displayed in the Toolbox. Because this is an HTML
    page, the server controls aren't supported.

5. If necessary, click the Design tab to display the HTML page in Design mode.

    The I-beam insertion point blinks on the page, ready for your input.

6. Type the following text:

    Car Loan Calculator

    The Car Loan Calculator Web site was developed for the book *Microsoft Visual Basic*
    2005 Step by Step, **by Michael Halvorson (Microsoft Press, 2005). The Web site is**
    best viewed using Microsoft Internet Explorer version 6.0 or later. To learn more
    about how this ADO.NET application was created, read Chapter 20 in the book.

    Operating Instructions:

    Type a loan amount, without dollar sign or commas, into the Loan Amount box.

    Type an interest rate in decimal format into the Interest Rate text box. Do not
    include the "%" sign. For example, to specify a 9% interest rate, type "0.09".

    Note that this loan calculator assumes a three year, 36-month payment period.

    Click the Calculate button to compute the basic monthly loan payment that does
    not include taxes or other fees.

7. Using buttons on the Formatting toolbar, add bold and italic formatting, as shown here:

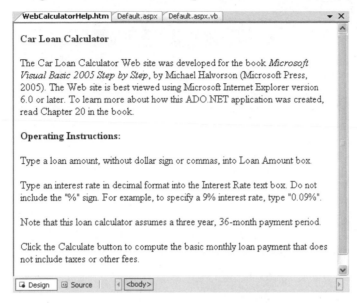

8. Click the Save All button on the Standard toolbar to save your changes.

Now you'll use the *HyperLink* control to create a hyperlink on the first Web page that opens the WebCalculatorHelp.htm file.

Use the *HyperLink* control

1. Display the Web page (Default.aspx) in Design mode.

2. Move the I-beam to the right of the button object on the Web page, and then press Enter twice.

3. Double-click the *HyperLink* control on the Standard tab of the Toolbox to create a hyperlink object at the insertion point.

4. Set the *Text* property of the hyperlink object to "Get Help".

   The *Text* property contains the text that will appear as the underlined hyperlink on the HTML page. You want to use words here that will make it obvious that there's a Web page available containing Help text.

5. Set the *ID* property of the hyperlink object to "lnkHelp".

   Naming this object makes it consistent with the other objects in the Web site.

6. Click the *NavigateUrl* property, and then click the ellipsis button in the second column.

   Visual Studio opens the Select URL dialog box, which prompts you for the location of the Web page to which you want to link.

7. Click the WebCalculatorHelp.htm file in the Contents Of Folder list box.

The URL text box displays the name of the file you want to use as the hyperlink. Your dialog box looks like this:

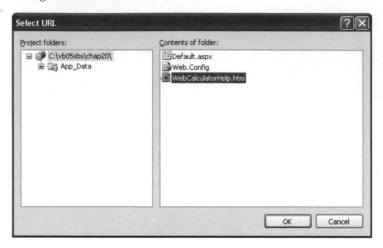

8. Click OK to set the *NavigateUrl* property.

    Your HTML page looks like this:

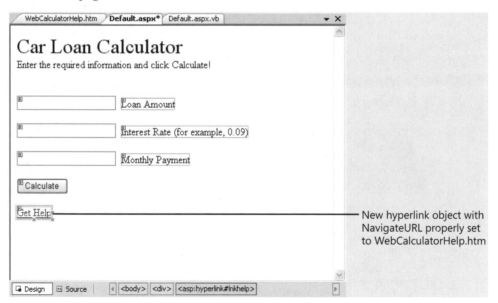

New hyperlink object with NavigateURL properly set to WebCalculatorHelp.htm

Your link is finished, and you're ready to view the Web site in your browser again.

9. Click the Save All button.

10. Click the Start Debugging button.

    Visual Studio builds the Web site and displays it in Internet Explorer.

11. Compute another loan payment to experiment further with the loan calculator.

If you want to test another set of numbers, try entering 20000 for the loan amount and 0.075 for the interest rate. The result is $622.12.

12. Now click the Get Help hyperlink to see how the *HyperLink* control works.

Internet Explorer displays your new HTML page on the screen (resize the window if necessary to see all the text). Your HTML page looks something like this:

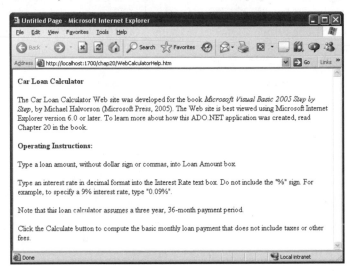

13. Read the text, and then click the Back button in Internet Explorer.

Just like any Web site, this one lets you click the Back and Forward buttons to jump from one Web page to the next.

14. Close Internet Explorer to close the Web site.

You've added a simple HTML page to your Web site, and you have experimented with using the *HyperLink* control to link together Web pages. Pretty cool. Now try something more sophisticated that shows how far you can take your Web site if you choose to include information from a database.

Displaying Database Records on a Web Page

For many users, one of the most exciting aspects of the World Wide Web is the ability to access large amounts of information rapidly through a Web browser. Often, of course, the quantity of information that needs to be displayed on a commercial Web site far exceeds what a developer can realistically prepare using simple text documents. In these cases, Web programmers add database objects to their Web sites to display tables, fields, and records of database information on Web pages, and they connect the objects to a secure database residing on the Web server or another location.

Visual Studio 2005 makes it easy to display simple database tables on a Web site, so as your computing needs grow, you can use Visual Studio to process orders, handle security, manage complex customer information profiles, and create new database records—all from the Web. Importantly, Visual Web Designer delivers this power very effectively. For example, by using the *GridView* control, you can display a database table containing dozens or thousands of records on a Web page without any program code. You'll see how this works by completing the following exercise, which adds a Web page containing loan contact data to the Car Loan Calculator project. If you completed the database programming exercises in Chapter 18, "Getting Started with ADO.NET," and Chapter 19, "Data Presentation Using the *DataGrid-View* Control," be sure to notice the similarities (and a few differences) between database programming in a Windows environment and database programming on the Web.

Add a new Web page for database information

1. Click the Add New Item command on the Website menu.

   Visual Web Developer displays a list of components that you can add to your Web site.

2. Click the Web Form icon, type **InstructorLoans.aspx** in the Name text box, and then click Add.

   Visual Web Developer adds a new Web page your Web site. Unlike the HTML page you added earlier, this Web page component is capable of displaying server controls.

3. If necessary, click the Design tab to switch to Design mode.

4. Enter the following text at the top of the Web page:

   The following grid shows instructors who want loans and their contact phone numbers:

5. Press the Enter key twice to add two blank lines below the text.

   Remember that Web page controls are added to Web pages at the insertion point, so it is always important to create a few blank lines when you are preparing to add a control.

Next you'll display two fields from the *Instructors* table of the Students.mdb database by adding a *GridView* control to the Web page. *GridView* is similar to the *GridDataView* control you used in Chapter 19, but *GridView* has been optimized for use on the Web. (There are also a few other differences, which you can explore by using the Properties window and Visual Studio online Help.) Note that I'm using the same Access database table I used in Chapters 18 and 19, so you can see how similar database programming is in Visual Web Developer. Many programmers also use SQL databases on their Web sites, and Visual Web Developer also handles that format very well.

Add a *GridView* control

1. With the new Web page open and the insertion point in the desired location, double-click the *GridView* control on the Data tab of the Visual Web Developer Toolbox.

Visual Web Developer adds a grid view object named *GridView1* to the Web page. The grid view object currently contains placeholder information and a tiny green icon, indicating that the object is a server control.

2. If the GridView Tasks list box is not already displayed, click the *GridView1* object's shortcut arrow to display the list box.

3. Click the Choose Data Source arrow, and then click the New Data Source option.

Visual Web Developer displays the Data Source Configuration Wizard, a tool that you used in Chapters 18 and 19 to establish a connection to a database and select the tables and fields that will make up a dataset. Your screen looks like this:

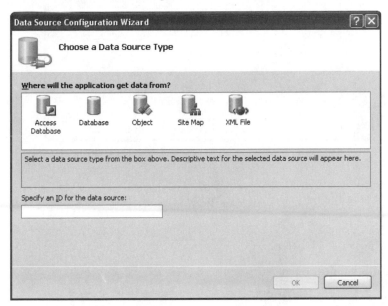

4. Click the Access Database icon, type **Students** in the Specify An ID For The Source box, and click OK.

You are now prompted to specify the location of the Access database on your system. (This dialog box is slightly different than the one you used in Chapter 18.)

5. Type **c:\vb05sbs\chap18\students.mdb**, and click Next.

You are now asked to configure your data source; that is, to select the table and fields that you want to display on your Web page. Here you'll use two fields from the *Instructors* table. (Remember that in Visual Studio, database fields are often referred to as columns, so you'll see the word "columns" used in the IDE and the instructions below.)

6. Click the Name arrow, and then click Instructors in the list box.

7. Select the Instructor and PhoneNumber check boxes in the Columns list box.

Your screen looks like this:

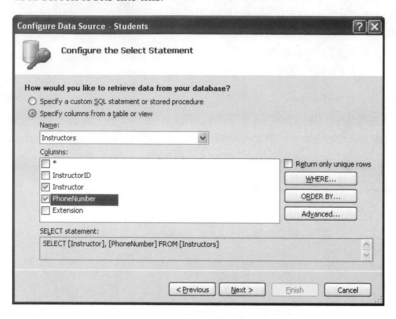

Through your actions here, you are creating a SQL SELECT statement that configures a dataset representing a portion of the Students.mdb database. You can see the SELECT statement at the bottom of this dialog box.

8. Click Next to see the Test Query dialog box.

9. Click the Test Query button to see a preview of your data.

You see the following information in the dialog box:

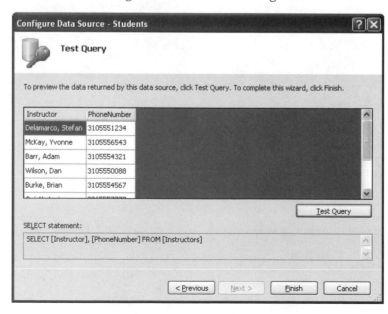

This data looks as expected, although if we were preparing this Web site for wider distribution, we would take the extra step of formatting the PhoneNumber column so that it contains standard spacing and phone number formatting.

10.   Click Finish.

Visual Web Developer closes the wizard and adjusts the number of columns and column headers in the grid view object to match the selections that you have made. However, it continues to display placeholder information ("abc") in the grid cells.

11.   With the GridView Tasks list box still open, click the Auto Format command.

12.   Click the Professional scheme.

The Auto Format dialog box looks like this:

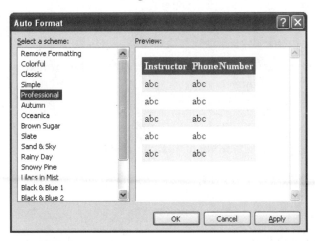

The ability to quickly format, adjust, and preview formatting options is a great feature of the *GridView* control.

13.   Click OK and then close the GridView Tasks list.

The InstructorLoans.aspx Web page is complete now, and looks like this:

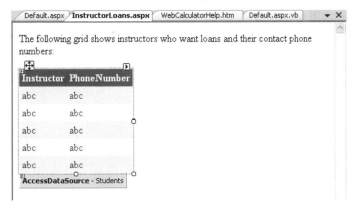

Now you'll add a hyperlink on the first Web page (or home page) that will display this Web page when the user wants to see the database table. You'll create the hyperlink with the *HyperLink* control.

Add a hyperlink to the home page

1. Click the Default.aspx tab at the top of the Designer.

    The home page for your Web site appears in the Designer.

2. Click to the right of the Display Help (*lnkHelp*) object to place the insertion point after that object.

3. Press Enter twice to create space for a second hyperlink.

4. Double-click the *HyperLink* control on the Standard tab of the Toolbox to create a hyperlink object at the insertion point.

5. Set the *Text* property of the hyperlink object to "Display Loan Prospects".

    We'll pretend that your users are bank loan officers (or well-informed car salespeople) looking to sell auto loans to university professors. Display Loan Prospects will be the link they click to view the selected database records.

6. Set the *ID* property of the hyperlink object to "lnkProspects".

7. Click the *NavigateUrl* property, and then click the ellipsis button.

    Visual Studio opens the Select URL dialog box.

8. Click the InstructorLoans.aspx file in the Contents Of Folder list box, and then click OK.

Your link is finished, and you're ready to test the Web site and *GridView* control in your browser.

Test the final Car Loan Calculator Web site

> **Tip**   The complete Car Loan Calculator Web site is located in the c:\vb05sbs\chap20 folder. Use the Open Web Site command on the File menu to open an existing Web site.

1. Click the Start Debugging button.

    Visual Studio builds the Web site and displays it in Internet Explorer.

2. Enter **8000** for the loan amount and **0.08** for the interest rate, then click Calculate.

    The result is $250.69. Whenever you add to a project, it is always good to go back and test the original features to verify that they have not been modified inadvertently. Your screen looks like this:

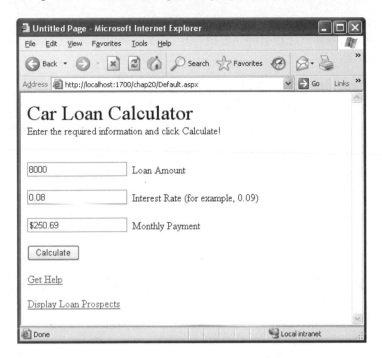

The new hyperlink (Display Loan Prospects) is visible at the bottom of the Web page.

3. Click Display Loan Prospects to load the database table.

Internet Explorer loads the *Instructor* and *PhoneNumber* fields from the Students.mdb database into the grid view object. Your Web page looks something like this:

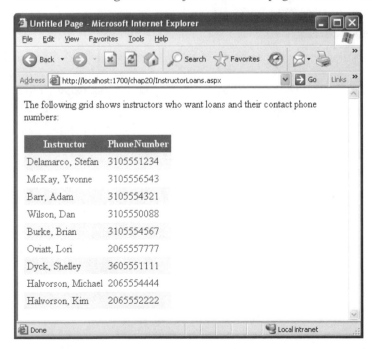

The information is nicely formatted and appears useful. By default, you'll find that the data in this table cannot be sorted, but you can change this option by selecting the Enable Sorting check box in GridView Tasks. If your database contains many rows (records) of information, you can select the Enable Paging check box in GridView Tasks to display a list of page numbers at the bottom of the Web page (like a list you might see in Microsoft Document Explorer or a search engine that displays many pages of "hits" for your search).

4.   Click the Back and Forward buttons in Internet Explorer.

     As you learned earlier, you can jump back and forth between Web pages in your Web site, just as you would in any professional Web site.

5.   When you're finished experimenting, close Internet Explorer to close the Web site.

You've added a table of custom database information without adding any program code!

One Step Further: Setting the Web Site Title in Internet Explorer

Haven't had enough yet? Here's one last Web programming tip to enhance your Web site and send you off on your own explorations.

You might have noticed while testing the Car Loan Calculator Web site that Internet Explorer displayed "Untitled Page" in the title bar when displaying your Web site. In other words, your screen looked like this:

You can customize what Internet Explorer and other browsers display in the title bar by setting the *Title* property of the *Document* object for your Web page. Give it a try now.

Set the *Title* property

1.   With the Default.aspx Web page open in Design mode, click the *Document* object in Object list box of the Properties window.

     Each Web page in a Web site contains a *Document* object that holds important general settings for the Web page. However, the *Document* object is not selected by default in the Designer, so you might not have noticed it. One of the important properties for the *Document* object is *Title*, which sets the title of the current Web page in the browser.

2.   Set the *Title* property to "Car Loan Calculator".

The change does not appear on the screen, but Visual Web Developer records it internally.

3.   Click the Start Debugging button.

Visual Studio opens Internet Explorer and loads the Web site. Now a more useful title bar appears, as shown in the following illustration:

Now that looks better.

4.   Close Internet Explorer, and update the *Title* properties for the other Web pages in your Web site.

5.   When you're finished experimenting with the Car Loan Calculator, save your changes, and close Visual Studio.

Congratulations on completing the entire *Microsoft Visual Basic 2005 Step by Step* programming course! Take a few moments to flip back through this book and see all that you have learned. Now you're ready for more sophisticated Visual Basic challenges and programming techniques. Check out the resource list in Appendix A, "Where to Go For More Information," for a few ideas about continuing your learning. But take a break first—you've earned it!

Chapter 20 Quick Reference

To	Do this
Create a new ASP.NET Web site	Click the New Web Site command on the File menu, click ASP.NET Web Site, specify a folder location in the Location list box, and then click OK.
Switch between Design mode and Source mode in the Web Page Designer	Click the Source or Design tabs in the Designer.
Enter text on a Web page	Click the Design tab, and then type the text you want to add.
Format text on a Web page	On the page, select the text that you want to format, and then click a button or control on the Formatting toolbar.
View the HTML code in your Web page	Click the Source tab in the designer.
Add controls to a Web page	Display the Web page in Design mode, open the Toolbox (which automatically contains Visual Web Developer controls), position the insertion point where you want to place the control on the page, and then double-click the control in the Toolbox.
Change the name of an object on a Web page	Use the Properties window to change the object's *ID* property to a new name.

To	Do this
Write an event procedure for an object on a Web page	Double-click the object to display the code-behind file, and write the event procedure code for the object in the Code Editor.
Verify the format of the data entered by the user into a control on a Web page	Use one or more validator controls from the Validation tab of the Toolbox to test the data entered in an input control.
Run and test a Web site in Visual Studio	Click the Start Debugging button on the Standard toolbar. Visual Studio builds the project and loads the Web site in Internet Explorer.
Create an HTML page for a project	Click the Add New Item command on the Website menu, and then add the new HTML page to the project. Create and format the HTML page by using the Web Page Designer.
Create a link to other Web pages on your Web site	Add a *HyperLink* control to your Web page, and then set the control's *NavigateUrl* property to the address of the linked Web page.
Display database records on a Web page	Add a *GridView* control to a Web page in the Web Page Designer. Establish a connection to the database and format the data by using commands in the GridView Tasks list box. (The Choose Data Source command launches the Data Source Configuration Wizard.)
Set the title displayed for Web pages on the Internet Explorer title bar	For each Web page, use the Properties window to set the *Document* object's *Title* property.

Part V
Appendix

Appendix

Where to Go for More Information

This book has presented beginning, intermediate, and advanced Visual Basic 2005 programming techniques with the aim of making you a confident software developer and Microsoft Windows programmer. Now that you've experimented with many of the tools and features in Visual Basic 2005, you're ready for more advanced topics and the full breadth of the Microsoft Visual Studio 2005 development suite.

If you have your sights set on a career in Visual Basic programming, you might also want to test your proficiency by preparing for a certified exam in Visual Basic 2005 development. In this appendix, you'll learn about additional resources for Visual Basic programming, including helpful Web sites, a source for certification information, and books that you can use to expand your Visual Basic programming skills.

Visual Basic Web Sites

The Web is a boon to programmers and is definitely the fastest mechanism for gathering information about Visual Basic 2005 and related technologies. In this section, I list several of the Web sites that I use to learn about new products and services related to Visual Basic. As you use this list, note that the Internet address and contents of each site change from time to time, so the sites might not appear exactly as I've described them. Considering the constant ebb and flow of the Internet, it's also a good idea to search for "Visual Basic", "Visual Studio 2005", and "VB.NET" occasionally to see what new information is available. (For the most specific hits, include the quotes around each search item as shown.)

www.msdn.microsoft.com/vbasic/

The Microsoft Corporation Visual Basic home page is the best overall site for documentation, breaking news, conference information, and product support for Visual Basic 2005. This site gives you up-to-date information about the entire Visual Basic product line and lets you know how new operating systems, applications, and programming tools affect Visual Basic development.

 Tip Remember that you can also access MSDN resources quickly from the Visual Studio Start Page within the Visual Studio IDE. The Start Page loads updated articles and news content each time you start Visual Studio, so its contents are always changing.

www.devx.com/

DevX is a commercial Web site devoted to numerous Windows development topics and issues, including Visual Studio and Visual Basic programming. Discussion groups of professional Visual Basic programmers provide peer-to-peer interaction and feedback for many development issues. In addition, DevX vendor partners offer books, controls, and third-party software for sale.

www.microsoft.com/learning/books/

The Microsoft Learning Web site offers the newest books on Visual Basic 2005 programming from Microsoft Press authors. Check here for new books about Microsoft Visual C#, Microsoft Visual C++, and Microsoft Visual J# as well. You can also download freebies and send mail to Microsoft Press.

www.microsoft.com/learning/training/

This is the Microsoft Learning Web site for software training and services, including testing and certification. Over the last few years, many Visual Basic programmers have found that they can better demonstrate their development skills to potential employers if they pass one or more certification examinations and earn a Microsoft certified credential, such as the Microsoft Certified Professional (MCP), the Microsoft Certified Systems Engineer (MCSE), or the Microsoft Certified Systems Administrator (MCSA). Visit this Web site to learn more about your certification options.

www.microsoft.com/communities/

This site of technical communities for many Microsoft software products and technologies offers opportunities to interact with Microsoft employees and your software development peers. Through this Web site, you can access blogs, newsgroups, webcasts, technical chats, user groups, and other resources related to Visual Studio development. Currently Visual Studio newsgroup topics are listed under the Microsoft MSDN (Developer Newsgroups) category.

Books for Visual Basic and Visual Studio Programming

Printed books about Visual Basic and Visual Studio programming provide in-depth sources of information and self-paced training that Web sites can supplement but not replace. As you seek to expand your Visual Basic and Visual Studio programming skills, I recommend that you consult the following sources of printed information (listed here by category). Note that this isn't a complete bibliography of Visual Studio 2005 titles, but it is a list that's representative of the books available in English at the time of the initial release of Visual Studio 2005. I also list books related to database programming, Web programming, Visual Basic for Applications (VBA) programming, and general books about software development and computer science.

Visual Basic 2005 Programming

- *Programming Microsoft Visual Basic 2005 Core Reference*, by Francesco Balena (Microsoft Press, ISBN 0-7356-2183-7)

- *Practical Guidelines and Best Practices for Microsoft Visual Basic and Visual C# Developers*, by Francesco Balena and Guiseppe Dimauro (Microsoft Press, ISBN 0-7356-2172-1)

- *OOP: Building Reusable Components with Microsoft Visual Basic .NET*, by Ken Spencer, Tom Eberhard, and John Alexander (Microsoft Press, ISBN 0-7356-1379-6). This book covers Visual Basic .NET 2003 but is still useful.

Visual Studio 2005 and Microsoft .NET Framework

- *Working with Microsoft Visual Studio 2005 Team System*, by Richard Hundhausen (Microsoft Press, ISBN 0-7356-2185-3)

- *Debugging, Tuning, and Testing Microsoft .NET Framework 2.0 Applications*, by John Robbins (Microsoft Press, ISBN 0-7356-2202-7)

Database Programming with ADO.NET

- *Microsoft ADO.NET 2.0 Step by Step*, by Rebecca Riordan (Microsoft Press, ISBN 0-7356-2164-0)

- *Programming Microsoft ADO.NET 2.0 Core Reference*, by David Sceppa (Microsoft Press, ISBN 0-7356-2206-X)

- *Programming Microsoft ADO.NET 2.0 Applications: Advanced Topics*, by Glenn Johnson (Microsoft Press, ISBN 0-7356-2141-1)

- *Microsoft SQL Server 2005 Express Step by Step*, by Jackie Goldstein (Microsoft Press, ISBN 0-7356-2184-5)

Web Programming with ASP.NET

- *Microsoft Visual Web Developer 2005 Express Edition: Build a Web Page Now!* by Jim Buyens (Microsoft Press, ISBN 0-7356-2212-4)

- *Microsoft ASP.NET 2.0 Programming Step by Step*, by George Shepherd (Microsoft Press, ISBN 0-7356-2201-9)

- *Programming Microsoft ASP.NET 2.0 Core Reference*, by Dino Esposito (Microsoft Press, ISBN 0-7356-2176-4)

- *Programming ASP.NET 2.0 Applications: Advanced Topics*, by Dino Esposito (Microsoft Press, ISBN 0-7356-2177-2)

- *Beginning ASP.NET 2.0 Databases: Beta Preview*, by John Kauffman, Thiru Thangarathinam (Wrox Press, ISBN 0-7645-7081-1)

Visual Basic for Applications Programming

- *Microsoft Office Excel 2003 Programming Inside Out*, by Curtis Frye, Wayne S. Freeze, and Felicia K. Buckingham (Microsoft Press, ISBN 0-7356-1985-9)

- *Programming Microsoft Office Access 2003 (Core Reference)*, by Rick Dobson (Microsoft Press, ISBN 0-7356-1942-5)

General Books about Programming and Computer Science

- *Code Complete, Second Edition*, by Steve McConnell (Microsoft Press, ISBN 0-7356-1967-0)

- *Code*, by Charles Petzold (Microsoft Press, ISBN 0-7356-1131-9)

- *Writing Secure Code, Second Edition*, by Michael Howard, David LeBlanc (Microsoft Press, ISBN 0-7356-1722-8)

- *Software Project Survival Guide*, by Steve McConnell (Microsoft Press, ISBN 1-57231-621-7)

- *Data Structures and Algorithms Using Visual Basic .NET*, by *Michael McMillan* (Cambridge University Press, ISBN 0-521547652)

- *The Art of Computer Programming, Volumes 1-3*, by Donald Knuth (Addison-Wesley Professional, ISBN 0-201485419)

- *Data Structures and Algorithms*, by Alfred V. Aho, Jeffrey D. Ullman, John E. Hopcroft (Addison-Wesley, ISBN 0-201000237)

Upgrading Index

This index provides an alphabetical guide to many of the upgrading topics in this book. It is designed to help readers who are familiar with Microsoft Visual Basic 6 and Microsoft Visual Basic .NET 2003 identify the new features in Microsoft Visual Basic 2005 and use them to upgrade their applications. Scan this index to find topics that you are curious about, and then turn to the page number indicated for a discussion of the upgrading material. Note that the comprehensive index following this table offers additional information about Visual Basic 2005 and Visual Studio 2005 features and programming skills.

Index

About the Author

Michael Halvorson is the author or co-author of over 30 books, including *Microsoft Visual Basic .NET Step by Step*, *Microsoft Office XP Inside Out*, *Microsoft Visual Basic 6.0 Professional Step By Step*, and *Learn Microsoft Visual Basic 6.0 Now*. Michael earned a bachelor's degree in Computer Science from Pacific Lutheran University in Tacoma, Washington, and master's and doctoral degrees in History from the University of Washington in Seattle. He was employed at Microsoft Corporation from 1985 to 1993, and he has been an advocate for Visual Basic programming since the product's original debut at Windows World in 1991. Michael is currently an assistant professor of History at Pacific Lutheran University, where he teaches courses in early modern Europe, the Middle Ages, Western Civilization, and interdisciplinary studies. In addition to his technical books, he is the editor or co-editor of two recent essay collections, *Loharano (The Water Spring): Missionary Tales from Madagascar*, and *A Lutheran Vocation: Philip A. Nordquist and the Study of History at Pacific Lutheran University*. He lives in Seattle with his wife and two sons.

Additional Resources for Web Developers
Published and Forthcoming Titles from Microsoft Press

Microsoft® Visual Web Developer™ 2005 Express Edition: Build a Web Site Now!
Jim Buyens • ISBN 0-7356-2212-4

With this lively, eye-opening, and hands-on book, all you need is a computer and the desire to learn how to create Web pages now using Visual Web Developer Express Edition! Featuring a full working edition of the software, this fun and highly visual guide walks you through a complete Web page project from set-up to launch. You'll get an introduction to the Microsoft Visual Studio® environment and learn how to put the light-weight, easy-to-use tools in Visual Web Developer Express to work right away—building your first, dynamic Web pages with Microsoft ASP.NET 2.0. You'll get expert tips, coaching, and visual examples at each step of the way, along with pointers to additional learning resources.

Microsoft ASP.NET 2.0 Programming
Step by Step
George Shepherd • ISBN 0-7356-2201-9

With dramatic improvements in performance, productivity, and security features, Visual Studio 2005 and ASP.NET 2.0 deliver a simplified, high-performance, and powerful Web development experience. ASP.NET 2.0 features a new set of controls and infrastructure that simplify Web based data access and include functionality that facilitates code reuse, visual consistency, and aesthetic appeal. Now you can teach yourself the essentials of working with ASP.NET 2.0 in the Visual Studio environment— one step at a time. With *Step by Step*, you work at your own pace through hands-on, learn-by-doing exercises. Whether you're a beginning programmer or new to this version of the technology, you'll understand the core capabilities and fundamental techniques for ASP.NET 2.0. Each chapter puts you to work, showing you how, when, and why to use specific features of the ASP.NET 2.0 rapid application development environment and guiding you as you create actual components and working applications for the Web, including advanced features such as personalization.

Programming Microsoft ASP.NET 2.0
Core Reference
Dino Esposito • ISBN 0-7356-2176-4

Delve into the core topics for ASP.NET 2.0 programming, mastering the essential skills and capabilities needed to build high-performance Web applications successfully. Well-known ASP.NET author Dino Esposito deftly builds your expertise with Web forms, Visual Studio, core controls, master pages, data access, data binding, state management, security services, and other must-know topics—combining definitive reference with practical, hands-on programming instruction. Packed with expert guidance and pragmatic examples, this *Core Reference* delivers the key resources that you need to develop professional-level Web programming skills.

Programming Microsoft ASP.NET 2.0
Applications: *Advanced Topics*
Dino Esposito • ISBN 0-7356-2177-2

Master advanced topics in ASP.NET 2.0 programming—gaining the essential insights and in-depth understanding that you need to build sophisticated, highly functional Web applications successfully. Topics include Web forms, Visual Studio 2005, core controls, master pages, data access, data binding, state management, and security considerations. Developers often discover that the more they use ASP.NET, the more they need to know. With expert guidance from ASP.NET authority Dino Esposito, you get the in-depth, comprehensive information that leads to full mastery of the technology.

Programming Microsoft Windows® Forms
Charles Petzold • ISBN 0-7356-2153-5

Programming Microsoft Web Forms
Douglas J. Reilly • ISBN 0-7356-2179-9

CLR via C++
Jeffrey Richter with Stanley B. Lippman
ISBN 0-7356-2248-5

Debugging, Tuning, and Testing Microsoft .NET 2.0 Applications
John Robbins • ISBN 0-7356-2202-7

CLR via C#, Second Edition
Jeffrey Richter • ISBN 0-7356-2163-2

For more information about Microsoft Press® books and other learning products, visit: **www.microsoft.com/books** *and* **www.microsoft.com/learning**

Additional Resources for Database Developers

Published and Forthcoming Titles from Microsoft Press

Microsoft® SQL Server™ 2005 Express Edition
Step by Step
Jackie Goldstein • ISBN 0-7356-2184-5

Teach yourself how to get database projects up and running quickly with SQL Server Express Edition—one step at a time! SQL Server Express is a free, easy-to-use database product that is based on SQL Server 2005 technology. It's designed for building simple, dynamic applications, with all the rich functionality of the SQL Server database engine and using the same data access APIs such as Microsoft ADO.NET, SQL Native Client, and T-SQL. With *Step by Step*, you work at your own pace through hands-on, learn-by-doing exercises. Whether you're new to database programming or new to SQL Server, you'll learn how, when, and why to use specific features of this simple but powerful database development environment. Each chapter puts you to work, building your knowledge of core capabilities and guiding you as you create actual components and working applications. You'll also discover how SQL Server Express works seamlessly with the Microsoft Visual Studio® 2005 environment, simplifying the design, development, and deployment of your applications.

Programming Microsoft ADO.NET 2.0
Applications: *Advanced Topics*
Glenn Johnson • ISBN 0-7356-2141-1

Get in-depth coverage and expert insights on advanced ADO.NET programming topics such as optimization, DataView, and large objects (BLOBs and CLOBs). Targeting experienced, professional software developers who design and develop enterprise applications, this book assumes that the reader knows and understands the basic functionality and concepts of ADO.NET 2.0 and that he or she is ready to move to mastering data-manipulation skills in Microsoft Windows. The book, complete with pragmatic and instructive code examples, is structured so that readers can jump in for reference on each topic as needed.

Microsoft ADO.NET 2.0
Step by Step
Rebecca Riordan • ISBN 0-7356-2164-0

In Microsoft .NET Framework 2.0, data access is enhanced not only through the addition of new data access controls, services, and the ability to integrate more seamlessly with SQL Server 2005, but also through improvements to the ADO.NET class libraries themselves. Now you can teach yourself the essentials of working with ADO.NET 2.0 in the Visual Studio environment—one step at a time. With *Step by Step*, you work at your own pace through hands-on, learn-by-doing exercises. Whether you're a beginning programmer or new to this version of the technology, you'll understand the core capabilities and fundamental techniques for ADO.NET 2.0. Each chapter puts you to work, showing you how, when, and why to use specific features of the ADO.NET 2.0 rapid application development environment and guiding as you create actual components and working applications for Microsoft Windows®.

Programming Microsoft ADO.NET 2.0
Core Reference
David Sceppa • ISBN 0-7356-2206-X

This *Core Reference* demonstrates how to use ADO.NET 2.0, a technology within Visual Studio 2005, to access, sort, and manipulate data in standalone, enterprise, and Web-enabled applications. Discover best practices for writing, testing, and debugging database application code using the new tools and wizards in Visual Studio 2005, and put them to work with extensive code samples, tutorials, and insider tips. The book describes the ADO.NET object model, its XML features for Web extensibility, integration with Microsoft SQL Server 2000 and SQL Server 2005, and other core topics.

Programming Microsoft Windows Forms
Charles Petzold • ISBN 0-7356-2153-5

Programming Microsoft Web Forms
Douglas J. Reilly • ISBN 0-7356-2179-9

Inside Microsoft SQL Server 2005: The Storage Engine (Volume 1)
Kalen Delaney • ISBN 0-7356-2105-5

Debugging, Tuning, and Testing Microsoft .NET 2.0 Applications
John Robbins • ISBN 0-7356-2202-7

Microsoft SQL Server 2005 Programming *Step by Step*
Fernando Guerrero • ISBN 0-7356-2207-8

Programming Microsoft SQL Server 2005
Andrew J. Brust, Stephen Forte, and William H. Zack
ISBN 0-7356-1923-9

For more information about Microsoft Press® books and other learning products,
visit: **www.microsoft.com/books** *and* **www.microsoft.com/learning**

Additional Resources for C# Developers
Published and Forthcoming Titles from Microsoft Press

Microsoft® Visual C#® 2005 Express Edition: Build a Program Now!
Patrice Pelland ● ISBN 0-7356-2229-9

In this lively, eye-opening, and hands-on book, all you need is a computer and the desire to learn how to program with Visual C# 2005 Express Edition. Featuring a full working edition of the software, this fun and highly visual guide walks you through a complete programming project—a desktop weather-reporting application—from start to finish. You'll get an unintimidating introduction to the Microsoft Visual Studio® development environment and learn how to put the lightweight, easy-to-use tools in Visual C# Express to work right away—creating, compiling, testing, and delivering your first, ready-to-use program. You'll get expert tips, coaching, and visual examples at each step of the way, along with pointers to additional learning resources.

Microsoft Visual C# 2005 *Step by Step*
John Sharp ● ISBN 0-7356-2129-2

Visual C#, a feature of Visual Studio 2005, is a modern programming language designed to deliver a productive environment for creating business frameworks and reusable object-oriented components. Now you can teach yourself essential techniques with Visual C#—and start building components and Microsoft Windows®–based applications—one step at a time. With *Step by Step*, you work at your own pace through hands-on, learn-by-doing exercises. Whether you're a beginning programmer or new to this particular language, you'll learn how, when, and why to use specific features of Visual C# 2005. Each chapter puts you to work, building your knowledge of core capabilities and guiding you as you create your first C#-based applications for Windows, data management, and the Web.

Programming Microsoft Visual C# 2005 Framework Reference
Francesco Balena ● ISBN 0-7356-2182-9

Complementing *Programming Microsoft Visual C# 2005 Core Reference*, this book covers a wide range of additional topics and information critical to Visual C# developers, including Windows Forms, working with Microsoft ADO.NET 2.0 and Microsoft ASP.NET 2.0, Web services, security, remoting, and much more. Packed with sample code and real-world examples, this book will help developers move from understanding to mastery.

Programming Microsoft Visual C# 2005 *Core Reference*
Donis Marshall ● ISBN 0-7356-2181-0

Get the in-depth reference and pragmatic, real-world insights you need to exploit the enhanced language features and core capabilities in Visual C# 2005. Programming expert Donis Marshall deftly builds your proficiency with classes, structs, and other fundamentals, and advances your expertise with more advanced topics such as debugging, threading, and memory management. Combining incisive reference with hands-on coding examples and best practices, this *Core Reference* focuses on mastering the C# skills you need to build innovative solutions for smart clients and the Web.

CLR via C#, Second Edition
Jeffrey Richter ● ISBN 0-7356-2163-2

In this new edition of Jeffrey Richter's popular book, you get focused, pragmatic guidance on how to exploit the common language runtime (CLR) functionality in Microsoft .NET Framework 2.0 for applications of all types—from Web Forms, Windows Forms, and Web services to solutions for Microsoft SQL Server™, Microsoft code names "Avalon" and "Indigo," consoles, Microsoft Windows NT® Service, and more. Targeted to advanced developers and software designers, this book takes you under the covers of .NET for an in-depth understanding of its structure, functions, and operational components, demonstrating the most practical ways to apply this knowledge to your own development efforts. You'll master fundamental design tenets for .NET and get hands-on insights for creating high-performance applications more easily and efficiently. The book features extensive code examples in Visual C# 2005.

Programming Microsoft Windows Forms
Charles Petzold ● ISBN 0-7356-2153-5

CLR via C++
Jeffrey Richter with Stanley B. Lippman
ISBN 0-7356-2248-5

Programming Microsoft Web Forms
Douglas J. Reilly ● ISBN 0-7356-2179-9

Debugging, Tuning, and Testing Microsoft .NET 2.0 Applications
John Robbins ● ISBN 0-7356-2202-7

For more information about Microsoft Press® books and other learning products, visit: **www.microsoft.com/books** *and* **www.microsoft.com/learning**

Additional Resources for Visual Basic Developers
Published and Forthcoming Titles from Microsoft Press

Microsoft® Visual Basic® 2005 Express Edition: Build a Program Now!
Patrice Pelland • ISBN 0-7356-2213-2

Featuring a full working edition of the software, this fun and highly visual guide walks you through a complete programming project—a desktop weather-reporting application—from start to finish. You'll get an introduction to the Microsoft Visual Studio® development environment and learn how to put the lightweight, easy-to-use tools in Visual Basic Express to work right away—creating, compiling, testing, and delivering your first ready-to-use program. You'll get expert tips, coaching, and visual examples each step of the way, along with pointers to additional learning resources.

Microsoft Visual Basic 2005 *Step by Step*
Michael Halvorson • ISBN 0-7356-2131-4

With enhancements across its visual designers, code editor, language, and debugger that help accelerate the development and deployment of robust, elegant applications across the Web, a business group, or an enterprise, Visual Basic 2005 focuses on enabling developers to rapidly build applications. Now you can teach yourself the essentials of working with Visual Studio 2005 and the new features of the Visual Basic language—one step at a time. Each chapter puts you to work, showing you how, when, and why to use specific features of Visual Basic and guiding as you create actual components and working applications for Microsoft Windows®. You'll also explore data management and Web-based development topics.

Programming Microsoft Visual Basic 2005 *Core Reference*
Francesco Balena • ISBN 0-7356-2183-7

Get the expert insights, indispensable reference, and practical instruction needed to exploit the core language features and capabilities in Visual Basic 2005. Well-known Visual Basic programming author Francesco Balena expertly guides you through the fundamentals, including modules, keywords, and inheritance, and builds your mastery of more advanced topics such as delegates, assemblies, and My Namespace. Combining in-depth reference with extensive, hands-on code examples and best-practices advice, this *Core Reference* delivers the key resources that you need to develop professional-level programming skills for smart clients and the Web.

Programming Microsoft Visual Basic 2005 Framework Reference
Francesco Balena • ISBN 0-7356-2175-6

Complementing *Programming Microsoft Visual Basic 2005 Core Reference*, this book covers a wide range of additional topics and information critical to Visual Basic developers, including Windows Forms, working with Microsoft ADO.NET 2.0 and ASP.NET 2.0, Web services, security, remoting, and much more. Packed with sample code and real-world examples, this book will help developers move from understanding to mastery.

Programming Microsoft Windows Forms
Charles Petzold • ISBN 0-7356-2153-5

Programming Microsoft Web Forms
Douglas J. Reilly • ISBN 0-7356-2179-9

Debugging, Tuning, and Testing Microsoft .NET 2.0 Applications
John Robbins • ISBN 0-7356-2202-7

Microsoft ASP.NET 2.0 *Step by Step*
George Shepherd • ISBN 0-7356-2201-9

Microsoft ADO.NET 2.0 *Step by Step*
Rebecca Riordan • ISBN 0-7356-2164-0

Programming Microsoft ASP.NET 2.0 *Core Reference*
Dino Esposito • ISBN 0-7356-2176-4

For more information about Microsoft Press® books and other learning products, visit: **www.microsoft.com/books** *and* **www.microsoft.com/learning**

What do you think of this book? We want to hear from you!

Do you have a few minutes to participate in a brief online survey? Microsoft is interested in hearing your feedback about this publication so that we can continually improve our books and learning resources for you.

To participate in our survey, please visit:

www.microsoft.com/learning/booksurvey

And enter this book's ISBN, 6-2131-4. As a thank-you to survey participants in the United States and Canada, each month we'll randomly select five respondents to win one of five $100 gift certificates from a leading online merchant.* At the conclusion of the survey, you can enter the drawing by providing your e-mail address, which will be used for prize notification *only*.

Thanks in advance for your input. Your opinion counts!

Sincerely,

Microsoft Learning

CL

005.
133
HAL

5000720036

 **Microsoft** | Learning

Learn More. Go Further.